PENGUIN BOOKS

THE KILLING OF BONNIE GARLAND

Willard Gaylin is a distinguished practicing psychiatrist and psychoanalyst; president of The Hastings Center, which pioneered in the study of society, ethics, and the life sciences; and Clinical Professor of Psychiatry at Columbia University's College of Physicians and Surgeons. His widely praised books include *Caring; In the Service of Their Country: War Resisters in Prison; Feelings: Our Vital Signs; Partial Justice: A Study of Bias in Sentencing;* and *Doing Good: The Limits of Benevolence* (with Ira Glasser, Steven Marcus, and David Rothman). Willard Gaylin and his wife, Betty, live in Hastings-on-Hudson, New York.

THE KILLING OF BONNIE GARLAND

A QUESTION OF JUSTICE

PENGUIN BOOKS

PENGUIN BOOKS
Published by the Penguin Group
Viking Penguin Inc., 40 West 23rd Street,
New York, New York 10010, U.S.A.
Penguin Books Ltd, 27 Wrights Lane,
London W8 5TZ, England
Penguin Books Australia Ltd, Ringwood,
Victoria, Australia
Penguin Books Canada Ltd, 2801 John Street,
Markham, Ontario, Canada L3R 1B4
Penguin Books (N.Z.) Ltd, 182–190 Wairau Road,
Auckland 10, New Zealand

Penguin Books Ltd, Registered Offices:
Harmondsworth, Middlesex, England

First published in the United States of America by
Simon and Schuster 1982
Published in Penguin Books with a new Afterword 1983

10 9 8 7 6 5 4

LIBRARY OF CONGRESS CATALOGING IN PUBLICATION DATA
Gaylin, Willard.
    The killing of Bonnie Garland.
    Reprint. Originally published: New York:
Simon and Schuster, c1982.
    Includes bibliographical references and index.
    1. Herrin, Richard.   2. Garland, Bonnie.   3. Trials
(Homicide)—New York (State).   I. Title.
KF224.H477M3   1983   345.73′0253   83-4001
ISBN 0 14 00.6727 2   347.305253

Printed in the United States of America by
R. R. Donnelley & Sons Company, Harrisonburg, Virginia
Set in Electra

Picture credits: Gene Gorlick/*New Haven Register*—10, 11, 12, 13, 16,
17. Wide World Photos—7, 18. Frank Leonardo/*New York Post*—14,
15. Bert Miller/Black Star—8. *New York Daily News*—9. *Los Angeles
Times*—20.

ACKNOWLEDGMENTS

I am deeply indebted to:

Those principals involved in this tragic event who — often at great personal pain, and some risk—unselfishly agreed to be interviewed for this book.

My colleagues at the Hastings Center for the atmosphere of informal consultation, collegiality and stimulation that so characterizes this place. While criminal activity is beyond the scope of the Center's concerns, the problem of justice is central to its work, and is argued here daily in other areas with other paradigms. I have learned and borrowed from that discourse.

Erwin Glikes, who transforms the work of an editor into that which it ought be — a creative art.

My wife, with the hope that she will someday allow to be acknowledged what everyone else about us already knows, that she is truly coauthor of this effort, as all others in my life.

Willard Gaylin
The Hastings Center
360 Broadway
Hastings-on-Hudson, New York 10706

CONTENTS

In this world of night, where a secret
equilibrium seems to reign, the victim is always
innocence.

—*Nellie Sachs*

PROLOGUE

Following Interstate Highway 87, one leaves the outskirts of New York City via the Tappan Zee Bridge, which spans the awesome Hudson River in seeming defiance at its most imposing width. In moments, the city is left behind and one enters the verdant foothills of the Catskill Mountains.

The beauty of the Catskills is obscured in the minds of most by the inundation of associations with the Borscht Belt. But unfamiliarity with the route forced my concentration to the surroundings, and annoyance at the frequent billboards only sharpened an awareness of the contrasting beauty of the countryside.

I was driving to the Napanoch Correctional Institution, a New York State Grade B Maximum Security Prison—like most prisons, buried away in a remote section, distant from the urban centers from which most of their residents are taken.

Nearing Napanoch, I found myself aware of a steady gnawing anxiety. Not normally an anxious person, I realized it was a feeling I had had many times before and was related to the approach to prison. I am a psychiatrist and had spent two years during the Vietnam War doing research on young war resisters in prison.[1]

It is the nature of prisons to make one anxious. The concept of being locked in a box is one of the terrors of childhood that few of us outgrow. It is the closest most of us can come to actually visualizing death. Locked in this particular box was the man I had come to see—Prisoner Number 78825118—Richard Herrin.

Richard Herrin, then twenty-three, had killed his college sweetheart, Bonnie Garland. He had hammered her to death in her sleep in her parents' home. This was the tragic culmination of a three-year romance. Richard Herrin, a poor Mexican-American boy, had been a junior at Yale University when he met seventeen-year-old freshman Bonnie Garland. Bonnie was a child of affluence. Daughter of Joan and Paul Garland, she had spent much of her childhood in Brazil, where her father was establishing a very successful international law practice. She had attended the fashionable Madeira School and went on to Yale, her father's alma mater.

Bonnie Garland was an unlikely victim of a killing. But then again, Richard Herrin was an unlikely killer. And the course of events following the killing was strange and unpredictable. Within two months of killing Bonnie, Richard Herrin was not in prison but attending classes at the State University of New York in Albany, working in a religious bookshop there, and being unstintingly supported both emotionally and financially by a Catholic community.

I am not a devotee of crime news; I rarely read it in the papers. But there was something unusually bizarre about this crime and its sequelae. I remembered one brief phrase from the reporting; Richard had been quoted as saying within hours of the killing, "Her head broke open like a watermelon." Who speaks in those terms? What kind of human being even thinks that way? One might expect a general revulsion, a turning away from the vile and indecent. But many did not turn away. The Catholic community at Yale University, where both Richard and his victim, Bonnie Garland, had been students, mobilized by Ashbel ("A.T.") T. Wall, a former roommate of Richard's and a member of an affluent and socially prominent New England family, along with Father Peter Fagan and Sister Ramona Pena, Catholic associate chaplains at Yale, began a crusade of compassion for Richard. The Garlands—her room in their house still soiled with their daughter's blood and brain tissue—started a countercrusade. This would eventually include hiring a private eye, appearing on a TV talk show, and interviews in such gossip sheets as the *Star* and *National Enquirer*.

The Garlands remain embittered and enraged. As a father of daughters, I can understand that. But what explains the wellspring of love and empathy for the killer? That circle of supporters, organized at St. Thomas More Church at Yale, formed a defense cordon that was to last to the day of this writing and beyond. Richard's first encounter after the killing—half naked and smeared with Bonnie's blood—was with a Catholic priest who was a stranger to him. It brought no revulsion, only sympathy and a desire to help. Father Paul Tartaglia, after twenty-five minutes with Richard, shed tears. Real tears for Richard. From my investigation it is clear that, except for the Garlands, more tears have since been shed for the killer than for his victim. How does this happen? Why does this happen? Should it happen? Is this good? Is this inevitable? What purposes are served? And where, in all of this, is the victim?

For at least twenty years I have been interested in questions of jurisprudence and concepts of crime and punishment and the role of justice; and how to define it; and in whose terms.[2] The story of Richard and Bonnie, of the crime and its consequences, seemed to drive directly to the heart of fundamental questions. In the story of their tragedy can be visualized much of the abstraction about crime and punishment, the individual and society, forgiveness and retribution, responsibility and compassion, and the nature of justice.

Our mechanisms of identification and empathy are central to our concepts of what is good and what is right. From the day of the killing, Richard attracted a host of concerned and compassionate defenders. When one person kills another, there is immediate revulsion at the nature of the crime. But in a time so short as to seem indecent to the members of the personal family, the dead person ceases to exist as an identifiable figure. To those individuals in the community of good will and empathy, warmth and compassion, only one of the key actors in the drama remains with whom to commiserate—and that is always the criminal. The dead person ceases to be a part of everyday reality, ceases to exist. She is only a figure in a historic event. We inevitably turn away from the past, toward the ongoing reality. And the ongoing reality is the criminal; trapped, anxious, now helpless, isolated, often badgered and bewildered. He usurps the compassion that is justly his victim's due. He will steal his victim's moral constituency along with her life.

It is not so in the world of the poets. They understood the necessity of maintaining a balance of sympathy. With them, the voice from the grave is present. The voice from the grave is a reality as profound, as startling, and as real a presence as the figure of the murderer. Hamlet's father's ghost dominates the opening action of the play and initiates its flow of events. But only in art. Banquo's ghost does not appear at modern banquets nor at modern trials. For while the courtroom is a drama, it is a drama without the voice of the poet or the voice from the dead.

Bonnie Garland's parents are tortured by unrequited needs for revenge. The concept of vengeance and the ways in which it has been absorbed by the legal principle of retribution require examination. Retribution was originally designed as a means of controlling the rage of the victim's friends. The criminal must pay for what he did by suffering in a commensurate way. The state, via the criminal jury, would inflict the punishment, thus assuaging and constraining the fury of the survivors and ensuring the King's Peace.

The concept of commensurate punishment is so vital that no punishment is almost preferable to an insufficient one. That some people "get away with murder" is simply part of the generic principle that "life isn't fair"—and we all know that. But when the opportunity for fairness is presented and when the institutions that carry the label of justice and are presumed to serve it seem to deny that purpose, the sense of outrage becomes unbearable.

So did the Garlands respond. This is not to say the punishment inflicted on Richard Herrin—a minimum of eight and one-third years in prison—may not have been severe enough. It is possible that nothing might have satisfied the Garlands, considering their loss. But obviously the mobilization of the Catholic community at Yale around Richard outraged Paul and Joan Garland. The Garlands describe the rallying around Richard as "the second assault."[3]

They were to be further offended when after thirty-five days in detention he was released on bail to the custody of the Christian Brothers in Albany. While there, he lived with the Brothers, attended classes at the State University under the assumed name of "Richard James" (according to SUNY officials), and began to build a social life with the young men and women who were his fellow students.

The fact that their daughter's killer was resuming a normal life, cosseted by concerned and loving members of the Catholic community, orchestrated through the Yale Chaplaincy at St. Thomas More Church, tormented the Garlands. They were bent on vengeance and felt no sympathy from Yale or anywhere else for their anguished cries for justice. They were viewed by some as a little indelicate and "unchristian."

Bonnie's parents felt that their battered child was already forgotten; her violation already forgiven. Where was the normal anguish for the innocent dead? Who listened to the voice from the grave? To the Garlands, it seemed, no one.

The verdict, when it arrived, was received like another hammer blow. Richard was convicted of manslaughter rather than murder with which he was charged.

"The jury let Bonnie down, let the family down, and the community down. . . . What happened today is another stage in our tragedy. Richard Herrin has successfully got away with murder," said a bitter Paul Garland after the trial.

"If you have a $30,000 defense fund, a Yale connection, and a clergy connection, you're entitled to one free hammer murder," Mrs. Garland said as she wept after the trial. "Because you're a Yale graduate shouldn't let you get away with murder . . . Because you can buy fancy psychiatric testimony shouldn't let you get away with murder."[4]

Two years later when I talked to the Garlands the bitterness was unabated, unmitigated, and in white heat. Paul Garland never referred to the Christian Brothers as anything but "the faggots," nor to anyone involved with the legal aspects of the case as anything but "conspirators."[5]

The nature of this crime is also special. Crimes of passion seem particularly tragic, because one always recognizes the ambivalence in them, the complexity of motive deriving from the unique relationship between the killer and the victim. A street thug and a paid killer are professionals—beasts of prey, if you will, who have dissociated themselves from the rest of humanity and can now see human beings in the same way that trout fishermen see trout.

In addition to there being different kinds of killing, there are different ways of killing. Richard hammered the skull of his sleeping lover. This is a different act from a shooting. I see no moral distinction between the two, but there is certainly a psychological one. The bayoneting of one individual is certainly less cruel than the dropping of an atomic bomb on a city, but a different kind of temperament is necessary to do the two things.

In defense of that which we value—children, grandchildren, country—most of us could shoot a pistol. Many could even shoot a pistol at close range. If frightened enough and under attack, some of us could wield a club, but there is something about the actual crushing of flesh which would make it more offensive. To wield a club against a *defenseless* human being would be as physically impossible for the majority of people, I suspect, as eating human flesh. Some few have been able to do both; most could do neither.

The insanity defense is another concern. Introduced to allow exculpation for those truly not responsible, it has been degraded to a point of professional embarrassment. It is a little difficult to know where the greater danger lies in the ever-increasing expansion of the definitions of insanity. Is the danger that too many who ought to be considered responsible will find in its ever-broadening reach a haven for evading legitimate justice? Or is it that disgust over its misuse will lead the general public to a cynicism that will demand a finding of guilt where indeed there is no real responsibility? Already, the cries for the abandonment of the insanity defense have passed from the lips of the evangelical and heretic pioneers, and are now being articulated by the cautious and conservative. And yet, the insanity defense has served the noblest spirit in modern civilization; while demanding responsibility for action, a compassionate society must excuse those truly not responsible.

There are urgent questions about the adversarial process and some of the unintended consequences of such an approach in a murder case. It is of the nature of such a process that in defense of the individual who committed the crime it may be necessary, or simply advantageous, to derogate and defame the victim. Some three and a half years later, in the same Scarsdale community where Richard Herrin killed his lover, another now famous trial occupied public attention.

Herman Tarnower, a distinguished internist and author of the *Scarsdale Diet Book,* had been shot to death by his former lover, Jean Harris. By chance I had been in Scarsdale giving a lecture the day after the murder. The grief evidenced in the group who came to hear my lecture forced me to deal with his death as well as the subject I had prepared. While Dr. Tarnower may have been known to the larger community as the author of a diet book, in Scarsdale he was foremost a respected internist and a popular member of the community. A mild eccentric, he was loved by many, known for his readiness to make house calls in the middle of the night (surely odd in the modern mores of medicine), and famous for the annual party he gave to which all of his patients were invited. He was understood to be something of a character and a man-about-town, but no more than was tolerable even in the bourgeois setting of suburban Westchester.

There is no question that if Dr. Tarnower had been hit by a truck a monument of sorts would have been erected to his memory, and a massive memorial service would have seen the outpouring of grief from his patients and friends. But Dr. Tarnower was not hit by a truck. He was killed by his ex-lover, and during the legal process of defending Mrs. Harris, Dr. Tarnower was made to seem mean, despicable, and unsympathetic. It was part of the adversarial process. To secure the maximum sympathy—to make Jean Harris pathetic and to make her crime less appalling—her victim must be diminished in value.

To me it seemed a double tragedy. Independent of my feelings for Jean Harris, I could identify with the dead Dr. Tarnower. For those of us who are not religious there are perhaps only two forms of immortality. One is that biological immortality represented by our children and their children. Here that genetic stuff of which we are made is shaped by the psychological and sociological qualities we each possess and handed down as a genetic component of children's children, whom we will never know and never see but who will contain some essential part of ourselves.

The second immortality is the immortality of memory. The dead continue to live in memories, and usually with the mythic distortion that time lends to those who need no longer pass muster in the real world.

"Reputation, reputation, reputation! O! I have lost my reputation! . . . My reputation, Iago, my reputation!" And we feel for Cassio, for we know our reputation extends around our being and beyond our presence. Dr. Tarnower was killed twice. Once by Jean Harris and the second time by her attorneys. I am not sure which is the worse crime. As one enters middle age a premature death seems less of an unmitigated tragedy. To be deprived of life and relieved of senescence, to be deprived of old age but to leave with full powers and full dignity and full respect, to have achieved most if not all of what one wants, and to have dissipated little of it in the potential indignity of senility or the destruction of character produced by chronic pain may, on balance, be less than a complete tragedy. But to be raised from the dead, to be taken from the coffin, to be mocked and degraded beyond any defense and beyond the rectification of events of daily living, is to lose more than the remaining few years of life; it is to lose your place in the love and memory of the community in perpetuity. It may be merely a measure of my age that I find the second murder as heinous as the first. And yet, how can it be avoided in the adversarial process?

So, too, would Bonnie Garland be on trial. Even with the utmost delicacy and solicitude, the victim will always be made an accomplice to the crime. To protect Richard, Bonnie must somehow be tainted. Her natural seductiveness will be seen as sexual entrapment, and her mature awareness of the limits of their relationship will be labeled betrayal. Her character will be—gently—impugned. To relieve Richard's culpability the defense must find someone to share the guilt. Bonnie must somehow share the responsibility for her own death. Bonnie, too, was on trial.

This killing and the responses to it illuminate the conflict between our concern for the individual and the needs of the group. The ultimate indication of the extreme to which we have come is the commonly heard statement about any crime: "What good would it do to put him in prison? Prison never rehabilitated anyone." I was to hear this phrase like a catechism from Richard's friends. I am not sure what the attractive alternatives are in those cases where protection of society demands isolating or disarming the dangerous; but, whatever, it is a humpty-dumpty view and demonstrates that we have come full circle. Prisons were not, after all, designed to serve the prisoners but rather the society at large. It was our humanistic hope that in serving our purposes we could also benevolently treat those within our institutions. I was told constantly that Richard required treatment. I suspect he does. But we must examine the assumption that it is somehow superior to attend to the criminal rather than the crime.

There is an increasing sense of diminution of the rule of law—and respect for law—often evidenced in the small erosions of everyday life: the readiness to steal, cheat, cut corners, attack, invade, trespass, insult, litter, jaywalk—the graffiti on the buildings and the graffiti in the soul. It is there and it is worrisome.

A social structure is a part of our biology and is a necessary part of our functioning, not a luxury. We need people not for company but for survival. We are social animals not by election but by nature. It is this obligation to live in groups which renders the destruction of social living so dangerous, and makes the neglect of the problems of public safety by the social and behavioral scientists so distressing. It *is* a concern when people can no longer walk the streets of our cities, when certain parks are declared out of bounds and no longer patrolled by police, and the answer is not in offering statistics on those who have succeeded in walking the streets with safety. The chance that only 10 percent of a facility is booby-trapped gives no comfort at all when walking through.

Now obviously a single crime of passion or a single criminal who commits such a crime does not threaten the public safety. But in the story of Richard and Bonnie we have an opportunity to examine the attitude of the public, the courts, and our system of justice on personal responsibility, to examine the theory that underlies the law, in order to clarify what emphasis it places on concern for individual good as balanced against concern for the good of the community.

Only the most mean-spirited individual will not find times when the general good should be sacrificed for the individual. Never can we, on a strictly utilitarian basis, defend some of the actions we are likely to take to protect one individual. And I am grateful. Think of the enormous cost necessary to save a child who has fallen into a mine shaft. We operate here on a nonutilitarian basis. We operate with our hearts as well as our minds.

Nevertheless, we must also face the fact that there may be times when the individual may be served with less than justice in order to satisfy the needs of the community.

The killing of Bonnie Garland is a focus in understanding the values that underlie the criminal justice system. Beyond that the announcements of the courts are one means of public enunciation of the principles of fairness and justice which prevail in the land.

For all these reasons, I was interested in Richard Herrin and his crime. And now, after two years of reading about him and the case, of reading over two thousand pages of transcript, over two hundred pages of clippings, over one thousand pages of typed manuscript of interviews, and after hundreds of hours of talking to those who hated him and those who loved him, I was about to meet Richard.

I had waited to see him until late in my investigation, when I felt I knew everything about him that I could from other sources. I wanted him to be the last person I would see. I almost waited too long. Richard's lawyers were filing a late appeal, and now, some two years later, his appeal was about to be considered. I was pressed for time to complete my research. My allotted period of "leisure" would soon be terminated. I did not want to jeopardize Richard's appeal, and I finally came to the conclusion I would have to go ahead without a personal interview. On Wednesday, June 10, 1981, however, I received the following letter:

Dr. Gaylin:

I received your letter of June 5, and since I haven't heard from my lawyers either, I'm going to go out on a limb and agree to see you this Friday, June 12. And even if I should hear from my lawyers during the week, I will go ahead and see you anyway on the 12th.

The prison is located on the east side of Route 209 in Napanoch. Visiting hours begin at 9:00, and all you need to do is give my name and number to the desk officer. There should also be a memo in the inner visiting room desk giving us the okay to use the private room.

There are vending machines and a dollar-bill changer in the visiting room. I will have no trouble recognizing you and vice-versa. I look forward very much to our meeting. See you on the 12th.

Yours truly,
Rich.

Ironically, I had finally reached his lawyer just two days before Richard's letter reached me and had gained his permission.

Napanoch looked like a fortress castle built out of sand, actually quite elegant from a distance, a huge pyramid with surrounding turrets. Yet, attached to it was a shabby wooden reception shed where the visitors were received. I waited outside of the doors, the only visitor there that early, and at precisely nine the guard came and ushered me in. The prison guard was a woman. Though not precisely courteous, she was efficient and not at all intimidating and arrogant as I had remembered reception guards to be.

There was, as anticipated, a question about my tape recorder. Richard, with the kind of precision that I later learned was a hallmark of his behavior, had guessed that I might be bringing one, and his written formal request specifically stated that Dr. Gaylin "might be bringing a tape recorder." I later asked him how he thought to include this in his request for visitation. He answered that from having read my book on the war resisters he knew I had conducted interviews by tape and presumed I would do the same now.

I then was asked to empty my pockets and pass through the kind of metal detector with which we are now all familiar from airport experiences. This one was so sensitive that after removing my watch, keys, coins, et cetera, I still sounded the alarm. The guard suggested my shoes, and as it turned out the nails in the shoes were sufficient to trigger that mechanism. Shoeless, I passed the test.

Collecting my belongings, I went through the double-doored system characteristic of prisons and closed wards in hospitals. First one door was opened electronically. I entered into an anteroom and then the door was closed behind me. Only then was another buzzer pressed to open the door into the main visitors' room.

Visitors entered into a large waiting room, perhaps eighty feet across by twenty, with rows of brightly colored plastic chairs. The prisoners entered this room from the opposite end, where, just around the corner and barely out of sight, there was a frisk room where the prisoners could be frisked before and after the visit. On one side of the large anteroom were three private visiting rooms, completely glassed in and reasonably soundproof. In each was a table and two chairs. The visiting-room guard suggested that I take the "palm room." It had one wall painted blue with a palm tree painted on it, and was used as a background for picture taking. The palm room unfortunately had no electrical outlet, but neither did the other two. The outlet in the waiting room tautly stretched the long extension cord I had brought with me to the limits of its reach. Richard seemed concerned about this and very early his solicitous nature became apparent. He carefully adjusted the extension cord so that no one on the outside would trip, and the one time we left the room he undid the cord without my knowledge. He then readjusted it as we came back.

Richard saw me while I was still examining the waiting room and before I noticed him. He seemed to recognize me instantly. I am not sure whether I would have immediately recognized him. He looked quite dissimilar from his pictures, less beefy (he had recently lost twenty pounds as he had indicated in a mimeographed letter that he periodically sends out to friends and supporters). He was slighter and shorter than I had anticipated, but he must have been at least five feet ten. He looked more Mexican than I had imagined, with his olive skin and Zapata-type heavy black mustache; and his eyes revealed his American Indian heritage. He would have been described as handsome by almost anyone seeing him. He was dressed tidily in pressed pants, in what seemed like a new pair of tie-style moccasin shoes, a yellow shirt, and rust Shetland crew-neck sweater.

It was a hot June day and I was aware of no air conditioning. By the end of the interview I had taken off my jacket, my tie, and rolled up my sleeves. Richard left the interview dressed precisely as he had entered. Despite my inquiries about whether he wasn't warm, he insisted he felt comfortable and, indeed, seemed unruffled.

It was impossible not to be impressed by Richard's solicitude. It was not an act, nor did it seem calculated and conscious. He was concerned about the way the seats were placed and my comfort and convenience, and when we were finished he demonstrated a fussy concern that we return the table and chairs to the exact position we had found them. He gathered the food remains from our snacks, brushed crumbs into a cup, and swooped it all off into a trash can. It was he, as I earlier mentioned, who was aware of the dangling cord and concerned that no one trip on it. He made sure that it was tucked in under the closed door.

After six hours of talk, I was exhausted and Richard seemed fresh. I took my leave of him aware that I must see him at least one more time. We made arrangements for another visit. We shook hands and said goodbye and then I turned to the waiting-room guard and said, "How do I get out of here?"

I was amused by my own syntax. It exposed that same anxiety I always have when locked behind closed doors, as if in some bad dream I will discover that while in there by mistake the officials will not know it and I will never be allowed to leave. Certainly, it would have been more courteous to simply ask, "Which way to the exit?"

As soon as I left the visiting room I called my wife from the pay phone in the receiving area. She asked me how it went, and I said what may sound peculiar to others but was to her a significant statement of the substance of the meeting. I said, "I sort of liked him." Surprisingly, and significantly, I was to feel *less* empathy after our second visit.

The rest remained for me to tell her when I got home. The fact that I liked him had profound implications. One's own personal emotional response means something special to a psychiatrist trained in psychoanalysis. Despite an intricate armamentarium of complicated devices for probing and evaluating personality, a psychoanalyst will trust, beyond all other measurements of temperament, that peculiar summation of subjective responses that adds up to the statement "I responded to him or I didn't; he touched me or he didn't." I liked Richard, more than I had anticipated.

And the fact that I liked him complicated my problem, for after all, I started with a bias and a thesis. Certain crimes demand certain punishments independent of their utility; individual justice must often defer to a sense of community morality; and the victim must be heard beyond the grave to balance the natural compassion of decent men to the surviving member of the tragedy. The fact that I liked Richard would make the proceedings more painful but would help me inevitably test my hypotheses at the most crucial level—the level of the heart.

When preoccupied, I have often experienced a certain mechanical takeover of behavior that seems to detach me from time and space and occupation of the moment. We have all experienced similar things. I will leave midtown Manhattan and only after arriving home will I recognize that I have maneuvered through time and space. I will ask myself how I got there.

It was precisely so as I was going home. I was thinking of Richard, a young man of twenty-seven, trapped behind bars for an as yet indeterminate number of years. I was aware, more than most who have never been in prison, of the subtle kind of torture prison can be. I remembered my own anxiety on leaving that day and I recalled the many departures I had taken from those young war resisters whom I grew to love in the two years I was visiting them in prisons. I thought of the fact that Richard could not leave. I thought of his waiting for an appeal that I was sure would be rejected, and waiting for executive clemency that I knew would not arrive. I thought of the loss of time and the loss of youth—and the waste, always the waste. And then I was startled by a rush of intense anxiety that worked its way through my chest ending in my throat. Something interrupted my train of thought, and I saw bounding across the highway a large beautiful doe.

There was no reason to be anxious. The deer had actually made the crossing a good fifty feet in front of my car, but the thought that I might have possibly hit her upset me and shook me from my preoccupation. I imagined the car hitting the doe, a wave of nausea seized me, and a chain of linked associations was initiated. I remembered another incident that had happened just two days before.

A woodchuck had been plaguing my neighbor for two years. It had tunneled throughout his yard, undermined his driveway to a point where he had broken an axle of his car. It was now tunneling under a stone wall between his yard and mine. For two years this neighbor had fought a losing struggle with this woodchuck—setting out poison and leg traps, sitting in wait with large sticks—and had never caught him. I myself had been totally oblivious of the ongoing battle until my neighbor discussed it with me and pointed out a hidden burrow beneath my rose bushes. I was intrigued by the woodchuck but also began to notice the damage he was doing. He had undermined part of my stone wall. I mentioned it to the gardener who comes in occasionally to help with heavy work. That very evening the gardener, with pride, called me over to announce that he had killed the woodchuck. He had hit it with a hoe handle and apologized that the force of the blow had broken the handle. He was sorry for the destruction of a three-dollar hoe handle, but with pride showed me the limp, soft, dead broken body of the woodchuck. I was surprised at how little blood there was and how soft and gentle the creature looked. And then, as thoughts will do, I was reminded of another incident of only a week before.

A small field mouse had entered our house, announced to us as always by the frantic behavior of our West Highland white terrier. We tracked the droppings and my wife baited a mousetrap. To her horror and dismay, the trap disappeared with the mouse. She was panicked at the thought of the trapped mouse going about the house half dead or injured. I located the mouse, struggling and running, bleeding, disabled, with the trap attached to its back legs. I had to "get rid of it," and without thinking did what seemed the logical thing to do. I picked up a broom and whacked the mouse. It must have died instantly and the thickness of the broom was sufficient that I could not honestly feel the contact with the fragile small body. Nonetheless, I was unable to go to sleep that night. I am not a sentimentalist about animals. I eat meat and have little patience with vegetarian philosophy, although I try to be indulgent of vegetarians. If the trap had done its job efficiently, I would have had no trouble, even though there is a certain squeamishness in lifting a trap with a dead mouse. There is a helplessness and a pathetic beauty to the small creatures, but I have done it many times and enjoyed a full night's sleep. It was the physical action of crushing flesh, even sub-human flesh, with the force of my muscles and blow that sickened me.

Then and only then—and for the first time since I had left the prison—I thought of Bonnie Garland. Richard had touched me, and I, too, heard no voice from the grave.

I
YOUNG LOVE

1
RICHARD AND BONNIE

The truth about Bonnie and Richard will never be knowable. It is buried in the past in multiple graves of memory. In John Barth's novel *The End of the Road* one character in an offhand manner repeats the cliché "You can't change the past," whereupon another contemptuously points out that since we are trapped by the present, and the future is never at hand, about the only thing we are free to change *is* the past.

From the first recounting of the "facts," they were blurred by the perceptions and the purposes of the viewers and tellers; and like some image fragmented in a hall of mirrors, each retelling merely presented another version of the truth reflected differently by those differing "planes" represented by the varying angles of the tellers.

The elaborate storytellers must all be heard. The religious believers with their special visions of love and compassion, the psychiatric believers with their new version of responsibility and determinism, the accusers and the defenders, will all have their turns. But first we must turn to those central actors in the drama, Bonnie and Richard. And here is the problem: Bonnie cannot speak to us.

So we start with Richard, as he tries to understand, explain, and justify what happened that converted a college romance into a tragedy; and everything he says must be balanced with the image of the mute figure of Bonnie. Richard offers us his history as he chooses to see it now. It will be the theme on which all the other variations will be played. It will be told in great part in his own words, for it is part of the thesis of a psychoanalytic author that manner and form often reveal as much as substance.

In the spring of 1971, 8,681 young men and women were "sweating out" their applications for acceptance to the Yale class of 1975. Richard James Herrin was not one of them. He knew where he was going. Despite SAT scores of only 580 verbal and 660 mathematics—not brilliant by Ivy League standards—he had early acceptance to Yale. He was valedictorian of his class of 415 at Abraham Lincoln High School in Los Angeles, but equally important in a period when colleges were particularly conscious of their obligations for affirmative action was the fact that Richard Herrin came from a poor Mexican-American background. Richard Herrin did not go to Yale. Yale came to him.

> When I was in the eleventh grade someone from Yale came to my high school and talked about Yale. I was mildly interested. I had always assumed I would go to UCLA or something. I knew I had the grades and talent to go to college, and I always knew I would.
>
> Senior year, again there was someone from the admissions office at Yale. (The admissions officer was later on very supportive after my arrest.) She came and talked to us about Yale, and there was another man with her who, on his own time, would try to get high school students interested in Ivy League schools.
>
> I had decided that I wanted to get out of the house and leave the conditions behind and go somewhere else where I would be far away from the violence and the yelling. What better opportunity to do that than to go all the way across the country to the East Coast.
>
> I applied to five schools—Yale, Harvard, Princeton, Williams, and the University of Pennsylvania. I was accepted at all five. My decision was based on the fact that there was a guy from my high school a year ahead of me who was at Yale. If I went to Yale I would know somebody there.

Yale was generous. They offered Richard a full tuition and expense package: an educational opportunity grant, a book and supply stipend, and a $1,000-a-year loan and a school job to cover incidental expenses.

The money I made from work was the money I used for spending money. That's the money I would save up to fly home for vacations. The first year I worked in the dining hall. Like Dr. Garland. We both worked in the dining hall the first year. He never mentioned I, too, worked in the dining hall the first year.

From the beginning Richard did not do well at Yale either academically or socially, and while some articles written about him had suggested that his academic studies suffered because of his outside interests, closer examination reveals that his attachments to people were tenuous and his commitment to causes minimal. Despite a record of some political involvement and some activity at the Catholic Church, he was not, as later described, a "big man on campus." None of his involvements in the first three years were significant distractions from his studies, and Richard himself knew it.

I wasn't really making decisions for myself. I got this job working with clams and snails, so now my interest was going to be clams and snails, although my interest was in human evolution. There were all these world figures right there working on human evolution, and I didn't even make their acquaintance. I might have played Ping-Pong with them, but I never even sat down to talk and tell them my interest and that I'd really like to know them. I was so wishy-washy that whatever I happened to fall into, I just went along with it, rather than make conscious decisions . . . saying this is fine for now, but I'm really interested over here. I didn't do that for myself.

Richard's behavior would not have been predictable. He would later be described as an "indifferent student" at Yale; in truth, he was a terrible one. And in less indulgent times he would have been dropped from the college. This valedictorian, this disciplined model boy, simply collapsed. On arrival at Yale, he abandoned whatever academic discipline, intellectual curiosity, energy, or industry that had sustained him through high school.

Beyond that, he simply did not seem to get involved—really involved—with anything. There were no activities to serve as substitute stimulations, no passionate commitments to some cause or pleasure. There was certainly no romantic life—none. By the third year Richard was determined to change that.

29

As soon as A.T. and Chuck and I arrived at our rooms in the junior year, I remember sitting down one night (this is before school started, and we were unpacking), and I said, "Guys, I've decided that this year I want to have a girlfriend. Okay? I went my first two years without a girlfriend and this year I want to have a girlfriend." So I made that pronouncement.

The girl Richard was about to find, or more accurately, be found by, was not Bonnie. But much—not all, not the horror at the end of the affair—that happened with Bonnie was presaged in his involvement with Ginny.[1]

I had some friends over at the college where Ginny lived, and I was over there visiting with them, and I kept running across this girl. I walked past her, and she'd look at me when I'd look at her, ran into her maybe half a dozen times in a couple of days. Finally I went to visit a friend of mine, and it turned out Ginny was one of her roommates. So I finally got to meet this girl that I'd run into. There was a party for new students at More House at the chapel, and Ginny managed to get herself invited. I think it was for Mexican-American students. Ginny knew I would be there, and she got friends to invite her.

So we left the party and had some doughnuts or something. I started going out with her after that, and like on the third date when I took her back to her room—the other times we had just sat on the couch and kissed and stuff—by the third time she wanted to get a little more involved, and there were other people in the living room, and she just kind of took me by the hand into her bedroom and closed the door. That was just petting and obviously we couldn't do that in the living room with all the people there. She was a virgin and wanted to remain so until "the right man" came along and she got married. So she actually took the initiative as far as the petting goes. So after that night . . . we would go back to her room or my room. We had advanced to petting now and eventually we got on to oral sex. I initiated that, and she was not averse to it. She made it clear that the first time she slept over she wanted to be as pure in the morning as she was that night, and I never bothered her about it after. She didn't want to have intercourse, and I wasn't going to push it.

Ginny seemed to be pure serendipity. Richard's resolve was hardly a factor. It was Ginny who felt the need for a sexual stopgap to tide her over between serious involvements. Richard was useful, and Ginny did not even bother to pretend that he was more than that. Richard was a passive instrument of her needs, not the aggressive, determined lover.

I had received from Richard no sense of Ginny as another human being. Richard had a "girlfriend," but was she even a friend?

—What was Ginny like as a person? Her background?

I believe her parents were first- or second-generation Poles. Ginny had gone to a Catholic girls' high school in Cleveland. She lived in the suburbs in a fancy neighborhood. She was pushed by her mother to achieve. She wanted Ginny to become a lawyer; she wanted Ginny to do this or that; Ginny worked hard.

She became a lawyer; she went to the University of Michigan Law School, and she married last year or two years ago to another lawyer who was about ten or twelve years older than she.

—Were you in love with Ginny?

I thought I was, but she didn't want me to be. She said, "Let's not get like that." It was convenient for her because she didn't get asked out a lot, and here I was.

—Why was that?

I'm not sure. She really wasn't that popular a person. She wasn't beautiful, she wasn't ugly, she was kind of in between. She was a conservative right-wing political type who was active in her political party. She was in the Tory party—was very active. It was a small group and kind of cliquish, I guess.

—So even though she wasn't that attractive, you found her so?

Yes. And she had expressed an interest in me. And she initiated our first petting session. And so now here someone liked me. A Yale woman that liked me, no less! And she's okay, and just last week I'd told my roommates I wanted a girlfriend. So gee, I just happened to run into this girl, and she likes me, so now I have someone to go out with, and she has someone to go out with, and she wanted to keep it on those terms. Of course I was head over heels for her. I wanted it to be more.

—You were pressing for more and she was pushing you off? How long did the relationship last?

It lasted from September, junior year, to February or March in the spring. The ending wasn't sharp and definitive, but towards the end there were a lot of unpleasant experiences, a lot of anguish. There was another fellow from the Tory party that she was interested in, but he wasn't interested enough. He was very, very shy and he wasn't interested enough to ask her to go out or maybe he didn't feel right in asking her out or he wasn't the kind of guy to ask a woman to go out. So I felt I was kept hanging on because I would take her out and go dancing; take her out and do what this other guy, Dave, wouldn't, even though she liked him and wanted him to. So I felt I was on a string. Whenever she didn't have anything to do and Dave wasn't going to take her out, there's old Rich.

Even as late as April for the prom she came over to my room and sat down on the couch and said, "Aren't you going to invite me to the prom?" and I said, "No." She said, "Oh, I can get tickets" (she was in a singing group and would be performing—she had free tickets) and said, "Ohhh, would you?" Dave's not a dancer, he's not a comfortable person, he doesn't socialize, so he wasn't going to ask her.

I didn't want to ask her. We had already gone our separate ways, but she pleaded with me, and I said "Yes." And I took her to the prom. That was in April. Back in February on Valentine's I went out and spent all the money I had on little different presents for her, and I wanted to take her out to a movie Saturday, and I went over and bought her roses and candy and perfume, and she said, "I can't go out with you; I have a meeting," and I was very disappointed and couldn't understand why she wouldn't be going out; here I brought her these presents and only had maybe ten minutes to spend with her.

Her roommates were there and they saw it happening, and they were feeling very bad for me, and in her room she had a calendar and on the calendar she had written "Dave" on that day. So, I don't know if I saw it that day or a few days later; at some point I did notice she had written "Dave" on it for that night when she told me she had a meeting. As it turned out, I found out she went out with Dave so I was crushed and heartbroken. In fact, one of her roommates called me over and said, "Rich, we like you and we just hate to see this happen to you—what Ginny is doing to you." I said, "What do you mean?" She said, "Every time she says she can't go out with you, she has a meeting, she's going out with Dave. Do you know she's lying to you?"

—But certainly you knew that. You saw the name on the calendar. What did you think that meant?

I don't know. I tried to believe she hadn't lied.

—Why did you take all that?

I wanted to have a girlfriend. I didn't want to lose her. I wanted to have that person who liked me; who I could go out with. It was a lot that I put up with.

—I don't understand why, when you saw the name "Dave" and she said, "I have a meeting," you didn't say, "Don't tell me you have a meeting, don't lie to me."

I confronted her with it later. Again, I don't remember the exact time when I saw the name on the calendar, but eventually I did confront her with it. She told me whatever I was accusing her of was wrong. She was innocent of whatever it was. Her roommates had told me at different times, and I brought it up, and she said, "My roommates are lying; it's not true, and I wouldn't do that to you." So . . .

I think the most painful time was during spring break in March. We both were staying on campus. I was going to be working a lot of overtime, and she was going to be working on researching papers and whatnot. Dave was also around at that time. I had hoped to see her every day—no pressure of classes and maybe I could have a lot of time with her. But no, there was always she couldn't spend this day or that. And one night was very painful. Three or four nights were very painful.

One night she didn't come back from Dave's room, and I asked her what had happened. She said they were sitting in the living room and she fell asleep on the chair, and he didn't want to wake her up. I believed that. [Laugh] Knowing Dave, I believed that. He was such a gentleman.

Another time during that spring break he'd invited her to dinner with some other people. They were going to cook the meal in the college. I sat at my window because my window overlooked the street, and I saw her on the way to dinner, and I waved to her and called out. She said, "Hi," and I sat at the window most of the day compulsively eating, and when I saw her coming back with Dave, they were walking hand in hand and that *really* hurt me. I just started crying and crying—just because I saw them walking hand in hand. That really was very upsetting to me.

—Did you confront her about that?

Yeah, I hastily scribbled a note, and I put on my coat and I went down and ran downstairs and caught up to them as they were going into their college. I looked at her, shoved the note in her hand, said something, and I walked away. I don't remember what I said. I was very upset. I don't remember what the note said either. It was something to the effect that I'm hurt . . . I want to talk to you about this.

—At that point weren't you in a rage about this? Didn't you feel humiliated, taken advantage of, lied to?

Well, here was this girl I hoped would still be my girlfriend walking down the street hand in hand with this other guy. Even though I knew she was interested in him and to see them walking just hand in hand, very innocently, it still symbolized here it was out in the open. I know she liked the guy, and now anybody can see this, and what are they going to think of me. I'm going to take her to the prom, and here she's walking with some other guy, and gee whiz. . . . I just sat and bawled and cried and sobbed. It was very painful to me, it just wrecked me inside.

The whole incident had an air of the unreal. It was remarkable and prophetic that Richard would build a love story out of this pathetic, thin involvement. Like a Rorschach test, he vested this meaningless thing with the significance of his needs.

He reveals more here. He indicates the importance of appearance. The image of love is more vital to him than even the need. The public display is part of that image; and hand-holding, I was later to discover, is a primary symbol for Richard—a signal to the world at large that he falsely assumes must be observing and judging him—of his success as a man.

—But you didn't feel rage with her?

I did to some extent. There were times . . . towards the end now when I felt more able to accept the breakup, I began to purposely initiate arguments just to get her mad and upset. Things that we had gone over before . . . you know, how could you do that, et cetera. I'd bring these things up on purpose just to rile her up. I confronted her with "I know what's really going on. How can you tell me it's not? I know different." And she would always deny it—doing any wrong at all.

—But you never used strong language, called her a bitch or liar?

No. The strongest it got was calling her "Creepo." After I met Bonnie that was my name for Ginny—Creepo. When I was a senior and going with Bonnie, she and Dave were not going together officially. They were Creepo and Marshmallow.

—Did you ever end up taking her to the prom in April?

Oh, yeah. Probably because I was a fool, but I did take her to the prom.

—Why did you take her?

There was still a chance to go out with someone, and I hadn't been all that successful at Yale in being able to ask Yale women to go out.

— Why not?

I suppose it was the same intimidation. How could someone like me dare ask this girl who might have gone to Phillips Exeter and gotten 800s, how could I ask her to go out with me? I didn't. .... I asked maybe two or three different girls to go out with me in two years. I wasn't dating. Most weekends were spent getting drunk at mixers with the other guys who were in the same boat as I was. Too shy to ask girls out, so we'd stand together and get drunk, and if we were lucky, at the end of a dance we'd meet a girl who came out on a bus and make out with her and put her back on the bus and that would be it.

They would come in from girls' colleges on buses to attend the mixers and at a certain hour they would have to get back on the bus to go back. Some of them came to go dancing and have a good time, others to find guys to go to bed with, and others, stragglers, would just want to make out and that would be it. Those were the kinds that I would chance upon.

—When did you finally break up with Ginny? Over the summer?

No. Over the summer I stayed at her house for two days. I was traveling back by bus, so I traveled to Cleveland one day, stopped over and stayed with Ginny, traveled another day, stopped in Denver, and stayed with Chuck, my roommate, and then the last day I was in L.A.

Ginny said, fine, I could come visit her. I was still not really her boyfriend any more, but when I got there we were cuddling and stuff in the back seat with her parents in the front seat. Holding hands and things.

—Did you like her parents?

I felt sorry for her father, and I didn't like her mother.

—What happened then? Did you still assume she was not your girlfriend but a friend?

Yeah. Again, it was an opportunity for that weekend at least to have someone to lie next to me in bed at night.

—But still you weren't having intercourse?

No.

—Did Ginny and you break up, or did it just peter out?

When I came back to school, the beginning of my senior year, I saw Ginny. I went over to her room to see how she was. I guess I wanted to hold her and kiss her, and she was kind of putting me off. That was really the last time I made any attempt to be that—to be close to her. For whatever reason, right at the beginning of the senior year she made it clear that we no longer had the same kind of relationship, that I couldn't come over and expect to spend the night with her or invite her over to spend the night with me. It was no longer like that. That was late August. So from that point on sometimes I would talk to her if I passed her in the street on the way to class, and other times I would not talk to her. Especially after I began going with Bonnie. I felt more accepting of having broken up with Ginny because now I had another girlfriend, and I had this sure thing over here. So there were times when I really kind of ignored her.

To the outside viewer the relationship between Richard and Ginny bears no relationship to *Love Story* and bears little relationship to a love story. He was a convenience. Duped, humiliated even, never really more than a stopgap or a convenience. Ginny, no different from many of her generation, saw casual relationships as fillers—as support systems—until more satisfactory ones came along. To Richard it was a romance, and whether Richard was in love with Ginny or not, he loved having Ginny.

He had demonstrated to himself and to others—and others were always important to Richard—that he was capable of having a girlfriend. The revelation of how tenuous was his hold on Ginny, and how minimal were her affection and commitment to him, might have been expected to erode the small reserve of self-confidence he had for himself as a sexual man. But Richard's appreciation and interpretation of the facts are always a little surprising, and after the affair he was capable of saying, "I had a little more confidence now. I asked a few girls out for dates."

The stage was set for Richard's next romance. Whether it was Richard's "new confidence" that triggered this involvement or Bonnie Garland's natural self-acceptance, insouciance, and high spirits is an open question.

Bonnie Garland, a seventeen-year-old freshman, had been assigned to Wright Hall, the freshman dormitory of Saybrook College, the college in which Richard resided, the college which had been her father's residence. Bonnie was—if that word is used for women undergraduates—a true "Yalie" in the way that Ginny was not and

Richard would never become. The daughter of an alumnus, Paul Garland, she had an international background, had spent many years of her childhood in Brazil while Paul Garland was building his immensely successful practice in international law. On their return to the States, she attended the fashionable Madeira School, which was to become infamous later when its headmistress, Jean Harris, killed her lover in that same New York suburb where the Garlands lived, Scarsdale.

In pictures, Bonnie does not seem like the classic beauty. She is somewhat too plump, and more important, her features are still those of a child rather than an adult, not yet shaped in conformity with character and experience. Yet, without exception, Bonnie was described as sensual, even sexual at times: "She was a bombshell—at her best, she really was. She was a wonderful combination of little girl and mature woman. She was seductive—whether consciously or not. Men were attracted to her, and she was used to it," one teacher stated. She was vivacious, open, exuberant, playful, seductive; and, as was to be constantly commented upon, there was that shining, extraordinary red hair—a feature mentioned by everyone who discussed her. And I was reminded how Eugene O'Neill focused on that kind of copper hair as his symbol of sexuality in another modern tragedy, *Mourning Becomes Electra*.

At midnight on November 1, 1974, the evening before Bladder Day, a day on which Yale students shove around a huge inflated ball, and label it a fall event, Richard and a friend decided to go to a movie.

My friend Paul Bardack and I had been good buddies since freshman year, and Paul was a Beatle fan, and I was. They were going to show a midnight showing of a Beatle movie, and Paul and I decided to go see the movie because we both enjoyed the Beatles. We would get together and jam. I would play Beatle songs on the guitar, and Paul had a recorder he played. So we went to see the movie, got out at one-thirty in the morning and got back to my room and he went back to his room and we met in the Towers of the College of Saybrook in the open air about two A.M., and we were playing and singing Beatle songs. Another friend of ours, Steve, came up with these two freshman girls he was kind of showing around. He was taking them to the Observatory where there was a telescope, and they could look at stars at that hour or whatever. He brought around Bonnie and one of her roommates, Kit, a Malaysian girl. He introduced us, "Rich, this is Bonnie, Bonnie, this is Rich," and something magical happened. There was an instantaneous attraction, and she liked Beatle music too, and she was a singer and she just blended right into what we were doing. I don't know how long it lasted, but Kit said she had to go back and go to bed. Then Steve left. Then Paul could see—he must have seen a look on our faces—he excused himself, and I asked Bonnie if she would like to help me carry my music books and guitar back to my room, and she said yes.

Paul, indeed, could see. "They started singing with us. Bonnie and Rich started getting closer and singing in unison, and it was like sparks flying through the night. I was overcome. Just started talking. After that, Bonnie and Richard was one word."[2]

We went back to my room; we talked for a few hours; drank some Kahlua . . . started playing around. She was into thumb-wrestling so we started thumb-wrestling, and that was our way to establish physical contact. I don't know how we did it, but we wrestled on the floor and stuff. It was kind of strange for us to be wrestling, having just met, but it was a way to feel each other out and see if, you know, do we get along, and the wrestling turned into making love.

Now the next morning was Bladderball morning. Bonnie was helping to make some banners or pennants. It's an annual event at the college. The people in each college try to devise plans to steal the ball. We had this plan at Saybrook College to steal the ball and get it into Saybrook courtyard. That would be the victory.

I was involved in setting up this elaborate apparatus that stretched across the street between two dorms. I had to go around six A.M. to help set this thing up, and Bonnie had to go finish painting the banners she was making, so getting close to six o'clock we moved from the living room where we had been rolling around. Chuck wasn't there, so we had the whole place to ourselves. Eventually we went to my bed, and we really didn't undress completely—just some articles. The sun was already coming up, and whatever stage we got to, I think I was the one that said, "Let's save it for later because we both have to go." The way she kissed me I felt like this was a very experienced woman. Very sexual and stimulating kiss—the way she kissed—and I started to feel a little panicky, like what if she wants to make love. I don't know anything about making love, and I hope that's not what she wants. But what I kind of implied was let's save it for later, so the pressure was off for that morning, and we put on what we had taken off and went our respective ways.

And that very morning while she was up on the tower putting up her posters in the same tower we were up the night before, I was also up there helping set up the apparatus, and somebody from another college—two guys from another college—were trying to disassemble the thing. We had some rope going down to the ground, and one of our guys was trying to tell them, "Don't touch that rope," and it was two against one, and so I saw this happening. I was way up in the tower, and I ran down and they ran out in the street, and I ran out there and I stood next to Dave, and there was Bonnie watching us all that time, and she saw me saying, "Look guys, that's none of your business; just leave us alone," et cetera. So the guys left.

And all this time I knew she was up there watching us, and here I'd made a hero of myself, defending the honor of Saybrook by not letting these guys destroy our work.

So . . . she had asked me what I had planned for that night, and I told her I didn't have anything planned; I was going to do laundry that night. And she said she had a date with Steve. So I felt, All right. They went to see a play. Right after the play was over she asked Steve to take her back home, she was tired and wanted to go to bed. She waited a few minutes till Steve left; then she went back to the college—she was living in the freshman dorms—she went back to Saybrook, came down to the laundry room looking for me. She didn't find me. She went back to her room, waited an hour, then went back. She went back to check three or four times looking for me because she wanted to see me. And the next day or during that week I managed to drop in on her room a few times. Eventually we started going out—that week. And by the following week she was staying with me in my room. That fast. That was in the beginning of November. We had the rest of that semester, plus the spring semester.

—I've never seen a good picture of Bonnie.

She's got big bones. She has straight reddish-blond hair. Thick lips, round nose, green eyes, big bosom. I considered her to be well proportioned. She always felt she was fat and heavy and ugly-looking. For being a big girl, I thought she was very well proportioned. She weighed anywhere from one fifty to one seventy during the time I knew her. She was five foot eight. And I thought she was beautiful. I didn't think Ginny was beautiful. She knew I didn't think she was beautiful. Bonnie, now, to me she was just a fantastic-looking woman. Here she was obviously very much infatuated with me, and I was head over heels with her.

Wow, I couldn't believe this was happening! This beautiful girl and she feels this way about me and gee whiz. . . . I can't believe it; it's too good to be true. How can someone like that . . .

—Your friends, did they find her attractive?

Yeah. So it was very important to me that we always held hands and always let people know that Bonnie and I were going together. Don't get any ideas—this is my girl.

—You made "pronouncements," so to speak.

Yeah, I was proud of her . . . very much so.

I was not sure that Richard understood what I meant by "pronouncements." I assumed that my choice of words was poor, but later on I was to realize that he had difficulties with abstractions and theoreticals.

Display was important to Richard, and no evidence of affection was more important than the physical act of hand-holding, which will run like a theme through Richard's description of his feelings about Bonnie. In Richard's mind, the public was never absent from even his most private moments with Bonnie.

A few short weeks later a significant member of the public was to appear on the scene. Richard met Bonnie's father, Paul Garland. Richard remembers very well his first meeting.

Richard, always extremely sensitive to appearance, seemed most offended by the things Garland was to say about his dress, which was trivial compared with his judgments of character. Paul Garland was not mild in his contempt for, and rage at, the man who had beaten to death his firstborn child. His comments about Richard were appropriate to a man who had experienced that which no man ought have to bear. Yet, Richard seemed to take most umbrage at other aspects of the statements Garland made to the newspapers. "I found a lot of distortion and inaccuracies, and maybe—or maybe not—intentional misstatements." When I asked him for examples, he said:

For example, the Garlands' recollection of my attire. I was portrayed as a slovenly person. On first meeting, Dr. Garland said I was wearing baggy pants, T-shirt, shoes with no socks.

That's not true. When I met him I was wearing corduroy pants, a pair of loafers, and a nice sweater and shirt. I remember that meeting very distinctly. I figured it would be nice to dress neatly for her father. It was after a football game. He had come down with her brother Patrick. They had attended the football game, and I had taken Bonnie to the game, and afterwards he was going to take Bonnie for pizza and she invited me to come along and meet her father, so I showed up dressed very neatly. He chose not to remember that as our first meeting, for whatever reason, and chose to say the first time he met me I was in baggy pants.

Richard Herrin was correct in his recall of Paul Garland's expression. Garland described him as "slovenly in appearance, slovenly in manners, difficult to talk to, physically unattractive."[3]

I asked Richard to give me a description or impression of Paul Garland.

He was a Saybrook alumnus, graduated in '52, came from the Midwest. Worked hard to get good grades; worked hard to get through Yale. Once at Yale he worked hard to get to the top of his class. He stayed at the top of his class to succeed. He sang in a group, got good grades, was involved in a lot of activities. He went to Harvard Law School. Very motivated. An achievement-oriented person.

In a certain sense he was entirely accurate. Paul and Joan Garland had also been college sweethearts. While Paul was an undergraduate at Yale, he had to work hard, working in the kitchen, waiting on tables at Saybrook College. His wife, Joan, too, had come from a poor family, her father being a superintendent of an apartment house. She, too, by all evidence was a hardworking and serious student. (Her interests and scholarship persisted to the day I met her; she was continuing to take courses and trying to find in her work an outlet for the miseries of her awful loss.) Paul Garland had been more than just a nominally successful student—or even a man. He was a summa cum laude graduate from Yale, graduating second in his class. He continued his education at Harvard Law School and then began to build a very successful practice centered in Brazil.

Coincidences abound in the similar and dissimilar backgrounds of the two relationships. It was Joan Garland—then Joan Bruder— who, when visiting Paul Garland at Yale, had attended Mass at the

St. Thomas More Church. She was then a practicing Roman Catholic. She is no longer. Paul Garland was interested in Spanish culture
and, like Richard, is also bilingual, indeed trilingual, speaking Portuguese too.

Richard continued:

> Bonnie told me most of what I know about him. Having met
> him, I saw that he was more concerned with success and mak-
> ing money and power than with feelings, the more emotional
> aspects of life.
>
> I found him to be cold, insensitive, not very understanding,
> aloof, unapproachable, uninterested about anything I had to
> say.
>
> —Didn't you have a feeling he was a good father?
> No.
> —More hostility towards her father or her mother?
> I think more towards her father. Now when she needed
> something she would most often go to her mother—like money
> or clothes or permission for something. I don't think she got
> along that well with her father.
> —What about her mother? What do you think she was like?
> Well, I felt a lot of the same feelings as with the father. I felt
> a coldness. Maybe it was the blue eyes and the black hair, a
> stern look like "I'm the mother here, and what I say goes." She
> seemed so self-assured and in control of things. She seemed so-
> phisticated. I felt inferior. I didn't know how to deal with peo-
> ple like this. They didn't really do anything to help me be at
> ease, to make me comfortable. They could have made me feel
> more welcome—helped me feel more at ease—but they didn't
> try.

Paul Garland, indeed, struck me as a reserved man. My first
meeting with him was a full two and a half years after his daughter's
death. He is an old-fashioned man, almost courtly in his behavior.
Bitter and sardonic, but always articulate, with tight-lipped control.
He seemed self-conscious and mannered and very, very much on his
guard. He had talked to many newspaper people and had felt that he
had opened up to really only one and then felt betrayed by the article.

My impression of Joan Garland was quite different. Again, it must
be remembered, this was years after Richard's meeting, years that
were centuries for the Garlands. And the relationship was different.

Nevertheless, there was an emotionality about Joan that was attractive. She seemed accessible. Her anger was evident, as was her hurt. Both were certainly present in Paul Garland to an extreme, but corseted and constrained by a personality that demanded self-control. Joan Garland was articulate and certainly sophisticated. Paul Garland seemed often naive, particularly in terms of human emotions and the human spirit. If one had to reduce impression to crude stereotypes, one would have seen Paul Garland as a typical engineer, and Joan as the typical social worker—which was precisely what she was. Paul Garland's formal, controlled manner was amazingly similar to that of Richard Herrin, except that there was, in addition, the rage and bitterness evident in every gesture and word.

I mentioned to Richard that, from what I had heard, the family seemed quite indulgent of Bonnie, granting her a great deal of opportunity for travel and certainly generous in their readiness to fulfill her material needs.

Yeah. She had enough for her needs. Later on she was put on a budget. But if she ran out of money she could always just call home, write home and get some more. The family traveled all over the world on vacations. Money had never been a problem. But the warmth and the love—that's what was lacking.
—Did they come up much? Bonnie was a singer. Did you go to all her concerts?
Yeah.
—Did the family come to hear her sing?
I can't remember. They might have been there. I don't remember knowing they would be there. She didn't like people she knew to be at her concerts. She was with a small women's singing group, and she told me she got nervous if she saw me there. She didn't like me to be there. I would go anyway. Any chance I got to hear her sing I'd go.
—So things were not good between you and the family, but they were never overtly ugly or mean to you?
No.
—Did you know that he was fluent in Spanish?
Yes, I knew that they were fluent in both Spanish and Portuguese. I thought it might be a way to ingratiate myself with them if they realized I was bilingual.
—Did you ever try?
I don't remember. I remember the maid was Spanish and hearing Mrs. Garland speak to the maid in Spanish. That

might have been one time I might have said something to her, but that's kind of vague. I don't recall other times speaking Spanish in front of them, although I made it known to them. They were asking me about myself; I told them I was Mexican-American. I was involved with a Chicano group on campus.
—Did you ever speak Spanish to Bonnie?
Oh yes. Mostly for fun. And endings to our letters we'd often end in Spanish. It seemed more romantic.

I specifically raised these questions because the Garlands had talked to me about how difficult and taciturn a person Richard had been. I pointed out to them certain crossroads of potential mutual interest and was amazed that Richard made no attempt to meet them at these points. In particular, I alluded to the fact that Paul Garland had more than a passing interest in Spanish culture and Spanish history, having taken his undergraduate degree and written his thesis in Spanish intellectual history. Richard's political activities in the Mexican-American student group might certainly have been a common ground for discourse. The amiable ability to share in the transfer of thoughts from one language to another is an intimate experience. That and the conviviality that comes from shared knowledge would seem to have been available to both of them.

The Garlands stated that Herrin did not volunteer the information that he spoke Spanish. Herrin, for his part, suggested that he hardly needed to volunteer it. One of the things they certainly knew about him was that he came from a Mexican-American heritage and was raised in a Mexican-American ghetto. The Garlands saw him as selfish, inconsiderate, and manipulative. "He had a gravy train mentality. He was a failure from start to finish, a passive glob, a giant sponge."[4]

He saw them as distant and unyielding.

They claim they had no idea I was bilingual. In fact, they knew very well I was, that I was a Mexican-American person from Los Angeles. They knew a lot about me. They chose to forget a lot.

Bonnie and Richard quickly then moved into a sexual relationship. I had asked him if she was a strongly libidinous person. He didn't understand the word "libidinous." I had to ask if she had a strong sexual drive. He responded that he initiated it most of the time, but that she was always responsive and she was never a passive sexual partner. To Richard's knowledge she was usually orgastic. He said:

> If she was faking, I didn't know enough to know it, if she were or not. But it was very satisfying to me because I believed she was . . . not every time, but a lot of the time she was.

He then described himself as a strongly libidinous person. They often had sex two or three times a day at all different hours, and Bonnie was always responsive.

It was clear that Bonnie was not passive and did not simply let him make love to her but made love to him. During all this discussion I had assumed the two of them were having sexual intercourse. He was describing, after all, a five- to six-month period when they were sleeping together. But it became apparent that this was not the case. I asked Richard if Bonnie seemed an experienced lover.

> She wasn't supposed to be, but . . . She had told me she was a virgin. We didn't have intercourse for a long time. About four or five months after we met. We had been sleeping with each other though.

—What did you do, mutual masturbation or oral sex?
> Right.

—And she was not averse to that?
> No.

—So you'd bring each other to orgasm orally or manually?
> Right.

—Why didn't you have intercourse?
> She said she wasn't ready for it emotionally, and when I heard that I was more or less relieved because I didn't want to push the issue. I was content to go along with her feelings. I hadn't had much experience myself and would not have . . . I would have been uncomfortable to force the issue. I was relieved when she said she didn't think she was ready to have sex, and I was perfectly willing to go along with that. It was no problem for me at all.

—Then how did you finally get around to having sex?
> Spring break. She went home for a week and for the second week of the spring break she invited me to her house. That was the first time I went to her house and the first night I was there in her room the feelings were very, very intense for both of us. Very excited and stimulated. By mutual agreement we didn't want to wait any longer. We both felt the time was right and

that was a very satisfying experience for the first time. She didn't have an orgasm the first time, but the next time we made love she did.

During the fall semester Richard and Bonnie were practically never apart. He describes that period as the heavenly part of their romance. Yet to an outside viewer it was hardly heaven. Richard was continuing his almost total lethargy in his classes and abdicating any academic goal, and Bonnie seemed to be doing the same. I asked him about this:

She was missing a lot of classes. She had a lot of commitments to her singing. She was in the freshman choir, another choir, in the singing group of hers, and that involved a lot of rehearsals, and there was the time she spent with me and the time with her roommates.
—Had she been a good student in high school, at Madeira?
I should recall this, but I don't remember her being an outstanding shining student.
—She was not a very ambitious person?
No, not when I knew her. At the beginning she was planning to go to graduate school or conservatory for music. She didn't have any clear idea of what she wanted to do that I knew of.
—Okay. So that fall was a kind of idyllic period, but both of you were messing up your college education. That didn't seem important. What happened after Christmastime?
During Christmas we were separated for two weeks. She was going to Hawaii. On the way when she stopped at the San Francisco airport she called my house, and I wasn't home, so I missed her. She sent me a couple of cards and a letter. The letter was written on hotel stationery, and it just said in big letters I LOVE YOU. There wasn't much else during that break. She was busy, and I was content. . . . I got a couple of postcards. My mother told me she tried to call while I was away, and I felt, Gee, she tried to call me!
Once we got back to school we just resumed where we left off before vacation.
—Was that the trip to her house when you first had intercourse?
That was in March '75. It was spring vacation. She told me she was going to be home for her spring break, and she suggested that I come up to her house for the second week. She wanted a week at home with her folks and family, and the sec-

ond week she wanted me to be there. I wasn't going home through the break; I was going to be at school, so I said sure, I'd love to come and meet the rest of your family and spend a week with them.

—You were not reluctant to get into the stickiness with her family—knowing of the hostility?

I was aware of her father's impression of me. The rest I didn't know. I'd met Patrick that same night, and there was really nothing . . . I liked Patrick. He was a football fan, and we talked about that.

—Do you ever hear from him?

No. Of any of them, I would think that he would contact me, either in ten years from now or two years from now. As he said on the witness stand when one of the lawyers asked him to describe his relationship with Rich, he said, "He was my friend." I killed his sister, but I don't think that ended totally our friendship. If anyone can forgive me, I think it would be Patrick.

Richard then described his coming to Bonnie's house in Scarsdale. It has been described as a $150,000 or $200,000 Tudor house in the newspapers, a testament either to the naiveté of the reporters or to the changing real estate values in Westchester County. A more appropriate estimate at this time would be over $300,000. Richard described it as

A big two-story affair, large lawn in front, two-car garage, large basement, attic, big kitchen, big living room with nice-looking furniture. Upstairs each child had his or her own bedroom. Bonnie had her own bathroom. Her room was set off a few steps above the other bedrooms in the corner of the house. A very well kept house. They had a maid. For me, it was intimidating to be in a place like that. The only other house comparable to that I'd been in before was A.T.'s house in Providence. His home was more or less the same, but I wasn't intimidated there, because I didn't feel any hostility. I did with the Garlands. With A.T. it was a new experience, and his folks were great people and warm and accepted me. The other guy that came along with us, Jim from Washington, he came by just for Thanksgiving. Jim and I had no other place to go except to hang around Yale, so A.T. said why don't you guys come up to Providence, you'd be welcome. We got up there, and we felt

very welcome. It was a different experience going to Scarsdale though. I already knew kind of what her father thought of me.
—How did you know?

She told me. His first impression of me was that I had no direction in life, no goals, no plans for the future, that I was just using Bonnie for my own pleasure and satisfaction. That I would wind up hurting her in the end. I was a bum, in other words. She did use that word; it was a direct quote from him. I was a bum. So I kind of knew where I stood, and I didn't make an impression on her mother either. I didn't meet her mother until I'd actually arrived at the house.
—Why do you say you didn't make an impression on her?

Apparently she felt the same way. I was not very outspoken. I was dying, kind of. I wasn't sure how to act—if I would make a mistake holding the wrong fork or the wrong spoon or the wrong hand or whatever. I was very self-conscious about my actions while I was there, knowing that people in that class do things certain ways that I wasn't used to doing. I didn't want to do things wrong and make a bad impression, but I was really clammed up. I rarely spoke, and when I did speak, I didn't say the right thing. I just didn't give a good impression at all.
—Are you saying that because of your nervousness you were at your worst with them?

I would say so.
—When did you meet Bonnie? Senior year. You'd had three years at Yale. That puts a polish on a young man, doesn't it?

It should have. I mean, I hadn't been to a nice house like that. I hadn't sat at a dinner table with people like that, and I felt pressured to be self-conscious with every move I made.
—You mean manners, how to eat an artichoke, et cetera?

Yeah. Little things like that I was very self-conscious about. At A.T.'s it wasn't for a very long time, and it was very informal and only a couple of days.
—And most of your friends were poor boys too?

Not necessarily, but I didn't go to their houses.
—You never felt like a "Yalie"?

Only in the sense that I was attending Yale. I never adopted that preppie mentality. But that speaks of the whole question of my attitude at Yale, my confidence, my self-confidence, which was almost nonexistent while I was there.
—Why was that?

Another factor of intimidation when I arrived on campus the first year was hearing people talk about themselves, their grades, their SAT scores, always talking about this. And I think what happened to me right off the bat, even though I was number one in my high school class, I had it made in high school, and here I was 2,500 miles away or so, and I could see other people who had achieved more than I had. They boast about it, and my reaction was to say, "Well, someone's got to get the A's and someone's got to get the C's, so I guess these guys will get the A's, and I'll get the C's." And there was a self-fulfilling prophecy, if you want to put it like that. I worked hard enough to get the C's, but I never worked hard enough to get the A's.

—Why was that? You were a smart kid. Why couldn't you have been in the half with the honors?

I hardly studied. I was independent now.

—Weren't you a model student in high school?

Model student, model son, model neighborhood kid. I didn't want to compete against these people. I can't really explain it more than my feeling inadequate amongst all these bright achievers. I just never gave myself a chance to even try to compete. Almost right off the bat I slacked off. Never really got started.

—So it wasn't that you were out of your depth?

I never gave myself a chance to see if that was the problem or not. I gave up before I started.

—But a lifetime habit of writing your papers, doing your work— what happened or why? What was there that was so awesome or intimidating?

I don't know.

If his relationships with the Garland family were strained, he was most content with the relationship with Bonnie.

I had the guest room in the bottom floor as my bedroom. The nights that I slept in that guest room— Well, the nights I slept in her room I would wake up early and go down to my room. We slept late every day. There were desks, papers, and things. A couple of times Patrick would have to come and get something, so they would think, Oh, here's Rich sleeping in his bed, so I guess this is where he slept last night—good. We'd get up very late, ten or eleven, have breakfast whenever we got up, and just kind of do nothing. Whatever we would do we would do together. Go for a ride, we really didn't do much . . . just kind of sat around and enjoyed each other's company.

—Didn't you want to walk in the country? Or didn't you have any curiosity about the city?

   I'd been to the city a couple of times. We did go into the city, but most of the time we just kind of sat around, goofed off.

Bonnie and Richard returned to Yale. At the tail end of the vacation an incident occurred which would have made it immediately apparent to a more sophisticated person than Richard that Bonnie's involvement with him was hardly as profound as he had described it. They returned before classes resumed. Bonnie went off to a "cheesecake party" in their very college of Saybrook. But without Richard. He waited alone in his room until she returned sometime after midnight.

Knowing the informality of college get-togethers, it seems inconceivable that Bonnie could not have, had she wished, brought Richard along. One of the dangers of the current informality is that when one invites a dozen people to a party forty may well show up. I asked Richard his response to this:

   I was kind of annoyed that I hadn't been invited. It wasn't really my group of friends. It was a different group that Bonnie was acquainted with. It was okay. I really didn't feel that bad about not going.
   While she was at the party, I was just alone there. We'd just come back from being together all the time, and she told me that the guy that had invited her to the party walked her back to her room. She wasn't as open about our relationship. Instead of telling this guy, "You don't have to walk me back to my room, I'm just going to Rich's room now," he walked her back to Wright Hall, which is across the street, another dorm.
   And then she told me that he wanted to kiss her when he dropped her off, and I asked her, "Well, what do you mean?" She said, "Well, I was facing him, and he put his arms around me, and kissed me good night." I said, "Yeah!" and I started putting on my shoes. She said, "Where are you going?" And I said, "I have to go talk to Hugh. I don't like what he did." I said, "I've got to go talk to him right now." I became very upset. I asked her was it just like a peck on the lips, and she said, "No, he wanted to . . ." and she said, "I didn't want him to kiss me passionately, but he wanted to."
   So my immediate reaction was to put on my shoes, go over

to this guy and say, "What do you think you're doing? Why can't you just kiss her on the cheek? Don't you know she's my girlfriend? What's wrong with you?" She said, "No, no, no. Don't go over. It's nothing, really. Forget about it." I explained to her that I felt very hurt. "Why did you even let him do that?" And she said, "I wanted to be kissed by another man."

That really threw me for a loop. We had just finished this week, first day back, and now she wants to be kissed by another man. So I was really messed up. I don't think I broke into sobs and wails, but I was really upset and crying a little bit and couldn't understand why she would do this to me. How could she feel that way. We'd had this terrific week. She managed to calm me down and soothe me and comfort me, and I forgot about going over to talk to the guy and never said much to him after that. I always viewed him with a lot of suspicion after that. . . .

So, now that we'd had intercourse at her house. we'd make love in my room, which we hadn't done before. Sometime during that spring we hit a point where neither of us went to class for a few days. We just did nothing except lay around in bed; we'd even get up too late to eat in the mess, and we'd go out and have a grinder or something and come back to the room. She might go to rehearsal and come back. We didn't look at books or classes or notes. Also during that time, a little bit later, the impending departure was beginning to come over our heads.

—Was that period when you didn't go to classes an "idyllic" period, or was it a period when you were both sort of deteriorating?

It was an idyllic period. We both just forgot about the problems and cares of classes and studies . . . we just laid around, slept late, and got up whenever we wanted to, and said, There's no outside world right now, there's just our whole world right here. It lasted—I don't know—it might have been only a few days, but it seemed like a month.

We did reach a stage later on. I remember we were going out to a party, she mentioned she felt our relationship had become stagnated, that it was not going anywhere. She didn't see a lot of future in it. In the course of that discussion we had flirted with the idea of going our own ways.

When she brought up the idea that the relationship had become stagnated—stagnant—that kind of touched a raw nerve. We actually became estranged for that night. Like "I didn't know it was that bad." Like, "Gee, what does that mean about me as a man, as a person, as your lover? Stagnant, gee! No future, gee! I didn't know you felt that way." "If that's the way you feel about it, then don't hold my hand, you know." "We could still go to parties. I don't know what's going on now." That was a bad scene walking to the party.

This is the spring of the first and only year Bonnie and Richard were to spend together. This will be later described as the apogee of their relationship. This will later be interpreted as an intense and "symbiotic" involvement. But everything in retrospect will be seen always and only from Richard's perspective. For Bonnie, this was no "symbiosis."

When we were in the party we made up. After that, everything was okay again. Some slow dancing, whispering, looking at each other. "Gee, that was really dumb what we went through coming over here." "I don't really feel that way." "I don't either." "Of course we're going to stay together."

And that's pretty much how the semester ended. That we were going to keep it alive and stay together, see each other when we can, write, visit, call, get together as soon as we can on a permanent basis.

I was allowed to participate in the graduation ceremony even though I hadn't really finished. That was a special decision by the executive committee. Yale, in the first time in history, was going to have a summer term, and so the conditions of my participating in the graduation were that I would take a course in the summer term in order to finish up and also I'd finish writing my senior essay, which I hadn't done. So I had my summer cut out for me.

For a time we had hoped to be together in New Haven that summer. Bonnie had called her mother and asked her if it would be okay if she stayed in New Haven. Her mother asked, "What are you going to do there? Who will you stay with," et cetera. Bonnie said, "Rich and I will get an apartment." Apparently her mother talked her out of it.

That night Bonnie'd talked to her mother she came to my room crying. She was just crying, sobbing. She was saying, "I don't see why my mother won't let us do what we want to do." She came right over as soon as she finished talking to her mother. Now I had to comfort her, she was very upset about it—that we couldn't spend the summer together. Somehow that got translated in the paper that Mrs. Garland said Bonnie sounded relieved to be denied the permission to spend the summer with me. Ten minutes later when she was at my door! I don't know how anyone can make up the emotions I saw on her face. They weren't crocodile tears. She was shaking. She was upset. She was angry that they wouldn't let her do it.

That summer Bonnie and Richard saw each other only occasionally. For a few weeks she was away on a Glee Club tour of Central America, and at every stop on her itinerary Bonnie was to find waiting for her a letter from Richard. And from every stop Richard was to receive a letter from Bonnie. This was a pattern of behavior whose breaking became a significant event in the tragic end of their affair. They would see each other for scattered days either in New York City or New Haven. He was not welcome in her home that summer.

Richard was, as always, "up to my usual tricks": missing classes, ignoring his studies, drifting and feckless. He had been accepted for a master's program in geology at Texas Christian University, contingent, of course, on his successful completion of his studies at Yale.

I was to leave in August, this is '75. I wound up passing physics with a D. I wound up having Bonnie type up my senior essay the night before it was due. It was last minute. I just passed the course, and I just got my senior essay done on time.

I turned in my senior essay like the day that I was leaving. I didn't give myself any time to spare. As I was writing it, Bonnie was typing it.

That's when we really talked about marriage. I asked her what her response would be if I were to ask her to marry me. She said, "I would say yes." I didn't make a proposal, but her answer was as good as a yes anyway.

So when we parted in August it was a very tearful farewell at the airport. I left her just . . . It hurt me because I was with her every second possible, yet I had to let her go and board the plane. She was just standing there, and I could see the shudders as she cried. There was nothing I could do about it. I couldn't go back and comfort her, take her home and hold her; I had to leave her. That scene has always stayed with me. Just seeing her with tears pouring down, just crying, it really hurt to see that, to see her like that and there was nothing I could do. But at least we both knew we had made some tentative plans for marriage in the near future. As soon as it would become possible. That takes me out of New Haven.

—That year you were studying for your master's?

Yes. The fall of '75 to '76.

—And things were good between you and Bonnie?

For the most part.

—What was some of the "non-part"?

Her dating. Although I had agreed it would be okay for her to see and go out and have a social life, one individual that she had told me she had gone out with, I didn't like it very much. The kind of guy he was. This is the guy they called her first Yale boyfriend. This was her second. *I* was her first.

I remember talking to him standing in line waiting for dinner, his telling me about his exploits with women. It was like he's from the Midwest. He would work all summer; he'd have some money. He was like a playboy, and the way he told me about his exploits, I could see that he didn't care about women.

So when she mentioned that this was the guy she went out with, I didn't like it. I tried to explain that this was not the kind of guy I approved of. She should reconsider. But she did not like to be told how to run her own personal act. Not angry, but she would make it clear that I was not to . . . that she was going to do what she wanted to do. But that I shouldn't worry. "Rich, please don't tell me who to go out with, but don't worry, I'm not . . . I know what our relationship is like. You have nothing to worry about."

—She'd tell you how? By telephone?

Yeah. We talked almost every night. So we'd have long conversations, sometimes three hours long. It would cost me a fortune. She was spending a lot of money too. When we were together at Yale she knew of my dislike of marijuana. If I was at a party and people were smoking, I didn't stay very long because the odor from the smoke was sickeningly sweet, and it bothered me. I couldn't stand it. I would leave the room or just leave the party. And she had indicated that she felt the same way.

Sometime during that fall she told me she had been over with some of the girls in the group and they got high. And I got mad. "But, Bonnie, you told me you didn't do that." "Well," she said, "I started. I'm with my friends and you have nothing to worry about."

To me, I guess, I kind of took a Moral Majority kind of mentality. Well, if she's going to start smoking grass, obviously she's on her way down, and the next thing she'll be sleeping with everyone she goes out with. I've got to put a stop to it right now. I can't let her do this. And she was stubborn. I couldn't tell her to stop smoking, she wouldn't hear of it.

But she was always so gentle and loving and she'd say, "Rich, I know what I'm doing. You have to let me to this. I'm not screwing around; I have to do something with myself, and here I am with my girlfriends from the singing group. There's no guys, just us, and we're getting high. What's your objection to that?"

I said, "I don't like it; I don't know what's going to happen. What if somebody takes advantage of you when you're high?" I didn't understand what being high was. I'd never had the sensation myself. I assumed you became helpless and would be easily taken advantage of by people like Johnny. I said, "You can't do that, it's messing me up. I can't deal with that." She said, "I'm sorry. You'll have to accept it." She was very firm. But she would always say, "You have nothing to worry about. Quit worrying about me." That fall she apparently was going out with this guy and whatever was happening . . . and yet on the phone she was telling me, "Don't worry."

—How do you know she was going out with this guy?

Well, her roommate told me. I visited in October. Her roommate got to me. "Rich, whatever you heard about Bonnie and John, don't believe it. It's not true. They're just friends." That's the trip where I formally proposed to her. That was in October of '75. She accepted.

—Did you confront her about John after the roommate?

No. I talked . . . Someone else had mentioned in passing, Bonnie and this other guy, who I thought were just friends. And I said, "What do you know about that? Tell me more. What is going on?" She didn't mean to imply there was anything going on. The way she said it, my suspicion was aroused, and I said, "What do you mean?" She said, "No, no, I didn't mean anything by it." So there were things in the air.

Richard's blithe acceptance of Bonnie's reassurances, both written and on the phone, was a gross denial of what common sense would have told anyone of his age and his presumed level of sophistication. He, particularly, should have been sensitized by his experience with Ginny. His totally distorted romanticizing of that relationship caused him great pain. Even by his own description of what transpired between him and Bonnie, it is difficult to see where he found evidence of a committed relationship.

In fact, it was general knowledge in the Yale community in that fall of '75 that Bonnie was involved with another man. Bonnie, this time, had told the other boy about her relationship with Richard; and with the kind of openness and casualness that characterize current undergraduate romances, they had decided that it would be a convenient interlude for both, since he was in precisely the same situation, having a girlfriend in a distant place. As the boyfriend reported later:

> Bonnie started talking about breaking up with Richard. She felt something was missing in their relationship, but she didn't know what. She worried he wasn't aggressive or ambitious enough. I said, "Why don't you just tell him you're dating me?" She said, not literally, "He'd kill me." She said she was afraid he'd hit somebody, either me or her.

The boyfriend continued:

> Despite her real desire to break off the relationship, she couldn't. Bonnie was a real procrastinator. Her motto was never put off till tomorrow what you could put off till next week.[5]

Instead of breaking off with Richard, she broke off with the new boyfriend. She indicated to him that Richard had been calling her room on Saturday nights, always when she was out, and when she came in at 3 A.M. she would hear the ringing telephone.

With the kind of denial that Richard used and the level of consciousness he possessed in respect to Bonnie's involvement with other men, it is difficult to gauge if he was capable of real anxiety and real anger.

Richard returned for a reunion in the fall of 1976, celebrating the second anniversary of his meeting Bonnie, where the following occurred. Nanette Rutka, a mutual friend, later recalled:

> "We were standing around listening to the Whiffs. I said, jokingly, 'I hope you've been keeping an eye on Bonnie, Rich.' He immediately grabbed my arm and said, 'What do you know?' He was the most serious and distraught I'd ever seen him. He said, 'I want to know exactly what you've seen, and I want to know what you know.' I said I had seen Bonnie holding hands. And that was *all*. He said, 'Nan, I really trust you, and I want to know if you're holding back on me.' He kept

asking it over and over. We had a 15-minute conversation about it. . . . And he said, 'I'm not going to be here after this weekend, and I'd like you to keep an eye on her and let me know if there's anything going on.' I said, 'Rich, I don't know anything. I'm just upsetting you unnecessarily.' But he was so very, very intense." . . .

Next morning Nanette saw Richard and Bonnie at brunch. "He mentioned it again. I reassured him again. He said, 'Well, I just want you to know Bonnie swore on a Bible.' He and I had been pastoral assistants together, and we were serious about our religion. It struck me as weird that he'd talk in religious language. I remember thinking, this is totally inconsistent with everything I know about Rich."[6]

Richard and Bonnie had spent the Christmas of 1975 together, but Richard needed constant reassurance about John. Richard more formally proposed, and with Bonnie's acceptance felt a measure of relief. It was a peculiar engagement.

—Was it public knowledge that you were engaged?

She explained to me in her society it was improper to announce an engagement if the marriage is not to be held within a year, and since we didn't really know when we could get married, she said there was no need to announce the engagement yet. I wanted everyone to know. I was happy about it, and I thought she was too. She was able to talk me out of making a public statement on it, to tell everyone in New Haven and maybe put it in the alumni news. So it just remained something between the two of us.

I gave her a bracelet I had bought in Germany that I had decided to give to the woman I would marry. It was a real charm bracelet, not worth very much, but its value was in what I intended to do with it—to give it to the girl I got engaged to. I made the decision to give it to Bonnie, and she accepted it.

In the spring of 1976 Bonnie Garland did seem committed to the relationship with Richard. She spontaneously made a trip to see him, flying down to Fort Worth, missing a full week of her own school since their vacations weren't consonant.

It was the usual happiness of being together. . . . Whatever problems we had over the phone, any doubts and suspicions always were cast aside when we were together. I'd say it was the usual happy days for the week or nine days, whatever.

That summer Richard and Bonnie were together in Los Angeles most of the time. "I showed her the sights, Disneyland, the beach, whatever." She then returned to New York, and Richard to Texas.

In the fall of '76, Richard was applying for Ph.D. programs, and Bonnie was attempting to accelerate so that she too could be free in June of 1977 and join Richard wherever he was accepted. They talked of marriage and future children, and they talked almost daily. "She even made a spontaneous visit to Fort Worth. There was no crisis for either of us. She just wanted to come and spend ten days with me. She took a week off from school."

—Did you assume she was faithful in this period?

I was still letting myself believe that she was abstaining from all sexual activities.

—You don't believe that now?

No. Now I've been able to accept it.

—But you have no evidence?

No. Jack was very tactful in court, in drawing out just enough evidence from the witnesses to give the jurors the idea that perhaps she was ... I don't know if that was in part to protect me and my feelings and in part not wanting to slander Bonnie in front of the whole world. Just enough to show she was not totally faithful to me. He just extracted one bit of evidence from one of Bonnie's roommates, and he left it at that. The testimony was that there had been guys staying in Bonnie's room for a few weeks in the spring of '77 or the winter. He didn't ask for more details. It wasn't me, it was someone else.

—Was it the guy she met on the spring tour?

I believe it was, but it wasn't identified. From other things that transpired that semester, I think it was the same guy. I think it actually began before the tour.

The fall of '76 could have been for Richard a replay of '75. Despite his stated confidence, he seemed to be drifting through his graduate training as he had his undergraduate.

—One of the things that's hard for me to understand is why you were doing so lousy in graduate school then. Here you had it all set up—the girl you loved. You had very good study habits in high school. You had to be number one in your class. How did you get turned around so?

Well, things came relatively easy in high school. I must have studied, but I don't remember really cramming or worrying about studying. I enjoyed learning. I really don't know why . . . I know what I was doing.

—What were you doing?

I was staying home and watching TV. Daytime, nighttime TV—all kinds of TV.

—Did you read much?

No, I was in a couple of book clubs, and I would read the books I got from them, but I very seldom would go to the library and read the books I should have been reading. I did have a reading habit when I was little. In school I read what I had to read for my classes. By high school I wasn't reading a whole lot of outside books. . . .

I watched game shows. I would go to class most of the time, but rather than stay in my office and do lab work or go to the library and do some research for my thesis or study for a class, I would go back to the apartment and turn on the TV. I'd maybe stay in school all morning, then go home for lunch and not go back the rest of the day. Turn on the tube and that was that. I should have spent five times more time in school than I did.

—How late would you stay up?

On an average, twelve, one o'clock. A lot of times I ended the day by talking to Bonnie on the phone in the late hours. We spoke on the phone five or six times a week.

—So you weren't depressed then?

No. Having recently sent off applications to graduate schools for a Ph.D. program, I would say I was optimistic. I had taken the next step and made applications. I had interviews scheduled at three graduate schools in the East. I was looking forward to making a good impression, hoping to get into a school where I could be in the same city as Bonnie. So there was a lot of plans, a lot of optimism that fall.

Bonnie and Richard spent Christmas 1976 together at the Garlands' house in Scarsdale. The Garlands had not changed their mind about the destructiveness of the relationship; they were simply bowing to a reality. At this time Bonnie seemed firmer in her commitment and had allowed her parents to know that she was spending the vacation with Richard, either at their house or somewhere else.

Bonnie, despite her peculiar childishness at some times, had a strong and independent nature. She was, after all, a firstborn, with many of the characteristics that are traditionally assigned to that role. It was to be Bonnie and Richard together, either in Los Angeles or in

Scarsdale. The Garlands wanted their child home. "It was clear that if he didn't come here, she would go to Los Angeles. We wanted her here for Christmas, so we had to have him. He seemed very smug. He felt he had Bonnie in his pocket. It seemed like 'I've got her, I can influence her, and you're out in the cold,'" said Joan Garland.

—And what was life like there? What did you do?

Not much. Kind of laid around, watched TV. We spent New Year's Eve in Times Square. We went to a Broadway show. We saw *Chicago* with Rita Moreno. Then we went to Sardi's and ducked out of Sardi's in time to see the ball come down in Times Square.

—Where did you get all the money for that?

Well, I brought what I had, and she did. We had to borrow a few bucks from one of her brothers. To have enough money for the evening.

—What was it like at the house?

I felt very uncomfortable and very uneasy. Conversations I felt were strained. I didn't think—even if I had not been there—I didn't think people were very comfortable sitting at the table together anyways. All the food was on the table. To be passed around. I wasn't used to eating dinner with people anyway. To be in that setting with Bonnie's parents . . .

—What do you mean you weren't used to eating with people? You were at Yale in the dining room.

That was about the only time I ever regularly sat and took meals with people.

—What about at home?

I always ate in my room.

—What did you call the Garlands?

I called *him* Dr. Garland, after the first time. When I was first introduced to him, I called him Mr. Garland, and Bonnie later told me that he was outraged that I dared call him Mr. Garland when he had worked so hard to achieve a Doctor of Law degree, and that I should henceforth refer to him as Doctor. From that point on I did refer to him as Dr. Garland and Mrs. Garland.

—What were the next developments?

Well, I would like to mention Christmas Eve. We exchanged our gifts on Christmas Eve. I'd been giving her clues as to what I had bought her. What I had bought was an opal ring. One of my students in my class sold jewelry on the side, and she had brought in some stones, and I chose a stone that I could afford and went through a book and chose a setting. Bonnie had always said she liked simple settings. She didn't like elaborate fancy settings. So I chose a simple setting, and I put in the stone. It cost me forty dollars. It wasn't bad for an opal. So I started giving her little clues like, like I already have your Christmas present. It's smaller than a grandfather's clock. She'd ask what color it was. I said it was a lot of colors. If we called each other on the phone and she didn't mention it, I would bring it up. I'd say, "Oh, by the way, would you like another clue as to what your present is?" I wrote a little message in Portuguese.

I bought a Portuguese-English dictionary and wrote her a little message which I attached to the middle of the box I had the ring in. I think the message read something like this: "This is the first but not the last." Something to that effect. Referring to the ring.

And we were in my room, the guest room, when we exchanged gifts.

So we decided to exchange gifts the night before, and when I gave her the little box and she could see it was a small box, and I had probably given her enough clues already so she could suspect it was a ring, and now I could understand her thinking a ring of different colors, she thought it was a diamond engagement ring. When she opened the box and saw it was—even though she loved opals—she told me it was her favorite stone—when she opened the box and saw it was an opal, I saw the disappointment. She couldn't hide it. At that point I felt very, very inadequate that I couldn't . . . Here I was engaged to this woman, and I could not even afford to buy her a diamond ring. Here I was giving her a measly opal, and she was so disappointed she was crying, and I started crying because I felt inadequate. I was crying because I felt "Gee, I disappointed her; I couldn't give her what she wanted." Gosh, so it was kind of a real bad scene.

—Did she *say* anything? Did she actually say she was hoping for an engagement ring?

I can't remember any specifics, but that was what she was registering was disappointment, and it was also why I felt so inadequate. I couldn't . . . I didn't . . . and it never occurred to me that when I would give her these clues she would think it was a diamond. I don't know why it never crossed my mind. I was . . . I always looked at it positively, like "Gee, here I was . . . I don't have a lot of money to spend, but here I spent forty dollars for an opal ring which I know she loves. And I know she's just going to love this ring. And she's going to wear it all the time. And it would be a really nice gift to give her. It would be something special."

And I was so buoyed up with all that thinking, and it was really a severe let-down when I saw the look on her face. She couldn't hide it; she couldn't hide the disappointment. She recognized it. So we talked about it. We discussed things that evening. She said that she did like the opal. It was a lovely ring. The intimation was that she had expected more, but she appreciated the sacrifice I made to get it for her and that she would wear it often. As far as I know she did wear the ring a lot.

—She didn't wear it always as she might have an engagement ring?

Right.

—So you were upset?

Yes. I hadn't been able to provide . . . It had always been at the back of my mind that she liked opals, and she liked Porsches, and I knew that she was accustomed to living comfortably, and I kept wondering if I was going to provide that kind of comfort. That was always maybe a secret fear that I had; wondering, "Gee, I've already spent twenty thousand dollars to buy her a Porsche and a nice ring and I'm already in debt and we're not even married yet." It was something that was always in the back of my mind. It's nice talking about when we get married, but gee, we start off in debt right off the bat. It's going to be tough.

—Did she have a Porsche?

No.

—Did the family?

No.

In the spring semester, Bonnie Garland made an unusual and significant decision. She decided to take a semester off. She presented it as a fait accompli. She did not discuss it in advance with her parents, nor with Richard. It was again a sign of a capacity for self-direction, and of a basic self-confidence that might have led to a mature young woman in a few years. Richard tried to talk her out of it.

It should have been apparent to him at that point that something was askew with their plans. She was still a junior, with a year and a half to go, but the two of them were talking about marriage that summer. Even when I asked Richard after the fact how he could have possibly considered marriage feasible, he talked vaguely about "acceleration," and "advanced placement credits." Her decision to drop out that semester meant that the already unlikely possibility of her graduating that June and joining Richard became an impossibility. The move predicted the end of their relationship.

Bonnie had turned a corner, and in retrospect, and perhaps only in retrospect, every action from then on indicated her intention to leave Richard. Richard didn't know it, the Garlands didn't know it, I suspect even Bonnie didn't consciously know it, judging by her ambivalent behavior toward Richard in the following month.

Two contrasting incidents, more than anything else, were revealing of the double signals Bonnie was sending, and the confusion of Richard's thinking during this period. The first occurred just prior to Bonnie's moving out of the dormitory.

I was talking to her on the phone one evening, and she had just finished telling me about this singing group she was in. Bonnie had been the pitch, the musical director. They just elected another girl to be the pitch. And I'd met this girl, Stephanie, on my previous visits. So in the middle of our conversation, there's a knock on the door, and Bonnie said, "There's someone at the door." She said, "That must be Stephanie; we're supposed to go out together." I said, "Okay, gee, why don't you let me say a couple of words to her to congratulate her on becoming the new pitch." Bonnie said, "No, no, we don't have time. I have to leave right away." I said, "Wait a minute, I just want to say a few words to Stephanie. Put her on the phone. She knows who I am. I'll just say this is Rich, congratulations." She said, "No, no, I have to go now. I have to hang up now."

I said, "Don't hang up."

She hung up on me.

So I called Yale information and got Stephanie's phone number and called Stephanie's room. Stephanie answered, and I said, "Is this Stephanie?" And she said, "Yes," and I hung up without telling her who I was.

—You called her because you knew Bonnie was lying?

I suspected it. The way she was talking on the phone, refusing to put Stephanie on the phone; what could be so urgent that she can't give me one minute to congratulate Stephanie. That made me suspicious, and that's why I called Stephanie. Stephanie was there in her room. She wasn't at the door going out with Bonnie. So, during the next hour I sat and fretted, and then I made reservations to fly to New Haven and see what this is all about. She had lied about who was at the door, and for another thing, she hung up on me as I was saying, "Wait, wait, don't hang up." That had never happened before, and I felt the situation was very serious. So I made reservations to fly to New Haven.

—Just on the basis of that?

Yeah. About an hour after she hung up. Oh, I tried calling back, before I called Stephanie, and the phone was apparently left off the hook, because I couldn't get through. So that's when I called Stephanie.

About an hour after that Bonnie called back, and she apologized for having hung up on me. She said she was very sorry, and she knows she shouldn't have done that. She knows it must have hurt me to have her hang up on me. She apologized profusely, and then said she had another confession to make—that it wasn't Stephanie at the door. And I said, "I know." Perhaps I should not have let her know that I checked on her, but I said, "I know." She said, "How?" I said I called Stephanie, and she was in her room so I know it wasn't Stephanie. So she became angry because I checked on her, but she was feeling guilt for having hung up on me, so she explained. She didn't really let that fact that I had checked up on her linger, because she still had this other confession to make. She said it wasn't Stephanie, and I said, "I know," and she said, "It was this guy named Bob, and we went out for a bite to eat and I came back." I said, "Oh, that's fine. Why did you have to lie?"

—Was Bob the boy she became involved with?

Right. This was in February. [Other printed reports place her first meeting with Bob in March.] I really don't know. All she gave me was his first name in February. She said his name is Bob. She didn't give me his last name. Later on I found out the guy on the tour was named Bob, and I figured it was the same guy.

—Didn't you get suspicious? She lied, and she was so panicky she hung up?

Yeah. As she was apologizing I was listening; she said, "It was Bob, and we're friends, and he came by, and we just went out to have a bite to eat and nothing more. Nothing beyond that. He's a friend of mine, and I need to have my friends and I need to go out and see people and go out to have a bite to eat if I get hungry. And there's nothing wrong with this." She said,

"I wanted to tell you about it. He's a friend of mine and don't worry; he's just a friend." That's how she—we were able to smooth things over again, and I said, "Okay, fine."

As it later turned out, this same guy had been living there in the room, so it was not the situation that she had told me about. Now again I assume it was the same guy. *Somebody* was living in her room. Her roommate testified that there was another guy living in Bonnie's room for at least a week or two in February.

—But do you mean you didn't suspect this?

Well, I was suspicious enough to call Stephanie and check and to get a plane reservation to come up and see what was wrong and why she felt it was necessary to hang up on me. To me that was a serious violation. But when she started talking and explaining it was just a friend—that "I was expecting Stephanie, but it was Bob instead," so I said fine, and smoothed it over.

In February, without notifying her parents, Bonnie moved off campus into the basement room of the Zeta Psi fraternity house. Richard didn't like this idea at all. One of the men who was a member of that fraternity was John, the boy Bonnie had been involved with the year before. As usual, Richard was looking in the wrong direction.

John lived in that house. She knew I didn't like John, but she told me John was one of the guys that lived in the house. Again, "Don't worry. I have my own room. I have a key for the back door. It leads to the basement where I have my room. I have my own little kitchen, bath. I don't have to interact with the guys. They're giving me a break by letting me live here, and I don't have to pay too much rent, so it's the best deal I can come up with. I don't have a lot of money, and I've decided to move in there." "Well, okay, you know what you're doing and I trust you. Everything's cool." She said, "Yeah, but I'm not going to tell my parents, because I know they would have a fit." I said, "Okay, I won't tell them."

Bonnie was reported to have met Bob after a rehearsal. It was suggested that she was not originally interested in him, but flirted with him as a means of attracting one of his Whiffenpoof friends. This was one of many signs of her declining interest in Richard.

Things were not going well for Richard in other directions. One after another his applications for a doctoral program had been rejected. His credentials at that point were hardly imposing, and he began to get frantic that he would be closed out of all programs.

The next incident was . . . I guess my anxiety was that I'd be rejected for the Ph.D. programs I had been applying for. I must have sounded terrible to Bonnie on the phone. Now, she's living in the fraternity house off campus, and I'm still calling her a lot, talking to each other on the phone, still writing letters.

It was a Sunday night, and we were talking on the phone, and she said she felt that I needed her, that I was so depressed about everything in general. She said, "I don't like the way you sound. I'm going to come up." She said, "I'll be up. I'm going to make reservations and fly up tomorrow. I feel that you need me now." I couldn't talk her out of it. I didn't really want to talk her out of it. It sounded good. Maybe she was right.

So the next day, there she was. She flew out Monday night. I had to give a presentation Tuesday morning in a seminar. Flubbed it royally—for the second time. The other time in October, she was there when I had to give a presentation in a seminar, and I blew that and again in the spring. I shouldn't have, because I had all semester to prepare this presentation, but I'd been saving everything for the night before, and now Bonnie's here the night before. Of course I didn't pay much attention to my presentation. It came out really bad.
—It came out bad in what sense?

I was ill-prepared. I made one great error in the presentation, and someone in the class brought it up—one of the students. [Laugh] Thanks a lot. He brought it up and said, "Hey, wait. If that happened, how could this happen? Doesn't the paper say this?" So I just sat down and got a zero for the presentation and a make-up presentation later on.
—Did you feel embarrassed or humiliated?

In front of the classs, yeah.

I told her about what happened. I didn't want her to feel guilty or responsible for it. I told her I had a lot of time to get it together and just blew it. I had put off preparing the presentation till the last minute. She was more important. She would always come first. She was very comforting. I didn't really take her out. I didn't want people to know she was there.
—Why not?

They would have connected my bad performance with Bonnie's presence. I felt it would make things worse to let people know that she was in town. And again I mentioned that in the fall, when she came out in October, one of my classes was supposed to have a field trip—an overnight field trip as part of the class. And it happened to coincide with the weekend when Bonnie would be in town. So the Friday before the overnight trip I had a meeting of the lab instructors, and we were supposed to prepare for the next week's lab. I feigned being real sick, coughing, pretending to gag as if I was about to heave. I tried to make myself look very miserable until finally one of the graduate students came over and said, "Rick, you look terrible." I said, "Yeah, but I have to go on this overnight trip," and she said, "No, go home and rest." My adviser, Dr. R., came over, and everyone agreed that I should stay in bed for the weekend. Inside I was going great. Bonnie and I had tried to figure out how I could get out of it—this overnight trip.

Now again, the coincidence was . . . here she was in town. I didn't want to go off on an overnight trip and leave her. She flew in to see me, and I didn't want to go off. I didn't want my adviser, this Dr. R., to know I'm going to give up this overnight trip, which was an integral part of the class, to be with Bonnie. She should be off studying, and I should be in the program. So I didn't want Dr. R. to know she was there. So I kind of kept her away. I didn't take her to the geology department and walk around with her. I kept her hidden.

—Were you ambivalent about her coming in?

No. It was worth her coming. It was still . . . Even though I flubbed the seminar and had to lie to get out of going on the overnight trip, to have her there with me was the most important thing in the world. So even though it did hamper my program school-wise, I felt good.

Richard's description of these events is, to say the least, peculiar. Bonnie has flown down to comfort him—out of her own guilt, compassion, love, and ambivalence—and he is subtly blaming her for his two major academic failures that year!

He did more. He tried to hide Bonnie's presence after the second failure because "they would have connected my bad performance with Bonnie's presence." Who would have possibly made such connections? Who cared? It was Richard who blamed Bonnie. It was Richard's anger, projected onto the outside world. The outside world had more than enough material from Richard's own behavior to account for his failures. This is the first clear evidence of his mounting anger with Bonnie and his need to displace it and, beyond that, his capacity to extend his anxiety about appearances to a paranoid degree.

In April Richard came up to Yale to be with Bonnie at the prom. He was unaware before he came that there had been a serious deterioration in their relationship. He was unaware during the dance. And he was unaware when he returned to Texas.

Bonnie Garland was about to begin her third and last romance. There was a near confrontation at the dance. Bob, being ignored by Bonnie and seeing her spend the entire evening with Richard, was determined to have a confrontation and force a decision from Bonnie then and there. Bonnie had what, in her case, proved to be a fatal flaw. She could not bear confrontations.

Richard discovered the truth of the prom only long after it ceased to have any importance.

> I've read about my being jerked off the dance floor to avoid a confrontation with this Bob guy, who was also there at the prom, and who couldn't stand seeing Bonnie with me. He'd made a decision that night to force her to make a decision, and when she saw him coming, she grabbed me and led me out the door.
>
> It was in a courtroom article. I didn't recall it. There was a point where she said, "Let's go outside and get some fresh air," and I said, "Okay." That's the only thing I can remember that approaches the incident described.

In different places, in different times, with different people, with different characters, making only slightly different decisions, that would have been the end of the affair. For Bonnie and Richard the end would be different.

2

THE END
OF THE AFFAIR

Bonnie did not want to hurt Richard, but she was afraid of confrontation. Richard loved Bonnie, but he could not face reality. And it was out of such common stuff of ordinary human frailty that uncommon tragedy was to evolve.

In early May 1977, Bonnie left with the Yale Glee Club for an extended European tour. She was not to return until June 30. Bob was with her. The Bonnie and Richard romance, which had endured two years of separation, albeit shakily, was to be dismantled during an idyllic voyage of travel, singing, and camaraderie.

And Richard was happy. At least in the beginning. It was a "good period." By getting an A in a difficult course, he had managed to salvage his course work for the semester. The A balanced out the C, an unacceptable grade in graduate school.

"I felt good," Richard said, "because when I did apply myself, I realized I could do well in school. It was just at Yale I never gave myself a chance. For once I really worked hard and I was really proud of myself."

And then he had heard from George Washington University. He had received a provisional acceptance to enter their doctoral program, provisional only on the successful completion of his master's thesis at Texas Christian.

Prior to Bonnie's leaving on the Glee Club tour, Richard, as he had in the past, received a complete itinerary with the dates, arrivals, and locations of all the places Bonnie would be staying. Additionally, he had written to her well in advance so that on her arrival at each town she would find a letter waiting for her.

The following is from direct testimony at the trial. Richard was being questioned by his own attorney, Jack Litman.

Q. During the first week of the Glee Club tour, did you get anything from Bonnie?
A. No, I didn't.
Q. Were you still living with Jack Edmondson at this point?
A. Yes, I was.
Q. How did you feel?
A. Well, I didn't expect anything the first week. I figured there wouldn't be enough time to get something from London or Paris to me within that first week. So, I didn't— I didn't think anything of it.
Q. During your second week, did you change residences at all?
A. I think at the end of the second week I moved out of the apartment with Jack Edmondson into a house.
Q. The house you moved into, was it— describe it.
A. It was—there were four small houses side by side. It was, like—well, it is four versions of a duplex. Four small houses side by side. It had two large rooms, kitchen, a closet and bathroom.
Q. Phone?
A. No phone.
Q. Roommate?
A. No roommate.
Q. Now, during that second week of the Glee Club tour, did you—did you receive anything from Bonnie?
A. No, I did not.
Q. What were you doing with respect to the mail?
A. [No response]
Q. The mail—did you receive mail at that point?
A. I went to check the old apartment anyway, just to make sure that there wasn't something from Bonnie sitting in the mail box. I checked a couple of times after I moved out.
Q. How did you feel at the end of the second week, having received nothing?
A. Well, I was beginning to think that the mail service was a lot slower than I thought they were. I was sure that Bonnie was writing and had written; it was just a matter of time before I started receiving correspondence from her.[1]

But Richard was anxious, whether he acknowledged the anxiety or not. His unconscious knew that which his conscious was unprepared to accept, the anxiety made itself manifest in the following episode. As he later told me:

> One time I was with a friend. We were watching television at her place, and there was the news report that came out about the Moluccan terrorists who hijacked a train in the Netherlands. I had Bonnie's itinerary, and I knew that she was scheduled to be in Holland right around that time. The news report said these terrorists hijacked this train, and on this train were some American students, and they didn't have any more details, and so I said to her, "Bonnie's in Europe, and she's supposed to be in the Netherlands around this time. And, gee, I wonder if that's . . ." It really bothered me. I was very worried she might be on the train and in great danger. And she was very sympathetic and comforting.
>
> I had even planned to call Dr. Garland. I'd worked on an introductory line saying, "I know you don't like me, but do you have any information about the hijacking. Is Bonnie on that train?" I'd gone over that time and time again in my mind. When I went back to my apartment, I checked her schedule and was relieved to see she wasn't due there for another two days.
>
> I was very lonely. I gave her a couple of weeks. I said I know for a week or two I won't get any mail from her, but after that I'll start looking. As you know, I never got anything. Week after week went by and nothing. My letters to her reflect how I was feeling then. One letter that I remember was telling her that I felt my guts were being torn out; what was going on? I was all by myself, isolated, lonely, and I wasn't hearing from her. I said my insides were being torn up—this is what's happening to me because I don't know what's going on. It didn't help to be in a house with no phone. I couldn't call her to find out what's happening. I had to rely on the mail box, and the mail box wasn't producing anything . . .

In court testimony Richard was even more specific.

Q. That brings us to the first week in June. In June, during the first week, the third week of the tour, did you receive anything from Bonnie?

A. No, I didn't.

Q. How did you react to that? How did you feel that week?

A. Well, I was beginning to think that I couldn't blame the Post

*Office for not hearing from Bonnie. Not after three weeks. I
thought of reasons why she may not have written.*

Q. *Such as?*

A. *Perhaps she was too busy singing and shopping and going out
with her friends to have time to write. Perhaps there was someone—another fellow on the Tour that she may have gotten involved with and, therefore, wasn't thinking about me any
more. I even went so far to think maybe she had eloped with
somebody in Europe, and I would never see her again. She
would stay in Europe for the rest of her life. I'd never see
her.*

Q. *Were you at this point still working on your thesis, as you had
been?*

A. *I was going into the office to—to work on the thesis occasionally. The more I thought about Bonnie, the less time I spent
thinking about my thesis.*

Q. *Where did you spend more time?*

A. *I spent more time at home, thinking about why I hadn't heard
from her. Just sitting around moping. I didn't know what was
going on. I was sure that I should have heard from her by now.
I wasn't getting anything from her. I didn't know why. I didn't
know why.*

Q. *Did you talk to anybody about the fact that you weren't receiving anything from Bonnie?*

A. *No. I was asked about it, but I didn't—I didn't bring it up.*

Q. *Why not?*

A. *I was ashamed to admit that I hadn't heard from Bonnie. Perhaps a person would conclude that Bonnie didn't love me any
more. That she had—that she had left me and—and I—I
would feel ashamed for people to think that.*

Here again, Richard seeks no comfort from others; he cannot.
Equally important to him as the possible loss of Bonnie is the symbolic, the "public," meaning of it. The possible shame and humiliation, the exposure, with all that signifies to Richard, prohibits his
taking comfort in the confidence of friends. Richard had friends, as
was proved by the extraordinary efforts of A. T. Wall (his former
roommate) and others who were to extend themselves to protect
Richard. Richard was kind, considerate, courteous, and tolerant; and
those around him appreciated it, but no one got close to Richard. No
one could later believe his crime; no one knew him.

Q. *At this time, were you having—thinking other things with respect to not hearing from Bonnie?*

A. [No response]

Q. Did you know why she did not send any letter?

A. I didn't know why. I was only speculating about the reasons. I was trying to justify why she hadn't written.

Q. What were you thinking about, as you say, as justification?

A. Well, I was giving her—I was giving reasons why she wouldn't have written. I was making excuses for her. Too busy or involved with someone else, or eloped.

This was not the answer Litman wanted and was probably not part of the carefully rehearsed testimony. Litman was preparing the story of an anxious, but not jealous, Richard whose betrayal came as an epiphany which destroyed him. Litman directed Richard back to the more favorable scenario.

Q. Did you know that she would be back soon?

A. I was expecting her back on June 30th, and I was looking forward to that date very, very much. I wanted to—figured at that time, I could talk to her, and she would explain everything away. She would explain why she hadn't written, and I would be satisfied and everything would be fine again.

Q. Were you having these thoughts at about the time you were having—during those same days that you were having the other thoughts you just told us about?

A. Yes. It was knowing she would be back on June 30th, was a reminder that things weren't—weren't too bad. When I would—when I would be thinking that I would never see her again, perhaps then I would recall that she would be back on June 30th, she would have to return with the Glee Club, she wasn't going to stay in Europe. She would be back, I could see her, talk to her; get this thing all straightened out, find out why she hadn't written. She would explain it, she would convince me, and we would continue to carry on as we always had been, had carried on.

Q. During this week, did you write anything to her?

A. I had—I continued to write letters to her in Europe.

Q. Let me show you this letter which has been already marked and received in evidence as People's 15E [handing]. When did you write that letter to Bonnie?

A. On Saturday, June 4th, 1977.

Q. Did you express your feelings to her in this letter?

A. Yes, I did.

Q. The fourth week now of June—or the fourth week of the

Tour, forgive me, the second week of June, did you receive anything from Bonnie?

A. No, I didn't.

Q. What were you doing with your time that week?

A. Was wasting most of it. I was going into the geology building, I had a job with the Department. I felt obligated to—to go in a couple of hours every day to work for the—for what I was being paid for. Even—even what I was doing there was starting to get sloppy.

Q. Did you work on your thesis?

A. I was spending less and less time on it. I had—I still had Lab work to do, and I wasn't—I wasn't doing the Lab work. I had research to do, and I wasn't doing much research. I had reading to do; I wasn't—what I was reading didn't have anything to do with my thesis. I was sitting around the house a lot, just—just wasting time.

Q. How did you feel?

A. I was—I was depressed for not having heard from her. I was still thinking, trying to make excuses for her as to why she wouldn't write. Some of the possibilities weren't pleasant, that there was someone else taking up her time. But there was still the hope that when she returned on June 30th that we could clear it all up. There was always that hope that I could return to her, that I would return to her periodically. She would come back and explain things and—and everything would be back to normal.

Then there were scenes popping into my head. They were like—like little nightmares that would pop into my head.

Q. Like what?

A. One scene, Bonnie and I were in a car or in my truck. The car—truck went into a lake and we drowned or we crashed into a barrier of some sort and were killed.

Q. What was your reaction to the scenes that came to your mind?

A. I didn't understand why they were there. I tried—I tried not—I tried to push them out of my mind. I was repulsed by having those thoughts.

Q. How long would they last?

A. Just—they were just a flash.

Q. Anything else?

A. There was another scene that would pop into my head, and I could see Bonnie lying naked with her breasts and genital area having been mutilated with a knife. And that was associated

74

with—with the idea that she had slept with someone while on the Tour.

Q. When did you return to Fort Worth?

A. June 27th.

Q. What were you thinking about on the way back from L.A. to Fort Worth?

A. Figured being away for a week, there—I would have mail. I would have a little pile of mail in the mail box when I got back home, and I was thinking there had to be something there from Bonnie.

Q. Do you remember going to the mail box that morning?

A. First thing I did when I got home from the airport was—was to bring in the mail, and there wasn't anything from Bonnie.

Q. How did you feel?

A. I was—was very, very disappointed. I had really built up an expectation of there being something there. It was shattering to just come back to a lonely place and not have something from Bonnie.

Q. Were you sleeping during that week?

A. Was trying to. It was—it was—for one thing, it was hot and uncomfortable. I was sleeping under an air conditioner to try to keep cool; and for another thing, I was alone in a small place with—with my thoughts, and I—I just kept going over and over and over what was going on, or trying to think of why I hadn't heard from her, what could possibly be going on.

Then I would look forward to—then I would look forward to talking to her when she came back, and wondering what was going to happen then. We—how we would resolve all of this, which I was sure we would.

Q. What were you doing other than trying to sleep and work a couple of hours in the Lab?

A. Sitting around the house, playing my guitar. I would go into the Geology Building to see who was around, just for companionship. Maybe somebody who'd want to go out to the Stables and get a beer now and then. I was hanging around the library, too, but I wasn't doing research for my own thesis. I was reading other material.

Q. Did you still have any hope with respect to Bonnie?

A. The hope was greater and greater as I approached June 30th. Hope that things would work out okay.

Q. Did you get any letter that week from Bonnie prior to the arrival of the Glee Club back in New York on the 30th of June?

A. No, I didn't.

Q. Were you aware, from the itinerary of the Glee Club or conversations with Bonnie, when the Glee Club plane was due to return to New York?

A. Yes, I was aware.

Q. What date was that?

A. June 30th, a Thursday.

Q. Sometime after the time of arrival of that flight, did you do anything?

A. I did what I had been looking forward to be doing for a long time. I called Bonnie's house.

Q. Where did you call Bonnie's house from, and how did you call Bonnie's house?

A. I had been accumulating a lot of small change, quarters and dimes. I didn't have a phone in the house, and I was going to use a pay phone and use the pay phone in the Geology Department.

Q. How many hours after the plane landed did you call?

A. Two or three hours after.

Q. Why?

A. Figured Bonnie would be home.

Q. Did someone answer the phone when you called at the Garland home on the 30th of June?

A. Yes, Mrs. Garland answered the phone.

Q. How did you feel?

A. Before making the phone call, I was trembling. I was very nervous. Probably a mixture of excitement at being able to talk to Bonnie, and maybe apprehension at what she might have to say. I was very—I was very nervous, shaking, but I knew I was going to get to talk to her, because she was—the plane was in, it was time for her to get home from the airport, and I was going to talk to her now.

Q. Were you able to talk to Bonnie then?

A. No. I asked for Bonnie. Mrs. Garland said she had gone—she had called her from the airport, and she said she was going straight to New Haven with some friends. I asked her if Bonnie left a phone number where she could be reached, and Mrs. Garland said, no, she hadn't, but she said she would be back Saturday night, back in Scarsdale Saturday night.

I asked Mrs. Garland if she thought Bonnie hadn't left a number because she didn't want to talk to me. Mrs. Garland said she didn't know what the reason was.

Q. You finished the conversation with her?

A. Yes.

Q. How did you feel?

A. I was—I was confused, upset. What I felt was that one of my fears that I had been thinking for a long time was being confirmed; that she was going to New Haven because she was with a guy from the Glee Club, and they were going off to spend a few days by themselves. I thought that. I really didn't know why she was in New Haven.

But I also felt that there could be a more reasonable explanation, one that wasn't so painful to me. That perhaps some of the people on the Tour wanted to have one final party together in New Haven before they all dispersed and went their separate ways. I thought that was just as plausible as any other explanation that I might also think up. And actually was prepared to give that story to anyone who had asked about Bonnie, since several people knew she was due to arrive that day.

Q. Do you remember what you did on the evening of Thursday, June 30th, 1977?

A. Yes. I—I went home after the phone call, but I didn't want to be alone. I was tormented by the thoughts that she might be with someone else in New Haven. But there were—but then I would think of other explanations why things wouldn't be so bad. And not wanting to be alone with these thoughts, that they were—were going from like hot and cold. I didn't want to have—to just sit there and think about these things, because I really didn't know. I had no basis for believing anything yet. I didn't want to be alone.

Q. Where did you go?

A. Well, I didn't go to the Geology Department. I knew that some of my friends had gone by that time—they were—it was the 4th of July weekend coming up, and I knew most people were gone. There weren't many people around. But a friend of mine worked at a Pizza Hut. I went there.

Q. Do you remember the next day, July the 1st?

A. Yes, I do.

Q. What did you do in the morning?

A. I awoke and went to the mail box, as I had done every morning that I was in Fort Worth. It was—it was out of habit by that time. I hadn't received anything from Bonnie up to that point. And just out of habit, I'd go to the mail box and—

Q. Was there a letter from Bonnie?

A. There was a letter from her from Norway.

Q. How did you feel when you took the letter out of the mail box?

A. Began trembling, shaking.

Q. Where did you go with it?

A. I took it inside the house and opened it up and started reading it.

Q. What happened?

A. Because of what the letter said, I started crying. Fell on the bed, crying, read the letter over and over.

Q. How long did you cry for?

A. I spent the next two or three hours reading the letter and crying, and I tried to tell myself that it didn't really say anything definite about the relationship. I had no reason to feel that it was—that everything was over. But I would read the letter again, and she would mention that there was another guy. I would go into despair that that fellow—that the relationship was definitely threatened. That maybe this guy was going to take her away from me. I just—was just crying. Composed myself and said, "It is not that bad. It doesn't say anything definite. I'll see her soon. I'll get it all fixed up. There is nothing to worry about." Read the letter again and went back into despair and crying, and I spent the next two or three hours just—just there in the bed.

Q. This is in evidence as People's Exhibit 13. I've removed the letter from the envelope.

Is that the letter you finally received from Bonnie on July the 1st [handing]?

"Dear Rick,

I know it has been an unforgiveable crime not to have written you all this time, but I have been trying to postpone action on something very important which has come up on this Tour. I still don't know what to do, but I must at least tell you what has happened. I have spent almost all my time on this Tour in the company of one specific man, someone I saw off and on during the semester. To make things short, he has fallen in love with me. I am in a total state of confusion, because I know I still love you just as much, but I feel an infatuation at least for him. I did not want to tell you, because I thought it would all be over when the Tour ended. But now I am not so sure. It makes me sick to write this letter, I couldn't lie and I didn't want to tell the truth. So, I just haven't written. You remember those conversations we have had about being constrained and feeling like I hadn't had a social life—well in a way, I

think the elastic finally broke into this. I can hardly believe that this is happening, and I hope to straighten things out with the help of my shrink when I get back. I need time to myself to think, but I also hope you will not turn your back on me. I know you feel hurt, betrayed, alienated, but you have always said that if it happened, you would want to know. I wish now more than ever that you will seek psychiatric help to help you deal with a flood of emotions which is probably beginning to overwhelm you. I hate this letter and this mess, but please be patient, and I'm sure things will work out because I still love you and I need your love as much as ever—please don't desert me. I'll be back soon, and we can talk. I've missed you a great deal.
Love,
Bonnie."[2]

Incredible as it may seem, Richard claimed to see the letter as partly encouraging. As he explained to me, it was not *really* definite.

"Is it over, is that it? But she still loves me." Back and forth. It was right there in the letter—the two-pronged thing. One good and one bad. She still loves me. There's this other guy.

I composed myself and went into the office, to the geology department and now made new plans for myself. I decided that I would forget about going to George Washington. I would move to New Haven so I could be near Bonnie and try to get a job; find a place to live; find a psychiatrist or someone to go to—but the most important thing, to be near Bonnie so I could see her as often as possible. This was the decision I made that night after reading the letter. So I went into the office. The secretary was there, and she happened to have an open Watts line right at the moment when I was there.

Richard had called a research office he knew in New Haven, requesting any kind of job that was available. He was told there were no openings at that point, but that he would be kept informed if anything opened up. This, in his peculiar fashion, seemed to encourage Richard. He felt he had behaved decisively.

I had made a decision. I'm not losing control; I'm going to have to set things up with George Washington to delay, postpone my admission for one semester. Again, as soon as any problems with Bonnie would crop up, the academic aspect— that was just totally shunned, automatically.

So now I'm not going to go to Washington; I'll go to New

Haven, get a job, maybe they'll defer my admission for a semester, but that's not important right now. The most important thing is to patch this relationship back up. Because I just
can't live without Bonnie—that's what I have to do. I have to
be near her and show her that she should come back to me, and
we'll live happily ever after. . . . Friday afternoon I went to the
bookstore and bought a few anthropology books to keep myself
company and have something to read. Of course I had tons of
books for my research, but that was not important at that time.

The next day I had an appointment to get my truck fixed—
new brakes. I wanted my truck to be in good shape. I wanted it
to be in good traveling condition because I was going to have to
drive halfway across the country, to New Haven, not Washington. I'd asked for some money from home because this was
going to be quite expensive—three hundred dollars—a muffler,
exhaust system, brakes, and my mother had sent the money to
help pay for all this. So I was investing a lot of money in the
truck.

I mention it because to me it shows that I hadn't really given
in. Forking over three hundred dollars cash—I still had a lot of
hope. . . . That night, my plane was going to leave at two
o'clock. I just kind of puttered around. I was still torn. I didn't
know what was going to happen. . . . At least I was going back
East to find out what the deal was. I had made a decision to go
back there and not wait to hear from her and not sit back. I'm
going to go back and find out. I had several stuffed animals
with me. One of them was a St. Bernard with a little plastic keg
around his neck, and I decided I would take that with me and
give it to her as a present, and I wrote a little note and taped it
to the keg. I remember that note—part of the note that said
that I would never be very far away from her again. I was
thinking that because I'd been in Texas all this time—that kind
of caused the relationship to crumble—so far away. Now I'm
planning to move to New Haven, and I would stay near her so
we would always be closer together. I felt that would help heal
the relationship.

During this period, Richard stated, he began to think more consciously of committing suicide. Certainly one of the most confusing
aspects about both Richard's behavior and his state of mind circles
around the question of suicide. Before leaving Texas, Richard had
written a cryptic note that was offered in evidence as a suicide note.
In addition, he had packed a length of rope in his suitcase. No

explicit suicide notes were written. The opportunities for suicide were plentiful, but no suicide attempts were executed, despite the statement of Mr. Litman. The preparations for suicide seem feeble or nonexistent. Even if one accepted Richard's current statements that the rope he brought with him to New York was intended for suicide, it seems ludicrous.

On the other hand, it could be equally said that no preparations were made for murder either. If one disbelieves that he ever entertained the idea of suicide, and interprets the rope as an instrument for murder, it seems just as foolish and nondirected.

The conversation I had with him after the fact clearly demonstrates this confusion and inconsistency in his story.

I must have made a decision that if Bonnie decided that she didn't want to try to heal the relationship and get back together and make a go of it—that life for me wouldn't be worth it. I had a brown cord that my mother had used to wrap around the suitcase. I had that cord there in the house. I bound it up and stuck it in my flight bag. I went over to the desk and wrote a little note. I said that if I'm not back in a few days, I would never be back. That's all I said.

—To whom did you write it?

It was intended for the Devereys [in whose house he was living]. And I referred them to the letter. The letter that I had received from Bonnie. I left it there attached to the note. I said this letter will explain. I intended to be back. I intended to talk to her, well, on my upswing I intended to be back. I intended to go out and talk to her for a couple of days. I knew the Devereys were due back on July twelfth, and this was now July first. I knew I had a few days' leeway. I could go out to New York, try to straighten things out, and then come back and nobody would know that I was gone.

On the other hand, there was the despair. You know, if I'm not back, that would explain why, and I did put the rope in the bag.

—Now why take the rope? That struck me as strange. You can get rope anywhere.

I just figured I was going to find a way to hang myself.

—Do you know anything about hanging yourself?

No. I wouldn't have known how to. I remember fooling around with string when I was a kid, but I don't know if I could have . . .

—Could you visualize yourself now hanging yourself?

I try to visualize how I would have done it—like when I went to grab the rope that night. I had the rope with me. I try to visualize what I could have done in the house to have hung myself, and I can't. All I see is failure, you know. The rope snapping or my not dying. I just can't see . . . I didn't know what to do. I didn't have any plans on how to go about doing it. But here's this rope, so if things don't work out, I'm just going to take this rope and just do myself in.

—In retrospect it doesn't sound very realistic.

No. The whole situation . . . Here's a suicide note that's not a suicide note. Here's taking a rope to kill myself, and I can't kill myself.

—What do you mean you can't?

I didn't. I couldn't go through with it.

—Do you think psychologically you could ever kill yourself?

Do you mean physically commit suicide?

—Yes.

No. If there had been a gun in the house or something that could have guaranteed a swift sure kill—maybe—all I can say is maybe. I don't know if I would have had the nerve to pull the trigger. If there was something there that was accessible that I knew could deliver a killing blow to myself, I might have gone ahead. I wouldn't have been the only person in history to have done that.

The circumstances in the house just prevented me from killing myself there, and then once I started driving around, I don't know how to describe it—the energy that I could have used to do it kind of gradually waned. Eventually I kind of just said, "There's a church. I'm going to go that route instead of . . ."

—Okay. So you had mixed feelings. How did you spend the night until two o'clock?

Earlier that day I'd been at the pizza parlor. There was no one I knew that I felt I could go to. Most of the evening I just stayed in the house. The pizza parlor—I was there just for the company. So I went there. Sometimes before I had washed dishes for them. They had been short of help, and said if you help us they'd give me a pizza. So I went back there, and I didn't mind, because then I was with people, and I wasn't alone. . . . Saturday I spent most of the day waiting for my truck to get fixed. That evening I spent some time at the pizza, but most of the time I was alone in the house—thinking.

—Thinking what?

Everything. How we would get back together. Of course once I'm there with her, she'll welcome me back, and everything will be okay. But wait, there's this letter with this guy . . .

—Did you have thoughts of killing Bonnie?

No.

—Did you have thoughts of her being dismembered, mutilated?

I don't remember having them that night. Those thoughts had occurred earlier during the six weeks—when the thought would be maybe she has this guy; maybe there's a boyfriend on the tour. Then I'd just sit there and let my mind dwell on these things, and I'd catch myself—gee, that was a gruesome thought—but yet I'd let it go for a few seconds or how long it took for that image to be complete of the dismemberment, the mutilation; also the scenes of driving in the truck, crashing into a barrier, a pond or lake or something to kill us. So those things were . . . I don't remember having anything like that that night. That night I was actively engaged in debate. I wasn't just sitting around. I was constantly thinking about it. I wasn't sitting back silently so thoughts could come in. I was actively pondering what's going to happen. Is there hope? Well, no, there's no hope. But wait. She still loves me. But wait, there's this guy.

—Was there a lot of crying?

No. Not at this point.

—Was there fear?

I would say yes. Fear of hearing what I didn't want to hear.

—What about anger?

I don't remember feeling anger.

—You didn't feel as angry as when she hung up on you.

No. I wasn't angry. Not that I can remember.

—So you took a two o'clock plane?

Right. The day before when I was getting my truck fixed I took a book with me and read *Sybil* that day. Nice reading sort of. About the multiple-personality person. And another book I had just finished reading that week was about a New York City policeman—a cop with a gun, and the psychologist with the city force who a—he was available to counsel—so I read a couple of psychologically oriented books.

The question of the books is a peculiar one—and never came up in the trial. Richard was not a reader. When I first asked him what the books were, he said, "Anthropology books." Later in the course of his narration he stated that the books were *Sybil*—a book about multiple personalities—and another book about a police officer who, having committed a murder, is defended by psychiatrists. He "couldn't remember" the title. These were books Richard specifically purchased, and their selection is open to some disturbing speculation.

Okay. So I took the two o'clock flight and arrived at the airport early in the morning, carrying the stuffed dog and flight bag, and got on a bus to get into the city to go to Grand Central. I remember asking someone for directions, exactly where I'd have to get off—something to that effect—and one of the stewardesses said, "Oh, you just get off. I'll let you know when to get off." As we were approaching her stop, she said, "Oh, I live there," and I remember thinking, I'll ask her if I could buy her a cup of coffee. I was thinking maybe I could prove something—I could go to bed with a stewardess. Maybe I'll ask her. She said, "I can't; my roommates are there." She got off the bus. But I did ask her. I did semi-proposition her. I didn't know how to do it, because I'd never been so forward before.

This incident, so peculiar, and so open to multiple interpretations, also never came out at the trial, and yet, even at this point one wonders what might have happened if the stewardess had not "had a roommate."

So I finally made it to Grand Central. I knew which train to get to go to Scarsdale. I got to the station and called. I assumed Bonnie would be there Sunday morning. I assumed she would have arrived Saturday night. I called the house. Again Mrs. Garland answered; I asked for Bonnie. She said she was out with her father on the boat, and they would be back later that day in the afternoon. I told Mrs. Garland I was there at the train station, which is just a couple of blocks away from the house. She said, "Oh, I'd better tell you there's another guy staying here." I said, "Oh." She said, "Would you like to come over here for lunch?" I said, "Okay." She said, "I'll leave the house open; I'll be in the shower. Come in. Make yourself comfortable." So I walked over to the house. Went to the back door, let myself in. I went straight up to Bonnie's room, where I left the stuffed dog with the note—put it on her bed. Came back downstairs to the kitchen, sat in the kitchen. Mrs. Garland came down. We started talking.

—Was she friendly?

Yes.

—Was she sympathetic?

To some extent. She asked a few questions that I didn't like. Which made sense. I didn't remember the questions until being reminded of them later on, but the gist of it was I told her I'd flown East to try to get Bonnie to come back to me, to try to patch things up, and I realized there was another guy, but there would still be some hope. We probably talked for a lot longer than I remember. And I didn't really feel like eating. My stomach was in knots, very tight ball. I had a cup of coffee. She asked me if I had a place to stay. I was going to try to come back to see Bonnie when this other guy left. So she suggested I try to find some friends to stay with for a few days until Bonnie could see me. At first I said, "I don't know anybody." I don't know why I did that. I was trying to force myself into the house and have them ask the other guy to leave to make room for me—something like that. At first I said I don't know where to go. Maybe I was just trying to evoke sympathy. Eventually I said there's a friend in Long Island. Maybe I could stay with him. She asked if I had his number, and I said no. She said, "Here's a phone book."

I said, "But I don't want to tell him. Mike knows Bonnie— he knows how involved I am with her. I don't want to tell Mike I flew from Texas to visit her and another guy is staying in the house. How can I tell him that? I don't know where the relationship stands right now. How can I tell him that?" She helped me come up with a plan. "Call Mike, tell him you flew in to see Bonnie, came to the house or called and there was no answer. You don't know if the family is on vacation or what, so you would like a place to stay until you can get in touch with somebody in the house." I said, "Okay, that sounds good." So I did.

I was invited to Mike's house in Long Island for the day or few days, however long. That was Sunday.

I called Bonnie on Sunday night. I talked to Patrick. I guess the guy had left by then. I don't know. He came back and told me that Bonnie was asleep. That was in the evening—seven or eight.

—Was she normally asleep at that time?

No. So I don't know if the guy was in the room or she was really asleep or she didn't want to talk to me. I rang up a few times, and each time she was asleep. I chatted with Patrick for a while. He invited me to a rock concert, and I said thanks, but no.

—Did you try to pump him for information?

No. Apparently he really didn't know much. He wasn't around the house very much. So I left the number there. I had planned to call back later, but she called instead, and her first words were "You nut, what are you doing out here." Very friendly, like, that's the old Bonnie. There was warmth in her voice, a little bit of a tease. So I told her, "I'm out here, and I want to see you," et cetera. I asked her if it would be possible for me to stay at the house. She said, "I'll go check." I don't know who she asked, but she came back—I waited on the phone—she came back and said, "Yeah, it's okay." So I planned to go up the next day.

This was Sunday when I was talking to her. She asked me right off if I could come up that night. It was so early that if I left I could be in Scarsdale maybe ten or eleven o'clock that night. I said, "No, tomorrow is the Fourth of July and I have plans to spend the day with Mike's family, but I'll come up in the evening."

—I don't understand. Here was the girl you loved, and she finally said come. Why didn't you just jump on the first bus and go?

I had already agreed to spend the day with Mike's family, but I don't know why I didn't jump, swim across the Long Island Sound to get to her that night. I felt . . . The way she was talking, she put me at ease as she always did. Maybe I felt it wasn't urgent. I really don't know why I didn't jump at the first chance to see her. It was kind of late in the evening.

—But you didn't go the next morning either?

No, I went in the late afternoon.

I wasn't letting anyone in on what I was feeling inside. I helped Mike cut down some tree limbs. We played badminton, and some friends or relatives came over. We went to see *Star Wars*—the whole family went to see it. The Fourth of July was a Monday. . . .

So Tuesday afternoon I left Long Island and did go to Scarsdale. I called her from the station and told her I was there. She said, "Okay, I'll come right over and pick you up." I could have walked to the house in fifteen minutes, but she came. I waited for her. When I arrived, I called her from the station, and then I waited for her so that we could walk back to the house together.

I thought she looked lovely. The greeting wasn't as warm as it could have been. It was not a long embrace or a long hug, but a very brief kiss. As we started to walk back, I didn't want to hold her hand or something like that. When we got near the house I didn't want anyone in the house to see us holding hands, because they would think I'm very much of a fool to be deceived by it because I know there's another guy now. If they see me holding her hand, they might think I didn't know what was going on. They'd think I'm a big fool and so we had a little disagreement. "Why are you acting like that?" I remember her asking. "Why are you acting like that?" Pretty much right off the bat there wasn't an immediate attachment like I had hoped. I hoped as soon as I arrived on the scene everything would be okay. Yet there wasn't. The greeting wasn't warm. I was acting childish by saying, "I don't want to hold your hand, because then they'll think I'm silly or that I'm an idiot."

At this intense moment of reunion, one part of Richard is still, as always, detached and observing. One part of Richard is still concerned about appearance and public display. He holds hands or doesn't hold hands not impulsively and unwittingly, as dictated by inner moods, but like a barometer, as an indicator of the nature of things to those who are watching.

When we got to the house her parents were home. I believe they were both home. I saw Dr. Garland, shook his hand and said hello. I might have seen Mrs. Garland and said hello. One of them might not have been there. . . . Most of the rest of the day was just spent talking to her, trying to find out what was going on. Where did I stand?

She was very firm. She was tender and loving and concerned, but very firm. She had made a decision for herself that she did not want to be tied down to one person, and she wanted to experiment, see different people; and very important for me, she said, "If I like someone, I might sleep with him—although I haven't done so yet." When she threw that part in—"even though I haven't done so yet"—that gave me a lot of hope. One of the things I'd been concerned with was Gee, she's been sleeping with guys, and it's one of the reasons she'd want to experiment more and more, but if she hasn't done so yet, then maybe I still have a chance to convince her.

—You believed it at that point?

Yes.

—Do you now?

No.

—Did you have some doubts about your capacity as a lover?

I felt as long as she didn't have any other men, I would be able to satisfy her, that if she were to sleep with someone else that she would enjoy that other person more than she would enjoy me.
—Why?
Probably the thing that I was concerned with was penis size. I felt that if she went to bed with someone who was bigger than I was that she would derive more satisfaction and therefore want to go with him.
—Do you have any reason to believe that you're small?
Yeah.
—Do you think it's real, or just your feelings about yourself?
I think it's real. When erect it's average. I'd have to say it's average from reading *Penthouse* and things like that. I would just say I fall in the average range. There's no problem there. But I still never felt that was enough. If she slept with someone who's bigger, she would get more satisfaction sexually and forget about any of the emotional attachment. When she had someone who was bigger, that would be it. I would lose her.
—Do you think penis size is important to a woman?
Intellectually I could argue against that, but I had this great fear. In fact, no one asked me about that. You're the first one who has asked me or who I've mentioned it to. But that was a tremendous fear that I had.
—All your adult life?
It might have contributed to my being satisfied with oral sex and not being terribly occupied with genital sex. But in Bonnie's case, at that stage now there was a tremendous fear that if she had anyone else who was bigger that she would go to him. I felt that when we did make love I satisfied her. That we had a very compatible relationship.
It was just something that I was terribly afraid of, so when she told me that she hadn't yet slept with anyone, naturally I jumped at it and believed it. Okay, that's one big problem out of the way. I don't have to compete with someone who's already slept with her. But it was a terrible fear. That might have played a significant part, and other people haven't realized it. It was a tremendous fear I had. Not for the amount of love I had for her, but someone else might be able to please her more.

Richard is not given to superlatives—particularly in the descriptions of emotions—but here when he is discussing penis size: "great fear," "tremendous fear," "terribly occupied," "tremendous fear," "terribly afraid of," "terrible fear," "tremendous fear," all within a momentary discussion of penis size. And it is the competitive aspect and loss that he emphasizes in considering his rejection by Bonnie, not the hurt and betrayal.

I got there on the fifth. I think. That first night I was there we talked about a great many things. About our relationship. Her telling me what she wanted for herself, and she didn't want to stop seeing me. She hoped I would still want to see her, but I had to realize that there would be other men in her life now. She was very adamant about it. I tried to talk her out of it, I tried to remind her of our commitment to each other. She did say, "Well, I know that I'm going to get married eventually, but I'm just not sure it's going to be with you." She had made that much ... We talked about the plans I had to go to New Haven and live to be near her instead of going to Washington. She talked me out of it. She said, "You can't do that. That's no good. You've got to think of yourself too." So by the end of that first day she had me agreeing that, yes, I would go ahead and go to Washington. That we would visit each other on weekends whenever we could. If I could get away for a weekend I would go up to see her, and she would come down for a week-end. We kind of agreed to that kind of a schedule. But I couldn't get her to change her mind about seeing other guys. That seemed to be the basic decision, that I would not be her exclusive, and she would have others.

—So, how did that night end? Did you go to bed?

Yeah. I was about to leave her room and go back downstairs to the guest room without us having any love. She was already in bed. I remember I turned; I saw her yearbook on the desk. She was already in bed, and I was kind of in the room and still talking; she was undressed and in bed, and I happened to see the yearbook on the desk, and I knew that this Bob was in it.

So I picked the yearbook up off the desk, and I flipped the pages. She had told me his name, which I hadn't known before. She did mention a little of what had gone on. She told me then that she hadn't opened all my letters. She got tired of reading the same thing. And she told me the guy's name, so I opened the book, and saw this guy who wasn't particularly good-looking, I didn't think, with curly blond, dirty-blond hair, and I kind of said, "That jerk or that twerp, that's the guy?" and I kind of slammed the book and put it down on the desk. I kind of shook my head, and I was trying to make her feel, "Gee, you could have picked a better one than that!"

Richard's anguish and his total incapacity to come to grips with his loss and grief are apparent in this pathetic attempt at disparaging his rival. The pain for Richard must have been enormous, and his methods for coping were so pitifully inadequate.

—Jokingly or angrily?

I was trying to say it angrily. Trying to make fun of her for her choice of the new lover or whatever interest. It didn't offend her. I was about ready to leave. I had already gone over and kissed her good night and was about ready to walk out the door, and I turned back and looked at her, and she was looking at me. I started to walk back to her, and she held her arms out to me—so I stayed with her that night. I got up early the next morning and went back to my room. I hadn't been with her for a long time, since April. I was maybe a little anxious, but it was a very pleasant interlude.

The next morning Patrick came in the room where I was sleeping. It was fortunate that I had gotten back to the bed when I did. Patrick knocked and came in when I answered, so I was glad I was in bed when he came in, because if there was ever a question of does Rich sleep with my sister, he would have thought, no, they don't. That day she was going to Columbia to register for summer school. In order to be admitted to Yale in the fall, instead of taking a whole year off, she had just quit in the middle of that previous semester, so she was catching up. She was going to try to go back to school in the fall. In order to do so she needed one more credit. So she was going to take a psychology course at Columbia.

So we drove to Columbia.

—Were you in good spirits?

Yep.

The next day Richard spent driving Bonnie to Columbia and accompanying her on her rounds. From Richard's description, it could have been a day on the campus at Yale two years before.

By now Richard, even Richard, assuredly knows that the game is lost. What reassurances Bonnie offers are the transparent words of her comfort offered to protect against despair. And yet Richard persists—in kindness, in concern, with solicitude and denial—in serving Bonnie's needs and pretending that he has not lost the dream. To a psychiatrist, at least, the denial is more heartbreaking than tears.

And the peculiar vulnerability and self-referential quality that made him assume that everyone was always noting his behavior were evident here too. That announcement to the world as he saw it— that index of his feelings, the hand-holding—once again was mentioned.

> We had a nice time. We were walking hand in hand, again. Very nice, lovey-dovey. She went through all the routine she had to go through to register. We walked around the campus, looked at different buildings. We hugged and held each other at different times and kissed and what-not.
>
> On the way back, driving back after her registration, we started talking about the relationship again. She still hadn't changed her mind on that point. I had hoped that after a nice pleasant day like we had and after the night before, the revelation that she hadn't slept with anyone, I thought that would be breaking the ice, and she could be reconsidering—but no, she was just as firm as before.
>
> In fact, en route to Columbia, I guess I tried to play her out of position. I said, "Well, if you're going to see other guys, I'll probably start seeing other women." I was hoping that would get her to reconsider. She said, "Well, if that's what you're going to do, go ahead." That wasn't the answer I was looking for. I was hoping she would say, "Oh, wait a minute. I don't want you to do that." Instead she said, "Well, okay."
>
> We had more discussion on the way back. We stopped to eat before we got home. I didn't say much all the time we ate. We stopped at a place we always stopped at—had a hamburger, whatever—and hardly spoke the whole time. We had had enough discussion in the car. I could see I wasn't getting anywhere with trying to change her mind, so we were pretty silent throughout the meal.

Bonnie was showing a resolution, a consistency, and a firmness that could not be misinterpreted. The relationship was over, and the "We'll see each other occasionally" motif was pro-forma reassurance. By this point even Richard had to know.

> We got back home and went right up to her room, and we continued the discussion. She told me that her mother had asked that I leave the next day, and had I made plans and reservations? I said no, I hadn't. Maybe you could talk to your mom and let me stay another couple of days. Nothing more was said on that. I don't know. I felt I was kind of being pushed out.
>
> Bonnie said, "My mother wants you to leave."

—Did you have the feeling *she* wanted you to too?

No. I didn't think so. I thought she said her mother wanted me to leave—her parents wanted me to leave—but here I am, holding Bonnie. How could she want me to leave?

We talked some more. She was still firm. I couldn't say anything that could convince her to change her mind. I felt, Well, I'm sure she will talk to her mom. I'm sure I'll get another couple of days. I'll just try again tomorrow.

The first night I was there she hadn't asked me to spend the night with her. It was something that happened spontaneously. Now Wednesday night she said, "I want you to stay with me tonight." I said, "Okay." She said, "We can set the clock, but I want you to stay with me." So Wednesday night I knew that I would spend the night with her.

All through the next day, after she talked to Mom, they would let me stay, I thought. I didn't have cash. I was going to have to have them cash a check for me for my plane ticket to get back. I had the money in my checking account. I had the money to get back to Texas, but I was going to have to borrow the money for the parking for my truck. I needed twenty dollars for parking, because I'd been gone a few days. I was going to say I lost my ticket, that's twenty dollars, instead of saying I was gone five days—that's forty dollars. But I felt I'm not going to make reservations. I'm going to wait and see if I can have a couple of more days.

So we kind of finished talking. We both settled down and got comfortable and turned on the TV, and around nine o'clock—I remembered that—*Policewoman* was on at nine—we got comfortable. We were both stripped to the waist, we both had pants on, no socks or shoes. I had my shirt off, she had her top off. And we were just sitting on her bed, watching TV, being very tender and warm and kissing and hugging. After the news and the *Tonight* show started, she said she was sleepy, and she wanted to go to sleep. I would have thought it unusual for her ordinarily to say she was sleepy, but she had some medicine. She had gotten sick on the tour. She said she had had a cold all throughout the tour, and she couldn't shake this cold or whatever it was, and she had medicine in this bottle, and she was taking or drinking it—a lot of it. So I thought maybe this medication is making her drowsy, and I said, "That's okay." She said, "Are you coming to bed?" I said, "No, I'm not really tired right now. I'll turn the TV off, but do you mind if I leave the light on?" She said, "No. That's okay."

So she finished undressing, got in bed, and she turned her back—well, she turned to face the wall so the light wouldn't get in her face. I leaned over to kiss her good night and said I'd be going to bed soon anyway, but I kissed her.

Then I sat down on the couch—she had like a daybed next to her bed—turned the TV off, left the light on. There was a *Sports Illustrated* magazine that I thought I would read until I got sleepy. That's what I did until the idea came to me to kill her.

I don't know how much time elapsed. It could have been five minutes; it could have been two hours. That elapsed time—I really have no idea how much time was involved. As I was looking through the magazine, I started looking over at her, put the magazine down. I started looking for a weapon. I started looking around the room. I'd decided, or whatever the term is, that we were both going to die that night. That decision, that thought, just came into my mind, and I accepted it, and set about to carry out the killing.

I don't remember feeling angry. I don't remember my heart racing. I don't remember my face getting flushed like I feel it is right now. I don't remember feeling my mom's going to feel pretty messed up when she hears this, that I'm going to die, that she hears I'm dead. I never considered what my mother would think. Never considered any consequences of what would happen. My life is over. That interval.
—Now how did you decide how to kill her?

The first scene I had was us laying in bed together with our wrists slashed, dying in bed together. I felt again that was it for me. There was no point in going on. Bonnie was there, so she was going to die too.
—Why didn't you just decide to kill yourself?

I still don't know why I killed her. I still don't really understand.

I've been told the dynamics, but it still doesn't . . . You know, they said it was a crazy act, and it defies logic. I still don't know. I'll never be able to answer why. I know it happened. I can tell *how* it happened. I'll never be able to say *why* it happened, because there's no explanation for it as far as I'm concerned.

The image of our lying in bed with our wrists slashed meant that I would have to slash her wrists, but in slashing her wrists she would most likely wake up, and I wouldn't be able to complete the other part of the scene—my lying next to her with my wrists slashed. She would undoubtedly resist or . . . I automatically knew that I should reject that idea, because I would not be—I wouldn't be part of the scene. I wouldn't be dying with her.

The next thing I saw was a glass or a mug on the table. We had had some cake and milk that evening. And I thought of using the mug as a weapon. It had a handle on it, but I rejected that. I saw a pair—she had a pair of stockings hanging over a chair back. I thought of taking the stockings and strangling her. I rejected that. I got up and looked in one of her closets where she had her guitar. I think I considered hitting her with the guitar—I think. I remember looking in the closet and seeing the guitar.

Then I walked downstairs into the kitchen. In the kitchen was where they have knives, but I guess by then the wrist slashing had already . . . I don't recall even thinking once I was in the kitchen that that's where the knives were kept. That had already been pushed out.

—There are other ways of using a knife. To stab someone.

Yeah. I don't remember thinking about stabbing. The wrist-slashing . . . There was not stabbing images I had. But I did know they had a workshop down the basement.

—And what were you thinking you'd find down there?

Something. You know, I didn't have anything in mind, but I knew they had a workshop. Something lethal would undoubtedly be found there. Now the door to the basement was in the kitchen. There's a doorway, then a little landing, then stairs leading down to the basement. So I opened the door, and right there on the landing I saw a hammer, on the little landing going down the stairs. So I picked up the hammer and closed the door. And that's what I was going to use.

—It was a heavy claw hammer?

Right. Now from the kitchen they have like the laundry room adjoining the kitchen and the living room is over here [pointing] and the guest room is over here. And I walked through the dining room, which adjoins the laundry room. I walked through the laundry room and picked up a yellow towel and walked into my room and on the bed was two pages of legal paper—a letter from Mrs. Garland in which she was asking me to leave the next day. It was a full page and part of a second page. The gist of it was that Bonnie was in an academic crisis again; she has to pass this course at Columbia; if I care about her, I'll leave her alone, leave her in peace so she can concentrate on the course. And would I please not call. Would I just confine my contact to writing letters till after the course is over. She said I hadn't been of any help to Bonnie in her previous crises in academic crises. And would I please try to do so now by letting her alone and be in peace to study and get through this third crisis so she could get into Yale in the fall.

I remember I picked up the letter and read it and put it back down on the bed. I reached in my flight bag and grabbed the rope. Put the hammer and rope inside the towel and wrapped them up. I walked back through the living room and through the kitchen and back up the stairs. Bonnie's room is—all the bedrooms are on one floor, the second floor, but in one corner of the house there is a small landing up a few stairs, and Bonnie's room is in that corner. She has her own bathroom and her bedroom, and there's a little hallway outside.

I set the towel—the towel with the hammer and rope—I set it on a box or pile or bundle of something out in the hallway, outside her room. Went into her room and walked over to the bed and leaned over to see if she was asleep. Saw that she was or she appeared to be asleep. Went out and got the towel.

—Didn't you feel any affection for her or . . . Seeing her lying there sleeping?

I don't remember feeling any affection. I don't remember feeling anything.

—So she was lying there still with her face to the wall?

Right.

Then what happened?

I went back out and got the hammer and the towel. I left the rope out in the hall. Went back into the room. I don't know. I must have just dropped the towel or put it on the couch. The towel got lost somewhere. I leaned over her again. She was still asleep. I hit her once around the temple.

—She was lying on her side?

Yes.

—Now when you say you hit her once, did you use both hands?

Yes.

I lifted it over my head. As far as using all my might, I can't say whether I did or not. I did lift it.

—It was a full swing?

Yeah. The way a lumberjack would raise a hammer. It wasn't the way a geologist uses his rock hammer. This was a two-handed . . . I had it with two hands.

—You hit her with great force on the temple?

95

Uh huh.

I saw a round bluish mark on the temple where the hammer had struck.

It didn't break through the skull?

It didn't break the skin even.

—So after the one blow?

I did notice blood start to come out of her ear. Her body jerked. Her eyes . . . This is the unfortunate part about my having this vivid recollection. This is what haunted me for the first six months. Her eyes rolled back, and she was making a little noise, a guttural noise. That's—at that point is when I lifted her head and cradled her head in my hands and called her name. Said her name once. There was no response, so I laid her head back down. The next blow did break the skin and break the skull, and the blows after that all penetrated into the same area—the temple area. It was the same area where the first blow had hit.

—The blows after. Was there blood splattered all over?

Yes.

—Were there multiple blows?

Yes.

—At the trial they talked about two or three.

I remember the first blow. After setting her head back down, I remember a few more. That part now is very vague in terms of how many blows there were.

—But you do remember that you said you had to pry the hammer away.

According to Chief Rea. He testified that I made that statement, and I probably said something to that effect. I'm sure it was partly true, but I was trying to convince him that I had indeed done this act. I was using the ball part of the hammer, not the claw part. And one of the blows might have penetrated, I might have had trouble pulling it straight out. I had to jiggle to get it back out, but that part is hazy in terms of how long I was there, hitting, and how many blows I delivered. But the blood was . . . I felt as though I was just covered with blood. I felt like the noise she was making was very loud, and I felt it was reverberating. It was so loud that people would wake up. I did see brain tissue oozing out of the wound. They recovered tissue from the ceiling of the room, so it must have got up there, but . . . I just remember the blood squirting, covering her, with this noise as loud as it was—as it seemed—not wanting to have people, other people in the house, wake up and prevent me from dying. I still wanted to die. I was as good as dead. I had to leave the house, to get away from the noise where people could wake up. The keys to the Impala were on that same little table where the mug and the plates from the cake were, so I reached down . . . I don't know where I set the hammer, but I set the hammer down and picked up the keys to the car and went downstairs.

—Before you left, didn't you also consciously hit her in the throat?

Oh, yeah, okay. The noise was continuing, that guttural gurgling or whatever it was. The blows to the head hadn't stilled her. She was still making this noise. I didn't remember hitting her on the throat. That was only because the medical examiner said the injuries on the throat were from the hammer, not my hand. But I remember hitting her once on the chest. That much I remember, thinking a blow to the chest would stop the heart. I did try to strangle her, but I didn't feel I had the strength.

—With your bare hands?

Yeah. So, I did reach down and grab her by the throat, but the noise continued, and I hit her with the hammer, and I hit her in the chest, and I tried to stop her; I tried to kill her with strangulation. She was still lying there making this noise. And that's when I grabbed the keys and ran. I had to grope my way downstairs—the breakfast nook—the door was locked. The back door was locked, and I couldn't unlock it, and I had to go back into the breakfast nook. The back door opened into the breakfast nook, and there was a light switch in there somewhere. I knew it was around there, so I was feeling my way around the wall. I found the light switch, and I turned the light on, and then I could see the door, see how to unlock the door to get out. I let myself out. Got into the car.

—Did you wipe yourself off at all, wash?

I didn't. I started wiping myself with my handkerchief after I got in the car as I was driving. I had my handkerchief and a comb and my wallet, a little bit of money in my pocket—that was all I had on me. I got into the car, started driving. I didn't know my way around driving. I didn't know my way around the area. I began driving up the Parkway. I don't know how long that lasted. I don't know time periods. The first incident that came about—as I was driving along I noticed a kind of hill on the road, a house on top of the road, a kind of building. I figured I could try to drive the car off the road to crash it. But I couldn't find a way to get up the hill. As I was driving through the downtown area of what city I don't know, what town it was, I realized that perhaps the police could kill me if they suspected me of—that I might try to kill them—if they got me and were in fear for their life, they might shoot me. I didn't get stopped. I was driving slowly, and I never got stopped.

I somehow managed to drive near the entrance to the Taconic Parkway. I associated Taconic with mountains, and again I was thinking of getting up high in order to drive the car off the road and kill myself that way. So I got on the Taconic. Also mistakenly thought that being a parkway there would be no tolls. In my limited knowledge of New York highways, I assumed there wouldn't be any tolls where I would have to stop and get grabbed. Now on the Taconic I was hoping there would be high speed trucks that maybe I could crash into. I thought about crashing into the railings, but I didn't see how being in a big car like that I could kill myself that way. I saw an exit for Sylvan Lake off the Taconic. And I thought, Oh, there's a lake, maybe I could drive the car into the lake. I got off the exit and drove to the lake. There were a lot of houses and things around. The lake was in front of me, but I didn't . . . There were a lot of people around—they were all asleep apparently, but there were a lot of houses and cars. I drove back, got back on the Taconic.

—Were you thinking of Bonnie during all this?

No.

—Didn't you think of her at all?

No.

—Didn't you assume that she was dead?

I didn't. Once I got to the priest and talked to the priest, I assumed she was dead. But up until that time I stopped outside the church I hadn't thought of her at all.

—You know, if you just go fifty miles an hour you could have gone into any wall and the Taconic is a mountainous road. More people have been killed by accidents there—it's a beautiful but treacherous road.

I've been on it since then in the day, but this was the night, and I couldn't see too far off the road, so I couldn't know how steep.

—There were a dozen ways you could have really killed yourself.

There were three more before I made my stop along the way. I saw a sign for the Van Winkle Bridge, so I got off to go to the bridge, and when I was over the bridge, I stopped the car and thought I'd dive off. That might have been the easiest one because the car wasn't involved. I felt the car was too big and heavy and protected me too much. But now here I could just jump into the water or hit one of the pilings or maybe just the impact of the dive would kill me, or whatever. I stopped momentarily. But I didn't do it.

—Do you think you really wanted to die?

I think I didn't really want to die. I continued over the bridge into the town of Coxsackie and . . . Now along the main street there are gas pumps so I thought of crashing into a gas pump, bursting the car into flames, and die that way. I made several runs up and down the street going faster than I had been driving out of the city when I first left, wondering if this would be the way to do it. I made several passes and just couldn't. I even drove into the gas station, into the lot. I didn't do it. I didn't really come close to it actually—barging into the pumps. I just continued back out into the street and made several passes. I drove a ways to the next town, and there was a pharmacy, so I figured maybe I could break into the pharmacy and just swallow a million bottles of pills and go out into the woods somewhere and just die. I thought about that, but I didn't do that. I finally turned around and went back into Coxsackie.

—Why back to Coxsackie?

I remembered passing a church. That's the point where I decided that I'm going to stop. I'm going to turn this over to someone else now. So I parked outside the church. I took a nap on the stairs to the church, which was next to the rectory. There was a clock in the car, so I knew what time it was when I arrived in Coxsackie. It was six o'clock in the morning. I slept.

—Did you have any trouble falling asleep?

No.

—Did you have any dreams?

No. I remember thinking maybe people would wonder what I was doing there and come and investigate, but I was so exhausted that I just stayed. Once I sat down and leaned up against the door, the side door of the church or whatever it was, I slept. It was a little cold, but . . . So when I woke up it was a little bit lighter. Around seven. So I went around the door and knocked at the rectory. Father Tartaglia answered. I told him I had just killed my girlfriend and I wanted to turn myself in. I was sure she was dead.

Father Paul Tartaglia described the scene in his testimony in the court.

Q. *What time was it, Father, if you recall, that you first saw the defendant?*

A. *It was approximately at 7:00 in the morning, because we have an Angelus bell that rings at that time. I was lying in bed, because—on Thursday, we had Mass in the evening instead of the morning. But I had awakened and heard the bell, and was just kind of relaxing before getting out of bed.*

And then the door bell rang, and I put a cassock on—which I use as a kind of a robe if I have to answer the door in the middle of the night—and at that point, I opened the door and saw Richard.

Richard was standing there with just a pair of trousers on, no other clothing, and nothing on his feet. And my first thoughts were that someone in the community had had an emergency, a fire, tragedy—and he resembled one of my parishioners—and I thought it might be the brother of a parishioner whom I never met.

And so, I immediately opened the door, saw that he was very much disturbed or distraught, and he said he had to talk to me.

So I opened the door, and he came in.

Q. *Father, I wonder if you could tell us now, as you first viewed the Defendant—you used the words "disturbed, distraught." Describe him. Describe how his physical appearance—*

A. *Well, kind of with the chills, in spite of the fact that it was July 7th, you know. And I learned later that he had been exposed to the night air, and that explained the chills.*

Wasn't hysterical; I don't mean that. But disturbed.

Q. *Did you let him into the Rectory, Father?*

A. *Surely.*

Q. *What happened?*

A. *Well, on the way in, I said to him, "What happened? What is the trouble?" and he said, "I killed my girlfriend." And my immediate thought was, we are dealing with someone who is hallucinating; perhaps someone on drugs, someone who doesn't seem in touch with reality. Those were my first impressions.*

And then I realized that that was not the case. And we got on into conversation, and I—I started to understand, you know, that we were—that I was really in the midst of a very tragic situation.

Because the boy did come through, you know, with sincerity. And—and I could definitely grasp on to what he was saying, you know. And, therefore, it became very tragic, in my own judgment.

As soon as I was aware of the fact that he was definitely with it, so to speak, I asked him for some particulars, because my first thought was that I had to be the bearer of this tragic news to someone. So that was uppermost in my mind.

So I took a piece of paper, and I jotted down the information that he gave me, as I asked him who the girl was and where it happened.

I said, "Do you think they know about it by now?" and he said, "Yes, I'm sure that they have—that they have found that out." And also, that he was sure that they would know that he was the one.

Q. And how long a period of time, Father, would you say you were with him on the morning of July 7th?

A. I would say about 20, 25 minutes.

I don't remember chronologically the way things came up, but I do remember that Richard was very disturbed at one point, wincing when I asked him—almost breaking down, when I asked him how it happened. And my impressions were this: That the whole thing flashed through his head, and he winced very, very horribly, as though he were ready to start crying. That was the first time.

Q. You said, as though he were ready to start crying?

A. Right.

Q. Did he cry at that time, Father?

A. No, he did not.

The second time, of course, was when he stated that he had planned to take his own life, and that he lost an awful lot of—I don't know whether you call it self-respect or courage, because he could not do it. And that is the second time that he showed that type of reaction.

Q. "That type," talking about the wincing, Father?

A. Right.[3]

Father Tartaglia saw Richard for all of twenty to twenty-five minutes (see Chapter 4).

A recurrent theme that clearly offended—no, outraged and tortured—the Garlands was that so many people, particularly members of the Catholic pastoral community, seemed able to pass with unseemly ease from revulsion at the crime to sympathy for the criminal.

Certainly this was the case with Father Tartaglia, and objectively it is not difficult to understand. What he *saw* was a helpless young man, frightened, bewildered, cold, disorganized, and lost. What he did not see was the ghost of Bonnie Garland. But for now, Bonnie's *ghost* could not have appeared, because Bonnie was not dead! Bonnie was still lying there as Richard had left her, her head split open, moaning and gurgling in the pool of blood accumulating in her larynx.

Father Tartaglia finally said to Richard, "What do you want me to do for you?" And Richard responded, "I have to turn myself in."

The priest called the police, and in twelve to fifteen minutes Chief Ronald L. Rea arrived. Father Tartaglia felt relieved. "My only thought was I don't have to call the Garlands." His second thought was to go out and put some hot water on for coffee because "The boy was cold." It was then time for Richard to leave with Chief Rea.

> Q. *All right. Did there come a time, Father, when Chief Rea left the Rectory with Richard Herrin?*
>
> A. *Yes. I was standing there, and Richard, in a sense of relief, put his arms around me, as just about—just as he was ready to walk out the door, and I realized that I wanted to see him again, because I didn't just like leaving flatly and coldly. And because of a certain tragedy in my own family at that time, I didn't get to see him later that day. . . .*
>
> *I have never seen Richard. I received information that it might possibly be better if I didn't. So, that is the very reason that I did not get in touch with him or didn't write to him. I just communicated through others that were interested in him, about prayerful support, and so on and so forth.*[4]

Most people, even innocent people, feel uncomfortable and intimidated in the presence of a policeman. Richard liked Chief Rea and, unlike the typical stereotypes, found him sympathetic.

> He was nice to me. He was totally at ease with my presence there. In other words, he didn't feel, even though I had confessed to a murder, he didn't feel threatened. He didn't feel that I was capable of any further violence. He didn't handcuff me until I got to the station. I got in his car, drove to the station, and we got out, walked into his office. He handcuffed me because other deputies would be in the office. If it hadn't been

for other people who might notice it, his unreadiness to handcuff me . . . If it had been just Chief Rea and myself, I don't
think he would have handcuffed me the whole day.

When Chief Rea finished reading the Miranda warning to Richard, he first asked, " 'Richard, are you sure she's dead?' and he answered, 'She has to be.' I said, 'Why?' and he said, 'I hit her with a
claw hammer.' "[5]

Patrolman Philip Porcelli of the Scarsdale police force was just
completing his midnight-to-8-A.M. tour of duty when he received a
call from police headquarters directing him to go to the Garland
home. By the time he arrived, Sergeant Valancia and Lieutenant
Donovan were already there. As he was to testify in trial:

A. *Lieutenant Donovan related that they received a telephone
call from upstate New York stating that there was a possible
homicide inside the house, and that they did not believe there
was anyone home. And requested we check the exterior for an
unlocked door, unlocked window, some way of getting entry to
the house.*

Q. *What did you do at that time, sir?*

A. *At that time, I started around the side of the house. When one
of the officers—I don't remember exactly which one—hit the
doorbell, and Mrs. Garland answered the door.*

Q. *Did you see Mrs. Garland open the door, sir?*

A. *Didn't see her open it, but I was there shortly after.*

Q. *Did you go into the house?*

A. *Just into the downstairs lobby at that time.*

Q. *What did you do there, sir?*

A. *Well, we spoke with Mrs. Garland and asked her if there was
any problem, et cetera, and where her daughter was. And she
said that she was upstairs, asleep. And that there was no problem. . . .*

A. *Mrs. Garland walked up the stairs, and entered her daughter's
room. At that time she screamed, and the Lieutenant ran upstairs to the room with her. . . . The Lieutenant called down to
get the stretcher.*

Q. *Okay. Did you do anything at that point, sir?*

A. *No, I didn't. I just—I went—I left the hallway and rushed to
the car to get the stretcher. . . . At that time, I took the
stretcher up to the top of the stairs, to a landing, went up a few
more stairs, into the victim's room. And approached the bed
that she was lying on.*

Q. What, if anything, did you see at that time, Sergeant?

A. I observed the victim lying on her back, staring at the ceiling. She was breathing very laboredly. It sounded as if she had either some kind of mucus or blood in her throat. However, she was breathing.

At that time, with another Officer, we made a type of make-fashion stretcher by rolling the bedding on either side, so we could carry the victim from the bed down onto the landing, where the stretcher was waiting.

However, before we could move her, there was a hammer alongside her bed, on the bed. There was a hammer, claw-type, red-brown handle. I scanned the floor quickly, picked up a yellow towel that was laying at the foot of the bed, and with two fingers and the towel very close to the claw, very close to the head of the hammer, I picked it up, turned to my right, and I laid it down on a piece of furniture that was right alongside the bed.

At that time, we rolled up the bedding on either side of her and used the bedding to carry her down the two or three steps onto the stretcher that was waiting there. . . .

She was lying on her back, her eyes were fixed straight up above. The hammer was on the bed, on her left side, about neck—neck high. . . .

There was a gash on the left side of her head, approximately over the ear and slightly to the rear, approximately half to three-quarters of an inch wide. It appeared to be right into the skull itself.

In addition, right on her forehead, just to the left of the center, there was one—one round mark that looked—that appeared to be right into the skull also. That is the best way I could describe it, as if you hit a very soft piece of wood with a hammer very hard, the same mark was on her head right here, on the left side [indicating].[6]

Joan Garland had slept soundly through the night on July 7, when she was awakened by a phone call.

A. . . . somebody called up and said, "Is this the Police Station?" and I said, "I'm sorry, I think you have the wrong number." And I went back to bed.

Q. Did you have a telephone in your bedroom, ma'am?

A. Yes.

Q. After that phone call woke you up, did you have occasion to wake up again, so to speak?

A. Yes. About ten minutes later the doorbell was ringing very insistently. And when I got down there, my father had opened the door, and there was several Policemen standing outside.

I asked—the first thing I said was, "I think you have the wrong house. We didn't call the Police." And somebody said to me, "May we come in?" and I said, "Yes." And he said, "Do you have a daughter named—" you know, he said first, "Do you know Richard Herrin?" and I said, "Yes." And he said, "Do you have a daughter named Bonnie?" And I said, "Yes." He said, "Are they here?"

I went running into the study and the bed was there un— you know, just sheets. And I went running upstairs, calling Bonnie. I opened the door of her room, and at first I thought she was crying. She was lying on her back. There was blood all over, and her breath was coming like she was sobbing.

I called her twice. She was lying on her back with her arms at her sides. She was completely naked and uncovered. I thought she had been beaten. I said, "Oh," twice. . . . I ran downstairs and said, "What did he do to her?" and the Police came running up; and as they started to take her out, I realized that she wasn't crying, she was unconscious, and she was gasping for breath.[7]

Bonnie Garland was not dead. Despite the assault some five to seven hours before, despite the assumption of Richard Herrin, Bonnie had managed to survive. She was taken to the emergency room of White Plains Hospital, where she was seen by Dr. Herbert Oestreich, a neurosurgeon who was on call at the hospital. He described the scene as follows:

A. When she came in, when first entering the Emergency Room, she had obviously evidence of multiple injuries to the scalp and skull and brain.

She was unconscious and had been bleeding and showed evidence of rather profuse bleeding by the fact that when she arrived at the hospital, she had no blood pressure or palpable pulse, and was in very marked extremis at that time. . . .

Very quickly, we took her to the operating room and tried to control the bleeding. As we gave her blood, she began to— she began to bleed again, and we tried to take out what bleeding, what clot there was within the brain and what broken fragments there had been driven into the brain, and tried to— we tried to clean up this controlled bleeding.

Q. Now, Doctor, in addition to the injuries that you've described for us on Bonnie's head, were there any other injuries that you noted, sir?

A. . . . We noted that there was a black and blue or ecchymosis about her neck and, indeed, when the anesthesiologist was placing the tube in the throat, in the trachea, just in preparation for the surgery, he also noted that internally there was bleeding and hemorrhage about the trachea there. . . .

Q. Now, the injuries that you observed to the head, what side of the head were they on, Doctor?

A. On the left front, on—the left front and the left temporal side of the skull.

Q. Did you operate on Bonnie, sir?

A. Yes, sir.

Q. How long did this operation take, approximately?

A. Perhaps two to three hours. . . .

She never woke, but she at least stabilized, and then rather abruptly towards evening, she became worse, and we knew there were problems. We suspected there were problems of bleeding and lack of ability to clot her blood. We felt that this was probably attributable to the fact that she had been without blood pressure for so long a period of time. But we worried that there might be further bleeding within the brain. And for this reason, we took her back to the operating room. . . .

We opened up the wound and found there was a small amount of bleeding.

But at about this time, she showed marked irregularities in her heart, which, again, we felt was attributable to the lack of blood pressure for an extended period of time. And despite a variety of measures, her heart ceased beating.

Q. Did she die, sir?

A. She died at that time, yes.

Q. Did you pronounce her dead?

A. Yes.

Q. Do you recall what time that was?

A. 10:38 P.M.[8]

And that is the story of Richard and Bonnie. At least that is part of the story of Richard and Bonnie. But what do we really know of Bonnie. Of the corners of her heart and the darker rooms of her soul? Who is witness to her passion, her ambivalence, her anxiety, her love, her self-deception, her insights, her selfishness, her love for Richard, her fear of him, her hatred of him, her desire to leave him, her desire to keep him—her passions and despair? Who is witness to the changing moods and plans and hopes and aspirations and fantasies of a teen-age girl?

We can look at her letters and diaries. But we psychiatrists distrust letters; they were meant for an audience and therefore for an effect. We even distrust diaries; they, too, are often meant for some imagined audience in some imagined future. We trust direct speech and fantasies, daydreams and night terrors. And where are Bonnie's?

Richard can share with us some of their intimacies, tell us what she felt, what she said, what she promised, how she lied, how she loved, how she gave, and what she took. But we must depend on Richard; it is the nature of the case. And if Richard chose to lie to us—and I have no reason to believe that he did—we would not know the truth. And if Richard told us the truth as he saw it, we would still not know the truth. Whatever truth may be, it is a multiple-faceted prism in which each person is but a surface reflecting the light according to the angle at which it is cut.

If we have heard little of what Bonnie felt or said, the jury will have heard less. One of the peculiarities of our legal system is that "hearsay" evidence is not admissible. Bonnie can never be quoted in trial. Every conversation must start with "I said," and end there. It cannot include the response—what "she said." So Bonnie's father, her mother, her lover, were only free to give half of every conversation with her. She must remain mute even here.

Bonnie was never present at her own trial. And she should have been. It was through the generosity—or shrewd psychological judgment—of Jack Litman that she was not openly maligned or held up for abuse. But she was diminished and, in suggesting that she was somewhat responsible for her own fate, made an accomplice to her own killing. She was on trial, and was given no voice, no presence. No real attempt was made by the prosecution to bring her to life. But she could have been. This was a girl whose character and personality were more flamboyant, more appealing, and more accessible than Richard's. One looks through two thousand pages of records for her presence. Barely the faintest of echoes. Hardly the lightest of footsteps.

There is a way in which a visual picture brings together the sense of a described person like a focusing lens. Those twelve jurors, casting the final vote on the end of her affair, never had the chance to see her; they were never even shown a picture. Perhaps she visited them in their dreams.

II
THE
STORYTELLERS

3

THE TELLER
AND THE TALE

"That's the gospel truth!" When that expression is used these days, most of us would readily replace the word "gospel" with "literal" or "absolute." But "gospel" did not originally mean God's honest truth. It meant a good story ("gōd," as in good or gut, not God). With the foundation of Christianity, Jesus and his Apostles were not simply offering a new religion—a reverential contract with God— they were offering "evangelian" tidings, news, information. A new story: of man, his relationship to God or the cosmos, his purposes and his intentions, the meaning of his actions in moral terms beyond the apparent terms of observation. In fact, a new way of perceiving the relationship of things, all things, our actions to our inner self, our relationships to others, our relationships to the common good and our relationships to the moral order. Of course it was heretical, like any new religion. But this heresy eventually became the Gospel and one of the half dozen visions that have dominated man's perception of himself. It offered a new morality. Essential to a new morality is a new concept of justice and a new vision of truth.

"We are willing to go to jail for our version of the truth,"[1] Philip Berrigan said when he appeared in a Pennsylvania court on July 19, 1981. He was given three to eight years. Not for the truth, but for his version of the truth.

Truth like beauty may be only in the eye of the beholder. There may be many truths, and there may be no truth. Or absolute truth may exist but only in an unknowable state. Psychoanalysis is aware of this. It draws a distinction between "actuality" and "reality," truth and perceived truth.[2] It reserves the term "actuality" for the world of events as they actually are; in doing so, it assumes an essential truth about things, existence, and events. "Reality" is our subjective perception of that actual world. Each of us perceives a different reality. All of us take the actual events and interpret them according to the biases of a lifetime of experiences. So that while all of us may occupy the same space and the same time and be exposed to the same actual events, we are living in different real worlds. We will define good and evil according to our personal reality and will make judgments and pursue goals varying according to the different stories we have built out of the raw material.

The actual events are Rorschach blots ready for our personal interpretations. We do not perceive that we are constructing images and stories that are uniquely ours; we will not see them as mere foci of our elaboration. We will define *the* truth in terms of *our* reality, not the actuality. We will, therefore, "see" different things without lying or any attempt at distortion; we will build from the same raw ingredients different structures. People may look at a lily and see in it the hand of God if they are religious; an esthetic, sensuous accretion of planes, textures, and colors if they are artists; or a relative of an onion if they are botanists. And the same person may be all three, seeing the same lily differently in different contexts at different times.

The killing of Bonnie Garland was a tragedy, but a different tragedy when viewed from the different perspectives of religion, psychiatry, and the law.

Central to the Christian vision of the purpose of life is man's relationship to a God of love and forgiveness. That relationship preempts the primary importance of life on earth.

Psychoanalysis acknowledges no God, only a prophet. But Freud's view of human behavior also encourages forgiveness, in this case by reducing personal responsibility.

The law, in distinction, is only concerned with earthly matters and demands a central assumption of personal responsibility. Where Christianity and psychoanalysis, in their separate ways, are concerned with individual salvation, the law must preserve the state and the social order. Criminal justice must respect the individual but serve the common good. It assigns two champions of absolute positions: a defender who will argue nothing but innocence and a prosecutor who acknowledges only guilt. They will battle in a court of law before a jury of peers. The jury, using standards of the community at large, will decide which advocate represents "truth"—therefore, where justice lies. This is the adversarial process.

Bonnie and Richard's story was to be the subject of four different and contradictory tellings—from the perspective of religion, psychiatry, prosecution, and defense. Each story reflects the values and convictions of the teller, and each leads to different judgments of right and wrong, of guilt and innocence. Because they are looking for different visions, they perceive different events. They tell different stories.

4

THE GOSPEL TRUTH: CHRISTIANITY

From the beginning and to an extraordinary degree, the Catholic community, particularly the Catholic religious community, rallied around Richard to provide an extensive organized network of support—an extended family, if you will, of co-religionists. Nor was their activity limited to comfort and religious succor. They became the active agency of his defense. The key figures of the Church in this battle were the two assistant Catholic chaplains at Yale—Father Peter Fagan and Sister Ramona Pena.

The opening paragraph of a letter dated July 13, 1977, part of a group mailing for bail application—later described by Judge John J. Walsh as "one of the most thorough bail applications I have ever heard"—begins as follows:

Dear Friend,

The terrible events described in the enclosed articles are most likely not of news to you. While we are left only to mourn Bonnie's tragic death, it is important, that having lost one life, we do what we can to salvage another.

This mailing, sent in the name of Ashbel T. Wall ("A.T."), Richard's former roommate, was the opening salvo in a barrage of petitions, newsletters, and solicitations that was to gain Richard release on bail, raise funds for that bail, place him in a social setting of love and comfort (rather than jail) while awaiting trial, organize his defense and hire a prestigious attorney, raise funds for that defense, hire the best psychiatric testimony available, campaign for a leniency of sentence after the trial, and continues to raise funds for legal appeals and personal expenses up to the present. It was all organized at More House, the seat of the Catholic Chaplaincy at Yale.

From the depths of despair, Richard called to the Church, and the Church responded.

> That first night I was in a regular cell block. I was so exhausted that I don't remember having any thoughts. I just went right to bed.
> —And then what happened? What was the next step?
> I asked to see a priest.

When the priest arrived, Richard asked him to contact another priest in Los Angeles to notify his mother. This first contact with a clergyman in his role as a clergyman (Father Tartaglia made it clear that his contact with Richard was not in his capacity as a priest) was to set the pattern of the dual role played by the Catholic religious community in Richard's life. Always it was a combination of practical mobilization and money, with comfort and reassurance.

And always the message was forgiveness. The first religious advice Richard was given after the killing was from Father Tartaglia.

> The hardest thing you are going to have to deal with is how to forgive yourself. Bonnie is dead, and she won't be back. Now you're going to have to learn to forgive yourself.

The next day Richard was talking with the public defender that had been assigned to him. As the public defender was asking whom he might contact on the outside, Father Peter Fagan, one of the chaplains at Yale, showed up. Richard told me:

> I was very relieved to see Peter. He was someone I could trust. He came to see how I was, and from then on, other people started showing up.

From then on, Richard never had to feel alone or isolated. One of the early visitors to Richard was Dr. Marie Brown. Richard did not know Dr. Brown, and I asked him how she got involved.

> She was a member of the Yale—the More House—community. She had seen me playing in church. I used to play folk music. I didn't know her personally.
> —How did she make this extraordinary gesture of mortgaging her house to put up bail for you?

She did come up to visit me in jail. She felt I needed some sort of reassurance, a show of confidence. I needed to get out of jail, out with people who would care for me. Those were her thoughts.

—Did she ever talk about the crime itself?

No.

For the Garlands the experience was different. Paul Garland was particularly bitter. Whether because of the nature of the horrible events or because of his character or simply his perception—whatever the reasons, Paul Garland felt particularly hurt and betrayed by the Yale community and outraged by what he saw as "a conspiracy" of the Catholic Church.

He did not want to hear that since one life was lost, we must now "do what we can to salvage another." He was bewildered by the outpouring of solicitude for Richard, and the readiness to accept Bonnie's death as part of the irrevocable past. He could not understand that from now on *Richard* would be seen as the helpless child in distress; Richard, not Bonnie, would be the focus of love and compassion; Richard would be assuming the role of victim. For Richard was alive and available for identification, and Bonnie was dead. The Garlands could not understand that. Bonnie still existed for them, if for very few others. It is the nature of things.

Paul Garland took his case to the Catholic hierarchy. In rage with St. Thomas More, he wrote to Cardinal Terence Cooke asking the Cardinal to review "the serious issues of propriety and morality" that he felt were present in the intervention of St. Thomas More and the Christian Brothers community in Albany, who were to offer Richard sanctuary while awaiting trial.

Hearing no answer to his communication only enhanced his frustration and anger. The day after Christmas, Mrs. Garland wrote the Cardinal that "five months after hammering my daughter to death, Richard Herrin continues to enjoy the hospitality of the Christian Brothers . . . while you have not even deigned to acknowledge the serious religious issues brought before you by the victims of his horrible crime."[1]

Eventually the Garlands were granted a meeting with Cardinal Cooke, but by that point the Garlands refused, fearing perhaps the futility of the meeting and sensing the Cardinal was not prepared to discuss "the moral and religious questions raised by the Catholic community's support in defense of Richard."

Paul Garland wrote to an aide of Cardinal Cooke's, "For eight months now we have lived in anguish, produced by the murder, by the inexplicable intervention of the Catholic clergy on behalf of the killer, by the successful efforts of the clergy to persuade the Judge to grant bail, by the uncertainty of what the killer at large might do, and now we must steel ourselves for a murder trial in which it appears the Catholic clergy will support our daughter's killer in his attempt to evade responsibility for his act, assisting him in an attempt to hide behind his alleged state of mind."[2]

These letters were released to the press by the Garlands in an attempt to publicize their plight.

But the Catholic Church is not a tribunal of justice. It is a church based on a specific testament and philosophy. It has always been prepared to "render unto Caesar that which is Caesar's." The purposes of a religion are different from the purposes of a state, and therefore its methods, procedures, orientation, and morality are entitled to be different from the institution of government.

Moreover, the "Catholic Church" is not a thing in itself, although it can mobilize itself to speak with a single voice. It is a collection of multiple and conflicting hierarchies and institutions. And it is a collection of individuals who are free to act on their own (within specified limits) and to exercise their conscience and their efforts, particularly when they do so in conformity with the Church's central commitment to love, charity, and forgiveness.

So the institution of the Church and the institution of the state are separate in purposes and intents. But not completely separate. A concept of justice operating through a system of trial by jury may involve the same individuals in two ways, for key participants may straddle the two institutions, being members of both the religious and secular community. Sister Mary Ann Walsh acknowledged the dual purposes of the Christian Brothers when she wrote, "Though the Brothers' rationale was to give a Christian response, some also wanted to take a stand against criminal justice . . . calling that system one which neither rehabilitates nor accomplishes a positive social purpose."[3]

There is always a concern whenever a priest speaks that the awe and reverence we have for his religious authority will be displaced, and grant him an "expertise" in political matters that is not necessarily warranted. Justice is always an amalgam of factual appraisal with moral inclination. The confusion between mind and soul, morality and mores, is a crucial issue, particularly when an insanity defense is introduced. In both these major institutions, the Church and the state, there is a role for the concept of evil, whether it is called sin or crime. There is a concept of payment, whether it is called punishment or penance. Only the language differs.

For the most part the clerics involved with Richard were peculiarly disinterested in the concept of penance. "Whatever became of sin?" Karl Menninger asked in another context.[4] Perhaps the Church, like the state—influenced in great part by a psychoanalytic view of human behavior (where all actions are determined and all individuals nonculpable in the broadest sense)—may have joined in finding "punishment" an unfashionable and uncomfortable concept. Or perhaps it was that we were dealing with that segment of the religious community (chaplains and teachers) that was most "social worker"–oriented.

If the Catholic community was to be the primary support mechanism, Sister Ramona would certainly be its cornerstone. Peter Fagan initiated the More House involvement with Richard, but it was Sister Ramona who took charge. This strong, dedicated nun, who had risen to the position of a Yale Chaplaincy, would become Richard's primary ally in distress. She would sustain his family, coordinate his support mechanisms, and nourish his pride and self-esteem. And she would pay dearly for this. Sister Ramona is, however, not the Catholic Church, simply one of its representatives. She is a person. And she is an extraordinary person, shaped by a unique background which directed her to a religious life. She is a woman of passions who one would have thought was made for motherhood and for romantic love. Her commitment to her profession as a teacher and her identity with the religious life are all the more rigorous, therefore, because she sacrifices greatly to them. Celibacy, one suspects, does not come easy to her, as it does to some, and is therefore a greater gift. She sublimates these energies in an evangelical pursuit of her religious convictions.

While she is not the Catholic Church, she is an instrument of it and an ornament to it. She defines her sense of reality in terms of her religion and creates her sense of truth through the specific visions of that religion. Sister Ramona will construct out of the facts of Richard's life a religious "story" that defines the essential truths. Maybe not *the* religious story (Is there such a thing?) but a religious story of the actuality of the events modified and manipulated to the tenets of her faith.

I had first heard Sister Ramona's name from Paul Garland. It was she who was seen by him as the locus of all that was topsy-turvy, unjust, and corrupt in the peculiar flow of sympathy toward Richard. When Paul Garland, in outrage that Richard was not convicted of murder, cried out, "The forces of evil triumphed here,"[5] it was Sister Ramona who was at the center of his accusations.

I had traveled to her new location—she had since left New Haven—and in my anxiety misremembered our appointment, arriving two and a half hours early. Standing at the entrance of her apartment, ringing a bell that would not be answered, I realized my error and was about to depart when she appeared, carrying a large bag of groceries. Immediately realizing who I was, she introduced herself and, although I offered to leave and return at the proper time, insisted that we start then so as not to waste my time. The groceries were some fruits and pastries she had bought in anticipation of my visit.

She is a short, somewhat chunky woman, with close-cropped black-gray hair. Energy, warmth, and vitality radiate from her. I think I would have known, merely by her manner and language style, that she was a politically active and politically committed individual in the liberal-radical tradition. If she were somewhat younger and somewhat prettier, she would have looked like Anne Bancroft; if she were somewhat older, one would have cast her as Pilar in *For Whom the Bell Tolls*. We talked for three hours, and I realized I would have to come back to talk some more.

From the beginning she was remarkably candid and open, and while I was impressed by her strength, I was also aware of her vulnerability. She had been badly hurt, and tears came welling to her eyes frequently during our conversation. It is not possible to talk to this woman tête-à-tête for six hours and not feel the love in her—and not respond to it.

I knew him, but not well. We weren't close friends. When I arrived, he was in his junior year. He was one of the musicians at the folk Mass at the chapel, which was basically an Anglo-Catholic WASP group. I'm not really partial to such groups.

He was not very vibrant. He rarely initiated activity. He was reliable, you would notice him for his constancy. There was no question that he would be there. He would not have come to mind if you wanted someone to lead a program or be a spokesman.

Sister Ramona was on vacation with her cousin and father in a rented cabin in Connecticut in July of 1977. Early in the morning on July 8, she heard that one of the young people in the Yale community had been involved in a killing. She did not know who it was.

I was not alarmed. We walked down to the village to get a paper. When I read who, I was astonished. He was not the kind of person you associated with anything dramatic. I was astonished and horrified. I finally got myself together to send him a mailgram to Valhalla prison telling him I knew. I went back home to the cottage and sat down and wrote a letter to the Garlands telling them how sorry I was. I also wrote to the priest. Then I called the chapel and only one priest was on duty [Peter Fagan] and he had called Richard's mother, and she was coming in and would be housed at the chapel. I told him I would come in in a few days, and if he needed me to call me. So I really didn't feel that central. I knew that, without thinking, Richard was going to need us, but I didn't see myself as a crucial person in his life. I hadn't been.

She wrote to Peter Fagan expressing how heartsick she was about Richard and offering whatever help she could. She also sent a mailgram to Richard advising him to "trust in us and to trust in God." She also wrote to the warden and Father Tartaglia.

The letter to Father Tartaglia brought a response some two weeks later in which he stated that in only twenty or twenty-five minutes he had formed "very positive and beautiful" impressions of Richard. He expressed his feeling that what made this affair so tragic was that this had happened to such an unusually "virtuous and good person"— meaning, of course, Richard and not Bonnie.

Father Tartaglia carried away from the meeting the memory of how warmly Richard had embraced him as he left, and the desire to help him and aid in his comforting.

I remember a clipping from the National Catholic Reporter in which Father Richard Russell, the Catholic Chaplain at Yale, had said, "We must love the sinner and hate the sin."[6] And I was reminded that by this time, having interviewed Father Russell and the Christian Brothers in Albany, I had not as yet felt from them any spontaneous "hatred" of the sin or, for that matter, of anything else. Of course, when I asked, they allowed that the crime was dreadful, but never did I "feel" their revulsion. In my interview with Sister Ramona, for instance:

No, never. I didn't think that, and not until people took such an opposite viewpoint was I aware of it. I guess inside of me, I felt that all of us are capable of killing someone. I just am very grateful that I have never been triggered. I, like Richard, had never touched anything—I don't even know what it is to be hit. It never occurred to me to think about it, but when people took such as astonishing attitude, I thought about it. It is my conviction that we are all lucky if we are not triggered.
—Do you think you could take an instrument and bludgeon a person?
I can't imagine me, but I believe if I was triggered, I could.
—Do you feel anything could trigger you?
I don't know. I can't conceive it, but at the same time I say to myself the mystery of killing and violence is precisely that. We're fortunate when it doesn't come out. My theory is that it cuts across upbringing, everything. I can't visualize myself doing it, but I feel somewhere inside all of us can be triggered.
—So you think that any of us could commit the most heinous crime?
I guess so. That's what I have been saying.

Then, returning to a sensitive subject, I quoted the press as having said, "Sister Ramona never left his side during the trial." I asked her if it was fair to say she became the central person. She bristled at this and seemed hurt.

The perspective is wrong when they say I was the central person. I went to see Richard as soon as they let me, but so did Father Fagan. I stayed on vacation. I had an obligation to my cousin. Knowing Father Fagan was on duty, I was confident of the fact that things that had to be taken care of would be. He said to me, "I'll see about a lawyer." I said, "Fine." I wanted to meet his mother, no question. My heart went out to her just as it had gone out to the Garlands. Richard's mother came in with her brother. Something constructive had to be done to keep her occupied when she wasn't seeing Richard. Someone had to be concerned about these two people who came across country and were all alone. So I contacted a few of the parishioners to say she was in, and they were able to stay at the rectory. That was no problem. But it would be good if a few would have them to dinner, and they did.

While Peter Fagan and Ashbel T. Wall were organizing mailings that were to become known as the bail letters, Peter asked Ramona to take charge of what was later known as the defense fund. It involved establishing a newsletter to keep friends informed and instituting a system for soliciting support money (and often crucial letters) to conduct this case. It was a matter of compiling a list of friends, family, acquaintances, anyone who might be sympathetic. It drew heavily, naturally, on the parishioners of St. Thomas More and members of the Yale community.

She went well beyond this. Ramona organized a file index and sent it to "All our friends, mine, his mother's, every name possible, to tell them what we needed."

It was only then, with her involvement with the defense fund and the frequent visits to the prison—when she became a constant companion of Richard's mother—that she began to know Richard as a person.

First, I saw him at his arraignment in Valhalla. I think it was two days after. He needed clothes. First visit, he was like a non-person. I had visited before with other young people who had been in trouble; it was through a plastic screen by telephone. But now as a chaplain I'm ushered to a contact visit, and after they got used to me I was ushered right into a cell block because all the time he was in Valhalla, he was in the psychiatric division.

But the first time, it was a contact visit in a hall. They brought him out—a non-person, absolutely depressed, supergrateful. It was a case of lending emotional, affectionate support, not of conversation. In a sense, what could you say? He was not denying he had killed Bonnie. It was an astonishing fact. You couldn't say, "Richard, how could you do this terrible thing?" It never occurred to me. We were involved in being horrified *with* him, not *judging* him. The girl is dead.

"The girl is dead." With this statement I began to have an appreciation of the nature of that extraordinary outpouring of affection and love for someone who had just hammered to death a twenty-year-old sleeping girl. Remember, Sister Ramona did not know Richard. Father Tartaglia spent only twenty-five minutes with him. Dr. Marie Brown had only seen him from a distance. Why was this response different from the response of most of us on picking up a copy of any daily tabloid in any urban center?

In every ghetto of every major large city, almost every day, an old woman will be brutally murdered, a child will be raped or molested, a teen-ager will be killed, a person may be tortured. Butchery and mayhem are part of our daily entertainment in the evening news. Most of us do not rush to embrace the criminal. If anything, we may do something more dangerous. Out of fear and loathing, we may generalize from the crime that was done to the population from which the criminal was drawn. There is no question that much of current political conservatism is identification of street crime with minorities and ghetto people. This compounding of anxiety with revulsion leads to alienation, anger, and a fortress mentality.

Here there was a difference. This was not an anonymous killer but indeed an identifiable actor. "Identifiable" in both meanings of that peculiar word. It was known who he was—his identity was established. And he was someone who looked, acted, talked, and comported himself in a way that was consonant with our own, in a way with which we could identify. New Haven is not just a college town. It is a large city with much of the ugliness of any large city. I was not aware during any time of the tenure of Richard Russell, Peter Fagan, or Ramona Pena, for that matter, that they had mobilized themselves for the protection of any urban killers who must have existed in New Haven during that period. On the other hand, they may not have been parishioners of St. Thomas More.

There had to be revulsion for this crime. To kill an innocent girl in her sleep by bludgeoning her with a claw hammer is an innately revolting and repugnant thing. Where was the revulsion? Lost, I suspect, in compassion. Faced with such a crime, there are two conflicting sets of emotions. There is the horror and disgust at the event, combined with an enormous frustrated and impotent compassion to do something about it. But what to do? There was no way to put that battered body of a young girl together again. There was no way to embrace that bloodied, broken creature who now lay buried.

Compassion is an alternative to and protection against facing the revulsion. And if there is only one person left to embrace, we embrace him, particularly if he does not offend our esthetic sensibilities by looking ugly, deformed, or simply different in color or comportment. "The girl is dead." Along with her, then, we will bury the emotional reality of the crime.

Ramona continued with her story:

> I went with A.T. when Richard was preparing to tell us who his lawyer would be. Peter and his mother interviewed all the lawyers—four. A.T. and I stayed outside while his mother and Peter described the lawyers to him, and the positions each lawyer took. So they went, and I wasn't there for the telling, but I knew they had liked Jack [Litman]. Once the decision was made, they asked us to come in, and I walked in and A.T. said, "Who did you choose?" and he said the first thing that reminded me of the Richard I knew. He said, "You're not going to be happy, A.T., because I've chosen a Harvard man." Now for the first time I felt that was a return to life. I guess people think it's so terrible that he could have made a joke two weeks after killing a girl. My response to that was "He's alive enough to say to another Yalie, I chose a Harvard man."

Richard, later, was to have a crisis of faith. By the time I met him, he said he was no longer a believer. Ramona felt that was good, a sign of his sophistication. True religion should be more thought through, she felt. She felt that this could well be an interlude on the way toward "mature faith." But the last time she had talked to him, it was not only the religion, but the *institutions* of the religion that he was questioning, and this she felt was ungrateful.

> The institutions in the Church were awfully good to him. He was very lucky with the institutions. It was not a usual thing. I know. I've looked back and felt that every single Church institution that touched him was 100 percent what you want a Church institution to be. It was so unlikely, and there, I have to say to Richard, there was the hand of God. Even in Albany, the vibrant laity and the vibrant clergy were unbelievable. When the bishop there was asked how could he give the Brothers permission to take him in, I'll never forget his letter. The Brothers hadn't asked his permission, because they didn't need it. However, if they had asked his permission, he would have given it. He sends Richard a card every Christmas.

The institutions were "awfully good to him." This was certainly true. Thirty-five days after he had killed Bonnie Garland, Richard

Herrin was living with the Christian Brothers in Albany at the La-Salle Academy, sharing their life and their community. The Garlands were furious and indignant and frightened. When they expressed concern about what forms of security were being taken, they were not at all reassured when Brother Thomas—head of the Christian Brothers community there—informed them that no particular special forms of security were necessary since "our security is God."

Sister Ramona had accompanied Richard to the Brothers' community in Albany:

> I wasn't supposed to, but it worked out that way because of the courts. That was another time his sense of humor suddenly rose, and I didn't know it. We had stopped to buy him clothes on the way. I should have realized the Brothers would have clothes, but I didn't. So we stopped, and I wanted him to pick out the clothes. I guess I was trying to have him make his own decisions instead of always asking what I thought. I was always saying to Richard, "You have to decide." So we got to the door of the monastery, and I said something like "Stand up straight and be a person. When the door opens I want them to be looking at a person." And as soon as I said it, I was aware he was teasing me, because he pretended to be a little boy and hid behind my back, and I said, "Richard, stop it and stand up," and as I said it, he was standing up straight.
>
> A man, whom I presumed to be a Brother [it was Thomas, the group's leader], opened the door and said, "Oh, you must be Ramona, and this must be Richard," and he said something like, "Welcome." And then, I'll never forget it, he said, "Richard, this is your key to the door. You've arrived at a good time. The Brothers are downstairs having a drink before supper. Why not come down and meet them."
>
> We met them, and Thomas went around introducing him. They were from twenty-two to eighty-six years in age. It was just the most gracious moment. Then Brother Thomas said, "Why don't we go above for dinner now." I said to Thomas, "Richard is going to have to stay here when I go, so I think he should start right in," and I sat with Brother Thomas, and Richard had to make his way. He did. And that night is when I heard the whole story for the first time.
>
> After dinner Thomas showed me where my room would be and where Richard's would be, and he said, "You two will want to talk," and he closed the door. We started to talk as he unpacked. Some of the things he was unpacking Bonnie had given

to him. He had asked for them. What triggered the tears was when he came to the turquoise scarf she had made. First the teddy bear, and then the scarf. That triggered him, and he started to cry. I had been told a thousand times not to let him tell me the story. In case I was called, the less I knew, the better off I would be. I realized that night there was no way of stopping him. He had to cry. He just cried and cried.

—How did he explain it?

He didn't explain. He just cried and cried. He never said because this or because that. He kept saying how much he loved her.

—Did he ever say, "If I could only go back and undo it"?

No. He never said, "If I had it to do over again."

I took a trip to Albany to interview two of the Brothers most directly involved with the decision to accept Richard. The third by that time had transferred to Riverdale, and I was to see him later. LaSalle Academy, a school for troubled and delinquent boys, is a most unprepossessing, one would have to say ugly, building in a run-down section of Albany. I stumbled into the one building closest to where I had parked and saw a group of men in rolled-up shirtsleeves scrubbing floors with mops and pails. For all the world I thought I had been transferred to prison. I then realized I was in the dormitory, the living section of the Brothers, and not at the academy.

One of the Brothers directed me around the corner to the main school building. The first person I interviewed was Brother Thomas, and it seemed completely appropriate, for in many ways he was quintessentially true to one of the most extreme positions of his faith, and therefore a firm spokesman for the concept of forgiveness.

Thomas was one of seven brothers and sisters raised in New York City; no other siblings entered the religious life. He left home for the Brothers after high school in 1958. He had been taught by the Brothers since the sixth grade, and after graduation from high school he joined the order. He had come to Albany in 1966 and, except for a two-year hiatus, had been there since. At the time of the decision to accept Richard, he was the religious superior of the Brothers' community. He was only thirty-seven years old. He looked younger. He was extraordinarily softspoken and reminded me of the actor Michael Moriarty, with steel-rimmed glasses. He had the same look of an adolescent choirboy—small-featured, fair, fresh, and slight.

Richard was only admitted into the community after gaining a consensus approval in meeting. That is the way decisions are made here. Some members had raised questions about the safety of bringing Richard into the community. An interview with Richard was arranged. Thomas took a colleague, Brother Robert, with him because Robert was a man of independent mind, and he had the credentials of a social worker. They were to bring a firsthand judgment back.

—Tell me what happened on the visit.

Well, we wanted to see Richard. To see what condition he was in. To ask him what he was asking of us rather than get this through Father Fagan. And to tell him what we would expect.

—Where was he?

He was in the Westchester County Jail at Valhalla.

—What were your impressions?

Richard appeared as an intelligent, overt young man. My feelings, to say what they were, to see a young life like this in such trouble, just feelings of confusion, why this happened—it was just two weeks after the crime. He was nervous. He didn't know us. We didn't know him. I think he was pleased to see us—for the human contact, that somebody would help. I think there was great relief.

We could offer a place that he could stay and kind of piece things together as best he could and start the healing process. We're essentially believers in Christ and we express this through a life of community, of prayer, and of sharing the Gospel values. Helping the needy and those who are in trouble.

—Were you worried about Richard?

We were. Whether we could offer him anything that would be helpful; we were strangers. [That was not what I had meant!] I think two things—contact with human beings and forgiveness. In prison, contact is kind of minimal. There are guards and lots of noise. Not really a place where someone can be restored, healed.

—So beyond a place to stay and kindness, you also had a therapeutic hope?

We hoped to help him spiritually.

—Were you worried about his mental status, that he might kill someone else, or kill himself?

Yes, we were. They were the reasons we went down to jail to see him.

—Which were you most worried about? And after you saw him, were your anxieties allayed?

They were. We spent about forty-five minutes with him. As I recall, we weren't allowed more time.

I was, to say the least, nonplussed. Forty-five minutes of gentle talk between two Brothers and Richard were sufficient to convince them that he was neither a potential runaway, a suicidal risk, or a threat to other persons. This despite the fact that the LaSalle Academy, the community in which Richard was to live, was a school for delinquent boys. I am aware of the lack of reliability of prediction by experts in the field and was appalled at and envious of the insouciance and confidence of Brother Thomas. It is, I suppose, part of the serenity that comes from feeling that everything is in the hands of God. I decided to press him on this point.

—You felt confident that he wouldn't commit another murder?
      We were.
—Were you as confident that he wouldn't commit suicide?
      I think so. Actually we considered those, but with what we had heard from others and what we saw of Richard, we felt that those feelings of worry were irrational. Of his killing others as he had killed Bonnie—there was an element of risk, but I guess we were willing to take it.
—Tell me, what impressed you in so short a time to make such an important decision? Tell me what it was in Richard.
      He made complete sense when we talked to him. He looked well. He didn't seem extremely depressed or he didn't give any outward sign of not being in control.
—Can you give me a little more about Richard as a person?
      I can. I find that Richard is a very loving person. People are important to him. He's still involved—just in life, music, taking up a job and helping out. I think he is a fine person. He fit in just beautifully. I don't know if this is explaining what he did, but I think he was so grateful there would be people willing to be with him and the initial transition from jail to living with us—he was so relieved, he was able to become part of us very fast.
—Do you mean true friendships emerged?
      I think so.
—Who were his best friends here?
      I consider myself a good friend of Richard.

Richard had been encouraged to enroll in the State University of New York. He had been attending classes there, making friends with young men and women, working part-time at a religious bookstore, and generally leading the life of a student. There was some question about whether he was registered in his name or under an assumed name. Later a fuss was made about this, and the State University insisted they had been deceived, that Richard had been enrolled under a pseudonym. The publicity was a product of Paul Garland's investigation. At that time he had hired a private detective to check on Richard's past and present. The publicity that issued from this announcement caused the State University to ask that Richard not attend classes, although he was allowed to finish the courses and take the final examinations at home with the Brothers.

Brother Thomas was upset by all this and felt it was "unfair" to Richard. "After all," he said, "the whole matter was unsettled and people were acting as though it was. The trial hadn't occurred." At this point I was somewhat confused, for while the trial hadn't occurred, there was no doubt about whether Richard had killed Bonnie Garland, so I said:

—You mean the presumption of innocence?
     That's right. Those are the legal terms. Something more basic, human decency. Any person shouldn't be mistreated without—well, they shouldn't be mistreated at all, but it wasn't good reason it seemed to me.
—What about the killing? Was that a good reason?
     I personally don't think so.
—Are you saying that just because it was before the trial, or would you say that after the trial?
     I think I would say that after the trial.
—What do you think would have been the just and fair thing?
     I think the just thing is the thing that has happened—that he has been found guilty of manslaughter. Evidently the jury felt that way.

Richard had been acquitted of murder but found guilty of manslaughter in the first degree. His sentence was the maximum allowable by law—eight and one-third to twenty-five years.

—What do you feel about the sentence?
     That it was too severe. I have a problem with incarceration. It's barbaric putting people into cages. I don't have a problem with punishment, but with that kind of punishment I have a problem.

—What would be the kind of punishment you would not have a problem with?

I'm not sure what would be a better punishment, but sometimes I think whipping is a far more humane punishment than incarceration.

—What would be a punishment you could accept for someone having killed?

In cold-blooded murder?

—We could start there.

I think the basic punishment of any person is ostracism of some kind by the community.

—How can one do that? Wasn't that the purpose of prisons?

Probably.

—If you want justice for society and you don't want prisons, you have to offer an alternative.

Have him understand the seriousness of his crime, how he has offended the community by his crime, and mete out a punishment that fits the crime.

—I assume you think of murder in cold blood as the highest crime, or would you not?

Oh, I think there are worse crimes. When millions of people are going to bed hungry, isn't that a great crime?

—Would you say that taking an innocent life is a high crime?

I am not sure.

—It has been generally considered as among the highest crimes. Would you, personally, *not* send the person who killed in cold blood to prison?

No, I would not; I would try some form of rehabilitation. I would be concerned that a person regret what he had done.

—So a sense of regret and a sense that he would not repeat would suffice for you?

Yes.

—What you're talking about is taking the person into the community to rehabilitate him.

Yes.

—But some people feel it isn't fair. The concept of just deserts seems important to them.

Yes, but then we have the question of whether we take *two* lives. This sounds like foolishness. One life has been lost. Should another be wasted and lost? Or should we try to salvage that life. It's going to be a pretty tough road ahead no matter what happens, even under the best conditions, and what can be done to help that life?

Nonetheless, Brother Thomas reluctantly recognized the secular community had a right to set its standards of proper punishment provided they were within certain limits. I pressed him about what those limits ought be.

—With Richard, what would you have liked to see happen?
　　I think that he has been punished enough as of now.
—Wouldn't you honestly have said that before he went to trial?
　　I would, but his serving in prison now is absolutely serving no purpose.
—Did it serve any purpose last year?
　　I think it did.
—What?
　　Carrying out the jury's decision.
—Supposing I had asked you this a year ago. Wouldn't you not have said the same?
　　Perhaps I would have.
—So one year in prison is enough?
　　I think a day in prison is inhumane. I think six months to a year would have served the purpose of a punishment that people decided was necessary for the crime, and anything more than that is of no service. I think what he did was horrible.
—Yet if we think of proportionality of things. If you were to destroy my home, burn it down, and you were fined fifty dollars, I would be outraged.
　　Most certainly.
—Now supposing the Garlands were to say, "We've lost a child, our daughter, and the Church especially has respect for human life, even a two-day-old fetus, and you talk about proportionality of six months."
　　I don't think I could speak to them like that.
—How would you explain it?
　　There is no explaining it. It was a horrible thing that happened. I guess I would try to say there is another way of trying to deal with something like this. There is, I believe, such a thing as forgiveness, and as such it is opposed to the idea of proportionality. There is in the human person the capacity to forgive. Most of the time we are incapable of that, but we do have that in us. And people do forgive.
—But should society forgive?
　　I hope so.

Before concluding my talk with Brother Thomas, I asked him about predictability. No one involved with Richard's release on bail seemed to have particular concern about his fleeing, committing another crime, or committing suicide. The latter is a constant concern of psychiatrists when dealing with clinical depression. I also asked everyone about another kind of prediction—whether they could visualize themselves, under any circumstances, committing a crime like this and in this manner. Predictions about our own behavior are of course no more reliable than our predictions about others, but our perceptions of our future say something about our philosophy. It should be remembered that Brother Thomas was the mildest, gentlest of men, with otherworldly qualities that would have made him perfect casting for a thirteenth-century scholastic monk.

—Is it irrational when someone has committed a murder to fear that he might do it again?

It might be.

—Are you convinced that Richard would not kill again?

I have no way of telling that, but according to my own judgment I could not see Richard killing again.

—The day before the killing, or the month, you might have said the same?

I guess I wouldn't have believed it possible.

—So much for human prediction. At least in terms of Brother Thomas.

Yes, foresight and hindsight.

—Does not the fact that he did it once make him a higher risk than someone who never did?

It does make him a higher risk, but not all that—it's something to be factored in.

—Now, could you imagine yourself ever taking a hammer and hitting someone?

I could. I could consider that I could not be in control. If something is so outrageous in my makeup that could be triggered and I could just lash out.

—Have you ever attacked anyone with an instrument?

No, I haven't.

—Yet you have been outraged by social conditions every day of your life?

Yes, I have, but it has been small and inconsequential.

—But you really could imagine picking up a hammer and crushing a skull?

I don't know the difference in picking up a hammer and shooting. I can see myself losing control and doing practically anything.

—Under what conditions have you actually ever lost control?

Well, driving in a snowstorm I have lost control in the car, gone out of control. I don't feel in control in such situations.

—That's fear. I mean in other relationships.

No, I have never lost control. But I pick up the newspaper and it seems to happen so much. If it can happen to one person, it can happen to me.

—I have confidence in saying I would never beat or torture my child.

I don't have that confidence. I see nearby a home for abused children, and I wonder how anybody could abuse them, but I see people are so distraught they get carried away.

—I know I could never beat my children.

I don't have children, but I couldn't say that even if I did. I couldn't conceive of myself torturing anyone. I could conceive of myself killing someone, but not torturing. I think the human heart and my own heart are capable of great cruelties, and I don't put that out of my own capacity.

Brother Augustine is a different story from Brother Thomas. He is a man of sixty-seven, one of three children, born in Minneapolis into a middle-class family. He has been with the Brothers since the age of fourteen. After finishing college, he became a classicist, but for the last thirty-five years he has been in administration. He is the executive director of the LaSalle Academy. He has a lean, angular look, something halfway between the actors Art Carney and Barnard Hughes. It was from him that I learned that Sister Ramona had become the link between the Christian Brothers and Richard. Through a friend, she learned there were two communities that had boarding schools for troubled boys and were open all year—Lincoln Hall in Westchester and LaSalle in Albany. Peter Fagan contacted Lincoln Hall with the idea of accepting Richard, but was refused. He then came to LaSalle.

One should not assume—as I wrongly did—that the basic objections raised to accepting Richard were on the basis of safety, reputation, criminality—the kinds of concerns that certainly would have been central to Phillips Exeter or Choate, completely different kinds of boarding schools and different kinds of communities. They were more concerned about what effect a stranger—any stranger—would have on the dynamics of their community.

Brother Augustine said:

This was an extraordinary, unprecedented kind of request. I knew the sensitivities of the members of the community who are used to living in a private community—a family. We were being asked to perform some kind of hospice role, that is, a sanctuary role, that in our recent history was unprecedented. My initial reaction was that it would be a beautiful thing and I knew Brother Thomas would not turn it down out-of-hand. But I did have misgivings.

Brother Augustine confirmed that Brother Robert had probably been picked by Thomas for essentially internal politics. Robert was a psychiatric social worker. He was, in a religious sense, conservative.

He's from New England. We hadn't done this in the past, and it has certain elements of riskiness about it.

One had the feeling that what Augustine was saying was that Brother Robert was less otherworldly and was generally known as a spokesman and leader of realistic and conservative positions.

When they came back from the visit, Brothers Thomas and Robert were both convinced that Richard was a safe person to live in their community; I suspect that Brother Thomas's deep religious, even mystical, orientation was a key factor and Brother Robert accepted the situation. The fact that the request came from the Chaplain of Yale University (Peter Fagan) and the fact that he had confidence in Father Fagan led Brother Robert to also put a religious value on what was being asked. In other words, both these men were now looking at the problem from a religious point of view.

Brother Thomas alerted everyone beforehand to what we were basically being asked to do—I don't know how he did that. I think he went around personally to each person. So when the community gathered at an unusual hour—we usually have four o'clock meetings, but this was at eight—and we met in the dining room, I don't know why, but it made this occasion a little different. Brother Thomas began the meeting with a prayer, so there was context set for it. We were not being asked to do something sociological. We were being asked to do something religious—with a very definite scriptural context.

It is important to appreciate that Augustine, unlike most of the others in the religious community, was prepared to draw a distinction between the religious and social contracts. Brother Thomas cast the problems in religious terms. Within that context, Augustine, at least, came to a very different conclusion about the right, goodness, and justice of things than he might have in a political frame.

I asked him if in their discussion the nature of the crime was considered significant.

> It was a significant factor. We would look upon the crime as a heinous crime, and most unfortunate that it occurred. I suppose the fact that it was a crime of passion to some extent mitigated our conception of it. We weren't dealing with a deceitful, particularly cruel, cunning kind of person. Admission to the community of that kind of person would put us all on guard because of the untrustworthiness.

—How did you make those judgments?

> Brothers Thomas and Robert, who had spent much time with him, gave us assurances that we weren't dealing with a psycho. Because of our work here and the psychodynamic dimensions of it, we are familiar with that, and to be told that this person is a sane individual and he comes through with all the normal reactions of time, space, et cetera. We knew there must have been a lot of underlying anger potential there, and I tend to use humor to alleviate a tense situation. At one point, after we had gotten through a lot of our discussion, I said, "Let's all agree that none of us will provoke him." We all laughed.

Brother Augustine had no worries about putting Richard in with the other boys, nor was he worried about Richard committing suicide. After all, he had the reassurance of Brother Robert, "with his professional skill." Indeed, he said, he had originally naively thought Richard was looking for a job with them; and since he had an M.S., he could do some tutoring work. Another expression of the naiveté of Brother Augustine was the assumption that they could do all of this in total "obscurity, anonymity, and secrecy."

> We had no idea of any publicity. In fact, we had decided among ourselves that the only Brother outside our community who would know about this would be the Brother Provincial, because it would only be with his permission that we would do something like this. We would not dare to do this on our own. We had already gotten permission. We were convinced that even with other Brothers who visited our community, they would be told simply that this is a colleague interested in our life. So that's another example of the total naiveté of the com-

munity. We had no idea that everybody would know about this, we figured that would not be called for. He'd be a college student living in our community. And he was just another member of the community like everyone else. He went to church with us, he participated. No one would be able to judge he was not a member of the community. He participated around the house and in light recreation and social things like having a drink. I used to play cribbage with him. Brother Thomas played cards with him in the evening a couple of times a week.

—What was your impression of Richard?

I already knew he was intelligent, and he gave evidences of that in his conversation. I guess I would say he was under anxiety and tension in the beginning, and that was understandable. He was a pleasant conversationalist, had a good sense of humor. He was always respectful. He was not inappropriately friendly, or imposing in any way. He was most discreet and appropriate in the way he integrated himself into the community. He was musically gifted, played the guitar with Brother Thomas. He was clearly religious. It was easy for him to accept the religious structure. It's not that high-pressured, but we have our community ways.

—Was he someone you grew fond of? Did you grow to love him?

I can't say that I grew to love him. I think my own personal relationship with him was one of respect, appreciation for his gifts, enjoyment of his company and desire to help him. I had no feeling of any kind of antagonism or animosity toward him, but some of the Brothers became good friends with him. I did not.

Brother Augustine was prepared to acknowledge the moral right of society to operate in a different frame of reference. He emphasized that "in a religious life you must think of forgiveness," but while it might be a better world if there were no prisons, he didn't personally see how society could operate that way. He could not conceive of a case-by-case individualization of justice or its feasibility.

"Given the way the world is now, I feel that Richard has received fair treatment," he said, although he emphasized that he was looking forward to a better world.

I also asked him if he thought Richard could do it again. He said, "He would not." And when I asked if he would have predicted before Richard's behavior that he would have done it, he said he would not have. We both laughed. But he went beyond this. He said that the question of certitude was an important one. He recognized that as long as one could not be certain, society has a right to protect itself.

We must remember that Augustine had been working for years and years in a school for young men in trouble. He was aware that there were "psychopaths"—his word. Unlike Brother Thomas, he rarely used words like "sinful" or "evil." He talked about "self-destructiveness," and he was aware of how truly difficult rehabilitation and change were for these young men.

Certitude was repeated constantly in his conversation, so I asked him, if the certainty that an action would never be repeated was his only concern. Would that be sufficient to release Richard? To my great surprise he said, "No." He felt there would have to be "a deep sense of moral change," and he introduced the word "repentance." "It is not enough to know the person will not do it again. You have to have a sense that the individual is contrite and repented what he had done."

I asked if he thought Richard was repentant, and there was a noticeable hesitation in his response. He said he felt prison had in many ways done Richard good, and that the crime itself must have caused certain changes in him.

He also surprised me by telling me that he did not feel Richard's sentence was too long, and he was sorry to observe in Richard "a bitterness growing about imprisonment." I asked if that implied a lack of repentance, and again he was hesitant before he said he guessed he would have to say so, because if one is truly repentant, one is at peace.

Richard was beginning to get bitter about his condition, despite the fact that actually things had improved. He had been moved to progressively less restrictive prisons; and because of his intelligence he was given work that ordinary prisoners could not do; and he was being useful, which, by Augustine's standards, would alone make for a good life.

Augustine felt Richard's life was not one of great duress. He had almost a library of books in his room, he was allowed a small stove to cook, and other luxuries. So he was distressed to see Richard beginning to feel self-pity and bitterness.

I asked whether he thought Richard was suitable for the religious life or intended to go into it. He said, "No, no, not at all." He thought Richard was now planning to go into business on the West Coast somewhere or other. He felt he could no longer go on with his Ph.D. That road was foreclosed.

I then asked him the same question I'd asked Brother Thomas: Could he visualize himself bludgeoning someone? He said, in all honesty, he could not, but then he said he did not want to second-guess. I said, "Brother Augustine, I simply want to know if ever, under any circumstances, you could imagine yourself capable of doing that." He answered, "No."

I told him Brother Thomas said he could imagine himself doing it, and I felt Thomas was if anything less capable of it than either he or I. He laughed and agreed he could not imagine it either. I asked if he had a temper. He said, "Yes, I do, rather a severe one."

I asked him if, with his severe temper, he had ever struck anybody in his life with an instrument. He said, "No, never."

I do not want to give the impression that Brother Augustine was entirely a pragmatist or an unholy man. There was a lovely religious quality about him, too. He was simply less ethereal than Brother Thomas. He constantly talked about the privilege of the community, to be able to serve in this way. He talked about the divine purpose evidenced in the fact that Richard had come to them; even in the fact that Judge Walsh, the judge who had decided whether Richard was to go out on bail or not, had shared a house for thirty or thirty-five years with Brother Thomas's family. He saw the hand of God in all that. He said, "While I do not believe in predestination, it appeals to the idea of a purpose in life, a design."

I was struck by his seeing "the hand of God" in all that. To me it was more likely the hand of "the old boys' network," which obviously exists in a Catholic religious community as much as it does at Yale or Harvard. It emphasized in a nice small way the difference in the way one can accept or interpret simple facts. What to him was a sign of heavenly design, to me was a matter of good homework and some luck.

No, it was not that Augustine was not religious. It was that, as a hard-nosed realist, shaped by years of working with delinquent and often psychopathic boys, he intuitively understood that the purposes of the Church and the purposes of society were not the same. While he lived within the Church, he respected the rights of society to pursue its own independent ends. He repeatedly emphasized the distinction between the religious goals and religious purposes, and the needs for social order in society. Recognizing the differences, he still hopes for the day when the two would be fused, and you could have a life of complete forgiveness and complete understanding.

We both allowed that such time had not yet arrived. But rather than letting it end there, he introduced a wry note of confidence by reminding me of Cardinal Newman's statement: "In a higher world it is otherwise, but here below to live is to change, and to be perfect is to have changed often."

By the time I saw Brother Robert I had a fairly complete feeling about the attitudes of the Christian Brothers. He, however, did outline and confirm both the impressions of Richard, and the nature of the decision-making, in the community. Since there was some conflict about the degree and the extent of Richard's emotional condition in the immediate period following the murder, this interested me enough to hear another report. I asked Brother Robert for his impressions of Richard on first seeing him. He gave me the following:

> Physically, he's about five-eight, five-nine, weightwise he's a hefty young man. I'm going to say he's about 180, 190, but very muscular. While he is Spanish-Mexican in origin, he doesn't look that. I think he probably looks more like his father than his Mexican mother. Handsome man, dark hair, dark features. That's the best way I can describe him right now.

—What about his personality?

> He's a very likable fellow. Almost instantly. That's what came across, a warmth in him. You know, you have in your own mind preconceived notions of what a murderer is going to be like, and that's built up because murderers are always bad people—that's what we're told by society—and yet, when Richard came into the room, and we sat in a regular room, it wasn't a cell or anything like that, and there was no guard, and we were talking with Richard, he was very open.

—He was not reluctant to talk about the events of the killing?

> He didn't go into great detail, and I didn't push him to go into detail. What I tried to ascertain was how he *felt* about the situation.

—How *did* he feel at that time?

> There was a certain amount of remorse; he did feel that he

had done something wrong; he felt very bad about it. That's a feeling he kept all along, and I think he still has that feeling—that he knew he had done something wrong and that he was sorry for it.

—Did he break down when you were talking?

There was no scene. There was very much of a calmness about him, and control. I think probably if there had been a lot of emotional crying and breaking down, my judgment might have been a little different. Because I would say that maybe there was a psychiatric problem here, and we might not be able to deal with it.

He had control of himself and was in control of what he was going to do with his future, his direction and his goal for his future. One of the things that came across was that he had already talked to a priest about what he had done, and in our tradition he had gone to confession, so that he felt good about himself.

If we are to believe Brother Robert, within weeks of the killing, Richard "had gone to confession [and] felt good about himself." But more interesting is that Brother Robert felt good that Richard felt good about himself. At the time, I had serious questions about this leapfrogging from sin to forgiveness over the neglected but hallowed principle of penance. Later, when I was to meet Richard and become aware of his "concreteness" and suggestibility, I was doubly doubtful. This ready forgiveness was no service to Richard. In fact, it may well have contributed to his bitterness. The Church had forgiven him, so he had forgiven himself, through their aid. Why then was society so cruel and recalcitrant? Richard's readiness to hear the voice of authority might have responded differently to a voice from the Church that emphasized sin and guilt, remorse and penance. This was a church, after all, that in its past had brought kings to their knees—and not simply for prayer.

Richard realized he had done something wrong, and that he owed some debt to society. He did not quite know in what direction to go. He was directed to self-forgiveness. This, despite the fact that the concept of service dominates the thinking of the Christian Brothers. Much of their debate on whether to accept Richard centered about whether *they* were sufficient, whether they had enough to offer him.

Brother Robert then hinted at some of the prices the Brothers had to pay for what they saw as a simple act of Christian charity.

For the first time we ran into the Garland wall, where we were going to be very open to them. That was our understanding, to offer them our sympathy and to tell them we really knew how hurt they were, and that what we were doing was in no way condoning what Richard had done, but what we were doing was trying to heal Richard and to help him through a very difficult time, but when we got down there, the wall was there, and in no way were we going to be able to meet with them or even convey our feelings towards them.

—Did you try to write them?

No, if anybody did, it would be Brother Thomas, but I don't know.

—When were you made aware of this degree of resentment?

Probably it was more after that initial hearing than during the trial. The second time we went down to get him, before we got back to Albany the TV cameras were there, it was on the radio, the newspapermen were all sitting in the courtroom. That's where we ran into a lot of difficulty publicity-wise. We got anonymous telephone calls. I don't know if Thomas got any letters. I only got one personally.

Fortunately, we had done our work ahead of time. We had gotten permission from the bishop to do this, from our local pastor of our parish, so that we had covered all the bases ourselves, so that they were all supportive of us. In fact, the bishop came out very strongly in favor of what we were doing. This of course quieted a lot of the local people. They realized we had done our homework rather well. But I do know it was a rather difficult time for us.

If the Christian Brothers were feeling the heat, they were not alone. In response to a critical letter, Peter Fagan wrote a letter defending the personal and pastoral support given Richard. He stated that his support was rooted in his belief that no one is beyond the pale of God's mercy, and that as a Christian his response to Richard ought to be a reflection of that mercy.

He alluded specifically to Matthew 9:11–13, wherein Jesus answered those who questioned His eating with sinners by saying "They that be whole need not a physician, but they that are sick."

Father Fagan acknowledged that the support of Richard might be seen as an attitude of indifference to the Garlands, but while regretting this misunderstanding, he knew of no remedy for it.

It became necessary for all principals to answer not just letters from strangers or anonymous vilifications but also letters from personal friends and supporters at St. Thomas More. In one of the letters of defense sent to a general mailing list, Richard Russell indicated that he, Father Fagan and Sister Ramona would continue to minister to Richard, with the deep conviction that no one of us is "beyond the pale of God's merciful forgiveness." If such a pastoral presence to Richard was interpreted by some as being "immoral" or "unchristian," he felt that words of self-defense would hardly bring understanding.

In that same letter, he indicated that he grieved deeply with both Bonnie's and Richard's families, closing with the statement that since one life had been irrevocably lost, by giving Christian presence and the full benefit of our nation's legal system to Richard, he would "continue to join those others to do what is possible to salvage what remains of the second life."

Another letter, sent out under the heading of "Dear Friend of More House," tried to make clear that the financial assistance that had been given Richard was:

> ... of private, responsive individuals; it is an effort separate from the official program and budget of the Chapel. ... for us and those who worship at the Chapel, the response is rooted in our common belief that God is always present to his people.

But no one paid quite the price of Sister Ramona. Her high visibility, her passion, her central role (despite a reluctance to see herself in this position), and the intensity of her personality were an affront to many, and she became the ultimate target. For Sister Ramona, the letters became a nightmare, particularly after the publication of a large picture of her on the front page of the *New Haven Register* on Friday, June 2, 1978, kissing Richard goodbye. Some of the letters were signed accusations, as the following:

> Dear Sister:
> I would just like to say that I think the picture that was in the paper of you kissing a murderer was a positive disgrace. I consider myself a good Catholic, being brought up by the Sisters of Mercy. We were taught the ten commandments, one being "THOU SHALL NOT KILL." How can you people make so much and protect so much a man who admitted killing a girl like this. I am beginning to think the Catholic reli-

gion is really going down the drain. How can I answer my co-workers when they see the way this trial is being carried out. You know what I tell them "If I were on the jury I would hang him." You know one time everyone had respect for religion but not with this sort of thing going on. As I said to Archbishop Whealon something had better be done to bring the Catholic religion back to where it used to be and get a little respect from people.

I really don't blame the coming generation to be falling away from the church. Again I must say I think this trial is the worst spectacle the world has ever seen.

Sincerely
Miss ———

But more of them were the ugly, unsigned ones:

Sister Penis—
    For your irreligious efforts to help the murderer herring, you deserve to have your cunt ripped open and then your head cut off. Then you and all the other Roman Catholic parasites at Yale should be shipped to Rome to screw the Pope.

Sister Ramona Pena was born in 1929 of a Spanish family in New York City. She had five sisters and a brother. Her intelligence was evident from childhood, when she was placed in a rapid advancement class for a group of gifted children. Her father had emigrated to this country at age eighteen. He had been in the Spanish merchant marine and he kept his Spanish loyalties throughout his life.

When Ramona was nine, the Spanish civil war broke out. "We were anti-Franco, so we ate, lived, slept the war. Fund-raising, helping immigrants, housing immigrants, working. That's where I became politically aware."

The strongest influence of her life was the father, with his political nature, and the fact that she was raised during the Depression and influenced by predominantly Jewish teachers with a radical commitment. At one time during her adolescence she was attracted to the Quaker style. She had planned to go to Syracuse University, but at the influence of her principal, an Episcopalian, she was urged to become reintroduced to her own religion and agreed to give St. Joseph's Catholic College a trial. It was there that she realized "the most total of all dedications that I could think of was the religious life."

I asked her if the idea of giving up marriage and children hadn't struck her as an enormous sacrifice, sensing her sensual nature. Her answer was interesting.

"There is nothing that doesn't have its price. I had and have a deep conviction that any religious person who doesn't have the potential to be a good wife—including being a good sexual companion—and also a good mother, would not make a good religious. The only good, happy, fulfilled religious are those who have all the potential for the other, who really made a sacrifice. It's the only way to feel valid. The idea of making a whole gift to God, the totality, means giving up what you like. There isn't a middle way for me."

She loved to teach. She loved the religious life, and she found herself in a perfect position as an assistant chaplain at Yale. All that was to change.

And a note of bitterness creeps in.

People think I make this case my life. I am a friend to Richard, but this is not my life.

—Who's making the assumption?

It's as if I did nothing at Yale except stand by Richard. It's as if I did nothing at the chapel, nothing in the community. I was never aware of what a small town New Haven is until it became impossible for me to shop at Macy's. It became an impossibility because the New Haven paper reporter thought he had some special privilege, and when he didn't, and when I took him up on some of the things he wrote—he was the only reporter who named the other young man in Bonnie's life. *The New York Times*, the *New York Post*, the Gannett papers, didn't do that. It was nobody's business. The other young man had nothing to do with what happened. When I confronted him, he took it very badly. So anyway, then I was so visible.

—Do you mean they then cast you as the main character?

Go to the files! The pictures! It was as if nothing else had ever happened or ever was going to happen. People stopped me on the street. Before that I could walk through New Haven anonymous. I didn't wear a habit. I didn't at the trial either. The jury didn't know who I was. At first they thought I must be his mother because I was there every day. I'm Hispanic-looking enough. When his mother went to the stand, they realized I wasn't his mother.

—You're implying it was the media that made your life difficult?

It sure did. The New Haven media. Painfully. I have all kinds of mail. I try to push it back. People asked me why I was doing this. The day they published the picture of Richard kissing me goodbye was the day I was presiding at the communion services at the chapel.

I hadn't seen the paper, but on my way to church someone gave me a copy. They caught the moment Richard had become the unafraid person he *wanted* to become. We had considered that a beautiful moment the day before. So to see that moment on the front page of the paper in the context in which they had it. I'll tell you!

The problem was that we were cut off from much support because we did not want to involve the parish, and had no right to, so we were walking a very narrow line. We were trying to do what we must—as chaplain and friend, leaving our entire community free to take their own position. So people who would ordinarily be called on to sustain us weren't. We felt we couldn't.

—You felt a great animosity in the Yale community?

No, in the New Haven community. At Yale only isolated instances. Most of Yale and the professors at Yale wanted to stay as far away from it as possible. They did not want to talk about it. They wanted to stay away from it.

We had never asked them, and I think it's true that though Bonnie and Richard had both gone to Yale, Yale could not express a loyalty to one above the other. In point of fact, they eventually had to, because it was brought into that position, scholarship, service . . . Yale administrators tried to keep as far away from actively supporting anybody as they could.

—Do you ever get seriously depressed?

Oh, sure. I don't think I'm over the depression.

—Is that partly why you left Yale?

No. I was fired by the chaplain [Father Richard Russell].

—Because of the case?

He never gave a reason. That's a more hurtful situation than the rest. He specifically said it wasn't because of this case. He refused to give a reason. It's all hurtful.

Many times during our discussion, Ramona's eyes would well with tears. These events were not part of some distant buried past, but occupied her present. She never completely lost control. In discussing her dismissal from Yale, she came close to it. She loved Yale. She hated to leave it. And she was hurt and felt badly treated by a man she loved, Richard Russell. Ramona uses "love" loosely. By that I do not mean she feels it loosely, but she is generous in her feelings. I had a sense that she was not using it generically in talking of Richard Russell, but in a more specific sense. I did not want to upset her, so I pulled away from the subject. Shortly after, she spontaneously returned to discussing her final days at Yale.

Paul Garland is so bitter about Yale, and yet Yale has been so self-righteous in disassociating themselves from the whole thing. They almost wanted to pretend they were not Yale students, the Yale community was not a significant part of the trial.

They let the Glee Club sing at the funeral. The Glee Club was Bonnie's group—she was first soprano there. There was a benefit performance for the scholarships the Garlands have set up at the music school which will have Bonnie's name. That's the only thing the Garlands didn't cancel. There is an active scholarship with her name on it. The university had a public memorial service, the Glee Club was there, the University Chaplain presided. We were forbidden to come—forbidden by the Garlands, which was transferred to Yale, and the Yale Chaplain forbade us to go—the three Catholic chaplains. They could not forbid our community because they couldn't identify them.

The word we got from John van Ardsdale, the chaplain, was that if the Garlands walked into Dwight Chapel and saw us, they would leave. Consequently, since we prayed regularly in our community for her, we put the memorial in the bulletin and urged our congregation to go. So many of our congregation, even those who didn't know them, out of respect for the girl, went and were part of the group.

The Catholic chaplains were responsible for the service. The other chaplains came to us and asked what to do. We said, "Start planning now for a memorial." That's the appropriate thing for the chaplain to do, and the university can do it without taking sides—to remember a girl who died in such a tragic way.

It was very crowded, very beautiful, it was an esthetic setting. It was done by a Lutheran priest, and even though we weren't there, we knew it was done in style. It was in October. Since I knew it would be better if I weren't there since I couldn't attend, I wrote the Brothers and went to visit Richard. I went to Albany. We didn't tell Richard about the memorial. I just had to be close to some part of that grief. Several times I asked the chaplains if they could intercede and try to work out some reconciliation, because people who would walk out when they saw us were concentrating more on *us* than on their *daughter*, but finally Richard Russell said to me, "I would prefer you not go."

—Were you good friends with him?

Yes. That was the trauma of the whole situation. Oh, yes. We were at a staff meeting, and after it was over, he said, "There's something else I want to tell you. I really can't work with you any more, and I would like you to leave." I said, "I won't stay with anyone who doesn't want me. But this is something the board has to deal with." He insisted that it wasn't, that it was his prerogative, so I was the one who brought it to the board, saying to them, "I am not staying under any circumstances, but I want them to make a statement." I never got a statement, except personal regrets, et cetera. Father Fagan had already left, and I felt that was enough trauma for a small ministry.

—Did Peter Fagan leave because of this?

No. Peter Fagan left because he was getting married. So Richard went to jail in August. Peter left on August thirty-first, and they fired me on October eighteenth.

—Certainly you must have demanded more of Father Russell? Did you say, "Why, we've been friends," et cetera?

Sure. Sure. He said that he couldn't tell me. So we carried that out till the end, and finally he said to me, his reasons would be "destructive to my reputation." I said to him, "That is worse than giving me a reason. Whatever the issue is, I ought to be confronted with it."

One of the major personal conflicts I've always had is my awareness that there are very few people who ever feel the gentle side of me. My very, very best friend in this world says to me all the time, and said it to me long ago when we worked together in the same office, "Why do you fight so hard to be gentle, when you *are* gentle?" People treat me as if I'm going to give them a battle.

After a brief diversion into her politicization, coming out of the family background previously discussed, she reiterated:

I was absolutely smashed by Richard's imprisonment. I knew it was going to happen, but it still doesn't change the

emotional smash. And Peter's leaving the priesthood—not the
marrying—I approve of his marrying—but just leaving us. And
Dick's firing of me—I was absolutely smashed.

Despite all this, perhaps because of all this, Ramona was as reso-
lute and firm about her ideas of justice and punishment and her conviction that her Christian point of view was somehow or other recon-
cilable with the political system.

The verdict was fair. I don't know if the sentence was fair. I
don't think the sentence was given objectively. My problem is
with the length of the sentence. If I could be convinced that
the judge pronounced sentence because he had come to the
legal conclusion about Richard that led to that sentence, I
would feel okay, but I don't feel that that judge was that objective.

You had a Westchester County judge who was one of the
leading figures in the Republican party, and the victim's father
was another leading Republican figure in Westchester. A judge
who when he was sentencing and described what had happened
described *murder*, not manslaughter, and then imposed the
sentence. If that judge had defined manslaughter and then
given Richard the maximum sentence, in the context of a criminal justice system that I don't approve of for anybody—Richard or anybody else—I would say he was given justice. I have
some question of the objectivity of this particular judge in this
case. The judge who was in the pretrial hearing—he seemed to
be going more according to what is the law, not personal.

—In a better society, would you say Richard should not have
gone to jail?

I would devise a system other than prison. If we as a nation
are willing to say we don't know what to do with people who
don't conform to society—we remove them to warehouses because we don't have a better solution—I wouldn't like it, but I
would feel we're being honest. I know nothing is being cor-
rected even though they're all called correctional institutions.

—What about the concept of punishment, not rehabilitation?

The only logical sentence then is a life sentence. Because
you are taking people who are being punished for being violent,
making them more violent in the prisons, and then returning
them to society.

—How do you think the Garlands would feel if Richard had simply stayed with the Brothers a few years and then done some
service?

I have no idea how you handle it, having a child killed. If a child died of illness, I'd be heartbroken. I do have a very strong sense that if I were to lose a child as horribly as they, it would be incumbent to me—while I would always remember my child—to have my life as unbitter as possible. I'd try not to concentrate on eliminating the other person, because that would not restore my loss.

—What about the case Litman is involved in now—the off-duty policeman? What about Eichmann?

One question I ask myself—Do you believe in change? Do you believe in redemption? Yes, the man was an SS officer thirty years ago. What does that say about the man today?

—Are you saying Eichmann ought to have gone unpunished?

Thirty years later is different. At the time, when he hadn't had time to re-examine his life, I would want to catch him up and have him think—either that or say to myself, this person is dangerously psychotic.

For someone like myself, who has been almost obsessed with the Holocaust and what its implications are for human nature and human institutions, the idea that it would have been appropriate with Eichmann to "catch him up and have him think" is about as antithetical as could be. Ramona seemed to be implying that what she wanted from him was some self-examination, unless, of course, he was psychotic. That would be a different story.

That's different. People that you know are psychotic belong in institutions. When you know a person has no inner control, they should be institutionalized. This is what I say about psychiatry and Richard. We all said this boy is abnormal. He can only have psychiatry now to adjust him to prison life, risking coming out of prison to normal life as disturbed as you were the moment you killed that girl.

—Then you're essentially saying you don't believe in punishment?

I really think I don't believe in punishment that effects no good. You want to prevent evil from occurring again. The social order demands that good come out of it. Someone like David Berkowitz, who hasn't got the inner conscience, has to be kept in an institution. Someone like Richard, I would like to send to a lifetime of service like in medieval times. You went to a monastery for the rest of your life and you served, fed the poor, nursed.

—You said you reached out to Richard because he was a member of your parish, and you would have done the same to anyone in the community. Now, what about, as a member of the community, your sharing the burden of guilt?

Yes. I tried to reach out to the Garlands, but they wouldn't have it. I tried indirectly to contact the Friends group in Scarsdale, and through that reach them, but the only answer was that I should then have nothing to do with Richard. I tried at the trial to reach Patrick Garland, because he seemed so broken and upset as he testified.

—Do you feel Richard is guilty of a terrible thing?

Yes. Anybody who kills anybody is guilty of the most terrible thing. It's awful. He knows it too.

—And do you feel he must do penance for this guilt?

For himself yes. Absolutely. It's the only way back to health.

When Paul Garland wrote his letter to the Archdiocese of New York in October 1977, he posed specific questions:

Is it appropriate for a church to participate in the solicitation of attestations of good character for one who has confessed in writing to murder?

Is it appropriate for a church to seek the release on bail, without psychiatric examination, and to an insecure facility, of one who has confessed to murder?

What is the moral responsibility of a church if Herrin escapes, commits suicide, or kills or harms others?

Is it appropriate for a church, without consideration of the impact on the family of the victim, to participate in efforts to secure the release of a confessed killer?

And what are the criteria which a church should use in determining when and how to offer aid and support in a criminal case?

Paul Garland may have meant these as rhetorical questions; I do not know. But they are questions which could be taken very directly and very seriously. There is no reason why any institution such as a religion or, for that matter, a family need conform the values within its internal structure to those inherent in the laws of society. Every institution has its own value system consonant with the purposes of that institution.

Different institutions may even share common words that connote entirely different meanings. You are allowed to inflict pain to help a child walk. That is the context of the medical model. We are not allowed to inflict pain to help a child read (although reading may be more central to his adaptation in a civilized society than walking), because that is part of the pedagogical model which does not countenance pain. Medicine is allowed to be bitter; painful indoctrination is torture. When the rehabilitative model intrudes too extensively into the justice system, gross injustices result. That which is unconscionable under the rubric of punishment—extended sentences and unlimited open-ended incarceration—is perfectly acceptable when seen as treatment. The reformist movement for the prison system came crashing down not in the traditional way—because it had not attained its ends—but because it had. And the results were not as anticipated. The disastrous implications of reformist politics on the prison system became apparent almost immediately after the reformists won their victories.

No, the question is not whether different institutions should have different values even while sharing the same language. We are all entitled to our myths. We are entitled to design our own stories and live in conformity to our own designs. The problem comes when we try to reconcile one definition of "reality" against another when we have respect for both and allegiances to both.

Sister Ramona wanted justice in both the religious world she espoused and the political world she occupied—certainly an honorable goal. But she wanted more. She wanted the *same definition* of justice to exist in both worlds. And in this case that can't be. Total forgiveness, love for your enemy, and turning the other cheek are ideals that guide human behavior to a perfection they may never be able to achieve. They are noble concepts that serve to make us better. They have yet to be proved as a pragmatic constitution for living. Even if the "perfectibility of man" and total forgiveness are realistic bases (as distinguished from useful ideals) for a political justice system, they are not the foundations of *this* political system.

Father William Ryan, Chaplain of the State University of New York in Albany, said, "After asking myself what Jesus would do, I don't know that the Church could have responded in any other way," and perhaps so. The Catholic religion is bound by the teachings of Jesus and the dogma of the Church Fathers. The County of Westchester in the State of New York is not. Perhaps, in a better world, it should be; but it is not. It is bound by the Constitution, the common law, and the Criminal Code of the State of New York, *plus* a whole different set of principles, definitions, perceptions, ideals—a whole different set of "truths" that define the myth and the reality of that secular democracy.

Sister Ramona looks at the real world, but with the vision, bias, and optimism of a New Testament prophet. She suffers because she believes in the eternal truth of her religious perception, and does not understand those for whom religious affiliation carries no religious conviction. She is looking for a Christian world that has yet to come.

5

A NEW TESTAMENT: PSYCHOANALYSIS

Some eighteen hundred years after Christ another storyteller was to offer yet another vision of human nature that would powerfully influence our perceptions of ourselves and therefore our definitions of truth. When Sigmund Freud commenced his studies in hysteria,[1] he was a physician looking for the cause of a crippling disease. He never found it. It was not as a pathologist—a student of disease—that Freud made his mark on our time but as a psychologist. It was his contributions to our understanding of the mind, our mental and emotional processes, and their influence on behavior; it was his precise elucidation of the actions, traits, attitudes, thoughts, and the mental states of persons and groups that contributed to his dominant impact on not only academic psychology but also on the literature of myth and on the self-perception of the average man.

He told us a new story—a good story, a gospel that a twentieth century in the process of replacing its reverence for God with awe of science and technology was prepared to accept as gospel truth.

But it is not gospel truth, and it does not lead to certitude. The psychoanalytic view is in no way "truer" than the Christian, or any other religious vision of humankind. The problem is that psychiatrists are not seen as storytellers. They are physicians, scientists, experts. The power of the psychoanalytic model is that it took a philosophical vision of man and cast it within the medical model, so that we approach it not with the incredulity that we bring to new religions but with a credibility that we grant to "scientific" discoveries. We accept diversity in religion. We do not in science. Where diversity occurs there, we constantly chafe until some resolution allows us the peace of mind of accepting one aspect of it as truth. When a doctor testifies in a court of law, he is not seen as a prophet or a preacher or a proselytizer but as a describer of scientific data—signs and symptoms—a reporter of that which is.

Two vast and yawning lacunae exist in the Freudian explanation of disease, both recognized by Freud himself close to one hundred years ago. The first is that the very dynamic explanations which are so intricately linked with pathological behavior also exist in normal behavior, so they cannot be explanations of "cause" in a disease. They are what philosophers would call necessary but not sufficient causes. Both the flasher and the actor may be explained in terms of narcissistic needs to please the mother and to gain approval, combined with a primitive residual exhibitionism. But acting, after all, is still a respectable profession, a "healthy" way to gain pleasure and gratification; whereas dropping your pants in public (opening your raincoat more likely) to entertain the passing ladies with the exquisite sight of your erection is not—at least not yet—considered acceptable social behavior.

The second deficiency in the Freudian theory of disease is just as significant. Psychoanalysis, although it has struggled admirably, has never solved the problem of why, given certain conflicts from the past, one individual solves his problems by hysterical solution and another by obsessive resolution, or beyond that, why one solution is confined to the real world (neurosis), while in another individual it is necessary to abandon one's hold on reality in order to survive (psychosis). No, it is not in pathology but in the psychology of everyday life that one sees Freud at his best, and in which he is accepted most comfortably. The average layman speaks of himself; he explains and apologizes, rationalizes and justifies, accuses and condones—all in Freudian terms.

What is this new story? Well, it is neither penis envy nor castration anxiety nor Oedipal complex. It is a complex analysis of human behavior—all articulated at the turn of the century—that offered a new story of why we do what we do.

Behavior, Freud said, is motivated. That is, it moves always with purpose, and toward a goal. It is never just random. There is an explanation for each action in terms of some anticipation or desire.

Behavior must also be seen as dynamic. No single action is the product of any single cause. Think of a giant game of Bladderball where hundreds of students may be pushing the ball from hundreds of different angles and the ball may remain still. That does not mean there are no forces in motion. It simply means they are balanced. If the ball moves slightly to the northeast, it is not that someone in the southwest has pushed it there; the balance of forces—of hundreds of forces—has led to that result. It was a concept, as many of Freud's were, borrowed specifically and directly from the emerging field of physics. All behavior, therefore, is dynamic—a resultant (in a mathematical sense) of forces and counterforces.

Behavior also must be understood in a developmental context. Nothing that happened today can be understood as a thing in itself, but rather as one in a continuum or sequence of events from the past leading to specific goals in the future. To read today's events without having understood the chapters that have preceded them is to ignore the essential truth of what is happening.

Freud further postulated that we are mostly unaware of the determinants of our behavior, for much of behavior is determined not in the conscious sphere but in the "unconscious." Freud divided the spheres of the mind into three separate functions: the conscious, the unconscious, and the preconscious. It is not necessary to elaborate the distinctions here; it is sufficient to appreciate that we are unaware of the unconscious and incapable (without extraordinary methods like psychoanalysis) of bringing this material to the forefront of the mind. Yet the unconscious determines our perceptions and our responses and influences our behavior. We are as likely to respond to something for unconscious reasons as we are for the rational reasons we offer for our specific behavior.

When one puts together the concept of unconscious determinants with the concept of motivation, the dynamic nature of behavior, and the developmental principle, what emerges is the profound doctrine of psychic determinism. If each piece of behavior is causally related to the past, if one does B because of an A ($A^1 + A^2 + A^3 + A^4$ ad infinitum) that preceded it, and if one is going to explain B on the basis of A, then one is forced to say that behavior is determined: You had to do that which you did.

This concept of psychic determinism is directly contrary to the perception of Christianity with its central emphasis on the individual and his need to seek his own redemption. Christianity is rooted in a sense of responsibility and freedom. In this aspect the law could be more comfortable with the Christian psychology than the Freudian. Christianity emphasizes not only responsibility but also rationality: In the beginning is the Word. But what Freud has created, to borrow William Barrett's term, is an irrational view of man.[2] It is this conflict between the Freudian concept of determinism and the law's demand for responsibility that has made such a mess of the insanity defense.

Beyond the concept of determinism, Freud clearly announces the nature of these determinants as being predominantly irrational. Those forces and counterforces that determine our emotions are primarily the passions, the instincts, the emotions, vested in the biological and animal nature of the human species. Reason and cognition are fragile shields against the onslaught of the passions.

To the Christian, thoughts may be sinful. The distinction between thought and action is blurred, unlike in the Old Testament, where the commandments are essentially instructions as to behavior. In Freud, instincts and feelings are never condemned (even behavior is never condemned except by labeling it "sick"), for we all share the same primordial unconscious. In our unconscious we are all killers, rapists, incestual, exhibitionistic, voyeuristic, aggressive, and homicidal. The difference between the criminal and the model citizen is not in his impulses but in his impulse-control mechanism. In this sense the psychoanalytic view is more accommodating to the law than the Christian. So while the mechanisms of Richard's defense may have been organized from the Christian community, the substance of his defense was defined in terms of the new gospel. If Richard was to be exculpated, if he was to be freed by the state, it would not be because Christ had enjoined us to love the sinner, nor because we had established the fact that he "didn't really do it" (he really did it, and confessed as much), but that the "he" who did it wasn't really Richard. Rather, it was a less rational, less responsible, less autonomous, and therefore a less culpable Richard.

Psychiatry can only exculpate; it cannot incriminate. But psychiatrists can do both. A psychiatrist can testify that the accused is not part of his constituency, that he is not sick, and therefore not entitled to the special mitigation and understanding allowed those seen as not responsible or less responsible because of mental disease.

Experts were, as is now the custom, sought by both sides in the Bonnie Garland killing. Testifying for the defense were Dr. John Train and Dr. Mark Rubenstein. Testifying for District Attorney William M. Fredreck were Dr. Daniel Schwartz, Dr. Abraham Halpern, and Dr. Leonard Abrams.

The "big guns" were Train and Schwartz—two men who feature in the majority of bizarre and newsworthy cases in the New York area.

Dr. John Train examined Richard for a total of nine hours within three to four weeks of the "incident in question." This was Litman's manner of referring to the killing throughout the trial. (It was also Richard's in his interviews with me.)

Dr. John Train is a professional at psychiatric testimony in court. He is a professional at constructing a convincing story to reinforce the case of the prosecutor or defense attorney he may be serving. He is paid to take complicated and often inconsistent threads of behavior and weave them skillfully together into a recognizable, consistent pattern. Out of the muddle of contradictions that is the human mind, he will find a direction that leads clearly to guilt or innocence, depending on the necessities of his client. He is a storyteller.

Here is his story as he told it in trial:[3]

A. I examined Richard Herrin on two occasions, on two occasions for a total of nine hours.

Q. Can you tell us when those occasions were?

A. On August the 2nd of 1977 and August the 5th of 1977.

Q. Approximately three to four weeks after the incident in question?

A. Yes.

Q. . . . by the way, where did those examinations take place, Doctor?

A. In Westchester County Jail. In the hospital—in the Mental Health Unit.

Q. Now, in addition to your examination of the Defendant of approximately nine hours, can you tell us what else you have reviewed in terms of documentation in connection with this case?

Train then listed individually—and therefore at considerable length—every document, report, and letter that he had studied for the case.

> Q. Now, Doctor, have you spent a considerable amount of time in consideration of the issues in this case, sir?
>
> A. A very considerable amount of time, yes, sir. I have spent over forty hours on this case.
>
> Q. Doctor, based on your examination of Richard Herrin, of your consideration of the matters in this case, of the documents you have referred to, can you tell us, sir, whether you have an opinion which you can state with a reasonable degree of medical certainty as to what Richard Herrin's state of mind was on July the 7th, 1977, when he struck Bonnie Garland?
>
> A. I believe that at the time that he struck Bonnie Garland, he was suffering from a severe mental disease or mental illness classified as a transient situational reaction, in which it indicates an adult adjustment problem.
>
> Q. Did the mental disease, serious mental disease from which he was suffering at that time reach, in your opinion, sir, to psychotic proportions?
>
> A. Yes, sir.

While I am reluctant to interrupt a good story—and Dr. Train is a very good storyteller—it seems propitious to insert some comments to highlight both what Train was doing and some of the difficulties with that which he was doing.

Here, in his introduction, with minimal prompting from Litman, he spelled out all the criteria for either defense that Litman was pressing for. In this case Litman was pleading two innately self-contradictory cases. First he was stating that his client should be acquitted because he was psychotic to a point where he no longer had the capacity to know and appreciate that what he was doing was wrong, in which case the law demands that he be exculpated, i.e., found not guilty. On the other hand, Litman was not sure this would be effective; and in case the jury would not buy that, he was at the same time setting the stage for an argument that Richard was operating under "extreme emotional disturbance" at the time of the killing.

Extreme emotional disturbance is a legal term. It is the condition which alters second-degree murder, with its massively larger sentence (a minimum of fifteen years), to first-degree manslaughter, which has a maximum of eight and one-third to twenty-five years and can carry sentences much less constricting.

Notice that Train, an absolute pro in the courtroom, did not use the words "extreme emotional disturbance," for then he would have been speaking to legal matters, and he was not recognized by the court as a legal expert. He was allowed extraordinary latitude—beyond that of most witnesses—because he was speaking as a professional, as a sworn expert witness, presumably with the impartiality that expertise in scientific matters should bring. If he had said, "extreme emotional disturbance," it would have been objected to by Mr. Fredreck and sustained by the judge. But he produced an impression as close to that as possible for the jury to carry with it. He said that Richard was suffering "extreme emotional reaction," in itself not particularly a psychiatric term any more than it is a legal term.

A. In psychiatric classification, we apply this term [transient situational reaction] to individuals who appear to be relatively normal, in that they have no history of being in mental hospitals, they have no history of attending psychiatrists. And they seem to be getting along quite well except that they are relatively unstable, and if one examines them a little more closely, we find that these particular individuals are unstable and not functioning the way we would expect them to.

The indication that Herrin was a poorly put together person, unstable, immature, and making only marginal adjustments, is indicated by the fact that this young man, with an I.Q. of 130, which places him substantially in the superior intellectual group, can only perform to 2.3 level, which is a—just about passing level, while attending a University. In people such as this, when they are exposed to an overwhelming external stress or situation, they do not have any psychological room to maneuver. Their capacity to adapt is limited. And because of this inability to adapt, whatever adjustments they were making, which were marginal, now become precarious and finally collapse.

Train had set up a theoretical discussion to serve the needs of his client. He had to convince the jury that Richard was crazy enough to be excused from responsibility for the dreadful acts that were done. But he could not frighten the jury. Richard could not "now" be crazy, because a jury need not be logically accountable, and culpable or not, Richard might be convicted simply because these twelve ladies and gentlemen might rest more comfortably in their beds at night with a potentially "crazy" Richard locked up. So Train allowed for a "slow return" to normal.

Under questioning from Litman, he related Richard to other cases of "transient situational reaction." It was important that Richard be placed in a class with those who normally and naturally elicit compassion. He discussed the depressed person driven to suicide, the soldier suffering from battle fatigue, the innocent girl being "pregnant out of wedlock" and driven to suicide.

Train betrayed a Victorian morality that often made his examples more appropriate to a nineteenth-century novelist than a post-Freudian psychiatrist. Few out-of-wedlock mothers nowadays are driven from the parental doorsteps into the unwelcoming snowy night. Besides the anachronism, there was a flaw in the analogy. Train's "diseased" victims were all driven to self-destruction. He had to get closer to Richard's case.

> I should say another type of example is where a man finds someone—where individuals who love each other, and then suddenly finds one is unfaithful, and there is suddenly this outburst of rage at this kind of unfaithfulness, giving rise to a violent action. That also would fall into that category.
>
> Q. Now, Doctor, the outburst of emotion that you were talking about, is that necessarily followed immediately upon the overwhelming environmental stress?
>
> A. Oh, no. With our advanced understanding of the human mind and with our understanding of how unconscious mechanisms can occur, that there can be so much going on in the human mind that the individual does not know about it—in fact, at one time it was stated that the human being only knows, is conscious of ten per cent of what is in his mind. The rest of his function is motivated by unconscious things.
>
> And so, with this understanding, the law has been changed so that we don't deal with just the issue of an immediate situation of heat of passion and then reaction immediately. Not at all.
>
> We are able to recognize that when an individual is exposed to stress over any protracted period of time, especially an individual like Herrin, who over the years has never really expressed emotion—he has learned to be an overdisciplined, overcontrolled individual—the emotions can simmer uncon-

sciously over that period of stress, and then inexplicably give rise to a sudden thought. And then at some time there will be an explosion—a volcanic outburst of this seething emotion that's become pent up in his unconscious.

There can be a period of time between cause and outburst.

Q. Did you find that in this case, Doctor?

A. This is a classical case of it.[4]

In this section Dr. Train was inconsistent and, psychiatrically speaking, simplistic and probably wrong. Nonetheless, it is the kind of thing that has a "scientifical" quality about it that might impress the jury.

Notice that throughout he talked about "outbursts of emotion," although later he would testify that there was no emotion during the period of the attack.

There are also very few academic psychiatrists who would talk about "our advanced understanding of the human mind." We are in the pre-kindergarten stage of understanding human dynamics and mental mechanisms.

The use of a percentage like 10 percent was sheer sophistry. We have no idea if it's 1/10 of 1 percent, in which case Train's figure was a hundredfold wrong. To use statistics in that manner would be intolerable at a scientific meeting.

Finally, if the term "transient situational reaction" is to be used loosely enough to excuse any violent crime in a person exposed to stress, the only persons not excused are the insane! Who else would explode without pressure or stress? But who can ever be said to be free of pressure?

Train then established the principle that all of Richard's history was essential to an appreciation of the nature of his behavior at any given time, particularly at the time of the murder. This is completely consistent with the concept of psychic determinism as previously explained. Train, of course, did not acknowledge that this type of explanation could be offered in defense of *any* individual committing *any* crime, since it is the very nature of psychic determinism to see all behavior as predetermined.

Train was going to take us through a long journey starting with Richard's illegitimate birth and listing all the traumata to which he was exposed in an attempt to show how those events in early years became the ingredients that currently concerned the court.

To do this he would emphasize all those negative aspects of Richard's childhood in an attempt to weave a story that carried with it the tragic inevitability of a Greek drama. Since Richard's childhood was not terribly traumatic, he had to find the symbolic meanings of the events that would most lend a somber portentous tone.

He described Richard's alcoholic father, who abandoned the family when Richard was only three, and his mother's remarriage when Richard was seven. He made a few statistical errors, having Richard's mother remarry when Richard was four, at the height of "the Oedipal period." He saw this as having a profound effect on Richard. He did not explain to the jury that by Freudian definitions all four-year-olds enter an Oedipal period in which they wish their mothers exclusively for themselves.

He described the stepfather as not particularly supportive. In many ways he was not, but he was not brutal; and Richard, unlike so many raised in a minority ghetto, did have a father figure in attendance. There was a sense of constancy in this man and vital support. There was, it is true, no love. Train described the stepfather as "harsh, critical, unaffectionate, not warm . . . and from the age of seven or eight made him work in a flea market where he was frequently ridiculed and humiliated and scolded." All of this is apparently true.

He then offered further evidence that Richard had problems as a child. He was "a bed-wetter well beyond the period where he should have outgrown it" and "suffered from eczema." He then added the following:

Q. What leads you to believe that even though he was within apparent normal limits, he had a personality problem?
A. . . . To further interfere with the wholesome development, there was the fact that his mother had to work. And so when he returned from school, he could not play with his school friends, and he had to go to a nursery school where he was kept until his mother could pick him up, which meant that he was involved with a structured kind of environment and never was exposed to be able to have the free spontaneous kind of play that children have in the streets. And he also had to answer to authority.[5]

It is peculiar in this day of the ubiquitous working mother to hear that his "wholesome development" was interfered with because he "had to go to nursery school" rather than experiencing "the free spontaneous kind of play that children have in the streets." The background that Train sketched was neither unique nor horrifying. Eczema, bed-wetting, and a second father do not represent a Dickensian childhood. This was not a slum horror story of hunger and brutality. Part of the confusion of psychodynamic explanations of behavior is that the background of pathological people often sounds so normal, while the background of normal people often seems pathological.

Train continued then to trace Richard's story of his childhood in Los Angeles much in the way that Richard has already done for us, but with one significant difference in narrative style. Richard told us what happened. Train told us what happened always as though it were an explanation of what was later to happen. In other words, seemingly innocent events of childhood were attached by a tenuous causal linkage to the horrible actions that led Richard to the courtroom, thereby lending those events an ominous note.

There were at least two major themes that Train stressed, both part of the "model boy syndrome." One was Richard's inability to ever express anger. The second was Richard's need to ingratiate. To Train, this was directly linked to fear of abandonment by his mother. The unanswered question, and it will remain unanswered, was why Richard, more than other children, should have felt this terror of abandonment. His mother, Mrs. Linda Ugarte, may have been remiss in some aspects of motherhood, but what came through was an enormously devoted and dedicated person who placed her child above all else. Of course, in the psychoanalytic libretto it is impossible for the mother to have a winning part. She's damned if she does and damned if she doesn't. If the child does not turn out well, it is seen as evidence of either too little love from her or too much love from her, even though she may have given no more or less than the mothers of thousands of children who never came to this particular grief. Dr. Train:

> A. And, so, he became what is called the model boy. Extremely polite, well-behaved, no temper tantrums . . . The kind of boy or child that parents might feel a great deal of joy in, except that they would have to be prepared later on to having someone who has a mental illness.
>
> And he goes to Yale, and we begin to see the signs now of

the marginal adjustments breaking down. Because he comes to Yale and he's immediately overwhelmed by this citadel of intellectual accomplishment. And he cannot compete and be top man. And so, begins to withdraw from actively being a student, becomes unmotivated, and is unable to perform according to his capacity. Already we are seeing now the marginal adjustments beginning to break down.[6]

Richard started to fall apart, then, three years before he met Bonnie. Why? What was the stress? These were the intriguing questions that were never answered.

The defense mechanisms that Train later described were *not* effective. He was not capable of substituting social and political success for intellectual failure. Train tried to make the case that Richard became a big man on campus, listing all of the organizations in which he was active. But it was only too clear from other reports that his position was passive and peripheral in most of these organizations.

It was here that Train introduced another dynamic factor on which he would rest a significant part of his case, the concept of symbiosis. Symbiosis is used in psychiatry to explain the intensity of the relationship between the mother and her infant, or for that matter the relationship between a woman and her dying husband. Here the relationship becomes a means of survival for both in which the seemingly independent member of the team is in actuality as dependent as the obviously helpless one. We know these conditions exist. We have seen where the individual who has supported a dependent loved one to a point of exhaustion and bankruptcy nonetheless thrives on the situation and collapses only after the loss of the dependent partner.

Train's new story was going to show that Richard formed "symbioses" with large groups of people, then ultimately with Ginny, and finally with Bonnie. I have never heard symbiosis used in this particular way. It is clearly a misuse and a sloppy one. He meant an excessive dependency, a passive, parasitic, and unrealistic attachment. It was Train at his least elegant and least interesting. It constantly led him into contradictions—and often led him into perilous statements—perilous for the case he wished to make.

A. *He becomes very dependent upon Ginny. Even though he was warned against it by his friends. And even though he knew that*

> *this particular girl was preoccupied with her own interests on campus . . . she could be quite manipulative or date people that might help her in this realm. But he refuses to accept that. Until when he began to have his doubts, and he began to feel rejected by her.*
>
> *We have the first evidence of not only the marginal adjustments breaking down, but the first evidence of it becoming so precarious that he was now acting in a peculiar, bizarre, strange way. And his behavior in this particular way bordered on being psychotic.[7]*

It is interesting that Train saw this behavior as suggesting "psychosis." It is important in light of the fact that part of the argument for Herrin's bail hearing, an argument that would be used constantly in the future, was that the peculiar combination of events that led to Bonnie Garland's murder could never happen explicitly in that way again. Yet Train was suggesting here a response close to psychosis even with Ginny (although I myself would not state it so). This would suggest that in both the major relationships—different as they were—he was capable of responding psychotically. If one accepted this concept, one would have to look differently at Richard's future in terms of his potential dangerousness.

> *. . . For instance, in order to spy on her, he crept out on the ledge high above the ground, risking his life, so that he could look into her apartment. And when he saw her with somebody in her apartment at a particular time, he ran down, ran to the apartment, knocked on the door, gained admission, and when he was asked, "What do you want?" he asked for a glass of water. And he asked for three glasses of water, hoping that maybe the man would leave so he could talk to the girl and confront her. But when the man didn't leave, he just up and left. . . .*
>
> *This is quite bizarre. But at no time did he have any overt, angry outburst at her.*
>
> Q. *Why did he not express anger in these situations?*
>
> A. *He never can. It is repressed. He is following a pattern of defense mechanism he learned as a child. He can't tolerate to have anybody angry at him. He can't tolerate having anyone dislike him. . . .*
>
> *It is interesting he had no sexual intercourse with her. In fact, he's a—quite a moral person on that ground. Unusually*

so for this day and age and for his particular relationships with his peers.[8]

It was odd hearing a dynamic psychiatrist using the fact that a man avoided sexual intercourse as indicating that he was a "moral person." Indeed, we know from Richard's story that throughout this period they were performing fellatio and cunnilingus. I am not clear if Dr. Train was suggesting a higher morality in that behavior than in intercourse. Besides, we know from Richard's own story that it was a condition that Ginny set on the relationship! Richard, judging from his reaction when Bonnie set the same condition, was probably relieved. He suffered from extreme anxiety about his sexual potential, in terms of both performance and equipment. Neither of these conditions would reflect any moral statement.

Litman then led Train to the relationship of Richard with Bonnie. Again, Train repeated the incidents and episodes with which we are now familiar, but he cast the events into categories of evidence. The relationship was seen as a symbiotic one from the beginning, "and it developed into a relationship where both were totally dependent upon each other symbiotically, as I mentioned before."

Yet from all evidence, Bonnie had doubts intermittently and throughout their relationship. From the very beginning there were periods of withdrawal of interest from Richard, attraction to other men, and at least one or two documented cases of sexual involvement. This is not to suggest that she did not deeply love Richard—or at least feel that she deeply loved him (Bonnie was a girl who loved being in love)—but it is an absurd use of the word "symbiosis."

Train then began to establish an extension from the idea of symbiosis: Richard's existence became totally dependent on Bonnie. It was important for Train to establish the fact early that Richard would see the loss of Bonnie as something beyond the painful abandonment of a loved object but as the loss of the very mechanism of survival. If this could be established, if Bonnie's interest in another man could be interpreted as a murderous assault on Richard rather than the withdrawal of the gift of love, then Richard's attack on Bonnie could be seen as a peculiar form of self-defense—a grotesque "survival mechanism." It was part of the technique of converting Bonnie from victim to victimizer, thereby making Richard a victim.

Train established this case in a way that was particularly helpful to Litman. He did it through the inadmissible letters. With some coaching from Litman, he constantly alluded to the letters and read those portions most sympathetic to his case. They could then be put in the record as psychiatric testimony, even though the judge had ruled them irrelevant. Train took these statements from love letters as though they were an essential truth. I wonder how many of such declarations of love, how many claims that "you are the essence of my being," were dissipated on relationships that lasted not through a semester but only a two-week summer cruise.

Train took them literally.

A. *Through her love and through the fact that she returned or responded to his love, he began to feel that he was a person of worth. He wrote one letter where he says something to the effect that she is his link to people, indicating that he has a social identity through her. Other times, he wrote something to the effect that she is the essence of the fire of his life, indicating that his whole sense of self-worth, his whole identity, his whole being of a worthy person was being nourished by her love. And, of course, that she responded to him with intense affection and passion, restored his whole essence or gave him an essence of being a masculine and acceptable person.*

And so, in three important areas, he could have a sense of identity, a sense of being, a sense of worth through this girl.

She became the fountainhead of his psychological being, and he was as dependent upon her as he was when he was a child dependent upon his mother.

In an extensive and prolonged set of questions and answers, Litman then led Train through the entire set of correspondence that had been ruled inadmissible. A typical example of this colloquy follows:

Q. *Doctor, let me show you Defense Exhibit E [Letter from Richard to his mother] marked for identification [handing]. Doctor, is that letter—of significance to you in arriving at your opinion in this case?*

A. *Well, it sure does. It is an indication of how intense he felt about this girl and how he idealizes her. . . . He's mentioning how difficult it is and, he hasn't seen this girl whom he loves so much in six weeks. . . . "She is a very special wonderful young lady." "I know she will never do anything to hurt me," indicating that in the back of the recesses of his mind, the same way as a child he was always afraid of being abandoned, being hurt . . .*

Now, this from a 21-year-old young man is quite immature to express his love for someone on those terms. Usually we think of it in the reverse. In the role playing of the sexes, it is the girl that is always worried about being hurt, jilted, not the fellow. But he plays this immature role, which is a continuation of his mental state.[9]

Dr. Train again seemed to be confusing the mores of his generation with the current one. There is absolutely no evidence that women are more vulnerable to rejection than men. On reading these letters, I have asked myself if, unaware of the eventual outcome, I would have found the letters remarkable. I would not. Where Train found "a beautiful letter to indicate the total dependency and symbiotic relationship and the intensity of the relationship that they were both dependent upon," I saw only a typical adolescent, idealized, hyperbolic, and somewhat embarrassing love letter to "Twinkletoes" from "Sunshine."

Q. What does this signify, that this type of relationship can be maintained over that distance for such a period of time.

A. It indicates what I've explained before, the essence of symbiotic dependency, so totally dependent upon each other. He lived through this girl and she, apparently, was living through him. They had, from a technical point of view—their whole essence of identity of being, of worth, was through each other and for each other.

But we all know, even Richard by now, that Bonnie was dating another boy during this period, and by all evidence probably sleeping with him. "Her whole essence of identity" was hardly through Richard. She was preparing her final exit from a relationship that showed clear ambivalence from the beginning. Examine the following letter, not admitted in evidence, from the *first month* of their relationship.

I'm scared to talk about this because I'm scared of hurting you—I don't want freedom from you—I love you—but sometimes I feel I have to report all my doings to you—whether you ask or not—because I get these "vibes"—if you will—that even though you say you're not, you are suspicious. I even feel odd sometimes when I'm just kidding around w/ other guys—something like "Would he approve? Would he be mad?" goes thru my mind. The line I was talking about was between my right to freedom and my responsibility to you—I've got to have freedom because I am rebellious by nature—I need elbow room—but I don't want to hit my elbows against you—do you understand? I hate feeling hemmed in by some *role* I feel I have to play—sometimes I feel you put me in a role where there are certain accepted behaviors & others that are taboo. What would everyone think? Sometimes it seems to me anyways that you become concerned w/your image (I guess which is natural) and our image but that is what I rebell against—images are extensions of roles—all I'm saying is just let me be me and you be you and put up with my "goings-off-on-tangents" because I have to do it—anyways, that's what was on my mind and you can punch me if you like or anything but I still love you.[10]

Bonnie was unsure and romantic—as she had every right to be at age eighteen. She did continue to confuse and confound Richard with declarations of love.

She did what countless others her age have done—tried to hang on to an old love while pursuing a new one. It is a common failing. Most, however, do not pay for it with their lives.

Train continued to see the relationship in terms of "symbiosis" up until, and even through, the phone call in February 1977 in which Richard caught Bonnie in a lie.

> A. *This is the first evidence in which he develops a doubt in the relationship....*
> *This time, he is quite distressed, apprehensive, doesn't become angry, but becomes fearful.*[11]

The myth of a symbiotic relationship will simply not hold, not for Richard, not for the jury, and if he followed closely enough, not for Train. That Richard was dependent on Bonnie is obvious. The matter of Richard's dependency is not to be taken lightly, nor is the nature of the dependency (see Chapter 8). But this is not symbiosis; and the poetic interweaving of a myth involving Richard's mother, his relationships with groups in general, and his relationship with Bonnie into some prototypic symbiosis was false from the start. A good story takes the known facts and conforms them to an attractive thesis. The thesis of symbiosis is silly and ignores the fact that Bonnie was not pathologically and completely dependent on Richard. She was experimenting, looking, and finding other interests.

Bonnie was falling in love—again. She may not have known it, but the door was slowly closing on her relationship with Richard. Of course she still had affection for him and fear of losing him and guilt about hurting him. During the winter of 1977, when things were not going well for Richard, she sensed his despair. She flew down to comfort him. Bonnie, like so many her age, was reluctant to give up that which she had until she was secure about that which was to come. In addition, she clung to old love with a nostalgia of those of few years. But everything was interpreted by Train as being clear and consistent with his line of reasoning. How simple life would be for all of us, and particularly for those of us who earn a living as psychoanalysts, if people moved in a single continuum from one point to another. Unfortunately, they do not. They move simultaneously in multiple directions, weaving and bobbing, pushing out and pulling back, in multiple forays, sending out loud and clear contradictory messages.

It is interesting that while Train was elaborating the detailed story of Bonnie's extraordinary and unwavering devotion toward Richard he did so almost completely uninterrupted by District Attorney Fredreck. By the time of the trial, Fredreck was aware, as were most of the principals, that Bonnie had affairs during the period, and certainly by the winter and spring of 1977 was having a serious relationship with Bob.

The interpretation of Bonnie's compassionate trip to see Richard as evidence of pathologic dependency was part of the regrettable fact that everything is always up for this kind of interpretation. It is just as likely a manifestation of her guilt over her affair with Bob, and her recognition that Richard was slipping into her past; and it is equally interpretable as a simple act of generosity and kindness—both of which were characteristic of Bonnie.

Q. All right. Doctor, could you tell us what happened to Richard Herrin after Bonnie Garland left on the Glee Club tour in the middle of May?

A. At that particular time, during that time, he became distressed, agitated, very disturbed, because he was receiving no mail. It affected his work, this agitation and despair as to why he would not receive any mail from her. And no matter what he would think, he became involved with the idea of being abandoned again—a return to his childlike memories and an extension of it. One can say it is like a reliving of it without this mail. And so, he wrote some letters indicating to what de-gree—to what degree he was suffering because he's not re-ceived any mail. And even though he knew that it takes a while for the mail, and he was hoping it was because of the mails that he was not receiving mail, he could not help but also think that she might have met a European and would live with this European in Europe, and he would never see her again.

Q. Is there any—

A. And there was no reason for it. It was just a continuation of the unstable element of his own personality. Something he's never gotten over since his childhood.[12]

Of course there was a reason for his anxiety. Richard, not being the automaton, the predictable stereotype, the cookie cutout of Dr. Train's cookie cutter, was finally reacting as a normal human being. He was anxious and frightened, and he had good reason. A phone call just prior to Bonnie's leaving on tour forced even Richard to ac-knowledge that Bonnie had been lying to him and in all probability was already involved with another man.[13]

Even if one argues that Richard repressed the ultimate knowl-edge, then he certainly unconsciously recognized Bonnie's involve-ment; and by the principles of dynamic reasoning with which Train was explaining this case, the unconscious recognition was just as ca-pable, one might say more so, of producing anxiety. Richard's behav-ior at this point seemed more reasonable than at many times in the past. His anxiety was a sign that his massive denial mechanisms were not working and that he was facing a tough reality.

Q. Doctor, let me show you this, which is People's Exhibit 15-D in evidence, a letter he wrote Bonnie on the 28th of May, 1977 [handing]. Were you aware of that, sir, and had you taken that into consideration in arriving at your analysis and conclusion in this case?

A. Yes.

Sat. nite 5/28/77

Good Morning Sunshine!
How's my sweet little hunk of beauty and inspiration doing today? I love you, Bonnie. I moved into the Devery's house yesterday and its the loneliest place I've ever lived in. There's nobody around and nothing to do. I've been thinking about you all day, babe. I've been thinking about you all day every day, babe. I've never missed you so much.
I've never yearned for you like I do now. That gives me a

great idea for your Tour Break!! But no, don't do it, don't fly back to Ft. Worth, I'll survive. You know, sweetheart, as of today (Saturday) I still haven't heard from you. 10 days!!! I can't stand it. Why me?!! Here's my new address:

Dr. Richard James Herrin * @ √
2304 W. Lowden St.
Ft. Worthless, Texas 76110

* = Future holder of the Cheetah Chair of Primatology, Smithsonian Institution.

@ Pretty nice guy, too.

√ Friend and lover to only you, Bonnie.

Well, Thursday I helped Jack move some of his stuff out. Yesterday I moved all of my stuff. This morning Denny and I helped Becky move out of her place. Tomorrow I'm helping Jack some more. Tuesday I'm helping two other people. Wednesday I'm going to collapse!!!

The new place is small and hot. Bath but no shower. Air conditioner, 2 large rooms, kitchen. At least I'm getting it rent free. All I pay is the electricity. I sleep on a double box spring and mattress but no frame. (it sits on the floor). Almost feels like a waterbed!!! All I have is my radio. Looks like a lot of time will be spent in the Geology Department. Becky offered to loan me her TV for the meantime but I told her no, that I was going cold turkey on T.V.!!!

I know you'll be going on your break pretty soon, and I assume you're still going to Venice. Hope you've found innocent companions and gracious hosts for the jog to Italy. My lucky little girl.

I put new spark plugs in TWUK yesterday, and it ran *worse* than ever, much to my dismay. Denny figured out that I put two of the wires back on in the wrong order, and that's why the truck ran bad *after* I had put in new plugs. I reversed the two wires and now TWUK runs fine. Gosh, I get more like Dean every day!!!

I just got a booklet from GW which lists apartments in the D.C., Alexandria, and Arlington areas. Single furnished *efficiency* apts. start at $176/month!! Regular singles start at $200–215 (up to $590/month). Even double furnished apts. begin at $460/month. Expensive city, sweetie.

I really do hope to start receiving your cards or letters soon, babe. I love you and need you always. With love from your lonely cowboy,

Rick[14]

Train continued:

Q. *Please tell us what significance it has.*
A. *In this particular letter, he again speaks of his great intense love for her and idealizes her again. He also points out to the fact that he is living alone in a friend's house, where he is very, very lonely, and the only thing that relieves him of this loneliness is the constant preoccupation about her, thinking about her. As he states in the letter, "I've been thinking about you all day. I've been thinking about you all day, every day."*

He describes how much he's missed her, and he states, "I've never yearned for you like I do now." This is even though the future of life looks more rosy than ever. Even though he is now only having to finish his thesis; he's been accepted to graduate school. Everything is programmed. He is in a direct direction for his life, and yet he can say he yearns for her, as if this is— and truly is the very essence, the very center of his being.

He is also thinking of how they would get back together when she comes back from the Tour.

So that on May the 28th, he's madly in love with this girl and convinced that she is equally madly in love with him.[15]

Train seemed to accept the literal truth of this letter. To me, there is a desperation here which indicates not at all that he is "convinced that she is equally madly in love with him" but rather that he is doubting that very thing. Remember, he had discovered that she had lied to him; she had been with another man. Then, she left on a trip, and in contrast to her traditional constancy as a correspondent, there was no mail. Perhaps I am projecting into this my knowledge of the letter that would come a short week later, but there is something pathetic about the attempt at joking and the joviality; the "humor" of his address has something of desperation about it; and the exclamation points after he says, "You know, sweetheart, as of today I still haven't heard from you. 10 days!!! I can't stand it. Why me?!!" seem to suggest the frantic. The reader will have to cast his own interpretation of this letter. The letter of June 4 represented a further deterioration, which is so explicit as to defy any misinterpretation.

Hi Babe
I'm sad sad sad, lonely lonely lonely, depressed depressed depressed. Today is Saturday, June 4, and I still haven't received any word from you. I didn't expect the mail service to

173

be so slow, because its tearing my guts out. Every morning I wait for the mailman, and every morning I'm disappointed. I can truly feel what you must have gone through last summer babe. I have never, never, been so sad and lonely. Its a wonder I get any work done.

As an alternative to slow mail service, there's the possibility that you've been too busy to write, but its a slim possibility. I mean, you should have written at least once so far, and it should have been here by now. You've been gone 17 days so far. Leanne just told me that her letters to and from Germany take up to 14 days or so to arrive, so that has eased my mind somewhat. I know in my heart that you have been thinking of me and that you have written. Its just slow mail service. You need not apologize for the slow mail, babe. Just keep writing, because that's as much as you can do. MWWAAAHHH!!!!!

I trust that your break was well spent and very pleasant. Hope you can remember everything that has happened, because I'll want to hear your highlights. I remind you that you need not tell me things you don't want to tell me. I'll try not to be too nosy. Okay? I love you.

Your trip is almost half over (from my end.) That means its only 3 more weeks or so before I see you, and even less time from your end once you receive this.

I hope I've been sending my letters with enough time to arrive while you've still been in the various cities to which they've been sent. If you didn't get one from any stop so far, rest assured that I did send one but *slow mail service* is the culprit.

We've had high-90° weather for quite a while now, and the only comfortable places in the house are right under the cooler (on the bed) or in a cool bath. Otherwise, its hot as hell!!!

The other morning I received the book "How to Take Charge of Your Life." I read it through before going in to the office. It is very interesting and confirms what you've been telling me all along about the value of analysis for understanding oneself. I'm sorry for having been so thick-headed, Bonnie, because you really are such a good thinker. I promise to give your advice top-priority and to really value it, because I realize that you're giving it to me because you care so much. Your love and concern for me is one of the fuels that keep my fire going. My love for you is strong as it is, sweetheart, and rest assured that with your love in return, the pilot light will never go out. Enjoy Deutschland and I'll see you soon.

With love everlasting yours,
Rick[16]

Richard discussed with no one his despair over Bonnie's failure to send him a single letter. He continued the false front and, as was typical of him, sought no counsel from those around him and looked for comfort to none of those people who thought of him as a friend. He sulked in sullen isolation. Train acknowledged the peculiarity of his behavior. Train said, "He would be embarrassed to tell anyone he's lost this love from this girl which would mean that he is diminished as an entity, as a person." Train also revealed the other edge of the paranoia. Bonnie was Richard's girlfriend. People must not think badly of Bonnie, because it would reflect badly on him. He must also protect her image. "So," Train continued, "it is to avoid his own humiliation, as he would interpret it, and also to maintain the image he would want people to have of her, he would not speak of this to anybody."

Train acknowledged that paranoid element which weaves in and out of Richard's story. It would seem to me a significant element, but it was not part of the main thread of Train's particular story, and to introduce it here would compound the diagnostic problem.

Mark Rubenstein, the other defense psychiatrist, emphasized the paranoid as he did the borderline character in Richard. But in addressing the jury with the complexity with which he would address a group of psychiatric residents, he lost his audience. True dynamics are too confusing to be understood in the adversary position of the court of law. It was good psychiatry but bad storytelling. Train, as Litman suggested, is a good storyteller.

Q. *Doctor, let me show you these letters, 15-H, I, and G, three identical letters which it has been stipulated were found in his room, dated June 8th, 1977, written to Bonnie, put in an envelope, stamped but never mailed [handing]. Tell us about it.*

A. *By June the 8th, this is now that he's received no mail for three weeks. The letters express depression. He is confused. He can't understand why he hasn't received mail. He is in doubt. He's very apprehensive. He hopes at this point—he doesn't blame the mail. He only hopes it is the mail that has been delayed* and *is frustrating him. He cannot understand why it is three weeks, and he then states, "I am F'd over by the Postal Service or whatever," and the "whatever" indicates to me that he is beginning to feel that he is being victimized by Miss Garland and that he is being abandoned. That she's not thinking of him. And by this time, we are beginning to see all the despair occurring more frequently, with less ability to pull himself up to hope, and it's been noticed by this time that his work is faltering, but it is also noticed that his appearance is changing.*

He is untidy, he is disheveled, and he's become irritable, so that when a co-student questions him about mail, he answers her in a very irritable way not to discuss it, not to bring it up, which is out of keeping with this young man's character and behavior.[17]

Hi,

Remember me? June 8 and still no mail from you. If it takes more than 3 weeks for mail to reach here, it must take longer for it to reach any destination in Europe, so I shouldn't bother mailing these last 3 letters to Denmark, Swede, and Norway. I'm sending them all at once which means they'll say the same thing; that is, nothing. You probably won't get them, anyway. I at least hope you're safe. I'm not angry with the postal service, yet, and I hope they're the cause of the delay in me hearing from you. But 3 Weeks? I'm depressed and confused, and at times I feel like I'm getting fucked over. By the postal service or whatever. I'm sorry I can't be more cheerful. 3 damn weeks.

Yours in love,
Rick[18]

He wrote three copies of one and the same letter, and then mailed none of them. And what a letter! It is a clear message of clenched-teeth rage. Yet rage was never mentioned by Train. That Richard never feels anger is part of the necessary mythology of the defense, and here Train was building the defense. The letter, if nothing else, should be sufficient to deny that premise. Richard never *expresses* his anger. That's another story and one I can believe. Like Bonnie, he cannot tolerate confrontation. But this is not unconscious anger. This is conscious rage and resentment. This is white heat, and barely contained. When he said, "I'm depressed and confused, and at times I feel like I'm getting fucked over," he ended that with a period—and we know by whom he felt "fucked over." Then, half apologetically, with a whimper instead of a bang, he said, "By the postal service or whatever." Whatever indeed! But Train described no anger.

Q. Now, doctor, during this time, in the month of June of 1977, while he is still in Fort Worth, are you aware of any scenes or thoughts that come to him?

A. Yes. As he is feeling abandoned, frightened, hurt, depressed, it comes to his mind nightmarish kinds of fantasies of dismemberment of her. And as soon as they come to his mind, he is so repulsed by them that he dismisses them. This is an indication that at this particular time his conceptual thinking is intact enough that he can appreciate, understand, comprehend what would be revolting or wrong. But it also indicates the beginning of the dissociation.

The human mind functions as a unit of thinking, feeling and doing. And at this point, suddenly a thought comes to his mind with no forethought; it comes almost out of the blue. And it comes from the seething emotions that are repressed in his unconscious, and suddenly intrudes itself upon his consciousness, and as quickly as it intruded, he still had the capacity to reject it [emphasis mine].

It is an indication of the decompensation that is beginning. It is called dissociation.[19]

Train finally acknowledged the anger and almost trapped himself when he said, "And it comes from the seething emotion that is repressed in his unconscious, and suddenly intrudes itself upon his consciousness." Recognizing that he was in dangerous waters, he quickly defended: "and as quickly as it intrudes, he still had the capacity to reject it."

Little was made of these mutilation fantasies by either Fredreck or Litman. No one knew quite what to do with them, for they did not serve either man's purposes. They are, nonetheless, a serious sign of severe pathology. Normal people do not have fantasies of seeing their loved ones with their breasts sliced off or the vagina ripped open. Litman avoided it because it suggested a kind of pathology that was inconsistent with the defense he was offering. Any kind of pathology would be avoided by Fredreck, because he wanted to paint a picture of Richard Herrin as a bad—but normal—boy. Anything that suggested illness was potentially troublesome to his case, which required total responsibility.

As Train continued his narrative and approached the moment of killing, he had to set the stage for an automaton-type Richard behaving in a way that was inconsistent with the model life that preceded this horrible evening. It was necessary that Richard not be seen as jealous or angry, because we all have experienced jealous anger and we all have been subject to it. As such we demand limits. Richard had to be seen as operating under a different set of directives. He would be portrayed as the desperate individual clinging to a life raft (Bonnie), not as an angry, rejected, humiliated, and somewhat paranoid ex-lover.

We finally came to the "Dear John" letter.

Q. What happened the next day, Doctor?

A. In the morning, he ran back to the—his usual morning of returning to the mail box and found a letter. And this letter was the final blow to his capacity to stay as a complete entity. It also was a very disturbing element to his stability, from the viewpoint that—it also portrays Bonnie Garland as something that he never did before—she's not living up to the idealized concept and image he had of her.[20]

This concept of the shattering of a "Madonna type" illusion is pure Train. Richard would have taken Bonnie back in a flash, given any opportunity. All his efforts were devoted to retrieving her—and perhaps to destroying her. It was not the loss of an illusion that bothered Richard but the real loss of an instrument of his pride, vanity, status, self-respect, and love. This sense of real loss was accompanied by fear, yes, but also anger and humiliation.

No anger. All during this Friday, he can't calm himself. He can't eat. He is suffering. He is agitated. And Saturday, he works—tries to work on his car, but he is determined now to go there on Monday, when the mother said that she would be back on Sunday night, and she definitely would be home on Monday.

But he can't tolerate the delay. He has to see her. And so, he takes the plane on Sunday morning, at 3:00 in the morning.[21]

This is an error in fact. Richard did not try to work on his car. He waited in the garage for his truck to be repaired while he read the two books he had chosen to buy—one a psychological study of multiple personality, i.e., dissocation, and the second a story of the use of psychiatry in the defense of a homicide.

Litman then directly led Train to an analysis of two extraordinary and ambiguous notes written by Richard, one of which Train interpreted as a suicide note, and which may indeed be one.

> If I do not return from New York soon (departure June 3) I will never be back. The enclosed letter will explain why.[22]

Then this most confusing and bizarre note:

> Real Strength involves confidence in one's ability to meet whatever problems arise without overreacting, to be able to think through the solution rather than panicking. Confidence comes From being in touch with your own Fears. Real strength means understanding yourself and your capabilities as well as your fears.
> I will be near you From now on, always within reach, to give you all I can. I will never desert you, will
> always, always
> Love You, Bonnie.[23]

Train interpreted this letter as a "sort of philosophical pep talk"[24] and concluded that it was a "note that he intends to give Miss Garland." But the letter is certainly more than that, and is open to multiple interpretations. Train himself admitted to confusion: "When I first read this, I thought she wrote it to him because . . . [of the] kind of material . . . He was the one who really couldn't deal with the problem."[25]

The note abounds in ambiguity. Was it intended for Bonnie? In no way is it like anything he had ever written her. It is almost a paraphrase of what she had written him! It was he who was "panicking." It was he who was now confronting his fears. Bonnie was in New Haven, happy with her new boyfriend.

Why would Richard leave without the letter? Richard is meticulous as to details. It is part of the spookiness of his story and demeanor. Was it really intended for Bonnie? There are other speculations that are simply not provable but that seem as likely. Was it intended to seem like a note *from* Bonnie; it was printed, and none of the others are. Look at the last line. Is that a statement from Richard to Bonnie? (It does not say, "*I love you, Bonnie*") or a closing phrase, a signature from Bonnie *to* Richard, "Love You, Bonnie." It is set off on its own line, and in capitals, and was a common form of closing used by Bonnie.

Assuming, as I am inclined to do, that it was a simulation of a letter to *him* from Bonnie, what in the world could such an exercise mean? It could have been intended for others, part of a simpleminded plot of obfuscation; it was left behind. Or, and I think this is more likely, it was a pathetic, childish, and very disturbed mechanism of fantasy reassurance—a pretend letter from Bonnie. If the latter, it would be a strong statement of Richard's pathology, albeit a different pathology from the one described by Dr. Train.

Train reiterated a detailed account of Richard's activities from July third through the killing of Bonnie, interpreting along the way Richard's various experiences, and making general undocumented assumptions as to how Richard was feeling at each moment. All such assumptions were educated guesses, but Train was capable of cloaking them in the absolute terms of laboratory findings, leading to the following:

> *Richard Herrin couldn't feel anger at all. He could only feel that he is denied, that he is being abandoned. That aspect in the jealousy he could feel. The anger, not at all. That is repressed. That it would be there, sure. That it wasn't there is an indication that he is now dissociating more and more of his feelings out of his consciousness.*[26]

The "fact" that Richard was not feeling anger now (the few days before the killing) cannot be "an indication that he is now dissociating more and more of his feelings out of his consciousness" if we are to accept Train's repeated and insistent argument that Richard was never ever in the least capable of feeling anger in his entire life. In that case it has been a modus vivendi, and its presence now indicated nothing, at least nothing new.

Train, nonetheless, was a good, and experienced, psychiatrist. He worked hard on this case, and he noticed much that he did not use, or preferred not to use. In discussing Richard's delay in returning to Bonnie when she invited him to the house, he came close to an essential statement about Richard's character—not his acute pathology but his transcendent character—that in one way or another impressed Litman, Rubenstein, Schwartz, and myself (Chapter 8). He said:

A. *There is an unreal quality about this young man. During my intensive interviews with him and examination, he gave as the reason that he had made a promise to help his friend around*

*the house, and he was going to fulfill that commitment. This is
so out of keeping with the situation, it is totally inappropriate.*[27]

There is much about Richard's demeanor, to this day, that has a
slightly out of focus quality. Train then continued the narration of
events to the night of the killing.

Q. *Do you recall if he notices anything about her right before she
goes to bed?*
A. *Yes. He notices that she had three bruises on her thigh, and
almost speciously and facetiously, he asks how she got it, and
she said she didn't know. But he, at this point—he gives it no
other consideration.*
Q. *What is he feeling at this point?*
A. *He is a little suspect about whether she might have gotten it
while having sex with someone else. Convinced it was not
while he—she was having a sexual relationship with him. But
it passes off and doesn't incite any anger or jealousy, and he
remains in the same state of mind that he was before he observed it. It has, in itself, no particular significance as to what
effect it was having on him, other than the fact that he was
now in obvious dissociation, in which he was repressing his
feelings and not letting his thoughts run freely.*[28]

One of the more remarkable aspects of Train's testimony was the
latitude he was allowed by Fredreck. In this massive account—close
to one hundred pages of direct testimony alone[29]—Train was rarely
interrupted by Fredreck, even when he was involved in the most flagrant flights of fantasy. Partly this is explained by the freedom
granted by the court to expert testimony, but Litman chopped into
the prosecutor's experts constantly. If nothing else, it impeded and
muddled their narrative lines. Fredreck did not—and why, I do not
know.

The explaining away of the bruises as having no effect on Richard
is an example of dismissing something which might have been seen
as the emerging jealous rage over Richard's growing awareness of her
new sexual life without him.

Q. *Please continue, Doctor.*
A. *He, not wanting to go to bed—she turns to go to sleep—he sits
up on the couch, turning pages of a sports magazine. And as
he sits there, it suddenly intrudes upon his consciousness, that
idea that he will kill himself and kill her. There is no emotion*

with it. There is no debate about it. There is no conceptual thinking about it. He does not bring to bear into his consciousness any of his religious training, moral training, education, comprehension, concern of anything. It is there in his mind.

Q. Where did this come—where did this intrude from?

A. As we understand the mechanism of the human mind, we can say that it comes from his unconscious, where much of the repressed emotion, anger, resentment was seething, building up, and then inexplicably at that moment just extruded itself into a thought. Still without any expression of or sensation or consciousness of any emotion with it. It became a fact in his mind. And once that occurred, he then went about thinking of how to accomplish it.

At that particular point, he is functioning without emotion, without a complete conceptualization of his thoughts, and he is functioning as a—one might say a computerized machine. He still has some concept formation to be able to—to think of how to act out what he intends to do.

As he goes through this, there is a little bit of apprehension developing as he approaches to accomplish his act, and he goes through some simple procedures to avoid detection of what he intends to do, so that he will not be interfered with. This is not a question in his mind at any time whether it is right or wrong, whether he should or he shouldn't. It is just an accepted thought and it is to be acted out.

Q. Now, is there any dissociation in his mind at this point?

A. Oh, yes. He is dissociated in two very important factors of his mental faculties. He is dissociated emotionally, he is seething underneath, out of his consciousness; and his conceptual thinking is impaired, in that he is not bringing to bear an overall thinking of what he is to do, why he is to do it, what can happen, whether it should happen. He is bringing in nothing of the rest of his thinking capacity to bear on the question, on the issue.

Q. Had he been able to do that in Texas, when he dismissed those nightmarish thoughts that he had?

A. Yes. He was still integrated then, but now he is suffering from a mental disease in which he is dissociated.[30]

Train continued to interpret Richard's actions during and immediately after the killing. Only near the very end did Fredreck interrupt:

Q. Is it a cold, calculating, planned murder, Doctor?
A. A cold, calculating kind of murder can only occur in a cold
   killer. That would be criminal.
   Fredreck. Excuse me, Doctor. I object to this, Judge. Ask it to
   be stricken.
   The Court. The objection is sustained. Strike the word "criminal."[31]

This small objection was pathetic in its inadequacy. Fredreck objected only to the use of the word "criminal," for that was passing
legal not psychiatric judgment. But he also had the right to ask on
what evidence Train based pages of assumptions about what Richard
was feeling and was not feeling, what Richard was thinking and not
thinking. If the testimony was based on what Richard said he felt or
thought, the jury should have known that. That was hardly an objective source. If it was based on Train's speculation, let him defend
those deductions. Fredreck seemed AWOL during this entire testimony.

A. (Continuing) If you mean by "cold," that he wasn't off the
   wall, raving, ranting, screaming, and you mean by "cold" that
   there was no display of emotion, then it appears to be cold.
   But that is not actually what is going on in the human mind.
   There can be no display of emotion, but underneath you can
   have a torrent of emotions repressed.
Q. Is that what was happening to Richard Herrin?
A. Absolutely.[32]

With this one word, one can understand why Train is a good witness and an inadequate psychodynamicist. "Absolutely"? I know of
no psychiatrist in his clinical practice or in his teaching experience
who would dare speak "absolutely" to what was going on in the unconscious of an individual at a time prior to the examination. Even
in the course of an analytic hour one is never sure—absolutely—as to
what is going on in the patient's unconscious, even though one has
spent four hundred (not nine) hours with that same patient peering
into that same unconscious.

Q. Now, Doctor, can you tell us what the word "affect" means in
   psychiatric parlance?
A. "Affect" is a term that we use to indicate the display of emotion, the expression of emotion.
Q. And what is meant by the term "inappropriate affect"?

A. When an individual in a particular situation shows an expression of emotion that is inappropriate to the situation or not harmonious with the thought at that time.

Q. What is that indicative of?

A. A split in the integration, functioning of his mind. It means that the emotional element is dissociated from his thinking, or his contact with reality.

Q. Now, Doctor, when you spoke to Richard Herrin and examined him, as you said, for about nine hours about three or four weeks after this event, did he display any inappropriate affect, sir?

A. He displayed inappropriate affect all during the examination, except when discussing the actual offense. He would smile, appear to be congenial, very considerate of my comfort. And it appeared to me that he was in a great struggle to not be in contact or reveal what he was feeling. Not to me, but to himself. He was struggling. And in a usual struggle, it is the same when a person is embarrassed and is too embarrassed to show embarrassment; they try to put on an air of amusement or smile, and this is what he was doing. This was an inappropriate expression for what we were discussing or for the situation he was in.

Q. Is that significant?

A. Yes. As I said, it is an indication of a split in the integration of the—all the faculties of the mind working together. We also see this in some very severe mental illnesses, such as schizophrenia, but I'm not—I don't say that that is what he was suffering from.[33]

Three years later I observed (see Chapter 8) precisely the same inappropriate affect that every other psychiatrist had seen, and if I may be here allowed some of the latitude granted other expert witnesses, I would guess that three years from now, and ten years before, I would observe the same. This inappropriateness is not event specific. It is a significant feature of Richard's character and emotionality that is always part of his adaptation to life. If that flatness, and splitting, is used even to suggest schizophrenia as a *defense against culpability*, it is a dangerous maneuver, for it could condemn Richard to a lifetime judgment, since no psychiatrist—outside of a courtroom—will ever guarantee its remission. If this is the "mental state" referred to in Train's final paragraph to prove him insane, Richard is still in this identical mental state!

Q. *Doctor, was Mr. Herrin, in your opinion, sir, with a reasonable degree of medical certainty, suffering from a serious mental disease or disorder called transient situational reaction or adjustment—adult adjustment—adjustment of adult life, to a psychotic degree, whereby in an extreme emotional reaction he killed Bonnie Garland?*

A. *Yes.*

Q. *Was there, from a person in his circumstances, and viewing the circumstances as he did, a reasonable cause or explanation not for the killing but for the extreme emotional reaction?*

A. *Yes.*

Q. *What was that?*

A. *The reasonable explanation rests in what this girl meant to him and how dependent he became upon her for his very essence of psychic survival, having a sense of identity, self-worth, self-esteem, and a sense of belonging to the world around him.*

   I should like to repeat a phrase that he said: "That she was his link to people and reality."

Q. *Doctor, in your opinion at the time, you said he was psychotic?*

A. *Yes.*

Q. *As a result of the mental—serious mental disease, as you have described it, can you tell us with a reasonable degree of medical certainty to what extent, if any, his ability or his capacity to know and appreciate the wrongfulness of his conduct was impaired?*

A. *In my opinion, he was in such a mental state that at the time, there was a significant cause of a mental disease that he was suffering from, there was a significant loss of his capacity to know and appreciate that it was wrong.*

   Mr. Litman. Thank you, Doctor.[34]

Jack Litman, the defense attorney, had told me:

> There is an accepted theory that when you have a jury in a tough case you make sure to tell them your story many times. You tell them in the opening; you tell them in the witness stand; you tell them in the summation a few times—and before you know it, they're going to start to believe what you're saying. Not because you're a Svengali. The repetition is going to begin to sound familiar and true, and you're going to convince them.

It's very difficult in a case like this to get a juror to say "I find him not guilty by reason of insanity" when he smashed a hammer into a girl's head, covered it up with a towel. It's a very difficult case, but if you say it often enough maybe they'll start believing you. The importance of John Train's testimony was that he made it sound like common sense to a layman and he gave me one more chance to have all that repetition of the entire case—and that was very important. John is very straightforward and that was of great value. Dignified, down-to-earth, very common sense. He doesn't use long words. Whatever you think of the psychiatric consistency of what he said [I had raised some doubts about the quality of his testimony], that's only one thing. More important is that he comes across to the jury as a dignified common-sense doctor. And he is very good at that. Besides, he got in a lot of the stuff the judge wouldn't let me use. All those letters between Bonnie and Richard. I had John testify about them.

District Attorney Fredreck didn't seem to understand this. Given the opportunity to cross-examine Richard, he spent *less than three minutes* questioning him (less than six pages of testimony including objections). He thought his case was established in the following brief dialogue.

> Q. *Mr. Herrin, on the early morning hours of July 7, 1977, when you walked into Bonnie's room with the hammer in your hand, did you intend to kill her?*
> A. *Yes, I did.*
> Mr. Fredreck. *I have nothing further, Judge.*[35]

Fredreck's assumption that Richard's character and the relation between Bonnie and Richard were irrelevant, was a disastrous tactical error. This was a jury trial, and the decision would be made in the hearts as well as the minds of that jury. Even for cold legal logic, we must understand Richard's emotions. "Extreme emotional disturbance" is the only thing that distinguishes manslaughter from murder. Litman understood this, and Train understood this.

The prosecutor's lead-off expert witness was a psychiatrist of a different color, and he told, as one might expect, a much different story. He also told a shorter one. In the roughly seventeen total pages of testimony, including objections, offered by Dr. A. Leonard Abrams, four full pages are devoted to articulating his credentials. He evidently felt he needed little time to "explain" Richard. Then again, he had only spent one hour examining him. His direct testimony about Richard was as follows: And this was his entire testimony beyond his credentials.

Q. *In this case, when you spoke with the Defendant, Richard Herrin, sir, what were you looking for?*
A. *I was looking for psychotic manifestations. I found none.*
Q. *Now, Doctor, we've heard some testimony in this Court— we've heard the word "psychosis." Could you tell us what that means, sir?*
A. *Yes. A psychosis is a major mental illness, which includes the inability to think, the inability to communicate, usually manifested by delusions, by hallucinations, disorientation.*
Q. *All right. Now, in relation to this Defendant, Richard Herrin, sir, do you have an opinion as to whether or not he, in the early morning hours of July 7, 1977, was suffering from a psychosis, sir?*
A. *It is my opinion that he was not.*
Q. *Did you find any indications of psychosis in the materials you've reviewed, sir?*
A. *I found no indication of psychosis. Absolutely not.*
Q. *All right. Now, Doctor, do you have an opinion as to whether or not this Defendant, Richard Herrin, again in the early morning hours of July 7, 1977, as a result of a mental disease or defect, lacked substantial capacity to know or appreciate the nature and consequences of his conduct, or that such conduct was wrong?*
A. *My opinion is that he was not psychotic, that he did not lack substantial ability to understand what was going on, or that it was wrong.*
Q. *All right. Now, Doctor, as a result of, again, your examination and the documents that you've reviewed, sir, did you find any indication that this Defendant suffered from a mental disease or defect?*
A. *He did not suffer from a mental disease or defect. There was absolutely no indication anywhere in all that I've reviewed— that there was such a situation.*
Q. *Just with particularity, referring to the early morning hours of July 7, 1977, when he struck Bonnie Garland in the head with a hammer?*
A. *That is my opinion.*
Q. *Now, do you have an opinion, Doctor, as to whether or not in*

the early morning hours of July 7, 1977, this Defendant suffered from an extreme, unusual, or overwhelming environmental stress?

A. It was my opinion that he did not. He did suffer from stress, in a sense of that there was a romance that he was having a problem with. But there was not an overwhelming stress.

Q. Okay. Now, Doctor, assume that this Defendant—and again, this is a hypothetical, Doctor—assume that this Defendant, sometime before hitting Bonnie in the head with the hammer—when I say, "sometime," I'm referring to thirty to ninety minutes prior to hitting her in the head with a hammer—made a decision that he would kill Bonnie and kill himself, and that after making that decision, Doctor, he considered the use of several weapons to carry out his intent to kill—that is he considered the use of a beer mug, stockings, and eventually settled on and used a hammer in this case, sir—does that tell you anything medically, sir?

A. Yes. It tells me that his thinking processes were going on, that he was intact. The very fact that he remembers this is of interest, too, because it indicates, for example, there is no impairment of memory, and that he was aware of what was happening or what was going on.

Q. What is the significance, Doctor, medically speaking, of no impairment of memory?

A. Well, if someone has impaired memory, that would indicate a psychosis, a form of psychosis.

Q. Now, assume further, Doctor, that after picking up the hammer, he went from the area of the kitchen, where he got the hammer, to a room on the first floor of the Garland residence, where he took the hammer and wrapped it in a towel, and while doing that, he noticed a two-page note written by Mrs. Garland, on legal paper, that he picked up the note, read it, put the note back on the bed, went upstairs to the bedroom in which Bonnie Garland was sleeping, laid the hammer down in the towel outside of Bonnie Garland's bedroom door, went into the bedroom, made sure that Bonnie was still asleep, came back out to the hallway, retrieved the towel with the hammer in it, went back into Bonnie's room, placed the towel with the hammer in it under Bonnie's bed, made sure she was still asleep, then took the hammer, and hit her in the head with it, Doctor. What does that tell you medically, sir, about the state of the man's mind at that time on the morning of July 7, 1977.

A. That he absolutely was not psychotic.

Q. And what are your reasons for that, Doctor?

A. Because somebody that would be psychotic might—would not behave in a way as not to be detected. After all, this is what he was doing. He didn't want to be detected, and this is what the activity indicated. So, he was protecting himself. Psychotic people do not protect themselves.

Q. Assume further, Doctor, that after leaving Bonnie Garland's bedroom, he took the keys—withdrawn. While in Bonnie Garland's bedroom, he took the keys to a family car, left the Garland house, began to drive this car around Westchester County, with the intent of avoiding detection by the Police. What does that indicate to you, if anything, medically speaking, sir?

A. It indicated the individual was not psychotic.

Q. And for what reasons do you say that, sir?

A. Because he is thinking things through. He does not want to be detected.

Q. All right. Now, assume that the—assume, Doctor, that the Defendant, in thinking about suicide, thought about crashing this 1974 Impala automobile into an abutment of some type, but thought that he might not die because the hood of the car was too large, sir. Does that indicate anything to you medically?

A. Yes. That he is thinking things through. He is making decisions. Psychotic people don't think things through. They spontaneously respond. They don't know why they respond.

But here there is mentation going on, there is thinking, ideation going on. He differentiates in his mind which way to commit suicide. This is not a psychotic way of functioning.

Q. When you spoke with the Defendant, sir, in January of 1978, in the presence of his attorney, did you discuss with him, sir, the various methodologies that he claims he thought about committing suicide with?

A. Mentioned them.

Q. Doctor, in examining this Defendant and in examining the various data which you already testified to, sir, do you find any history of previous psychiatric treatment, sir?

A. There was absolutely no indication from my examination or from the examinations of the other doctors that there was any previous psychiatric help or hospitalization.

Q. What does that indicate to you medically speaking, sir?

A. That the individual is not psychotic. There was no basis to make a determination that he was psychotic.

Q. All right. Now, you mentioned earlier that you had occasion to

review the Report of a gentleman by the name of Lawrence
Abt; is that correct, sir?

A. Yes. He is a psychologist.

Q. Did you read his report, sir?

A. I certainly did.

Q. And what did that Report indicate to you?

A. Indicated to me that this individual had a high I.Q. and that
there was absolutely no indication of psychoses in the psychological testing. Absolutely no indication.

    And it is interesting, because psychological tests—very
often where there is psychosis in an individual who then becomes well or goes into remission, very often you find a residual of psychotic manifestations in the psychological testing. In
this case, there was absolutely no indication of any kind of psychotic manifestation.

Q. Doctor, you also mentioned to us that you had occasion to review a Report of the Forensic Unit at the County Jail; is that
correct, sir?

A. Yes.

Q. All right. What, if anything, sir, did that Report indicate to
you?

A. Well, I think that is a very, very significant Report. That Report was made on July 8th, the day after the incident. It revealed that there was no psychosis present. This was done by a
Dr. Harvey Lothringer at the Jail, who indicated that there was
no psychotic manifestations of psychosis at that time. This is
the next day.

Q. And what does that mean, the closeness in time, Doctor?

A. Well, I think that is as close as you possibly can get to the situation, to know what the situation was at the time of the incident.

Q. Doctor, you're aware, sir, are you not, that the Defendant
struck Bonnie several times in the head with a hammer.

A. Yes.

Q. Could you tell us, Doctor, based upon everything that you've
studied in this case—that is, the interview with the Defendant
and the other documents that you've outlined for us—what
was, in your opinion, sir, based on a reasonable degree of medical certainty—what is the state of the Defendant's mind at the
time he struck Bonnie?

A. Well, the very fact that he remembers in detail what happened
at the particular time indicates that he was intact and that
there was no psychosis. That is what it means. If an individual
was psychotic and was responding and doing this in a psy-

chotic state, they wouldn't remember the details, the completeness; the gurgling, the eyes falling back. They wouldn't remember this. This does indicate a psychotic individual.

Q. Doctor, what about the memory for details in a person who—if a person suffered an extreme reaction to an overwhelming environmental stress, sir?

A. I don't quite understand what you're saying.

Q. Yes. In a person—if a person suffered an extreme emotional reaction to an overwhelming environmental stress, would they be able to recall the details of their actions while under this stress, sir?

A. Not if they were psychotic.

Q. Did you, sir, find, in any of your interviews with the Defendant, or any of the other documents, any indication of mental disease or defect in Richard Herrin, sir?

A. Absolutely none.[36]

This was Dr. Abrams's entire direct testimony. "Absolutely none," Dr. Abrams concluded, and yet I am willing to guarantee that if we chose any individual at random and submitted him to examination by any ten psychiatrists, and if we asked those ten psychiatrists if there were any indications of mental disease or defect, there would be none who would answer, "absolutely none."

Dr. Abrams, then, can be viewed as an extension of Mr. Fredreck's thinking, just as Dr. Train will expand Mr. Litman's argument. Fredreck argued as though he had a relatively simple case. He had the confession; therefore he need not be interested in subtlety or nuance of personality. The murder was certainly a brutal crime. He kept it spare, assuming, I suppose, that the mere brutality would offend the sensibilities of the jury and allow them to bring home a verdict of murder.

But the brutality of the crime is not a legal factor in distinguishing between murder and manslaughter. It is not that murder is one step more awful in the nature of the crime. It is the nature of the criminal not the act that changes murder to manslaughter. There is only one factor that bridges the distinction; manslaughter encompasses everything that second-degree murder does except it is done under "extreme emotional disturbance."

The law reads that a person is guilty of murder when:

1. With intent to cause the death of another person, he causes the death of such person or the third person; except that in any prosecution under this subdivision, it is an affirmative

offense that: A. The Defendant acted under the influence of extreme emotional disturbance for which there was a reasonable explanation or excuse, the reasonableness which is to be determined from the viewpoint of a person in the defendant's situation under the circumstances the defendant believes them to be.[37]

The New York State law explicitly states in 125.25 that homicide committed under the influence of extreme emotional disturbance constitutes a mitigating circumstance reducing murder to manslaughter in the first degree.

Fredreck seemed to act as though he were arguing a murder case where the jury had only the options of finding Richard innocent or guilty, but the jury was perfectly free to ignore the charge and find a person guilty of the lesser charge of manslaughter—which is precisely what it did.

By limiting his case, he may have effectively made sure that Richard was not acquitted by reason of insanity—which was never very likely—but he left his flanks open by not adequately considering the emotional conditions that preceded Richard's actions, and by allowing his psychiatrist to offer such simple and skeletal testimony as was presented here.

After the decision of the jury was announced, Prosecutor Fredreck blamed the jury. He contended that the murder was "cold and calculated" and said that "the jury's decision had been sympathetic instead of intellectual. This will be a very hard decision for me to live with."[38]

The jury's decision was not "sympathetic instead of intellectual." It was very proper. And this should have been a hard decision for Fredreck to live with. In arguing his murder case, he had *not* argued in opposition to the manslaughter mitigation. The jury, as it so often surprisingly and extraordinarily does, followed the logic of the arguments and decided precisely what the balance of evidence would have had them do.

Abrams felt that Train's report "read like a movie scenario." In a sense he was correct. It certainly did not read like a psychiatric report, with its emphasis on dynamics and its Freudian bent. There is little in the way of data in his report. There is none of the stuff of the traditional psychiatric evaluation. One looks in his testimony for the basic ingredients of the standard Mental Status Examination, and looks in vain.

Abrams's testimony is also peculiar. In its absoluteness, terseness, and lack of descriptive quality, it reads more like an autopsy report. He went through his checklist as though he were eliminating every trace element of toxicity, proudly announcing he had found no evidence of strychnine, arsenic, lead, or the like.

It seemed to me as though both were acting as dutiful agents of the men who were paying their fees.

Doctors Rubenstein and Schwartz told more complicated stories and played more complicated roles. (Dr. Halpern's testimony will be discussed in Chapter 7.) Rubenstein was never comfortable with the prescribed role of the psychiatrist in the court of law—a salesman for a point of view. He was more comfortable in an academic position where the teacher's primary job is to indicate how little we know, not how much. A teacher, like Socrates, must counter students' self-assurance by showing the complexity of issues and raising doubts. The advocate must use certainty to relieve the anxiety and confusion of the juror. As a result, Rubenstein was totally ineffectual in the courtroom, and it is doubtful whether his testimony played any significant part in the verdict.

Schwartz, on the other hand, became, by general consensus and direct indication of jury members, the decisive factor in Richard's conviction for manslaughter rather than for murder. Schwartz, like Train, was a consummate master of the art of storytelling to a jury. While neither of them has any particular reputation in the larger intellectual academic community of psychiatry and psychoanalysis, they are treasured by members of the criminal law establishment in New York. Both prosecutors and defense attorneys often vie for their services, and it is extraordinary to note how frequently their names appear in the kinds of murder cases that transcend the run-of-the-mill (e.g., involving establishment people rather than ghetto people), the kinds of cases that will be featured in the major newspapers.

Dr. Rubenstein is a young forty-five-year-old, dressing in the casual manner that most psychiatrists over forty would find uncomfortable. He has a full beard and an easy, soft-spoken manner. An extremely well-intentioned and serious person, he was, to use his own phrase, "beyond [his] depth" in this trial. He is best understood outside of the courtroom where he could talk, face-to-face, one psychiatrist to another on intellectual and personal terms.

He started almost immediately discussing the enormous pressures that were put on him at the time of the trial, in preparation for the trial, and ever since the trial. I had an instant sense that he regretted his involvement.

> Oh, yes, there was enormous pressure. Well, one of the constraints I have in talking to you is that within the defense itself there was, and continues to be a great deal of pressure on me.
>
> Even to describe those to you would involve my making assumptions, speculations, about the motives of the people involved in the defense which I feel wouldn't be proper. I have to make my own interpretations about the behavior of everybody involved in the defense, and I have my own sense of obligation to Herrin; and then I must maneuver my way midst the various pressures I was getting from the defense; the kinds of information I was being given, not given, impressions that were being created, not created, so I had to make some very independent judgments about the nature of my own role in the defense, my obligations to Herrin.

—Did you see yourself as part of the defense or an expert witness?

> Well, I was trying to preserve some role as an expert witness against all kinds of pressures that were constantly making me an instrument of the defense. That would be a good way of summing up the difficulty.

This dilemma was to be a constant feature to a man of Rubenstein's sensitivity and integrity. He was trapped in a situation which seemed contradictory to this normal role. It led later to the following dialogue:

> Neither the prosecution nor defense conducted themselves very well, in my estimation. I have to leave for a later time any discussion about what my understanding was with Litman and what I was doing and why and how he conducted the direct examination in the court. It would be best to simply not say anything at this point.
>
> I felt Herrin had a right to the best psychological exposition he could get of what happened, and I felt a personal commitment to do this. That exposed me to a number of pressures and vulnerabilities. I was not really in control. I was being used. In retrospect I'm not sure I exercised all the options I had but . . . In the rehearsals that was clear.

—Did you feel you were being pressed to the point of compromising your position as a psychiatrist by your role in the defense?

Oh, yes. It's ordinarily not much of a problem in most insanity defense because the stakes aren't so high. I was being pressured. I don't know to what extent I was being compromised. The one issue I tried not to lose sight of was my sense that I really owed it to Herrin to develop the best I could a psychological case for him.

This is in many ways an appalling statement—that a defendant is entitled to the best possible "psychological case." Certainly a defendant is entitled to the best possible defense in an adversarial system, but the psychiatrist is being called as a "witness," to the court, if not of the court. That word is used as a most sacred principle of a religious conviction: to give testimony of facts, to be a servant of the truth. An *expert* witness is swearing to the facts as seen by a man of special expertise, in this case a physician. In theory at least, Rubenstein's statement continues to be repellent to me—that a physician should marshal different facts according to who is hiring him. This is sworn testimony, which involves his character as a human being and his integrity as a professional. A pathologist does not interpret laboratory findings in the way that would please the referring physician. He does not indicate remission when there is none—or at least he should not—and he would not if it were under sworn testimony. I said as much to Rubenstein.

—The word "witness" really means that in the law. Not to make a case, but to say what you observed publicly. You are not free from your responsibilities as a physician. You are not Herrin's physician. You are a public witness on that stand.

Well, yes, that's true, but that's also a naive description of what happens.

—That I know.

Let's say that you attempt to maintain such a perspective and you discover that the lawyer and his client are feeding you information that is designed—which is clearly designed to manipulate your opinion. I'm not talking about this case—at which point it occurs to you that you can't formulate an independent judgment very well, so you pull out of the case. At this point the prosecution becomes aware of this and that's fine: "We're going to subpoena you as *our* witness." At which point you then willy-nilly become the instrument of the other side. The idea of being a neutral witness for the court is fiction under the circumstances. From a pragmatic point of view, the courtroom is a kind of theater set up to play to either a judge or the jury and you're the witness cast in a role, depending on what side you come out on, your lines are going to be read one way or another way.

—You found this uncomfortable?

Yes.

—What made you do it? Do you do it quite frequently?

Well, not so much. I'm a small-town boy basically, and I had never been in a situation like that. So much pressure. Sister Ramona was at the house a lot. I don't know how she is these days, but she was very intense, driven, passionate. If I had let her, she would have taken over the child care, housekeeper, she was very invested. There were lots of people involved one way or another. I mean just on Richard's side. Giving me information, documents, so on.

Rubenstein is a sensitive, trusting person. He's still wondering what his proper role ought to have been or indeed is. It's what makes him so likable.

His was a circuitous involvement in the case. He had been recommended by Alan Stone, professor of psychiatry and law at Harvard Law School, and then president of the American Psychiatric Association. Jack Litman desired a Connecticut doctor to lessen in the Westchester jury's mind the local association to the killing.

Rubenstein's off-the-record impressions of Richard may sound confused, but they are the confusions inherent in the complexities of a person like Richard Herrin. They are the most accurate descriptions of him that I heard. At least, that is to say, they resonate the most with my own views.

Rubenstein described his first meetings with Richard:

I saw him a couple of times, and this is sort of typical of the case. I decided that I couldn't decide very much, that he looked more than anything at that moment to be suffering something like a traumatic neurosis. He seemed childlike, glassy-eyed. I saw him in two fairly closely spaced interviews—within two to three weeks after the murder—close enough in time for me to feel that what I was seeing was something colored by the trauma—a reaction.

He talked with appalling clarity about the murder itself. One of the striking things about this crime—the thing that is easy to feel and hard to find words for—is the nature of the crime itself. I mean, if it had been an ordinary gunshot or even a knife, if he had even slit her throat, in something that would have been relatively quick, but there was something about the idea of the repeated hammer blows. I'm not sure.

—Did it influence you?

Oh, I think so. That was something I had to cope with, particularly because he was in this kind of depersonalized state when I met him. Childlike, naive, as though he was repeating some kind of not exactly affectless way, but with the affect not really appropriate to what he was describing.

—Is it possible that that is his essential personality, not just a post-traumatic state? He's been described like that before. [I had not at this time seen Richard.]

At that time I didn't know it. But yes, I was seeing a heightened version of his normal self. I had to cope with my own repugnance with the story, and at the same time I found myself baffled, trying to find some structure. Did he have a psychotic disturbance? So I came away from that with a number of feelings, not all positive, about him, and a great many questions.

Rubenstein continued to describe a "puppy-doggish-likable" aspect to Richard's personality. He immediately added, "Not charming. I didn't find him charming. Many people did. I didn't."

"Were you touched by him?" I asked. "No, not really," he responded. Rubenstein instinctively knew what I meant. It is part of the quasi-scientific, quasi-artistic quality of psychiatric diagnosis that the psychiatrist uses his own emotions as a means of evaluating the patient.

There is a quality about certain borderline psychotic states that is best diagnosed by the fact that one feels no direct involvement and empathy. Rubenstein said, "There was no empathetic rapport. Even by the time of the trial—when I had many conversations with him—there wasn't."

Rubenstein then went on to a long, intelligent discussion of borderline personalities, an area in which he has obvious expertise. It is a difficult area for the layman to understand. Originally designated borderline schizophrenia, the "schizophrenia" was dropped from the label because of the often unwarranted malignant implications of the term.

Schizophrenia is the most complicated of conditions, and the one least understandable to laymen, partly because it encompasses such a divergent and dissimilar group. At one end of the spectrum is the decompensated schizophrenic who is delusional and hallucinatory, while at the other end one can find a *compensated* schizophrenic, who may never break down and will serve effectively as a senator, judge, head of a major organization, president of a school, distinguished surgeon, psychiatrist, and in all probability, if the grapevine is reliable, among presidents of the United States.

Rubenstein obviously felt that this was the case with Herrin. He admitted he could not make the case in court.

> I didn't ever see anything I could, for legal purposes, refer to as a schizophrenic process; and even for my own purposes, I was struck by the relative absence of anything resembling thought disorder. But there was a definite defect of ego function, a disturbance of his capacity for empathy, a primitiveness in object-relations [i.e., capacity to form mature love relationships] that while approximating psychotic individuals, isn't quite psychotic itself.

This is a good capsule summary of part of his diagnostic statement and explains why Rubenstein would say that while he sympathized with Herrin, "I never grew terribly fond of him. I never did. I don't see him or write to him."

There are two major aspects in describing an individual's state of mind—his emotionality or affect, and his capacity for reason or cognition. Much had been made of the peculiar emotional state of Richard. Rubenstein went beyond that and during the course of the trial said that Herrin's "cognitive capacity was impaired," his thinking ability damaged. He freely admitted that it would be hard to defend scientifically the premise that Herrin was not aware at the time he struck the blows. When I pointed out the extraordinary recall of extensive detail, Rubenstein acknowledged that and said, if anything, he was "supercognitive" and that added to an eerie sense of unreality in those areas.

> One of the horrible things about this crime was a sense of supercognitive clarity of the whole chain of events: having it come into his head that he was going to kill her; getting a hammer; wrapping it in the towel; putting it in the hallway to check if she's sleeping. I went over all of that with him a great many times. It seems to me there is something wrong about the clarity of that, too. In reality, I suspect, it pointed to a reasoning

defect—the anonymous relationship to the events, to the emotions, and the quality of reasoning.
—Did you sense any contrition?
Not by my terms, no. I don't think so.

We then discussed questions of jurisprudence, of punishment, of equity and justice. He drew a distinction between the two, suggesting that in Richard's case, while justice had been served, equity had been violated.

> I've always been impressed by the fact that those cases where there wasn't the same kind of public interest, but where the crime was no less, people are paroled after two years all the time.

At the same time Rubenstein was capable of saying:

> I felt justice was adequately served by the verdict of the jury. I felt the needs of the community were served by the maximum sentence. The position I took about the length of the sentence was that from what I understood about his character, his relative level of ego development, that it wouldn't hurt him, or us, for him to have eight and one-third years in which to grow a bit older. That if nothing else, that might be beneficial; that if nothing else, he might be able to grow. That's very primitive psychological kind of guesswork about what kind of growth might take place.

And when finally I asked Rubenstein, "If you had to do it over again, would you get involved in this?" the answer was immediate: "I would not!"

Dr. Daniel W. Schwartz is an old hand in the courtroom. He is a pro in the same sense as Dr. Train. Both exhibited a command of the laws of insanity and the conditions which must be fulfilled to satisfy those laws; of the rules of evidence and the means of testifying within those rules so as to avoid constant interruption by objections which when sustained begin to make a witness seem as if he did not know whereof he spoke; and a need to make a clear, simple, and apparently integrated story for the jury to understand, despite the fact that in real life psychiatric conditions are always a snarl of loose ends and inconsistencies.

Unlike Train, who tends to the romantic style, Schwartz is all business. He is polite, not tendentious, and generates an air of self-assurance, while being totally prepared to acknowledge limitations of knowledge. It is his capacity to say, "I wouldn't know about that," or, "That is not within my area of expertise," that particularly lends authority to those things he does address. The assumption is: Here is a man who will tell us when he doesn't know something; therefore, when he tells us that which he knows, it must be so.

He wears horn-rimmed glasses, a short brush mustache, and has the manner one identifies with a good accountant or lawyer. He is bright, knowledgeable, and articulate without being eloquent. At the times of my interview, Dr. Schwartz had been involved with two particular cases that had inflamed large segments of the public: the Robert Torsney case and the Kevin Durkin case (see chapter 7). Schwartz was testifying for the prosecution against Herrin, but he played a most peculiar role.

The prosecution acted as though Litman were arguing one case. He was actually arguing two: not guilty by reason of insanity; or, if guilty, only of manslaughter because of extreme emotional disturbance. This dual-pronged defense was quite unique in the courtroom—because of its essential contradiction. Its effectiveness, however, was such that Litman and others have begun to use this double argument routinely.

Fredreck was determined that Herrin not be acquitted on grounds of insanity. Litman never saw this as more than an outside chance, a crap shoot if you will, and was working primarily for that which he would have settled for in the beginning—reduction of charge from murder to manslaughter. So that while Schwartz was winning Fredreck's case against insanity, he was at the same time blithely and effectively arguing the defense case for mitigation. He turned out to be the *defense's* best witness!

A. *It is my professional opinion at the time he was undergoing an adjustment reaction of adult life, and that part of this were features of what I've called depersonalization.*
Q. *Could you tell us, Doctor, what "depersonalization" is?*
A. *Yes. It is a—it is a symptom or a condition in which, to a certain degree, a person has difficulty fully recognizing everything about himself or about the things around him. It is not a disease any more than fever is a disease. There may be feelings of vagueness, unreality, of detachment. A person might feel himself changed in some way at that time without any delusional*

explanation for this, without any understanding of this. At times, in such states, his actions could be mechanical or automatic. It is not a change in personality. Absolutely not. What he experiences is a kind of sense of loss of limits of his own personality. It is a feeling of indistinctness and, perhaps, even confusion.

Q. *Okay. And did you say that this is not a mental disease or defect, Doctor?*

A. *No. This is a symptom as—as I say, I can liken it to fever, which is a symptom of physical illness but not a disease in and of itself.*

That statement that he was only suffering from a symptom of a disease was offered by Schwartz to show that Herrin was not suffering from the disease itself. But it was completely and totally misinterpreted by the jury.

The jurors clearly stated that Schwartz had influenced them in both of his statements. They would not acquit Richard, because he was not technically insane; but they would reduce the charge, because he was obviously suffering from something. And one later said, in total inaccuracy: "After all, where there is a symptom there is a disease." I had a sense that Schwartz was personally satisfied with the end result of the case. I put it to him:

—You thought it was a fair decision and fair sentence?

I don't pass judgment on the sentence. I'm even reluctant to pass judgment on the decision. I've long since adopted the philosophy that whatever a jury decides in its own county is right. It's presumptuous for me to think what a jury ought to do. These are the people who live there. This is what they want to tolerate or not tolerate in their county.

It is this capacity for self-examination combined with the aura of exactitude that makes Schwartz such a good witness. He immediately established a good working relationship with Litman. Remember that he was called by the prosecution, not the defense!

Are you familiar with labor-management negotiations? You ask for the moon and settle for the earth. Okay. I came in from the prosecution's side. I examined Mr. Herrin in Jack Litman's office. I didn't know him before, but I've met very, very few lawyers who work as hard as Jack did on a case. He felt it was absolutely crucial that I read all the correspondence in this matter. When I examined Herrin he was staying with the Christian Brothers. Jack had him come down. I remember very vividly the location of the examination—it was in the conference room. We conferred, we talked, he made sure I read all this material. He told me that's what he wanted—extreme emotional disturbance—that the prosecution wouldn't give it to him. He then had psychiatrists Train and Rubenstein come in in effect with the insanity defense, but I knew all he was hoping for was manslaughter.

He asked me then what my conclusion would be as to extreme emotional disturbance, and I said to him I had no such opinion. However, it was clear to me that there was something wrong with Herrin. He is not a picture of health. Jack was satisfied, knowing my thinking about it—we discussed the case at length, that through cross-examination he would elicit from me enough pathology that he would then use in his summation to the jury and he would then tell the jury that all the stuff I had said equaled extreme emotional disturbance. *He* would make the transition from psychiatry to law, which I think is fine. This was an excellent transition and Jack did it excellently.[39]

Jack Litman had done his homework. Schwartz was a doctor who would tell his own story. Litman now knew the nature of that story and was capable of incorporating Schwartz's opinions into the detailed narrative he was prepared to present to the jury. It was not just chance that in his summation to the jury Schwartz was quoted by Litman as much as, if not more than, the psychiatrists he himself had procured. Schwartz by then had become a part of Litman's story. He had been called by the prosecution and appropriated by the defense.

The psychiatrist always enters the courtroom at his peril and will always be an awkward and inappropriate presence in that adversarial environment. To be physician and advocate, to see ambiguity everywhere and feel committed to certitude will inevitably undermine the integrity of his standing and statements, and confound the purposes of justice.

The psychiatrist must respect the meaning of the word "expert" and the role of witness. In order to do so he must leave the adversarial role to those reasonably assigned this purpose—the defense attorney and the prosecutor.

1

2

In the spring of 1971 (1), Richard Herrin was the pride of the Los Angeles barrio. Graduating first in his high school class of 415, he had accepted an offer from Yale of fully paid tuition and expenses and had turned down other Ivy League colleges, including Harvard and Williams. Four years later (2), only the pose was the same. After a poor college career, he was permitted to graduate despite an incomplete program. Richard's only palpable success at Yale was his love affair with a seventeen-year-old college freshman, Bonnie Garland. Rich, vivacious, a talented singer, she was a "dream come true" for Richard (3, 4).

3

4

5

Bonnie had doubts about Richard from the beginning and expressed them in writing within a month of the start of their relationship (6). Nonetheless, through two years of separation, the illusion of commitment was maintained. Bonnie continued her singing career and her social life (5). During a spring tour through Europe, however, the illusion

6

I'm scared to talk about this because I'm scared of hurting you— I don't want freedom from you— I love you— but sometimes I feel like I have to report all my doings to you— whether you ask or not— because I get these "vibes" up you will— that ever though you say you're not, you are suspicious. I even feel odd sometimes when I'm just kiddin around w/ other guys—something like "Would he approve? Would he be mad." goes thru my mind. The line I was talking about was between my right to freedom and my responsibility to you— I've got to have freedom because I am rebellious by nature— I need elbow room— but I don't want to whit my elbows against you— do you understand? I have feelings lemmed in by some role I feel I have to play— sometimes I feel you put me in a role where there are certain accepted behaviors & others that are taboo. What would everyone think? Sometimes it seems to me anyways that you become concerned w/ your image (I guess what is natural) and our image but that is what I rebell against— images are extensions of roles & all I'm saying is just let me be me and you be you and put up with my "going,-off-at-tangents" because I have to do it— anyways, that's what was on my mind and you can punch me up you like or anything but I still like you...

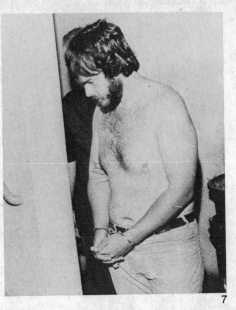

7

ended when Bonnie found another love. The "dream come true" became a nightmare when Richard, shown here (7) at the time of his arrest, bludgeoned the sleeping Bonnie to death in her Scarsdale home (8).

8

On July 13, 1977, Richard was arraigned for murder in Westchester County, New York (9). The prosecutor was Assistant District Attorney William M. Fredreck (11). Defending Richard was a brilliant young criminal lawyer, Jack Litman (10).

10

11

12

To pay the costs of the defense, funds were raised through an effort organized by a network of supporters from the Catholic community at Yale centered on St. Thomas More Church. A pivotal figure in that defense was Sister Ramona Pena, assistant Catholic chaplain at Yale, seen here with Richard and his mother, Linda Ugarte (12).

13

The Garlands with their surviving daughter, Kathy (13). Their sons, Patrick (14) and John (15).

14

15

16

County Court Judge Richard J. Daronco (16) presided at the trial, but the key figure may well have been psychiatrist Daniel Schwartz (18). Bonnie's presence was felt only in the limited number of her letters (17) admitted in evidence.

17   18

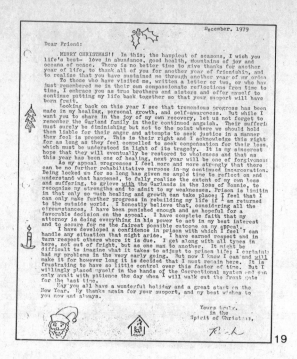

19

Richard, continuing to write cheery letters (19) from prison to his supporting cadre, masks a growing bitterness about his conviction for manslaughter and a sentence for eight and a third to twenty-five years that he now feels is excessive and unjust. And the Garlands (20), left with only a portrait of their dead firstborn, seethe with resentment that Richard was not found guilty of murder. Bewildered by the sympathy and support offered Richard, they feel that only they mourn their daughter in a society where the compassion due the victim is granted instead to the criminal.

20

6

THE ADVERSARIAL
CREDO: GUILT
OR INNOCENCE

In theater and movies the inevitable climax of the process of justice is visualized in that tense moment when the foreman of the jury rises to announce the verdict. But real life rarely bears any recognizable relationship to popular entertainment versions of it. In real-life courtrooms, guilt or innocence is not ordinarily the critical question. That, in the majority of cases, is decided in advance by mutual agreement in a haggling, coercing, often sordid, and always wearisome game called plea bargaining. The vast majority of criminals brought to trial plead guilty to accommodate the court, which in turn has accommodated them by agreeing to lesser charges and lesser ranges of sentences. It is the sentence which is the real pivot around which the emotions, tensions, pressures, hopes, and fears revolve. Sentencing is the province of the judge. He can decide that even the convicted man may be allowed to return to his everyday life, relatively free of punishment, or he may send him to jail for a maximum sentence stipulated by the law.[1]

In Richard's case, his lawyer, Jack Litman, was fighting on two fronts. The Westchester District Attorney's office had refused his offer to plead guilty to the lesser charge of manslaughter and charged Richard with murder. Murder carries with it a *minimum* sentence of fifteen years. Manslaughter has a *maximum* sentence of eight and one-third to twenty-five years.

Litman was going to try two self-contradictory defenses. First he would argue that Richard was not guilty of murder by reason of insanity, in which case Richard would not be punishable by law. It was an outside chance. He knew he was unlikely to win this argument, but it would allow him to introduce the kind of evidence that might soften up the jury for his second argument. And, one never knows, the unlikely number sometimes comes up. The second and crucial debate was to convince the jury that Richard was, if not insane, at least less culpable because he was operating under extreme emotional disturbance. It is this latter that differentiates manslaughter from murder. The legislature makes this distinction allowing for a more severe judgment to be made on the professional criminal-killer, as distinguished from an individual who kills in a crime of passion. With the lesser sentences allowable in manslaughter, Richard could conceivably serve no more than one to two years. This was Litman's goal.

While there may be confusion about the proper role of friends, clergy, and expert witnesses, almost everyone has clearly in mind that the courtrooms of the United States operate under an adversarial condition. This means that neither the prosecution nor the defense will seek objectivity, impartiality, or even necessarily equity or justice, but the best case. They will take all of the facts and emphasize those, and only those, that make the best story. All ambiguities will be argued away or interpreted as though they represent substantiating evidence pointing the arrow of certitude in the direction of either guilt or innocence, depending on which side of the case they are pleading.

The courtroom is a drama of spectacle and debate, and while there is no substitute for diligent preparation, intelligence, and professionalism, what a great criminal lawyer requires beyond those is a sense of style and excitement. He must never bore. Like a good storyteller, he must weave his web around you and bind you to his version of the truth. He must keep you excited, enthralled, and always sympathetic. He must use himself as a bridge to transfer the jury's affection and empathy to his client, who is often a most unsympathetic and unempathic individual.

Jack Litman is a good criminal lawyer and a total professional. He is bright, charming, and extraordinarily knowledgeable. For instance, he could argue aspects of psychiatry with me like a pro, and where he was unprepared he was smart enough to avoid argument. He is articulate and quick-thinking. He believes in himself:

> I like to think that I'm more intelligent than most of the prosecutors I've faced. My arguments are therefore going to sound more reasonable. Sincerity is my big key. I come across terribly sincere.

This should not be interpreted as being said in a cynical way. It is the candor of a very open man and a very confident one. He is right. He does come across as very sincere.

Litman was recommended to Richard, once again, by members of the Catholic community at Yale Law School through connections at St. Thomas More House. He was a relatively young man but had already a reputation in the New York area as a major figure in the criminal law. When a case is as dramatic as this, with the assured media coverage, a defendant will usually have his choice of lawyers, independent of his financial situation. This was the case here. As Sister Ramona told us, Litman was one of the four interviewed by Richard, and the one he selected. Richard showed good judgment.

You can tell a lot about a man by his passion for his work.

> I was a prosecuting attorney for a number of years. I was prosecuting chief for Frank Hogan. I love to do criminal law practice but I do a large number of civil litigation as well. I handle the large criminal cases. I prefer the defense. You can be much more inventive, more creative; it's much more difficult and therefore much more challenging and also much more rewarding. There's no comparison in the way you can feel when you get an acquittal as opposed to the way you feel when you get a conviction as a prosecutor. There's no comparison in terms of pride in what you've done, in emotional feeling, satisfaction. Even if it's someone who deserves conviction you don't get the feeling of total emotion and satisfaction. I used to only handle the most venal, egregious killers, and I felt it was a job well done, but it wasn't the same.
>
> As a defense lawyer I get that same satisfaction even if I know they're killers.
> —So that speaks to you as a person?
> Yes, beyond the job well done. Because you've saved that person from the clutches of society. You get that feeling in different intensities with different people and cases.

The "clutches of society" is a term which reflects a bias against the common good. If we live in an evil society, the predatory image is warranted. While we do not live in perfect justice, I do not think of our society as innately evil. I doubt that Litman does. More likely the term—whenever used—expresses the bias of our time that sees goodness as vested in the individual, and the individual as alien and antagonistic to the state, rather than as a component of the community.

—Will you take any case?

No.

—What kind of case will you turn down?

It's very hard to say. I've had a few people who come in to me to say here's a case, here's the way we defend it, please tell me the names of the people you want as alibi witnesses, I will furnish it. That witness is no problem. I will take care of him. I will not take those cases.

—That would involve your being a criminal yourself. But on the venality of the person or the crime, what would offend you? A professional hit man?

I've never faced that situation. I can't answer it. My intellectual reaction is that it would be no problem.

—You'd take the same pride in getting him off? Saving him from the "clutches of society"?

Certainly pride in a job well done. I view a criminal defense role as trying to save a person who's hanging by a thread, a person without anyone who's willing to champion his cause and I don't do it for free. Without people like me, we'd be in a lot of trouble, because I don't trust the good sense of prosecutors.

Since he was such a staunch defender of the adversarial role, I raised a question that has always disturbed me: that the defense of a defendant may require an attack on the victim. We have all been witness to this. It was particularly so in the trial of Jean Harris for the murder of Dr. Tarnower. It was an ugly case, defended in an ugly manner and with an ugly conclusion. Jean Harris was convicted of second-degree murder, although by most people's community standards there was certainly extreme emotional disturbance in her case. This kind of attack on the victim has always seemed particularly offensive and constitutes "a double murder" in my mind. I mentioned this to Litman and asked him if that bothered him at all—if he was averse to doing that.

It's obviously part of the adversarial position. There are some people who say you resuscitate the deceased so that the jury can kill them one more time. I don't think you always have to do that in a very overt way. Specifically, if you want to go back to our case I can tell you what I did in respect to Bonnie. First of all I did it minimally for a variety of reasons. (A) She's not a venal person to begin with. (B) What she did was not venal. She was a young girl who did not realize what she was dealing with. She made some very critical mistakes.

But it was important to taint her a little bit so the jury would not believe as the parents wanted, that she was this ingenue who fell in love for the first time to this wily man. She was a lot more sophisticated than Richard ever was and probably than he is right now, even though she was four years his junior. She was a freshman and he was a senior. She had gone about the world and met people, he hadn't. She knew more about the relationships between boys and girls than he knew about them.

—Do you mean sophisticated sexually as well?

That I can't tell you for sure. Richard still believes she was a virgin. I don't know. That's not significant. I mean the ways of people. Bonnie was a very sophisticated seventeen-year-old and Richard was a very immature twenty-one-year-old. I didn't want the jury to be left with the impression that the prosecutor tried to create, and certainly Mrs. Garland did in her attempt to portray that he stole this girl out of her cradle. That's not true. And we just brought it out very, very cautiously. I have nothing bad to say about Bonnie. I wasn't trying to downplay her. What I was trying to do and what I was successful in doing at the trial, and what the prosecution in a strategic matter did poorly is to make the jury see my client. They never let the jury "see" Bonnie. The one person missing from the trial—obviously she's missing because she's dead, but beyond that—is Bonnie.

"It was important to taint her a little bit," and here we see that inevitable part of the adversarial process that demands a "second assault" on the victim. Bonnie must be made—at the minimum—an accomplice to her own killing.

All I did was try to dispel the idea she was this young girl . . . I didn't attack her—I thought that would backfire. And I had a very good group of jurors. Jurors who were really into wanting to know why a person would do this kind of thing. That's what the whole case was about. The best juror was over seventy, and in New York either side has a chance to challenge a person if he is over seventy without exercising a peremptory challenge, a free challenge, as though people over seventy shouldn't be allowed to serve. Here's a fellow who told me he had traveled recently, taken a world cruise for the first time in his life, and I wanted to know was he the kind who saved up $4,000 only to play canasta all day. I asked him what he found interesting about travel. He said, "Seeing all the different people." I said, "That's my juror," and he's the one who influenced people in the jury room.

I could sense this. I'm pretty adept at picking jurors. I had that kind of a jury. The jury really liked me. They looked up to me. They thought I was the moral force in the courtroom. They respected me. I wouldn't lose their respect by doing idiotic things—so why would I put down Bonnie. What value?

It must be remembered that the attorney not only prepares his story, and not only prepares an answer to the story that is being prepared by his opponent, but in the voir dire (the jury selection) has the opportunity to select an audience that he senses would be the most sympathetic to the kind of tale he is about to spin out.

At a trial you have to know your audiences. I had the kind of jury that liked children, that understood the difficulties of raising children. One of the examples I used when we talked about the differences between "knowing" something and "feeling or appreciating" something. I kept using examples like "You've all baby-sat?" "Yes." "But you really couldn't appreciate what it was to have a child before you got married and had one." I used that example because all of us know people who from a very early age had a problem with some kid. That's common among people.

This kid [Richard] had difficulty from age one; look how bad his parents were; one turns out bad and you forget about the ninety-nine who turn out good. It's an ordinary thing that people can grasp. So if you show them a childhood which is a little bit screwed up, that doesn't necessarily mean the person is crazy, but it's the type of thing the jury can fasten on.

Remember, in a case like this where you have an educated boy who obviously had never been hospitalized, you can't say he had been a schizophrenic; you still have to give the jury a picture of how can a person who on the surface looks great be all screwed up.

Litman was fighting a battle to keep Richard out of jail, or more likely, to keep the incarceration time to a minimum. It is important to see how he constructed the defense of Richard. It is understood at its most elegant by reading the entire trial record, starting with his opening statement and ending with his prolonged summation, but it can also be appreciated by examining his summation in abbreviation, with emphasis on his construction of a story that will save his client from the "clutches of society."

> The issue in this case is not—it is not did Richard Herrin intentionally inflict wounds on Bonnie Garland which caused her death. That is conceded. That is not in dispute. That has never been in dispute. That is the starting point for the serious inquiry upon which you're about to embark, which is: When he intentionally inflicted those wounds, those blows, was he suffering from a mental disease or defect; or was he under the influence of extreme emotional disturbance? Those are the only issues, really, for you to consider here. In essence, what was the state of his mind at the time, as the evidence so clearly shows, he attacked a woman he loved, the center of his universe and, in essence, destroyed his own existence.
>
> Ladies and gentlemen, if you have a reasonable doubt, a reasonable doubt that Richard Herrin was suffering from a mental disease or defect, and that as a result of that mental disease or defect, he lacked substantial capacity to know and appreciate the nature and consequences of what he was doing—or, more importantly, the wrongfulness of his conduct—then you must, as you have sworn to do, return a verdict of not guilty by reason of mental disease or defect.
>
> On the other hand, if you find that the Prosecution has proved beyond a reasonable doubt and to a moral certainty that Richard Herrin did not have a mental disease or defect, as a result of which he did not lack substantial capacity to know or appreciate—and appreciate the wrongfulness of his conduct, then you must consider the lesser but still very serious charge of manslaughter in the first degree. And if you find that the scales tip in favor of showing that at the time that Richard Herrin struck Bonnie Garland on the early morning of July 7, 1977, that he was under the influence of extreme emotional disturbance—that is, he was acting under overwhelming stress, which was reasonably viewed as overwhelming by someone in Richard Herrin's position, someone in his shoes—then you must, consistent with the law as his Honor will give you, re-

turn a verdict of guilty, not of murder, of first-degree man-slaughter.[2]

Litman clearly defined the issue. He told the jury it had nothing to do with what Richard did that night. They should not concern themselves with that. It would best be forgotten, he implied. It might color their judgment of the difficult psychological questions they were going to have to wrestle with. No, the question was not what he did, but rather what he was feeling—his mental status.

In addition, Litman gave them two peculiarly restricted choices. On one hand, he suggested that they find Richard innocent by reason of insanity. On the other hand, they could find that he was merely suffering from an extreme emotional disturbance, in which case, they must mitigate the charge from murder to manslaughter. He did not complicate the problem for the jury by suggesting that they might find Richard guilty of murder as charged. "I will ask you, ladies and gentlemen, to consider these two verdicts, and to return a verdict of one of them."[3]

He then returned to the body of his case. Since it had nothing to do with action but only state of mind, the case had to be made by the psychiatrists. Litman immediately suggested that all four psychiatrists agreed that Richard was suffering from "mental disorder." The fact is that all four did not agree, as was evidenced in the previous chapter.

It doesn't really matter. Testimony is difficult to follow, and people are not always sure of what they heard, particularly when experts use different languages in testifying as to different things. Litman devoted the first few pages of his summation to assuming that in general agreement existed, and to derogating the one psychiatrist, Dr. Halpern, who did not agree.

Having co-opted, for the moment, most of the expert witnesses, he proceeded to make his case.

> Ladies and gentlemen, at this point in the trial, I suggest you know more about Richard Herrin than he probably knows about himself. Was he functioning normally on the early morning of July 7th, 1977, when his emotions were cut off from conscious awareness? Were his normal mechanisms intact when he, in an essentially machinelike fashion, went about to do what he did? Was smashing the skull of the woman who was the center of his life, without conscious mo-

tive, the action of a sane person? Or were they the irrational acts of a mind so overcome with the loss of self, so overwhelmed by his stress, a mind unable to be fully aware of the enormity of the horror of what was happening?

As I said to you in my opening statement, ladies and gentlemen, and even before, we are not contending that Richard Herrin was a major psychotic, that he was a manic depressive for the last 20 years of his life, or a paranoid schizophrenic, or that an image appeared in the sky and directed him to rid the world of infidels, and because of that, he went about doing what he did. But I suggest to you, if you analyze the evidence in this case carefully, there will come a point in your analysis of Richard Herrin's state of mind when you'll be unable to follow it, unable to appreciate his mental functioning at some point on the early morning of July 7, 1977. For I suggest to you, as the evidence shows, Richard Herrin literally went beyond the pale and crossed into a machinelike state of, essentially, unfeeling destruction. Why else did all his controls fail? Why else was he unable to debate or reflect on the thought to kill Bonnie and kill himself? Why else could he not call upon his excellent and previously unimpeachable morality, as has been testified to by people who knew him well over the years? Why else was he unable to call upon his religious training, his intelligence, and his background? . . .

Were his actions on the morning of July 7th—not the result of a mind pressed beyond its endurance, literally broken down, as the doctors testified, attempting to resolve conflicting and uncontrollable, unconscious drives and emotions, in a way that is so bizarre and so inhumane and so unlike the Richard Herrin that you have come to know? Were his normal mechanisms working?

Richard Herrin, as you've heard, keeps things under control more than most of us. He never experienced in an overt way anger or rage, and you have that not from Richard Herrin—and, certainly, not just from a psychiatrist—but from the people who knew him. The person who raised him, the people who roomed with him at Yale and knew him at Yale, the people—the person who lived with him for two years at Texas Christian University.

How many of us can state that position, that we've never externalized our anger or even rarely done so? And yet, the first time he does anything which is suggestive of anger or rage, is to pick up a hammer and put it through the skull of another

person and of the woman he loved, without any conscious mo-
tive, profit, self-protection, revenge. Nothing. Is that not a dis-
eased mind? How else do you understand, ladies and gentle-
men, the inability to juxtapose two thoughts? One to kill, and,
two, not to cause pain? It may sound poetic from a distance,
but it is inhuman and irrational to be able to consider these
two things without appreciating, while you're considering
them, the enormity and the horror of what you're doing.

In short, how can a highly moral, gentle, religious, sensitive
young man perform an act which is so totally foreign to his
character, to the way he has acted for the first twenty-three
years of his life? . . . Mr. Fredreck, as he told you in his open-
ing statement, wants you to believe that this is a planned, cold,
calculating killing, as if, somehow or other, Richard Herrin sat
down and reflected about whether he would kill Bonnie or not,
as if, like going on a robbery, he cased the bank, he figured out
where the guards are, what the best escape route was, had to
change license plates on a car, to get a car, choose a good
weapon, loaded it, weighed the benefit to himself—that is, the
money he could possibly get, against the risk, which is getting
caught, getting tried, getting convicted and getting pun-
ished—and then making a decision to do it? Is that the type
of thing you think happened here? Is that in accord with
anyone's common-sense view of the evidence, as you have
heard it?

A moment's reflection, ladies and gentlemen, will show that
there would be no way for Richard Herrin to get away with
this. Halfway across the country, from his home, from where
he was at school, without $5 in his pocket, dressed only in a
pair of pants—he had no thought, no desire to get away with
it. But simply a desire to get on with his death.[4]

Litman then continued his anticipation of Fredreck's case. He
was worried about those statements of Richard where he used the
word "planning," which might seem to imply calculation and pre-
meditation. After all, Fredreck had ended his cross-examination of
Richard on that note. Litman, therefore, tried to show that when
Richard had used the word "planned," as in "I planned to commit
suicide," it was merely a figure of speech, meaning, "I thought of" or
"I contemplated." He did not want it to be interpreted by the jury as
a calculation in advance.

If there is a plan, then there has to be not in the law, but in
common sense—there's got to be a motive for it . . . But,

ladies and gentlemen, you've heard from the psychiatrists that there is no conscious anger, there is no conscious revenge; that is not in his conscious mind when he goes about doing it. They have no reason to doubt his credibility, and I suggest to you that you have none either. . . .

Just look at what happened and ask yourself, was there a logical progression from a step logically, "Well, this happened, and I must do this and, therefore, I will do this. Therefore, I am going to plan to kill?" Remember his last conscious feeling, which is hope for the next day. "I'll be able to talk Bonnie out of it. Things will be well." He may even go to bed with her on the night of the 6th, as he had done on the night of the 5th. That was his last conscious hope.[5]

The question of motive is actually irrelevant in the issue of homicide. Intention is all that is necessary, but Litman wanted to introduce motive here, or rather the absence of motive, as the means of discrediting a logical, calculated action. A motiveless homicide is a more irrational act.

He was not above stretching the facts. He said, Richard is hoping to go to bed with Bonnie on the night of the sixth, as he had done on the night of the fifth, but Richard had that option. He told me as much. Bonnie wanted him to go to bed with her. It was he who chose to kill her instead. Litman then confronted a damaging piece of evidence. Richard had admitted too much, too soon, to too many people and in signed statements. The statement of Chief Ronald Rea was particularly damaging in its simplicity and brevity. Litman did not want the jury to hear any description of what happened on July 7 without considering the twenty-some years of Richard's life that preceded it, and the state of his mind at the time. So he emphasized Richard's essential honesty, his "sincerity." He made the confession into a virtue, a "badge of his honesty."

Chief Rea tells you he has no doubt about his honesty, and he has no doubt about his sincerity. He is essentially arresting him for a murder or attempted murder, and he doesn't even handcuff him, because he sees how passive and how totally out of danger Chief Rea perceives himself to be.

Remember when Richard Herrin does not remember and is told by the Chief about the crushed larynx? "Oh, my God, what have I done! What have I done! Why did I do it?" Is that the expression of a person who planned and coolly and calculatedly went about an event?

And yet, ladies and gentlemen, they will read the statement to you. It is in evidence here. And you will see it is a very short synopsis of what happened, as if Richard Herrin is trying, as a Yale student who's asked to dictate 100 words or less something that happened, to give a brief essay about something like this, about a killing—that is, at best, a thumbnail sketch of what occurred. And if you look at it, you'll see there are inaccuracies in it.[6]

Litman then devoted pages of testimony to tearing apart the statement that Richard signed, finding really quite minor discrepancies and errors, because, unfortunately for Litman, Richard is an extraordinarily direct observer and narrator of events. Litman attacked the syntax of the statement as a sign of how disorganized Richard was. The syntax of the statement, a dictated statement, therefore an oral one, remember, is, if anything, superior to Litman's syntax in general and vastly superior to Fredreck's. It is then and only then that Litman felt free to move away from the events of the killing and into the past, where he felt safer and more comfortable, into the more halcyon days of Richard and Bonnie's love affair.

The psychiatrists have told you—and much more importantly, the lay witnesses, the people who knew Richard Herrin and who knew of his relationship with Bonnie Garland—have all told you how Richard Herrin's life was centered around Bonnie Garland. The depth of their love is evident from many, many sources. . . .

To Richard Herrin's view, his love was reciprocated. Whatever might have been known by the Garland family—you know, from the external circumstances—they spent literally, whenever they had the time, all their time together. Whether Bonnie completely reciprocated his love, as a real matter, or was ambivalent, that is hard to discern, but that is not really that important. You can't deny the extreme depth of their love, of their relationship.

Here, Litman was really handicapped by the judge's refusal to admit the early correspondence. Bonnie was ambivalent from the very beginning; but she was a loving person—perhaps she loved too easily—and her love letters to Richard are compelling.

Look at the travel together. Look at the time spent together. The phone calls, essentially, every night for hours and hours

on end. *The letters. The plans for marriage. To do graduate
work together in the same city. Even the little details about
sharing a credit card, as if they are a married couple, and guar-
anteeing an application for American Express, both of which
occurred right before Bonnie left on the Glee Club Tour in
May of 1977.*

*Ladies and gentlemen, Dr. Train and Dr. Rubenstein, the
only doctors who had an opportunity to examine Richard Herrin, have explained to you how and why Richard was so dependent on Bonnie. But, you don't need a psychiatrist in this
case to know that he was, in fact, dependent on Bonnie Garland. When he has a crisis in school, who comes down to as-
suage him? Bonnie. When there is a Prom, where does he fly?
Immediately to Yale. Who is on the phone every single
night?*[7]

Litman then summarized the state of mind of Richard during the
period of Bonnie's European tour, starting with a Richard who was
blissfully happy, functioning well, and presumably at his best. He
will attribute the deterioration as being caused by Bonnie's heartless-
ness and failure to answer his letters. He will show Richard at his
most despairing and at his most sympathetic. It was an intriguing attempt to divert the jury from Richard's guilt to Richard's pain. It was
Richard who was victimized from May 7 to July 7, so it is to this period that Litman returned in great detail.

Richard was in a state of despair, and it was Bonnie's fault for not
writing, for leaving him stretched out with doubt. This would, Litman hoped, mitigate one's anger with Richard and reduce sympathy
for Bonnie.

He then returned to the theme of Richard's essential vulnerability
even before this trauma by relating this rejection to the earlier rejection by Ginny and to other traumas.

*In the fateful letter he received on July 1st, she says,
"Maybe you should see a psychiatrist finally, to deal with the
overwhelming flood of emotions which I know are going to
come upon you." Obviously Bonnie saw in Richard Herrin
what is obvious to us, that he certainly needed some help. He
was totally dependent upon her, and unable to express any
feeling other than despair.*

*How about the devastation that he feels about learning of
his illegitimacy? I mean, obviously, that is not a nice thing to*

learn. But this is a 23-year-old fellow. It is a guy who is already going to college. He's in graduate school. And he's literally devastated by it.

Or the things you've learned about the fear of abandonment with respect to his mother, when he was a child. You've heard about his childhood; these apparently psychosomatic rashes, and the explanation you've heard of them. Bed-wetting! I mean, that is somewhat unusual, to go to the age of 12 or 13.

Obviously, Bonnie saw something in Richard Herrin. Look at her letters that he wrote to her of June 8th. He puts them in an envelope, three identical letters. He stamps the envelope, but he doesn't even mail them. Okay? He doesn't mail them because, maybe, if he doesn't get mail, why should he send mail. Or he is not happy with what he wrote. But does he take them and throw them out? No. He leaves them right there, as a constant reminder to him. The letters are still there when the Police—or whoever retrieves the items in July—go to the room. They are still sitting right there. And the letters are written June 8th, are a constant reminder of his utter despair. And again, "Maybe it is the Postal Service."

He says in the letter, he is depressed and confused. Is there any doubt that at this point, that he can hardly function and hardly work on his thesis that he was so eager to work on just a couple of weeks before?

Even his appearance suffers an outward manifestation of it. You heard Leanne Watson's testimony about that. Only the thought of seeing Bonnie again sustained him.

Look at the June 24th letter that he wrote from Los Angeles, when he was at his mother's home. "I've been in the pits of depression. But with you coming back, hopefully, I'll reach new heights." Again, swing, with profound alterations of feeling. Overwhelmed by these feelings.

Not only are they a part of psychiatric testimony, but they show, obviously, an increasing inability to deal effectively with the problem.

I mean, each time, if you view a situation, your mood changes so radically from one to the other, each time you view it, you have to rearrange the facts to coincide with your feelings—if you feel great about a situation, you view things one way. If a couple of minutes later, you have a total alteration, you've got to reorganize the facts. And in addition to sustaining himself, he has to create wishful thinking about this. And this, as Dr. Schwartz testified—their psychiatrist—is the center of his life. The center of his life!

> *It is like a piece of metal. How many times can you bend it*
> *back and forth, back and forth, before it will eventually*
> *snap?*[8]

The image of a piece of metal snapping is precisely the impression Litman would have liked to leave with the jury. The concept of a broken mechanism, of a "nervous breakdown." The volitional person converted into a psychotic zombie. Litman then returned to Bonnie, only casually and briefly and again, suggesting her complicity without directly attacking her.

Her letter devastated Richard. He offered "to give up his career just to be near Bonnie."[9] But Richard had as yet nothing that could be called a career. Litman constantly contrasted the provocations to Richard—by Bonnie, Bonnie's mother, the world at large—with a psychiatric exculpation of Richard himself. Richard's disarray had to be compounded. Every shred of evidence was used to make Richard appear the pathetic and tormented victim. The story of Richard was gradually being converted into the story of Job.

> *But before he leaves Texas, he does two important things:*
> *He writes this note—yes, this could be, obviously, construed*
> *reasonably as a suicide note. It doesn't say, "I'm going to kill*
> *myself." He had the exact same elements of the hope and de-*
> *spair as has been going through his mind. If things will work*
> *out with Bonnie, if the relationship can be restored to where it*
> *has been, the central part of his life, obviously, he is not going*
> *to kill himself. He will return. That is why he takes the check-*
> *book with him. If things work out. But if they don't, "I will*
> *never be back." And to understand it, "Read the attached let-*
> *ter."*
>
> *What other reasonable explanation can you give to that let-*
> *ter? And if you want to see how distressed he was when he*
> *wrote it—and you can look at it, because it is in evidence—*
> *even Mrs. Garland, who identified his handwriting, said it is*
> *much more sloppy than it ordinarily was, and you will see the*
> *date that he writes, "Departure, June 3rd"—he even has the*
> *wrong month, as if he doesn't know this is the month of July.*
> *He's been, you can imagine, sitting by a calendar, checking*
> *each and every day, as he goes to the mailbox, looking for a*
> *letter, and he has "Departure, June 3rd," "If I do not return*
> *from New York soon, I will never be back. The enclosed letter*
> *will explain why."*

> *And he has, as Dr. Schwartz told you and as has been testi-*
> *fied—and Dr. Rubenstein—a certain feeling of depersonaliza-*
> *tion now. Feelings of unreality.*[10]

As Litman continued to narrate the story of events leading up to the killing, he tried to cover each point that indicated directly the sickness and despair of his client—often incorrectly utilizing the testimony of the psychiatrists and wherever possible the testimony of the prosecution psychiatrist. Beyond that he was also touching each point of the specific story that he sensed would be damaging to Richard. By anticipating such statements from Fredreck he hoped to defuse them in advance. We had been told, for example, that Richard never lied. I suspect that Richard is an honest individual, but honest individuals tell lies; and the only person I know who never told a lie was George Washington. I myself caught Richard, not to mention other principals in the case, in a sufficient number of lies to know that they share—with me and the rest of humanity—the capacity to do so.

> *Then he goes to the Greenwalds' and makes it apparent as*
> *if everything is fine. No problems. And you know there are*
> *problems. You've got the letters. You've got the letter mailed*
> *July 1st. That can't be denied. You know about the phone*
> *calls. You know about the immediate, impulsive trip to New*
> *York. You know there is a problem. But to him, there is no*
> *problem. Things are going to be wonderful. "We're about to*
> *be married. We're going to go to Washington." But we know*
> *that is not so. Maybe he is still hoping against all rational hope*
> *that everything is going to be okay. Still hoping to deal effec-*
> *tively with the feelings of abandonment and despair.*
> *And he tries to call Bonnie on the 4th, and she won't come*
> *to the phone . . . she will call back. And she does call back.*
> *And there is no anger and no confrontation. Needless to*
> *say, he is overwhelmed with happiness, with finally having*
> *heard from her for the first time in seven weeks on July the 4th,*
> *1977.*
> *And yet, knowing, as he must, what might happen, he is*
> *even fearful of seeing her right away. He didn't want to leave*
> *the Greenwalds'—fellow who left Texas so fast—and here he*
> *has the opportunity and "Well, I'll come the next day." Be-*
> *cause obviously, he is fearful of facing the ultimate and despair*
> *that might happen to him.*[11]

Richard postponed meeting Bonnie! This is bizarre. It certainly indicates the important role that fear of public humiliation and exposure played in Richard's life. But how does one explain the peculiar paranoid twist that would allow him to actually "enjoy" the fireworks, movies, and the weekend with his friend, without ever utilizing the friendship as a means of comfort and understanding at a moment of agony.

> And Bonnie, clearly unintentionally—but nonetheless—is sort of dangling. She doesn't realize how precarious he is at this time, because he doesn't express—he is just so overwhelmed with happiness, being in her presence. He cannot express his anger to her, because he is afraid of losing her.
>
> Yet, on July the 6th, as firm as ever, she tells him, "No. You know what I said yesterday, is the way it is going to be. You'll be one of the fellows." And he can't believe it, especially after what had happened the night before. Is that not—not reasonable? Is that not conceivable, as a fact, the way it happened?
>
> He says, "But, Bonnie, I can't live that way. If you want me just to hang around and be by a phone, maybe it is better for me to leave completely." And there is a—psychiatrists called it like a trump card—not played that way—"But, Bonnie, I may have to leave you." And for the first time in two and a half years, she tells him, "Well, if that is the way you want it, although I don't want it that way, so be it." She's expressed for the first time, the center of his universe, that she can afford and is willing to do without him, if necessary.[12]

Bonnie was never directly attacked. It was to Litman's purpose to make her neither a villain nor a heroine. The less she existed in the minds of the jurors the better for his story. The slight suggestion of her complicity and insensitivity was sufficient. Even an attempt to make her the villain would be treacherous, because it would make her appear. And one never knows what the jury will think if they are reminded of Bonnie. They might visualize that long red hair drenched with red blood. No, she must only exist as an agent—unconsciously cruel, slightly insensitive, but nonetheless always the source of Richard's despair.

Obviously Bonnie couldn't win in Litman's mind. When she did hedge—and she did hedge—she was seen as teasing and tantalizing. When she was positive she was seen as cruel and rejecting.

But Bonnie's hesitation is not mysterious to me. Bonnie's behavior is always easier to understand than Richard's. It is typical. In this case it is that of a young girl, torn and ambivalent, and sharing with Richard the inability to bear confrontation. In her it was a fatal flaw. In Richard it was not.

This is a narrative, a tale, like that of Faust or Oedipus, and as such it must lead to a climax that has to it the quality of the inevitable. Once more, Litman skirted the dangerous ground of the actual killing.

> There is no fight. There is no dispute in the room. There is no disorder in the room. Her state of undress, his state of undress, the emptiness of the milk glasses and the cookies there, they all corroborate what had happened at the end: They were cuddling and kissing, watching television there that night, before she retired and went to bed.
> Ladies and gentlemen, it is hard to say with specificity, obviously and exactly what is going on exactly in his overwrought mind at the time, of feelings of abandonment and the loss of self. Even as he consciously tried to agree with Bonnie's position, and had hopes for the next day. But, you know that his psyche did respond by pushing this thought, this inhumane thought into consciousness, a thought he could not and did not debate, a thought whose command he had to carry out. If he wasn't crazy, ladies and gentlemen, consciously, how can you not experience that terrible flood of emotions that are overwhelming you and directing you to kill, and to kill the person you love more than anyone in the whole world?[13]

And immediately after quickly indicating that the murder did take place, but "with tenderness," he proceeded to Richard's "attempts at suicide." It is interesting that Litman, whose job was to minimize the importance of events and to enhance the importance of feelings and perceptions, seemed to have confused the two himself, either unwittingly or wittingly. He constantly referred to "attempts at suicide in this case."[14] At one point he even stated, "Mr. Fredreck may try to argue that there was no real suicide attempt . . . did any one of the witnesses that testified for them doubt his sincerity in this regard."[15] There were absolutely no attempts at suicide. There were thoughts of suicide; but if thoughts were the same as attempts, each and every one of us would be suicides and murderers.

In all probability this was not an accident of words but a piece of sophistry. Litman is an articulate, bright man, sensitive to words and their meanings. Richard's sincerity was not at issue, it was his actions we were evaluating. We all know what the word "attempt" means. It means to try. Richard himself denied having made any attempts. Litman continued:

> Why was there no suicide? You've heard an explanation given by the psychiatrists who've examined him at great length. Psychiatrically, perhaps because in a sense by killing Bonnie, he had actually killed himself—and with the spent emotion, the rage which he lashed out with that hammer on the numerous occasions that he did, that the emotion that is necessary to kill yourself—that is why suicide is so morally repulsive—he didn't have what was necessary to overcome that instinct for self-preservation.[16]

Here, Litman announced that it was not necessary for Richard to commit suicide—he was already "dead." And then he blithely suggested that suicide is a morally repulsive thing. As distinguished from homicide? He implied that Richard, after taking one life, had acted morally, consonant and consistent with the preachings of the religious community that would support him in this, in at least not compounding it by taking another.

Litman was now pressing. He went through a dramatic fandango about the presence of a rope in Bonnie's room. It was not consistent with his usual technique. He got a little too clever for himself. He chastised the Scarsdale police (the more villains the better), whipping out a photo of the scene of the killing that had been produced in evidence by the prosecutor, and said the following:

> But when Detective Rizzo walked into the room, he didn't see the rope. You look here, and you will see one sitting right here on the couch [indicating]. Their photograph in evidence.[17]

It was not one of Jack Litman's better moments. The "rope" turned out not to be the rope that Richard purportedly brought along to hang himself, not even a rope at all, but the cord from a hair dryer.

The next forty pages, the last of Litman's very lengthy summation, are devoted to mobilizing the psychiatric aspects of his defense to emphasize the degree of Richard's mental illness. But at one point he realized that he was going to have to confront the fact that this very sick client of his—who had been living unfettered with the Christian Brothers, attending school, and making a new circle of friends—had neither felt the internal need for nor, heeding the direction of his compassionate friends and his wise counsel, sought psychiatric help.

> Clearly, now, the fact that he hasn't, as had been brought out, seen a psychiatrist since the incident—you can imagine what would happen had he been seeing a psychiatrist since the incident. They would say, It's been manufactured to make it sound like it is a good defense, because look what happened since the incident.
>
> People, as you know and as you heard testimony here, can get sustenance from what they need—from religious, as well as psychiatric sources—and I suggest to you that is what happened in this case. And, in any event, is nothing of import with respect to your consideration.[18]

This suggestion of Litman's offered many new opportunities now for the insanity defense. It may well be that we should propose a modification—giving the offender acquitted on grounds of insanity the option of going to either a mental institution or an unsecured religious community.

At the beginning of the lengthy restructuring of the psychiatric testimony, which does not warrant re-examining, he carefully attempted to build up the reputation of his psychiatrists while denigrating two of the opposition psychiatrists, Abrams and Halpern, and co-opting the third, Daniel Schwartz. Then, in anticipation of Fredreck's argument, he carefully prepared the jury for any impending argument which might depict insanity as grossly psychotic with hallucinations and delusions. He correctly wanted to show that the insane need not be bizarre or eccentric. He was not prepared for, and was chagrined and dismayed at, the closing statement of the judge, which described insanity in images of nineteenth-century lunacy.

> As I told you before, ladies and gentlemen, with respect to what we colloquially referred to as the defense of insanity, as I've told you from the very beginning, there is no argument of an ongoing major psychotic illness, that he's been in a blithering state and hallucinating for the last five years of his life. That is not what we are discussing here. Not an ongoing psychosis, but a psychotic episode which, as you all know in your

lives, happens to human beings. Because Dr. Schwartz told you it can happen to human beings for a short or lengthy period of time. A mental disorder, during which Richard Herrin lacked a strong and solid capacity—during which he lacked a sufficient and significant ability to be fully aware of, to see the full impact of the wrongfulness of his actions.

Listen to the law as his Honor will define it for you either today or, more likely, tomorrow, and apply it when you analyze the facts in this case.

Was he, in fact, acting, in essence, like an intelligent man on that night? Or, as Dr. Schwartz said, automatic or machine-like, when one is depersonalized? Is it a mental disorder, Transient Situational Disturbance? Is it a mental disorder, as his Honor will define it, with the condition that Dr. Schwartz calls "Depersonalization," troubled, with the mind fully recognizing everything about one's self, or things around him? That is what Dr. Schwartz said. Listen to the words his Honor charges you on what know and appreciate means, to be fully aware of, to understand the full impact of.

Based on that testimony, can it be said that Richard Herrin was fully aware—this is Dr. Schwartz's testimony there—can it be said that he was fully aware of what he was doing? Did he see the full impact of it? Was he alive to the full value that it was wrong to do it? Or was Richard Herrin's capacity to appreciate impaired because, as Dr. Train told you and Dr. Rubenstein told you and Dr. Schwartz told you, there was no integration of mental faculties? He could not call upon conscious emotion. . . .[19]

It is wrong to kill. We all know that. You don't need a Penal Law of the State of New York or the State of Massachusetts to tell us that it is. We know that. You feel that. And when that state of consciousness or when that aspect of the mental functioning—whether it is repressed, cut off, dissociated, depersonalized, or whatever—when it is not available to you, can one say that one did not lack a substantial capacity to fully be aware of what one was doing?

Things of this magnitude, ladies and gentlemen, you don't have to reason alone. When people become machines they do this, as we have seen in history. But when people can feel what is happening, it is not done.[20]

Oh, would that it were true! But I suspect that as many murders are committed in blind rage as are in cold blood. Generally, we tend to be more sympathetic to those that are done in blind rage. Cold-blooded and unfeeling murder is the "M.O." of the psychopath, the professional hit man, or simply the street thug who kills for convenience and pocket money.

Litman needed the presence of emotion in case he did not win the insanity defense. He would need it for the mitigation. And here he seemed to be arguing against it. But do not worry. In this case, at least, he had discovered that one could have his cake and eat it too. He would claim that Richard lacked the restraint of *conscious* emotion while being driven by unconscious emotion. It was a confusing and somewhat illogical juxtaposition of facts.

There is an ongoing debate in psychoanalysis as to what is meant by unconscious feelings. It is a little like talking about unconscious pain. It seems a non sequitur. You either *feel* pain or it doesn't exist. We do, however, use this concept of unconscious emotions in psychoanalysis despite the debate. One thing we do not confuse; we know that it makes very little difference whether the emotion we are talking about is conscious or unconscious. It is capable of playing its part in determining the behavior of an individual.

Litman did not get away trouble-free in his tiptoeing across the barrier between conscious and unconscious. He wanted to show the presence of the feeling of guilt to legitimize the seriousness of the "suicide attempts." But it was difficult to demonstrate guilt feelings while he was arguing that Richard was totally detached from his emotions. Observe the following:

> *Although he said he knew it was wrong, obviously, afterwards, as you know, when Richard Herrin—although he had not even been thinking about this for five or six hours, I suggest to you when he was riding around—because the credible testimony, when you consider the time it got right into the Johnny Carson Show—and then the time between the time it came to him to kill Bonnie and himself, and the time of the car ride, all told, as one of the doctors said, thirty to ninety minutes.*
>
> *But if you try to figure out what went on in that time, looking at a stocking, looking at a belt, looking in the closet, picking up a hammer and picking up a towel, and going to the room, and if there is not very much time—and if you analyze it as Dr. Schwartz did, it is closer to midnight or 1:00 in the morning, and he winds up in Coxsackie at about 6:00 in the morning. And thereafter, obviously, when he cannot bring*

himself to taking his own life, as he wished he had then, obviously, his full knowledge of the action—and he probably knew, in the sense of perceiving the wrongfulness of what was going on.[21]

The complications of the double offense abounded, and the contradictions were all through Litman's testimony as he concluded his summation.

It may not make any difference. Juries will form a general impression from an oral presentation that will smooth over logically inconsistent details, particularly when told by a forceful, impassioned, and "sincere" advocate.

> Do you think in his state of mind at that time he is debating is this right or is this wrong? The only thing in his mind is that he has to do it, and he goes about doing it.
> Was his capacity impaired? Would it have occurred to a person in Richard Herrin's state of mind at that time, as you've seen it progress and deteriorate over a time, from the middle of May onward, to consider the wrongfulness of his acts? Clearly not. Did he not consider the causes, as a moral person? Clearly not. He couldn't consider it. He didn't consider it, because he couldn't consider it at that time.
> Even Father Tartaglia, he asked him on redirect examination, "Well, did he indicate to you that he had done wrong?" Obviously he knew he had done wrong, but that is not what—do you remember Father Tartaglia's answer? "Not as such." He didn't come out and say, "I had done wrong." That is not what is going through his mind at the time. Certainly not as his Honor will define the word "appreciate" for you, to be fully aware of, to be alive to the value of.
> Even when he was asked—and he certainly knows, as you've heard of his religious background—he was asked for absolution, and he said or indicated that he didn't want it.
> Did he know—was he fearful of being stopped because it is wrong. Or did he have an appreciation, much like a child has, who is fearful of being punished because, for example, when he is being toilet trained and he relieves himself other than where his mother or father wants him to go, he fears being punished. But punished for an appreciation of what he is doing? No. But because it's been told, but there is no full appreciation of it. And the law requires both, to know and appreciate.[22]

If you are confused by the above statement, it is because Litman was confused, or more likely trying to obfuscate. Father Tartaglia implied that Richard was guilty and remorseful, but here Litman was using his refusal of absolution to suggest lack of remorse. Even Richard's lack of remorse was interpreted in his favor.

What is more amazing than this, however, is that Litman—who had been arguing all along that all of Richard's careful precautions against detection (the towel, the stealthy leaving) had nothing to do with escape from punishment—should now be telling us that this represented a childlike fear of punishment!

Litman than proceeded with a careful and always homely analysis of the meaning of terms in the insanity defense: "know," "appreciate," and "substantial" capacity. He said, "A guy who is a good baseball player and has a badly swollen ankle, lacks substantial capacity," for instance. He proceeded with an absurd (whether intentional or not, I do not know) distortion of Schwartz's discussion of signs and symptoms. It was to have a profound effect on the jury.

> A sign. What does "sign" mean? It means an indication of some kind of major illness, he testified to, under oath, for Mr. Fredreck no more than a couple of months ago.[23]

It is important to understand the nature of signs and symptoms. So I repeat, thirst is a symptom of diabetes. Everyone who is thirsty is not a diabetic. A swollen ankle is a sign of a failing heart; it is also a sign of a twisted ankle; and it is also a sign of having stood on one's feet all day.

"Where there is a symptom there must be a disease" was suggested to the jury by Litman, and it is patently foolish and wrong. A disease is indicated when an aggregation of signs and symptoms define it, and when it is confirmed, where we have such confirmations, by a diagnostic procedure.

The latter part of Litman's argument was studded with contradictions. It may have been that he was tired. It may have been that in weaving so many strands, the threads of one story began to interfere with another. In attacking Dr. Abrams he said, "He doesn't even ask him during this interview, 'What happened during the crime?' which is the only relevant period of time." But Litman had built his case on the fact that the time of the killing was *not* the only relevant period. And Fredreck lost his case because he would insist that it *was* the only relevant period.

In attacking the same testimony, Litman said that Abrams made a great deal about Richard's recollection of detail and then got confused:

> I'm not saying he doesn't have any recollection, and I'm not telling you that he wasn't in a fog—that he was in a fog. But look at it. What kind of detail are you talking about?
>
> And remember, psychotics of long-standing nature, as Dr. Schwartz told you, like Son of Sam, they can remember enormous detail, meticulous detail and preparation. . . . Do you really have that type of detail here?
>
> Sure, you have recollection and, sure, as Dr. Rubenstein candidly told you, that underscores the horror of it, that he can, as if rationally, go about remembering what is happening.[24]

He was trying, I think, to make the point that Richard did not have great recollection of detail, but all of us have been amazed at how clear and precise Richard was about so much of the minutiae of the killing. Litman knew he was on bad ground and threw in the fact—even while he was claiming Richard did not have a significant recall of detail—that psychotics have a great capacity for detail. He was trying to set up a heads-I-win-tails-you-lose situation.

> Again, I'm not suggesting, ladies and gentlemen, that he has no recollection. But to say he remembers the incredible, specific details, I think, is just belied by the reality of the facts that you've heard presented to you.[25]

At one point he attacked a fundamental component of the psychiatric examination.

> Dr. Abrams told you under oath—and I suggest that you don't have to believe that he put in 30 hours of work in this case. Read this thing here [indicating]. Look at this, and you try to find out what his conclusion is based on, and you find out it is based on the fact that Richard Herrin knew that one hundred minus seven is ninety-three; Jimmy Carter is the President of the United States; that he examined him in the month of January of 1978, who the Vice President was, Walter Mondale, and that a pound of feathers weighs the same as a pound of lead.[26]

Those questions that Abrams asked are part of a Mental Status Examination—a basic aspect of the diagnostic interview. Some of the psychiatrists, in their rush to be identified with a more elegant psychoanalytic position, forgot that they were physicians and psychiatrists. A more careful Mental Status Examination might have elicited the strange concreteness and literalness that clouded Richard's thought (see Chapter 8).

Litman then reiterated the "alternatives" available to the jury; that is, they had their choice of acquitting him as being insane or finding him guilty of a lesser charge. He closed as follows:

> Do you remember, as Dr. Schwartz asked Richard Herrin, as part of his interview, "Richard do you think you were crazy at the time?", and as he said, Dr. Schwartz did, he has no reason to doubt the sincerity and the honesty with which he answered it, and he said, "Yes, I had to be out of my mind. No question about it. I was crazy." That is not the Richard Herrin as you know him, as you've learned to know him throughout this trial. "I don't see how the Richard Herrin I knew could have done that." That is what he answered.
>
> And that is what, I suggest to you, ladies and gentlemen, the credible evidence in this case shows you.
>
> Dr. Schwartz didn't doubt that, and I suggest to you, as I just have, that the evidence shows here that you shouldn't either.
>
> Ladies and gentlemen, we are not looking for sympathy for Richard Herrin, for his background or his youth, or his religion, or good deeds. We are not looking for it; he's not entitled to it. He is not entitled to your sympathy. But he is entitled to your impartial fairness and he is entitled to justice.[27]

Fredreck's summation took much less time than Litman's did. That may be explained, however, by the fact that Litman's story had to go back to Richard's birth, whereas Fredreck's started with Bonnie's death.

> You told us, each and every one of you told us, as you were sworn as Jurors on this case, that you would apply your good, God-given everyday common sense, and objectively judge the facts of this case. Judge it objectively means without sympathy, without speculation, and most importantly, without fear. You promised me one thing at the outset, and I believe that I did ask each and every one of you individually to promise me that you would call it the way you see it, without copping out.
>
> Now that all the evidence is in and I'm about to begin my

> closing remarks to you, let me make my purpose in that question very clear. I submit to you from the credible evidence, the believable evidence in this case, that a verdict in this case of first-degree manslaughter is a cop-out. . . .
>
> Let me talk with you people about something that we haven't spoken about in, perhaps, seven or eight days, and that is, the facts of this case.[28]

Fredreck made it clear he was simply going to dismiss the concept of emotional status and deal with the facts. He was going to prove a murder case in an old-fashioned way. It was behavior, not emotion or the realms of the unconscious, that would interest him.

He then proceeded very quickly, and with little explicit detail, to outline the facts of the case:

> These are undisputed facts. Now, the Defendant's lawyer stood before you this morning and told you that is where the case begins. That is where the case ends, ladies and gentlemen. Bonnie died that night as a result of the intentional infliction of fatal wounds from Richard Herrin. That is the end of the case.[29]

Within the first few minutes, Mr. Fredreck had lost his case. Surely he must have been aware that the laws of his state allow mitigation for murder to manslaughter on the basis of extreme emotional disturbance. He simply could not ignore Richard's emotional state. To ignore it was to allow the constructions of Litman's story to stand without contradiction, or even without attractive alternatives.

He then proceeded to deal with Richard's statement to Chief Rea, making sure to point out to the jury that

> This was at a point in time when the Defendant had not been to court, had not seen a psychiatrist or seen an attorney. Now, you better believe, ladies and gentlemen . . . I'm going to talk to you about the Defendant's words at a time before he had an opportunity to contrive a defense.[30]

Fredreck pointed out that Richard said he had already "entertained the thought of killing her in her sleep," and quoted from Richard's testimony:

> I entertained the thought of killing her in her sleep. We were in the room . . . I was going to stay the night in her room.

229

She went to sleep first, and I told her I would join her when I was sleepy.[31]

Fredreck established, evidently to his satisfaction, what in his view were the pivotal issues of the case—calculation and intention.

> Dr. Schwartz also told us, "I think the fact that, as he told me—that he was afraid of others in the house seeing him. Why? Because they might call the Police. Indicates that he knew that what he was doing or was about to do was something that in the eyes of the law or society was wrong. The kind of thing you would call the Police for.
>
> "He also spoke about wanting to avoid toll booths when he was driving after the act, because he was covered with blood. That he feared that somebody at a toll booth would inquire or stop him should they see the blood. Again, indicating, in my opinion, good appreciation that what he had done was not— was wrong.
>
> "The fact that he sought out an appropriate weapon and used it effectively enough to cause somebody's death, I think is a good argument that he knew the nature and consequence of his acts."
>
> That is Dr. Schwartz's testimony, in part, verbatim. Ladies and gentlemen, based on the testimony in this case which is credible, believable, I submit to you that the Defense of mental disease or defect is an insult to your intelligence. Let us see what we know about that aspect.
>
> The Defendant loved Bonnie Garland. That is not in dispute. I know he had eleven or twelve witnesses to come in here and tell us that the Defendant loved Bonnie Garland, and nobody is arguing that.
>
> Bonnie loved Richard Herrin. I think she probably did. At least he believed that she did, and that is what is important here, what he believed.
>
> He wanted her exclusively and Bonnie said, "No, No. I am 20 years old. Let me grow. Let me spread my wings." But Herrin wanted her exclusively. He didn't want to be humiliated in the eyes of his friends; Bonnie was his. You heard what he said to Mrs. Garland on July 3rd: "I've come here to reclaim her." Well, he was unsuccessful. Unfortunately, he was unsuccessful.
>
> So, he killed her, and then he got in the car, and he drove, and he wound up in Coxsackie, New York, and he spoke with

a priest and with a Police Chief, and admitted his guilt to these two men.[32]

Fredreck then attacked some of the weakest parts of Litman's summation. First, the reasonableness of the provocation and secondly the confusion in the defense's story about whether there was or was not emotion. If there was no emotion, how could there be extreme emotional disturbance? But he did it in a cursory manner, briefly, too quickly, too unanalytically to allow twelve people to follow his reasoning.

> Mr. Litman told you this morning that it is not reasonable for a man who doesn't like his shoes—it is not reasonable for you to kill him. Perhaps if he curses at you, it is not reasonable to kill him. Perhaps if he defames your religion, he said—this one is unclear—but it is not reasonable to kill him.
>
> I submit to you, most respectfully, and appealing to your common sense, that it is not reasonable to kill a young girl who you love, because she has changed her mind about you.
>
> Where is the emotion in this machinelike Defendant? The Defense—one of the Defenses that the Defense wants you to consider is entitled "extreme emotional disturbance." My first question of Richard Herrin, on cross-examination, was "Mr. Herrin, did you tell your attorney this morning, sir, that at the time you killed Bonnie, you felt no emotion? A. That is correct."
>
> Give me emotion, ladies and gentlemen. Never mind extreme emotion and never mind an extreme emotional disturbance for which there is a reasonable explanation or excuse. This Defendant, by his very words, told us that he felt no emotion.[33]

These were valid points and made clearly. If Fredreck had had the persistence and the common sense to hammer away at the absence of emotion, the jury would have had to acknowledge that Litman also denied the presence of emotion. Fredreck then might have driven the jury to consider a different verdict than the two alternatives offered by Litman. If there was no extreme emotional disturbance, there was no manslaughter. Then the jury had only two other alternatives: Richard was either guilty or not guilty of murder; and, given the nature of the crime, it is inconceivable that the jury would have acquitted Richard out of hand.

It was in Fredreck's best interest to devote all of his time to the extreme emotional disturbance argument in order to eliminate it as an alternative, trusting that the jury would not allow a person who hammered to death a twenty-year-old girl in her sleep to be exculpated from personal responsibility. Richard simply didn't look or act crazy, except for the craziness of the murder itself. He didn't look it to those who had spent the July Fourth weekend with him before the killing, or to those who saw him immediately after the killing; and he surely didn't look it to the jury.

After the trial one juror said, "At no time was he close to being acquitted. . . . Hell, his Yale degree doesn't mean anything to me. Graduates of Yale can commit murder too." He proceeded: "The part about his childhood didn't enter into my thinking. He's not the only guy who had a rough childhood." What the juror meant was that he didn't *think* it had influenced him; and in the sense of believing that Richard's childhood should excuse the killing, it didn't influence him. But it did affect him in a crucial indirect way, for the same juror said, "At first I was going to convict him on the murder charge . . . [but] . . . the defense gave us a more complete picture of Herrin."[34]

The danger for Fredreck was in the extreme emotional disturbance argument, because it was a reasonable argument and Litman presented it well. It was Fredreck's responsibility to carefully, specifically, and persistently hammer away at *that* defense, and he failed to do that.

He did make clear that the irrationality of the act itself could not be used, under law, for mental illness. It was Litman's job to fudge the issue. But the law is clear here, and Fredreck was correct.

> Let me make myself perfectly clear. I'm not contending that this Defendant was rational when he killed Bonnie. Rational people don't kill. Or that he was normal. Our Penal Law doesn't outlaw rational acts. It only outlaws the irrational acts. That is not the criteria here, was he rational. Hey, take the law from the Judge, not from Mr. Litman, when he defines mental disease or defect.
>
> Again, normal isn't the criteria, I submit. Normal people don't kill. Normal behavior is not outlawed. Normal behavior is not criminal.
>
> Were his normal mechanisms working? That is not the criteria. That is the question the Defense Attorney put to you, but that is not the criteria.

> *No motive here. I submit to you, this Defendant had the oldest motive in the world: Jealousy.*
>
> *He said this act was so totally foreign to this Defendant's character. It was, it was. Whose character is not foreign to killing?*[35]

Fredreck correctly but too briefly pointed out that the irrationality of the act could not be evidence of extreme emotional disturbance. There had to be other evidence of *emotional* distress. But he made so little of this. Perhaps he did not persevere because he knew that by law the *defense* has the burden to prove mitigation. But Fredreck failed to recognize that the jury would not understand the technicalities of the law; they would continue to think that the burden of proof always rested with the prosecution. Besides, they would be struggling with their own guilt; no one wants to condemn a young man to jail for the rest of his life.

Fredreck resorted to simply attacking Richard. Whereas Litman came across as sincere and empathic, Fredreck ran the risk of seeming smarmy and sarcastic.

> *I told you at the outset, ladies and gentlemen, in my opening statement, that there would be a smoke screen put up before you. Was I ever right? Look, what is in issue here is the early morning hours of July 7th, 1977, and not the fact that Bonnie loved Richard Herrin at one point, that she sent him letters from Central America, and that she called him from Panama.*
>
> *"You can't deny the depth of their love," says Mr. Litman. Well, that is true. It is true as long as it was going the way the Defendant wanted it to go. But he showed his love in July of 1977, when a young girl of 20 years of age, whom he loved, wanted to see other people. Then that love changed to possessiveness, revenge, and vengeance.*
>
> *Yes, it was a time, I guess, as Mr. Litman said in his opening statement, that Richard Herrin was a big man on campus. Nobody says no to Mr. Number One. That is the depth of his love.*[36]

Fredreck proceeded then to outline Richard's behavior in terms that would be understandable to an average person—Richard in a rage at being rejected:

> *What does a person do who loves someone dearly and they are losing that person? Well, they get depressed, they feel bad.*

They will do anything they can to keep that person that they love. And they will impulsively fly from Texas to New York, if need be, to keep that person. They will write letters to the person, telling him how they are in the pits, and they can't wait to see them, and "I can't wait to see you again," and "I love you, I can't live without you, I'm so lonely without you." This is all normal behavior.

Dr. Train wouldn't know about this, because he's never seen correspondence to this effect. But this is all normal, perfect behavior. And Dr. Rubenstein said so on cross-examination. Doctor, it is not pathological that the Defendant impulsively flew up to see Bonnie; is it? Oh, no. Doctor, it is not pathological, is it, that he turned over in his mind just what he wanted to say to Bonnie? Oh, no. As a matter of fact, I did the same thing today, driving down here from New Haven, said Dr. Rubenstein. So, this is perfectly normal behavior. Nothing abnormal in this. Don't let that smoke screen divert your attention.[37]

Fredreck then attacked briefly the "suicide note." But that suicide note was a very ambiguous statement and Fredreck should have made more of it.

We get the statement, bold, blanket assertion, that the note attached to Bonnie's letter is a suicide note. I thought that Mrs. Stoddard came in here, called by the Defense, and told us that this man wanted a job in New Haven. So, when he writes to his roommates—to people for whom he was apartment sitting, "I might not be back," that is perfectly normal. That is perfectly normal. A suicide note, "I might not be back"? He's already called up for a job in New Haven.[38]

Fredreck is bright and knows the law but he did not seem to know how to effectively argue the law. Litman drew extensively on the concept of transient situational disturbance, because it is one of the few things that are listed as a defined disease in the Diagnostic Manual that is roughly analogous to extreme emotional disturbance.

When they talk about this Transient Situational Disturbance, part of the definition is—says, this is a diagnosis made in those people who have no apparent mental disorder.
Dr. Train doesn't count that very much when he comes in here and says, not only was he—did he have a mental disease or defect causing him to lack substantial capacity to know the

difference between right and wrong, he also had extreme emotional disturbance or Transient Situational Disturbance. Was inconsistent. By the very Manual adopted by the American Psychiatric Association, this is for people with no apparent underlying mental disorder.

You can't have it both ways, you see. Dr. Train wanted it both ways.[39]

Indeed, Dr. Train should not have had it both ways. This was a crucial point and was not, I submit, articulated with care and elegance. At another point Fredreck had an opportunity to trap Train in a contradiction. One of the problems with a psychiatrist seeing himself as an adversary is that unless he confines himself to one side of the case at all times he will be caught in previous constructions from previous cases. Schwartz avoids this, because in essence he kept his case close to that which he saw. Train confused his role with that of the defense attorney—always a bad thing for a witness who is supposed to be an expert.

> Chief Rea and Father Tartaglia told us that sometime, whether it be four—three, four or five, six hours after the Defendant inflicted the fatal wounds on Bonnie, they spoke with the Defendant, and he spoke clearly, coherently, productively, candidly. And again, Father Tartaglia told us he was able—the Defendant was able to give him a wealth of information.
>
> I asked Dr. Train on cross-examination if these things would be important to him. "Yes," he said, "they would." On this issue, Dr. Train, of extreme emotional disturbance, speech is very important, isn't it? "No."
>
> Then I read to him what he said elsewhere in another case. Then he changed his answer—"Oh, yes, well, I didn't understand what you said before." Another case where, based on a tape recording of the Defendant's voice eight hours after the attack, and that man's tone of voice, he determined he wasn't suffering from an extreme emotional disturbance. And why not? Because that other man spoke productively, coherently, relevantly and candidly.
>
> In all the 40 hours of so-called work that Dr. Train did, why didn't he pick up the telephone and call me? He knows me. Why didn't he pick up the telephone and call Chief Rea or Father Tartaglia? Because he, himself, says speech is important. "And said, how did he talk?" "Was he productive, was he candid? Or was he not?"

> Four months ago from that very stand, Dr. Train said, and I quote: "Now, in an extreme emotional disturbance, the individual is not going to be able to remember details. They don't. When an individual acts in an uncontrolled, impulsive, irrational, blind outburst, that makes up the criteria for extreme emotional disturbance, he doesn't know what he's doing. He is just acting out without any reasoning, without thought. It won't register in his memory."[40]

It was a telling point and Train had not looked that good in cross-examination. But Fredreck was too impressed with Train. He ought to have given the jury credit for being as perceptive as he was in sensing that Train's story was indeed too much like a movie scenario. He should have spent more time bolstering his most credible witness, Dr. Schwartz, and resisted his being taken over by the defense.

He also should not have indulged himself by being derogatory to the psychiatrists. The average person, despite all jokes, respects physicians, and is intimidated by expertise. Litman knew this and, with the one exception of Abrams, attempted to claim not that the opponent psychiatrists were fools but they in essence agreed with the defense. Fredreck did otherwise.

> Remember we talked about this in jury selection? These guys are going to come in here, going to have credentials as long as your arm. But if the basis of their opinion does not jibe with your good everyday common sense, then you people, who judge the facts, are totally free to reject their opinion.[41]

Fredreck then continued his summation by attacking the testimony of Rubenstein and Train; attempting always to identify insanity at its most extreme, and insisting on the presence of anger—explaining the killing in terms of "blind irrational rage."

He tended though to collapse all of these arguments together, giving them too little time and insufficient detail. Finally he returned where I think he would have been most effective to stay, that is, to the scene of the crime and of what Richard did:

> What happened? What happened July 7th, 1977, in Bonnie's bedroom? That is what you people have to decide. Well, we know what happened, but was the Defendant in control, based on the evidence in this case? Did he have a mental disease or defect? I submit, the credible evidence shows he did not.

But suppose he did? Suppose one of you prospective—one of you Jurors feels that he did or might have? Well, that is not where it ends. You see, you've got to go further and say, well, did this mental disease or defect cause him to lack substantial capacity to know and appreciate the nature and consequences of his actions and that his actions were wrong? Or that his actions were wrong.

It doesn't end—if there should be one of you Jurors who feels he did have a mental disease or defect, it doesn't end there. You must go further. If there is any question in that regard, I ask you to have the testimony, in its total, direct and cross, of Dr. Schwartz read back to you. Or the scholar—not the Courtroom buff, the scholar, Dr. Halpern. Because, Dr. Abrams came in here and was indignant; this case was a disservice to psychiatry. You might appreciate the exchange that he had with Mr. Litman in this case. But he was recognized by Dr. Train as being an expert in psychiatry. And you heard his credentials.

No mental disease or defect.

Why didn't Dr. Train read to us, and why didn't Mr. Litman mention in his closing argument this morning, the last seven words in Dr. Harvey Lothringer's Report of July 8th, 1977: No signs or symptoms of major psychosis. Why didn't Dr. Train read that to us on direct examination? He read it on cross, because I asked him to.

Ask yourselves that question. Because there was no psychosis. There was no mental disease or defect.

This, I submit, most respectfully, is a concoction to avoid criminal responsibility for a planned, controlled killing of a young girl in her sleep, and nothing more.[42]

Fredreck returned to the scene of the crime, but only to get somewhat legalistic.

The following confused and muddled statement became the final word from Mr. Fredreck on the specifics of the case. He made a very short closing statement:

I, ladies and gentlemen, have done my job to the best of my ability, as I'm sure Mr. Litman has. Shortly—that is, tomorrow—it is going to be your turn to do your jobs, consistent with your oaths as Jurors, to call it as you see it, without copping out. We know from the intensive questioning during Jury selection, and from your undivided attention to us, that you

*people are aware that this Defendant is entitled to that pre-
sumption of innocence, and he has it. That he is entitled to
representation by counsel, and he's certainly received that.
That he is entitled to a fair trial, and you people have given
him that.*

*But the People of this State are also entitled to something,
and that is justice. And justice can only be served by the truth.
And I submit to you, that based on the evidence in this case,
which is credible, that truth and justice in this case can only be
served by your returning a verdict of guilty of second-degree
murder. To call it the way you see it and don't cop out, under
your oaths as Jurors.*

I thank you for your time. Thank you, Your Honor.[43]

Jack Litman had skillfully absorbed the gospel of compassion and
love and the new testament of psychoanalysis with its suggestion of
limited individual responsibility. Fredreck had only the old-fashioned belief that a killer should be punished. He assumed that the
jury would remember the crime, and would separate the crime from
the criminal. The facts were otherwise. The jury was drawn from a
general public that respects and values the two new gospels. The
jurors were part of a society that in recent times has often pre-
cariously placed individual concerns beyond social needs.

Tactically, he made another mistake. He acted as though he were
an employee of the state. He should have been more than that. He
should have been an advocate for Bonnie. I suspect, since he is a decent and successful lawyer, he is technically more correct than I am
in defining his role. But in his hands rests that concept of justice that
sustains our conviction that things are working, that prevents us from
feeling alienated and hostile to the community which supports us,
and which we must support in kind. Justice must not be trivialized.
It is an honorable and glorious word and no full concept of social
justice can exist that does not consider the victim and the nature of
her tragedy.

Where was Bonnie? We'd heard so much about Richard and so
little about her. Fredreck never described her. Her letters break your
heart, because they reveal a girl of great charm and vivacity and,
above all, a delicious and delightful sense of humor, something of
which Richard is totally devoid. Bonnie should have been singing
through that summation; that beautiful red hair should have been
tossed in the eyes of the jury at every opportunity; she should have

been brought back to life so they could have appreciated the enormity of her death. She was not incidental to this case! The jury should have been made to mourn for her.

Justice must not be used in such a limited way as to mean only that which the law requires. The law requires certain things rather than other things, because they define a moral sense. At the end of the trial, Fredreck was outraged by the jury's decision. If during the trial he had expressed some of the outrage over the killing of Bonnie, he might have had a different decision. Shakespeare would have done better. Dickens and Tolstoi would have done better. Mozart would have done better. And Jack Litman would have done better.

This may not be explicitly understood as the function of a prosecutor, but it is essential for winning. In the adversarial processes, you must tell the best story. Fredreck told the wrong story. We should not have been asked simply to consider whether Richard was sincere or not; whether Richard was insane or not; Richard was honest or not; Richard was grieved or not; Richard was guilty or not; Richard was suicidal or not. That would be telling Richard's story, and that was Litman's job.

We should have heard of Bonnie and the Garlands; and the loss of a daughter; and the loss of a sister; and of a twenty-year-old girl who had beautiful red hair and a beautiful soprano voice and would never sing again.

Bonnie deserved a requiem in the courtroom as well as outside of it. The jury should have been reminded constantly of Bonnie, because it was her loss that the state was concerning itself with. They should have been moved by the richness and promise of her life in order to appreciate the magnitude of the crime that deprived her of life. When Fredreck was speaking, they should have heard a missa solemnis, they should have been moved as if hearing the Verdi *Requiem*. In this case there was no voice from the grave. There was no poet to speak of and for Bonnie.

So Litman won his case. He had not really hoped for more than the mitigation of offense from murder to manslaughter; he would have accepted that without a trial. And now all that remained was the sentencing. He went back to work and wrote a brilliant pre-sentence report and then awaited the decision of Judge Richard J. Daronco, the sentence of the court. When the sentence was passed down by Judge Daronco, Litman was dumbfounded. The sentence was the maximum allowable by law for manslaughter: eight and one-third to twenty-five years. The sentence, he felt, was grossly unfair and unwarranted. Litman had won the battle and lost the war.

At the end of our discussion, I asked Litman for some reasonable conclusions that ought be drawn from the case. He said:

> I think we learned the inevitability of murder. I think we learned that Aristotle was right, that moderation is an important key to learn. And Richard was unable to do that. I think we learned that the ability to deal with the problems in the frenetic world we live in are so overwhelming to people that if they do not have an anchor—as profound as the one Richard had in Bonnie—they cannot deal with life.

His mention of Aristotle made me return to an essential theme of mine. I said to him that he seemed very un-Aristotelean in his emphasis on the rights of the individual versus those of the community. I reminded him that Aristotle, with his biological orientation, saw the human being as a political animal, and I asked him whether in the pressure for individual rights the sense of the community might not be unbalanced. There is, after all, dangerous unrest that occurs when people think that justice is not done. The sense that we live in a reasonably fair society is a necessary anchor for all of us—"as profound as the one Richard had in Bonnie"—in this world that tests us all.

He answered forthrightly, and consistent to the end.

> I disagree with you. I think that it's important to have cases where people say things "aren't fair" because of an acquittal. Lord knows, if we lived in a society where everybody was convicted right down the line, it would be much too repressive. It's important to maintain a balance, to have those cases where people are obviously guilty and get acquitted. That's what gives you faith in the system.

Religion, psychiatry, and the law serve different aspects of the human condition. We are free to listen to each story in its place. The courtroom may generously invite these alien storytellers to its affairs, but it is the law that is at hand here, and the truth we must consider is the legal truth. The purpose here is to do justice. For the state requires it, and both Richard and Bonnie deserve it. To do justice, Bonnie Garland must be heard.

Bonnie Garland was never invited to appear at her own trial, and it was her trial. Her life and her worth were being tried and tested, along with Richard's. Nowhere in that courtroom was there anyone present to tell her story. Without the voice from the grave, she appeared only as a chapter in Richard's story. They approached her only as a vehicle for understanding Richard, and in so doing they violated that fundamental imperative of Kant that one never use a person only as a means to an end. But then, by the time of the trial, Bonnie was no longer a person.

III
JUSTICE

7

RATIONALITY
AND
RESPONSIBILITY

The laws of the land define the state's interest in individual behavior. The law is an announcement of that which is permissible, and that which is not permissible and as such punishable.

Obviously there are many things people refrain from doing that are not against the law. There are the moral codes of conduct that may serve as more powerful constraints on behavior than the threats of a punitive state. Professional achievement and standing among one's peers may allow a newspaperman or even a physician to see going to jail in protection of a professional principle like privacy as a symbol of pride rather than humiliation.

People have faced imprisonment or death in the service of principles they cannot even articulate. Honor, pride, duty, shame, guilt, fear, embarrassment, are all strong vectors driving behavior in specific directions. Conscience will often force an individual into acts which will seem foolish even to the person himself. Guilt is a powerful spur to behavior, as are shame and pride.

The law exists in those areas of moral behavior where the state is seen to have some interest in the definition of right or wrong. In one sense, the law always serves the purposes of the state, not the individual.

The law, by implication, as well as explicitly, does more than list that which is punishable; it defines the needs and morality of the state. It serves the survival of the state, and the concept of justice each government defines for itself. The law implies some of its morality in terms of the criminal punishments; the respective weight of each crime suggests the seriousness with which we hold its violation. It is assumed that those crimes which demand the death penalty are more heinous than those that involve a fifty-dollar fine. We therefore have to assume that our society holds human life at higher value than a parking space. Although to live in New York is to begin to doubt that.

Often there will be cases where the dual purposes of law, i.e., to preserve the common weal and to preserve a sense of justice, will come into conflict. Coercion is one example. The coerced act, whether killing or stealing, is, as an act, just as damaging as the voluntary one, but to punish the coerced individual is patently unjust. A bank teller who gives away his employer's money with a gun pointed at his head is certainly not seen as an accomplice to the robbery, nor held guilty of any crime. We recognize the action was not "voluntary." We acknowledge that the giving away of the bank's money was not the product of a criminal mind, mens rea. We understand that there was no intention to do wrong.

Recently there has been a concerted effort to extend the limits of the concept of coercion to something called coercive persuasion—that which used to be called "brainwashing." The Patty Hearst case led some people to feel that even if Patty had voluntarily held up a bank, her behavior ought be understood in terms of that which she had been exposed to before. Most of us assume that had Patty Hearst not been kidnapped, kept in isolation, and "brainwashed," she would have probably led a reasonably uneventful life. At least she would not have been involved in the events that led her to prison. A sense of fairness suggests that she ought to be seen as operating under reduced responsibility, somehow less culpable, or even not guilty.[1]

But the coercive persuasion concept is a slippery slope that everyone seems frightened to ascend. Once you acknowledge that a person intended to do something, but say that the intention was conditioned by events over which she had no control, you are opening the door to total exculpation of all behavior, because in each of our backgrounds must be some sociological deprivation, some psychological injury, without which we might not have found ourselves in whatever calamity is at hand. This, in great part, is an analogy to that which has been happening over recent years to the insanity defense.

Since classic times there were special allowances which placed the insane in special categories under law. The English common law since the thirteenth century has allowed that there was an essential injustice in *trying* a person during the period he was insane. Very much in the manner of modern law, he could be found not fit to stand trial "by reason of insanity" and would be simply detained, with his trial deferred until such time as he had regained his senses.[2]

Complete exculpation of actual criminal behavior can be traced back at least four and a half centuries—Nigel Walker,[3] in his classic study of crime and insanity, cited the first case of a man actually freed by a jury because he was insane—back in 1505. Nor was the crime a trivial one; he was charged with infanticide.

By the eighteenth century, the insanity defense was increasingly common, but until very recent times one had to be really and totally insane to be even considered for freedom from responsibility on the basis of insanity. The definitions of insanity were extreme and dramatic, with the courts often demanding a precision of diagnosis that was impossible, that only those unknowledgeable of the state of the art would have deemed feasible. As a result, total confusion reigned in the courtroom, and still does. So much so that some of the most distinguished forensic psychiatrists in the country refuse to ever testify in courts of law, and for most, every national trial is a source of embarrassment. Alan Stone, describing with disgust and contempt the spectacle of competing teams of psychiatric "experts" contradicting one another's diagnoses in the modern courtroom, considers them a humiliation in the field. He said, "The psychiatrists who participate are like clowns performing in a three ring circus."[4]

Whenever a major criminal case hits the front pages—Jean Harris, Sirhan Sirhan, the Son of Sam, Jack Ruby, and at the time of this writing, John W. Hinckley, Jr., the man who attempted to assassinate President Reagan—whenever these public spectacles occur, one segment of the population knows that along with the defendant they too will be on trial—and those are the psychiatrists.

Criminal activity is the bête noire of the modern psychiatrist.[5] It is the kind of human behavior about which he is most ignorant, and perversely, about which he is called upon to give the most certain opinions—in testimony under oath. The conditions that bind the relationship of psychiatry and the law today are such that confusion and contradiction are guaranteed.

For years the M'Naghten rules had been the basis throughout most of the United States for establishing a defense on the grounds of insanity. As defined by the English judiciary in 1843, the rules required proof "that at the time of the committing of the act, the party accused was laboring under such a defect of reason from disease of the mind as not to know the nature and quality of the act he was doing, or if he did know, that he did not know he was doing what was wrong."

In the early days of modern psychiatry this was seen as an adequate, although stringent, application of medical knowledge to the law, for "disease of the mind" was traditionally divided into psychosis and neurosis, with the psychoses being roughly equivalent to the common use of the term "insane." Definitions in criminal law, however, require precision, not rough equivalence, and some felt the M'Naghten rules achieved precision at the cost of defining insanity at its extreme.

As medical understanding of mental processes increased, the terms "insanity" and "psychosis" became progressively less congruent. The borderline between psychosis and neurosis became more difficult to define. Pre-psychotic conditions were recognized. Motivation, perception, and their influences on behavior were seen as more subtle and complex, and the term insanity was dropped from the medical vernacular. Insanity is now a legal term exclusively; it has no medical meaning. The typical psychiatrist today, when asked if in his opinion a defendant is legally insane, experiences the same frustration he might feel if asked whether a specific action was a function of black bile or phlegm.

The "test of right or wrong" was viewed as archaic and, medically speaking, unjust. More suitable as a gauge of feeble-mindedness than insanity, it arbitrarily endowed one form of mental impairment with an immunity denied to other forms equally debilitating, controlling, and restricting. Like other unrealistically rigid laws, the M'Naghten rules have constantly invited evasion and encouraged sophistry. ("Temporary insanity" is a legal defense in only a few states, but what in the world is it? More disturbing, what irrational act could not be so considered?)

As the dissatisfaction with what were seen as the deficiencies of the M'Naghten rules increased, pressure mounted—partly as a result of the tradition of humanizing the treatment of the criminal, and partly as a result of scientific progress—to redefine the insanity defense in a way more in line with current psychiatric concepts. Therefore, when in 1954 Judge David Bazelon handed down his opinion for the United States Court of Appeals in the now famous Durham case, it was not surprising that most progressive social thinkers considered it a major advance. (In Washington, D.C., the jurisdiction of the Durham case, the "irresistible impulse" test had been added in 1929.) Judge Bazelon proposed a new, far broader test: that "an accused is not criminally responsible if his unlawful act was the product of mental disease or mental defect."

Whereas the M'Naghten rules may have been stingy in denying clemency to many of the "psychologically innocent," they at least defined the *type* of defect involved, a defect of "reason" and the severity of the defect, so "as not to know the nature and quality of the act." As some were aware, a good scholar had a great deal of flexibility. He could play intricate variations on the theme of "knowing." What does "know" really mean or for that matter what is the definition of "reason" or "wrong"?

To absolve the accused from criminal responsibility, the Durham rule would merely require that the unlawful act be "the product of mental disease." This broadened the insanity test with a vengeance and, if nothing else, had the potential to introduce more psychiatric concepts into criminal law than we may care for.

When I first wrote about this subject in 1965, I naturally used the standard diagnostic headings of the American Psychiatric Association. I rarely use these diagnoses in my informal communications with colleagues. I never use them in my own perceptions. Most of us are aware how trivial, ephemeral, descriptive, and meaningless are psychiatric diagnoses. But they constitute the official language with which the law contends. I will keep the examples that I used in those days, because they defined the conditions at the time that the Durham rule was enunciated, and it makes very little difference what examples are used, out of what statistical manual. What is intriguing is that some fifteen years later none of the terms are acceptable, although the same conditions obviously still exist. They have either been relabeled or, in such dramatic cases as homosexuality, delisted by popular vote. The *Diagnostic and Statistical Manual of Mental*

Disorders of the APA is known as DSM. We have in less than fifteen years seen the emergence of a Son of DSM—known as DSM II, born in 1968, and now a Son of Son of DSM—DSM III, proudly adopted for the APA in 1979.

With this in mind let us begin with a few conditions then universally accepted by psychiatrists as mental disease. In addition to the classic phobias and obsessions, this category included alcoholism, drug addiction, and sexual deviation. Most thoughtful people, lawyers and psychiatrists included, then held that the excessive drinking of alcohol, the taking of heroin, and the homosexual act were per se symptoms of disease to be treated by a physician rather than crimes to be punished by law. Nevertheless the latter two were still crimes in more than half the states. The liberalizing influence of the Durham rule could indeed be useful to help correct this situation, but the logic implicit in it extended a good deal further. Society could not afford to exempt from criminal responsibility *all* actions that could be described psychiatrically as "the product of" these conditions. Would we grant immunity to the addict who steals to "feed his habit," while we hold liable the pauper who steals to feed his hunger?

A much more difficult group consists of the psychosomatic disorders—such as mucous colitis, tension headache, and neurodermatitis. No one is going to be jailed for scratching—his own skin at least—but who is to say what an itch can drive a man to do. Theoretically at least, any action of a person at the end of patience over, say, a migraine headache, might be exempt from liability, if innocence depended only on establishing a causal relationship between a criminal act and a mental disorder. As *reductio ad absurdum,* consider the case of an accused criminal whose lawyer, citing the Durham rule, enters a plea of not guilty because the crime was "the product of" acute heartburn (listed as an example of mental disorder 006-580 Psychophysiological gastrointestinal reaction, in DSM I). A novel defense, indeed; yet it would seem to satisfy the logic of the Durham rule.

Finally, there is a third category that defies all definition, those mental illnesses called character or personality disorders. In modern psychiatry these diseases are distinguished from classical neurosis, in which certain kinds of behavior patterns, often isolated, represent anxiety and the defenses against it. With the character disorder, since it is the very nature of the developed personality that is viewed as disturbed, *all* behavior would be considered by the psychiatrist to be "the product of" mental illness. Indeed, the concept of the character disorder leads to sheer legal irrationality, for it is the fact that a person indulges in antisocial behavior that *defines* him as being sick.

This third category of mental illness at least had been recognized for the legal anomaly it was in the Model Penal Code of the American Law Institute. The section dealing with criminal responsibility states, "The terms 'mental illness or defect' do not include an abnormality manifested only by repeated criminal or otherwise antisocial behavior."[6] The Model Penal Code, which was approved in 1962 by the institute, is just what its title suggests, a model which it was hoped would serve as a guide for states wishing to reform their criminal law; as such it represented a consensus of some of the best legal minds in the country. The code's suggested article for the insanity test is as follows: "A person is not responsible for criminal conduct if at the time of such conduct as a result of mental disease or defect he lacks substantial capacity either to appreciate the criminality (wrongfulness) of his conduct or to conform his conduct to the requirements of the law."

With the exception noted above, this is essentially a combination of the M'Naghten rules and the Durham rule, and although certainly more generous than the former, logically no improvement over the latter from the psychiatrist's point of view. Indeed, Judge Bazelon himself put the problem well in his learned opinion in the Durham case: "In attempting to define insanity in terms of any particular symptom, the courts have assumed an impossible task."[7] As a psychiatrist I can say that defining insanity itself is equally impossible. No, the problem is not, I think, one of finding a definable test for mental illness but of finding *any* test.

For strangely, psychiatrists as a group have never been able to define mental illness. Professional opinions range from the assumption that all human beings suffer from mental illness in varying degrees to the opposite extreme, that there is no such thing, that "mental illness is a myth." I do not mean that there are no objective criteria in the field of psychiatry. The case is quite the reverse. Present a patient to a group of psychiatrists—not in a courtroom—and they will agree to an amazing extent about the nature of the illness, severity of impairment, areas of malfunctioning, prognosis, and indicated therapy. Indeed, a common reaction of the doctor in training is surprise that his first patient talks and acts as though he had read the textbook.

ITS SOCIALIZATION THAT CREATES events for the INDIVIDUAL

But when the psychiatrist attempts to abstract from clinical data general concepts of mental functioning—concepts of responsibility or the essence of mental health that might be useful to the law—he is on his least sure footing. Even in those areas of mental malfunctioning about which there is the most agreement, psychiatry will not serve the law well. For fundamental to the psychiatric view of man are principles antagonistic to the social view of man upon which criminal law is founded.

Before psychoanalysis, psychiatry was a descriptive science without a psychology—without any explanation of mental mechanisms in health or disease. Modern psychiatry now uses general psychological principles borrowed from psychoanalysis. Although many psychiatrists reject psychoanalysis as a treatment technique and dismiss some of its developmental concepts, two axioms of psychoanalytic theory are so widely accepted that they are now represented in almost every psychiatric frame of reference. The first axiom: Every individual act of behavior is the resultant of a multitude of emotional forces and counterforces; this is the "psychodynamic" principle. The second: These forces and counterforces are shaped by past experience; this is the principle of psychic causality.

Taken together, these two principles dictate a way of viewing any act of behavior. Suppose three men are threatened by a man with a gun. One flees; one stands paralyzed with fear; one attacks. The stimulus for all three is the same. But the stimulus is only one factor in determining the resultant behavior. Acting on the complex machinery of the human being, it triggers associations, perceptions, and response patterns already "programmed in" by previous experience. This view of behavior rejects the possibility of an isolated or chance act and, whether we like it or not, places psychiatry in the camp of determinism. All acts—healthy, sick, or not-sure-which—share one property: *They are predetermined.*

Many psychiatrists in fact do not like it, and are personally unhappy with determinism; they "believe in" free will. But professionally—and it is in his capacity as a professional expert that the psychiatrist testifies before the law—we have not been able to incorporate "chance" as a relevant phenomenon into the theory of psychiatry. Deterministic it remains and antithetical to the social concept underlying criminal law, which must assume free will, or choice in action. It really is not important which concept is "true"—or if either is true. For certain purposes either assumption

252

may be useful, or necessary; but to assume both at the same time is logically impossible. Whenever a psychiatrist testifies in an insanity defense, he is doing so not under the M'Naghten or Durham rules but under the rule of the impossible.

This logical impasse has a further unfortunate consequence for the relationship of psychiatry and the law. The social view of behavior is in essence moralistic; an action is approved or disapproved, right or wrong, acceptable or nonacceptable. A person is guilty or innocent as more or less clearly defined in advance by law. But psychiatrically speaking, nothing is wrong—only sick. If an act is not a choice but merely the inevitable product of a series of past experiences, a man can be no more guilty of a crime than he is guilty of an abscess.

I do not mean that psychiatrists are amoral or that they preach amorality. On the contrary, it is the psychiatrist's job to help a person adjust to his environment—and our social environment operates under ethical and moral systems. (The degree to which values and judgments enter treatment is an entirely different brouhaha now raging in psychiatry.) What I do mean is that guilt and innocence, as used in criminal law, are not functional concepts in psychiatry. To the typical psychiatrist, guilt is an emotion—and innocence an age.

The remarkable Dr. Karl Menninger was reported to have said, on being invited to examine Mr. Jack Ruby, that he would be delighted to do so after the verdict was in. The implications of this statement are far-reaching. It says that the psychiatrist does not belong in the court of law.

As long as there has been law there has been, however primitive, a concept of justice. And long before psychiatry existed our ideas of justice dictated that behavior be evaluated in terms of the intention giving rise to it. "Thou shalt not kill" became "Thou shalt not kill" *except*; except in defense of life, ideals, country, home, property, bomb shelter; except in propagation of the faith, a political system, an economic principle, a prejudice. Indeed, so strong is the humanistic tradition that even God's commandment can change. In the new translations of all three major faiths (Judaism, Protestantism, and Catholicism) of the Holy Scriptures, He legalistically cautions, "Thou shalt not *murder*."[8]

In the beginning it must have seemed easy to enhance the effectiveness of justice by introducing into the law considerations of intention and personal responsibility. A century ago the jurist and social scientist were united in their ignorance of the mechanisms of human behavior. But at the turn of the century a revolution occurred. Psychology produced its first creative genius; as Copernicus shook the heavens, Freud shook man, and nothing since has looked the same. The explosion that transformed psychology from a nosological discipline to a dynamic, though primitive, science not only illuminated human behavior as never before, but necessarily began to shift our view of the laws governing that behavior.

The reason for introducing psychological considerations into the criminal law in the first place was to secure justice, and so, as understanding advanced, the test for insanity has been progressively exposed as grossly inequitable. The answer to many has seemed to be to revise criminal law in the light of the new knowledge of human motivation. This, in fact, had been the trend to the present.

Greater understanding of the implications of Freudian psychology, however, would reveal the futility of using psychology to leaven the law. In the psychoanalyst's view, if guilt is based on free choice, then no man is guilty, for behavior is predetermined. If guilt is based on intention, then every man is guilty, for every action is intended—if not consciously, then unconsciously, and the borders between the two are amorphous. The criminal law as it now stands is using false and, perhaps worse for legal purposes, indefinable psychological concepts.

Two hundred years separate two similar expressions of concern about excessive dependency on psychiatry by two distinguished judges. In 1760 an English solicitor general said, "My Lords, in some sense, every crime proceeds from insanity. All cruelty, all brutality, all revenge, all injustice is insanity. There were philosophers, in ancient times, who held this opinion. . . . My Lords, the opinion is right in philosophy but dangerous in judicature. It may have a useful and noble influence, to regulate the conduct of men; to control their important passions; to teach them that virtue is the perfection of reason, as reason itself is the perfection of human nature; but not to extenuate crimes, not to excuse those punishments which the law adjudges to be their due."[9]

In 1961, Warren Burger, then not yet Chief Justice of the Supreme Court, stated in a circuit court decision, "Not being judicially defined, these terms mean in any given case whatever the expert witnesses say they mean. We know also that psychiatrists are in disagreement on what is a 'mental disease' and even whether there exists such a definable and classifiable condition. . . . No rule of law can possibly be sound or workable which is dependent upon the terms of another discipline whose members are in profound disagreement about what those terms mean."[10]

The theoretical examples that I choose to dramatize the essential conflict between psychiatry and law may have seemed cavalier, but truth is always more exotic than anticipation. The cases that have caused the most public discussion and outrage are less trivial and no less absurd.

These days, those exotic cases in the criminal law that make headlines in the New York area are more than likely to include the names of Dr. Daniel Schwartz and Dr. John Train, and, increasingly, the name of Jack Litman. Schwartz's most famous case was undoubtedly David Berkowitz, the Son of Sam; but Berkowitz, despite the urging of his lawyers, refused to use the insanity defense—a piece of behavior that may well be a significant index of his insanity, for the insanity defense is increasingly used and increasingly effective.

Schwartz has said, "Some people are—literally—getting away with murder. Psychiatry is just part of the problem. People cop pleas, and in no time flat they're back on the street."[11] Many people have expressed the feeling that one individual who "got away with murder" may have been Officer Robert Torsney, a New York City policeman who, as reported by James Gleick in *New Times* magazine, shot an unarmed fifteen-year-old black boy in front of a number of witnesses who saw no sign of struggle or provocation.

Traditionally, in a situation where a white policeman shoots a black boy the defense is that the officer was operating in the line of duty, seeing himself, rightly or wrongly, as threatened by the appearance of a weapon or seeming appearance of a weapon. At least two other police officers had been acquitted in the same year as Torsney with that defense. But Torsney's action was too public. A dozen witnesses could testify that there was no weapon, no scuffle. Torsney first tried that plea, but found he could not garner any corroboration even from his fellow police officers, that the young boy made any gesture which might conceivably be interpreted as either reaching for a weapon or signaling an attack.

The lawyer, Edward M. Rappaport, entered a plea of not guilty by reason of insanity and had his client retain Daniel

Schwartz. He remembers the day Schwartz called to tell him he had settled on a diagnosis—it was an exciting moment, Rappaport says.

"I've got it," he quotes Schwartz as saying. "Now I know what was wrong with him—he had epilepsy." That was a surprise to Rappaport, and it was a surprise at the trial, not only because Torsney had no previous record of epilepsy—or any other mental problem—but also because an electroencephalogram had been normal.

But Schwartz explained that Torsney suffered from a rare form of epilepsy called "automatism of Penfield," which occasionally does not appear in an electroencephalogram. As a result of the epilepsy, Schwartz testified, the officer—already in a "dissociative psychotic state"—had a "psychomotor seizure."

"Dr. Schwartz said he was, like, in a trance—he did everything automatically," Rappaport says.

For Schwartz, the telling point was the complete absence of any motive for the killing, and the apparent absence of any emotion about it afterward. "No way does it make sense," Schwartz says. "Torsney acted in a way that was totally irrational."[12]

When confronted at the trial with the false story of self-defense that Officer Torsney had first offered, the insouciant Dr. Schwartz, quick as a wink, labeled it "involuntary retrospective falsification," as though the term he had just invented was recalled from an official diagnostic manual. Schwartz's performance was the source of encomia from all professional witnesses. One lawyer called it "sheer bravado."

For Schwartz, the gratuitous nature of the shooting—the irrationality of the act from an otherwise completely sane person—was in itself a sufficient sign of insanity.

According to reporter Gleick's coverage of the trial, Dr. Schwartz shared this feeling with a psychologist, Frances Gunnels, who in an entirely different case testified in defense of Robert Lewis Burns, who was being tried for the killing of Willie Maxwell.

When Maxwell had the effrontery to appear at the funeral of Robert Burns's niece, when most people in the community had assumed he had murdered her, Burns simply took out the pistol from the holster he was accustomed to wearing and put three bullets into Willie Maxwell's face at point-blank range. He pleaded not guilty by reason of insanity. He was acquitted with the help of testimony from Professor Gunnels and was sent to a mental institution. He was released after six weeks. He then continued his normal life.

Psychologist Gunnels was later quoted as saying that Burns was not really insane, but she also believed that anyone who commits a sudden, violent crime like Burns is, "in a way," insane for that short moment.

> "I testified that he was not aware of what he was doing at the time," she says. "I don't really believe in temporary insanity, but I do think that anybody who just goes berserk and commits a real violent crime is temporarily insane—I mean, society teaches us right from the start you just don't do things like that. You don't cut the cat's tail off right behind the ear and you don't flush the puppy down the commode." She used a technical term at the trial to describe Burns' mental state, but does not remember what it was.
>
> "In a way, though," she says, "killing Willie Maxwell was the sanest thing anybody did all summer." She says she doubted a jury could have been found that would have convicted Burns. "He was just doing what the law ought to have done sooner. Why, I probably would have killed that man myself."[13]

I asked Schwartz about his involvement in the Torsney case. He said, "It was a nightmare for me," and then went on to compare Torsney with Richard Herrin.

> Torsney was involved as far as I could see in a much more complex, strange piece of behavior than this man [Herrin] was. It was entirely different behavior. This man first of all has some motive for being angry at the girl who was rejecting him. He sat with her in her room. He then made a conscious decision to kill her. He then went searching for an appropriate weapon and, as I recall, for a towel in which to wrap the weapon so that if he were seen coming back from the kitchen to the room he wouldn't have to explain what he was doing with a hammer, and then he proceeded to hit her on the head and then he proceeded to try to get away from there at least consciously with the idea of killing himself. But he was also careful enough, if you recall, to drive on the back roads so he did not have to come to a toll booth where he might have to explain what he was doing covered with blood.

257

Torsney comes out of a building and, barely realizing it, starts to take out his gun. Richard, by the way, used the cover of night—it's after midnight by the time he's killed her. With Torsney, true, it's night, but if you understand the surroundings there, it's Thanksgiving night and there are a lot of people outside the building. It's not a private residence. It's a housing project. A youngster comes up to him, asks him a perfectly banal question, and for no rational reason, Torsney takes out his gun, shoots him, ejects the shell, keeps on walking, maybe breaking his pace once, maybe not, walks to the car and when his fellow officer says to him, "My God, what did you do?" he responds as though he doesn't know what he's talking about. He appears to have no awareness of what he's doing. He makes no attempt to escape. He doesn't flee. He walks at his same pace down this area to the car, and the fellow officer, Williams, asks him what's going on, he doesn't realize he's being spoken to. Later on when an assistant district attorney tries to take a statement from him he talks gibberish, the words don't make sense.

—What do you call that kind of condition?

I believed he was in a psychomotic seizure at that time. I don't know now for sure, but at the time of testimony I did believe it was psychomotor epilepsy. What happened was that he then went to the Creedmoor psychiatric hospital and became a nightmarish problem for the judges. Creedmoor applied for his release, and the question was then, Was he still dangerous? The Court of Appeals held that you couldn't pose the question of whether he was dangerous until you found he was mentally ill, and if he was *not* mentally ill it didn't matter how dangerous he was. He had to be released from the state hospital. The courts were furious, and their last sentence was that they hoped the legislature would clarify this matter further.

—Are you worried about his being out on the streets?

No. I was very sorry about all the judicial headaches. The second department where this occurred had, and still has, a fine appellate division. I was aghast to read the opening sentence of their Torsney opinion, which for no reason whatsoever includes the fact that the victim was black. To discuss the legal question of whether Torsney should be held in Creedmoor, the whole question of dangerous mental illness, it wouldn't matter if the victim were black, yellow, white, or tan. There was so much racial stuff introduced by black demagogues that even the court was contaminated by it.

—But isn't it possible that there is such a racist who doesn't consider blacks as people—and could use this same defense?

But nobody had suggested that Torsney had committed this
act because he was racist. No more than your average Irish
American.

—But do you worry about a man who can go into an "acute state
of psychomotor epilepsy" and shoot somebody, walking around
the streets?

I don't worry. Maybe I should.

In this case, the aftermath was as newsworthy as the trial. Torsney
was ordered released by the Court of Appeals because he was receiving no treatment at the Creedmoor Psychiatric Center. It is becoming part of the increasing national policy against warehousing that if
an individual is not receiving any treatment and is not predictably
dangerous he must be released.

Torsney was receiving no treatment because the psychiatrist at
Creedmoor said there was nothing to treat! There was nothing wrong
with him.

With complete chutzpah (in exact parallel with Dorothy Thomp-
son's classical example of the man convicted of killing his parents
who begs for leniency in consideration of his being an orphan),
Torsney filed suit for a disability pension from the New York City
Police Department. After all, he logically argued, insanity is a disability, and it was because of his insanity that he lost his job. The
Court of Appeals was relieved of the necessity of doing that which
might have brought them into a position of *legal* logic, but would
have been seen by the public as sheer madness. It did not have to
rule on the substance of the case, because Torsney had taken too
long to file court papers for the appeal. As is so often the case in law,
technicalities saved the day.

Jack Litman had argued that in many ways the whole problem
was only theoretical. When a person is found not guilty by reason of
insanity, it is likely that he will serve the same amount of time, only
in a mental institution. Professor Abraham Goldstein expressed the
same feeling in his careful and intelligent analysis of the insanity defense in 1967. As recently as five or ten years ago, this was probably
true. It is certainly not true today. The concept of rights, including
prisoners' rights, the rights of the mentally retarded, and the rights of
the mentally ill have made it increasingly difficult to keep a mental
patient hospitalized even when there are clear signs of dangerous-

ness—the analogy of preventive detention is made—let alone in the usual case where there may be no signs of dangerousness, even with a patient who later turns out to be dangerous.

Litman not only believed that a defendant would serve the same amount of time in either institution, but accepted the propriety of this, assuming that the purposes of the institutions were somewhat similar.

—Would you have felt justice was done if you had gotten an acquittal in Richard's case?

I never asked for an acquittal. I asked them to find that on the basis of mental disease and defect commonly called the defense of insanity that Richard should go to a hospital, alternatively.

—But to go to a hospital is to be found not guilty.

By reason of insanity, yes. I absolutely feel that would have been just.

—How does that fit in with your previous statements about retribution?

The fact that I said retribution is the cornerstone of criminal law means that it still has to be there. I think the state would have a certain amount of retribution in keeping Richard in the hospital. The hospital is not very much different from prison. Richard would have been sent to a closed institution with locked door and hopefully he would have received some therapy. . . . Not that I'm a great believer in psychiatric therapy.

The idea that a hospital ought to be used as a place of punishment is a reprehensible one to a psychiatrist. It ought to have been offensive to an intelligent layman like Litman if he had thought about the implications of his statement.

The distinction between therapy and social control is an absolutely essential one in the precarious position of a doctor who, as is the case with a psychiatrist, deals in symptoms which are expressed in behavior rather than internal pain and disability. The capacity for corruption is enormous. That which we do to an individual to serve his purposes alone would be abhorrent if done for political purposes. In medicine we inflict pain, amputate limbs, enucleate eyes, scar and disfigure—and institutionalize for life. They would be intolerable if done by the state for political purposes. The crude justice of Islamic states where hands are still severed for stealing is anathema to most of us.

The use of therapy as an excuse for social control reaches the ultimate degradation in the Soviet Union. While most of us have simply become numb to the brutishness of the Soviet Union, its use of psychiatry and mental institutions as a means of controlling dissidents has in recent years introduced a new wave of revulsion.

The trial of yet another police officer, Kevin Durkin, was occasion for a reunion of some of the principal agents in the Richard Herrin case. Jack Litman was once again the chief defense lawyer, and two star witnesses for the defense were Dr. Daniel Schwartz and Dr. John Train. Presiding was Justice John J. Walsh, the same jurist who had been so impressed with Litman's bail appeal for Richard Herrin. Bronx District Attorney Mario Merola had unsuccessfully tried to remove Justice Walsh from the trial, contending that he was biased.

In this case, Schwartz and Train were on the same side testifying for the defense, but they were testifying in completely opposite defenses. Here, too, Jack Litman was playing both sides against the middle. He was offering two defenses, mutually exclusive and contradictory, allowing the jury to buy either one. Litman did not care, since both led to acquittal. Schwartz would argue that Durkin was not guilty because of insanity, implying that the action was a criminal one but he should be excused because of the nature of his mental disease. Train would argue that the action was not a criminal action, that it was normal behavior of a police officer who thought he was defending himself.

Kevin Durkin was twenty-nine years old, handsome, white, and for eight years had been a model police officer. More than that, he had been a heroic one. His record was studded with courageous acts and citations. He was known for tenderness, for taking chances. On more than one occasion he had disarmed criminals without use of guns or force. He was popular in the community and, unlike many other police officers, was viewed as a friend to Hispanics and blacks. On February 21, 1979, Officer Durkin entered a bar at about 3 P.M., and despite the fact that he was known as a light drinker, he consumed quantities of beer.

Durkin later claimed that two Hispanic men he met in the bar wove a story of intrigue involving the F.A.L.N., implying that they were both members of this terrorist underground organization. They threatened him and, beyond that, his wife and child. One of the two men, Martinez, had a reputation for baiting people. Durkin was off duty, in civilian clothes, but he carried the .38-caliber revolver which off-duty officers are obliged to carry. The witnesses said Durkin pulled his gun out of its holster and fired five bullets into the two unarmed men at point-blank range. Durkin contended that he saw a suspicious movement as though one of the men were reaching for a gun. No one else saw the movement.

The Bronx District Attorney saw this as a classic case of racial bias and abuse of power by a police officer. Durkin was charged with murder and, as is increasingly popular these days, hired Jack Litman as his lawyer. Litman promptly hired Daniel Schwartz and John Train as his chief defense witnesses. Litman was, again, to use both sides against the middle, assigning each psychiatrist a different role. He first went all out for acquittal—seeing this as a classic case of self-defense. Train would argue that position. If the jury was unimpressed, he would offer an alternate argument, that Durkin was suffering from paranoid schizophrenia with delusions and should be acquitted by reason of insanity.

The case was one of the most dramatized, publicized, and longest criminal trials in New York City. Daniel Schwartz "lost" this one. Litman won with Train.

Dr. Daniel Schwartz:

> The jury did not agree with me in Durkin. I testified that he was suffering from mental disease at the time. Jack Litman, who was his defense attorney, also asked John Train to examine him. Train felt the man was not mentally ill at all at the time and he was acting in a reasonable way to defend himself. Given the reality of several hours with two men—one of whom proved to be intimidating to him, and the other who seemed to be a gunman—he had every right to reasonably interpret these two as posing a life-endangering situation. I felt that he had misinterpreted or overinterpreted, that he was paranoid. Both possibilities were presented to the jury, and the jury acquitted him as factually innocent. It was not on my testimony but on Train's.
> —Are you worried about his walking the streets? A man you diagnosed as paranoid and who has killed?
> No, he was at one given moment of his life put under that extreme pressure.
> —Are you saying then what Sister Ramona says, that there but for the grace of God, go any one of us?
> No. I don't think I'm in the same position as Durkin was.

Durkin, you have to understand, was a hero. I have met few people as heroic as Durkin. He had any number of cases in which he would disarm civilians by literally throwing down his own gun and saying, "I want to talk to you." He would then talk these people into giving up their weapons and lead them down.

—But when you introduce the idea of a paranoia so transient, then it becomes measurable only by the action; that gives you a peculiar kind of law. Any nonprofessional act of violence, murder, et cetera, by definition of the act itself, is so disproportionate to what a normal person would do that you have a built-in exculpation of any heinous crime.

I still follow the New York laws. It wasn't just paranoia. Paranoia is just an attitude. I might be suspicious of somebody, I might be doubtful of somebody, but this man had the true belief that these people were ordering him out of that bar; that they knew exactly where he lived; that his wife and child were in danger; that if they got him outside they would probably kill him, and his wife and child would be killed.

Dr. Train and the jury felt the baiting, the teasing, the confrontation, that those men had inflicted on Durkin was enough. That any normal person would also believe he was in danger. I called it psychotic because of what he had told me about his own position. Would he do it again? I don't know.

Litman, in discussing this case, said:

People were outraged! He walked out of the court scot free. The good thing about the insanity defense for the lawyer is that you are free then to bring in everything—all the background. And in the case of Durkin, the prosecutor fell into our trap. Instead of arguing the *reasonableness of the act* as a police officer, he argued the *sincerity of the belief* of the officer. He made the issue: Was he sincere and actually fearful? The jury believed he was sincere and they made that self-defense. That's not *necessarily* self-defense.

—As a person, do you think it was just?

I can't reconcile all things. That's one of the impossibilities of the system. You appear before judges, some of whom are miserable, don't know anything, are biased apparently against all defendants, some of whom are humane, intelligent, and fair people; and you say to yourself, "Why is it that some of my clients are lucky and get one and the others get the other?" You just can't deal with it. I deal in an imperfect world and do the best I can. I don't like to play God. Things are irreconcilable.

—Why do you say playing God? We do have to establish rules for society. We must draw lines—and we do.

With Durkin, I was very happy he wasn't convicted of murder. He shouldn't have been. The judge in that case also submitted lesser accounts. Personally, I think the best verdict in that case was probably the insanity verdict; but self-defense is also a just verdict.

—In what way was he insane?

He sincerely believed these men were threatening himself and his family, that they were members of the F.A.L.N. and about to kill his family unless he did A,B,C,D.

—You think he was suffering from delusions? People don't suffer from delusions for only one night, do they?

I disagree. I know people who have had psychotic episodes just during a certain period.

—If that's a logical excuse, with no past history of delusions and no pathology, we will simply have to trust the truth of every defendant on whether he had delusions or not on a given night.

No, you just don't have to trust them. We then give the opportunity to the jury. It is *they* who have the unfettered discretion to say, "This is not that bad a guy. We don't want him to go to jail for the rest of his life. We want him to go to a hospital for however long the community wants to hold him."

That was the way with Durkin.

The insanity defense has been under intense re-evaluation in the past ten years because of the rapid increase in both its use and its effectiveness (at an almost geometric rate in homicide cases in the past few years), and because of the high visibility and dramatic nature of the kinds of cases in which it is introduced. Recently it has gained further attention because of the assassination attempt on President Reagan.

As a result of this, presidential adviser Edwin Meese III has publicly suggested that the insanity defense be abolished altogether; and Senators Orrin Hatch and Edward Zorinsky have introduced bills that would either eliminate or severely curtail the use of this defense in the federal courts. Even here, the insanity defense would be allowed in a limited number of cases of homicide.

It is, however, the test of mental illness short of insanity, as a means for reduction of sentence and mitigation of charges, that has vastly expanded the role of the psychiatrist in the courtroom. This aspect has further inflamed the public, which sees it as a subversion of justice in specific and, beyond that, as a sign that society at large is a less than just place (see Chapter 9). It is to appeal to that sense of outrage, that feeling that justice is not done, that the Hatch Bill and others like it are formulated. It would return us to the earlier days of 500 years ago, where only lunatics in the traditional sense, the delusional and hallucinatory, people who simply did not occupy the world of you and me, would be exempted from full responsibility for their actions.

It is not just the politicians who are exercised by and divided on this issue. The community of jurisprudence—those lawyers, philosophers and psychiatrists who devote their lives to the fundamental issues on which these cases rest—is split wide open. The split goes beyond the traditional concept of political orientation. There are political conservatives and liberals on each side. It cuts across the ideological alliances that bind people together on other issues. It is the politics of strange bedfellows.

The distinguished on one side are no less distinguished than those on the other. In one New York Times article,[14] there were quotations from Professor Alan Stone of the Harvard Law School and Professor Norval Morris, professor of law and criminology at the University of Chicago, favoring the abolition of the psychiatry defense. And on the other side were Professor Alan Dershowitz of Harvard Law School, Professor Abraham Goldstein of the Yale Law School, and Judge David Bazelon of the Federal Appeals Court, District of Columbia. Judge Bazelon was the architect of the expanded concept of the insanity defense, although he has since become disillusioned. These five represent some of the best and the brightest we have.

Alan Dershowitz was quoted as saying that to abolish it would "be a disaster. You would have exactly the same swearing contest, you would just have it over intent rather than insanity."

Professor Goldstein felt that at this point the concept of a culpable state of mind is so intrinsic "to our common law as to be the equivalent of being imbedded in our Constitution."

It is indeed difficult to see how one could remove the concept of mens rea, the culpable state of mind, from the law. It has been suggested by many. I myself had done so some fifteen years ago (and now publicly recant). Of course there are other alternatives. Karl Menninger has argued that guilt and innocence ought to be determined by the facts, and then disposition could be determined on the basis of the condition of the individual who might be found "guilty." This is an attractive premise that is built on an optimism about psychiatry's capacity to treat the typical criminal that is becoming an increasingly rare point of view.

Another authority, Herbert Fingarette, has emphasized the concept of rationality as an alternative to the concept of mental disease. He would use this as a definition of criminal insanity: "The individual's mental makeup at the time of the offending act was such that, with respect for the criminality of his conduct, he substantially lacked the capacity to act rationally."[15]

This would indeed offer the apparent advantage of allowing psychiatrists and others to talk about the *rationality* of the behavior without being caught in the inanities that result from trying to conform to a set of constantly changing and meaningless definitions of mental illness.

Dr. Abraham Halpern, an opponent of the insanity defense, still offers exculpation based on the emotional or mental processes of the individual. He simply takes it out of the hands of the medical profession and removes it from the medical model. He offers the following standard which he titles "the justly acquitted doctrine":

"A defendant is not criminally responsible if, in the circumstances surrounding his unlawful act, his mental and emotional processes or behavioral controls were functioning in such a manner that he should justly be acquitted."[16]

While this would indeed get the psychiatrists out of the courtroom, or at least might do so, it might bring others in who are less capable of testifying about mental status. It also, in Halpern's own words, only speaks of "the defendant's not being criminally responsible," implying that he *is* responsible in some unstated way, but "even though responsible, can, if the conscience of the jury dictates, be acquitted."

I suspect it will be simply another case of *plus ça change, plus c'est la même chose.* But there will be a change. The unholy alliance of increased use of mental status as an excusing condition, added to increased sensationalism and publicity about crimes of violence, added to our inability to keep people in mental institutions for an equivalent time to what they would receive in a jail sentence, is creating a public impression that things are not working—always a dangerous state of affairs.

In the long run there is still a place for the insanity defense and a need for considering mental status in evaluating the seriousness of a crime. We will want to distinguish between the killing that the professional does in the course of his lifetime pursuit of criminal gain and, let us say, the depressed widow who kills her child in a fit of desperation. We know these crimes to be of a different order. While we may never be able to analyze the distinction into logical factors, we want to maintain the distinction. The primary purpose of the insanity defense is to allow a jury to lead with its heart. There are many cases in which by legal standards the facts seem to point directly to guilt but where a jury will emotionally feel different and wish to honor its feelings.

It also works in the opposite direction. Those people who are most completely and obviously crazy rarely are acquitted on an insanity plea. Not when their crimes capture public attention and involve public trials. Some crimes are so atrocious that the jury, like the public at large, simply will not hear that the individual is insane: David Berkowitz; Richard Speck; the Manson family; Sirhan Sirhan. And one could predict that John W. Hinckley, Jr., the Atlanta killer, and many others will fall into that category.

The truly crazy will either not come to trial, or else will be convicted despite all the evidence. A jury will function as a jury in the same way as Freud stated we all do in everyday life. Our rationality will generally be subservient to our emotions, but out of respect for reason we will protect ourselves from feeling foolish by finding some "rationalization" which will allow us to conform the "facts" to please our intentions.

When Patty Hearst was being tried, her attorneys argued two ways. They insisted that Patty was coerced and they also said that she was "brainwashed." The two simply cannot exist logically together. They mean opposite things. To be coerced means someone is holding a gun or the equivalent to your head; forcing you to do that which you do not wish. Brainwashing implies that you have been forced to wish that which you do not, or would not normally, wish. The brainwashed person acts in such a way that he no longer needs to be coerced. You do not have to hold the gun to his head. You have "convinced" him.

It was difficult for the jury in the Patty Hearst case to buy coercion, because she was seen acting and doing things months later when it was obvious that she was not being held by physical force or fear of violence. With Patty Hearst, brainwashing, if there is such a thing, was a more likely explanation of her behavior than coercion—at least in the later phases of her captivity. Were I her attorney, I would have had her argue that way. I would have had her get on the stand and say, "Nobody held a gun to my head. I held up that bank of my own free will. I would have done anything they told me to do. Had they at that point asked me to shoot my mother, I probably would have done it. Today, saying this, it sounds unbelievable and irrational and crazy to me; but they had me so confused and so convinced that they were right that I would have walked through fire for them. It now seems like a totally different me. But that's the truth, and that's the way it was."

In all probability the lawyers were afraid to take that chance, because brainwashing has no respectability in the law, whereas there is a long tradition of excuse and exculpation for coercion. They hedged their bets and they lost. They were probably afraid that in his charge to the jury the judge would have cautioned them that if they did not feel Patty was actually coerced—i.e., had the gun to her head—they were to find her guilty, that they must not and could not find her innocent because of brainwashing, because that concept has no legal standing.

The judge might have said that. So what! I am as sure as I can be in predicting any behavior that if it had been so argued she would have been acquitted. Juries do not have to listen to judges. Even legally, they are not so required—as was established some three hundred years ago.

In this case "upon an inquest to try an indictment against one Pen and Mede, upon a tumult and unlawful assembly; and because the jurors did acquit contrary to the evidence, and the direction of the Court, they were fined forty marks a man, and committed till they paid the fine." Bushell, one of the jurors, "brought his habeas corpus." Various counsel argued the merits of the case: "The Judges are to open the eyes of the jurors, but not to lead them by the nose." "(Although they went contrary to the evidence), they (the jurors) are judges and are to satisfy their own consciences." "(Although they did not pursue the direction of the Court in matter of law), it is possible the court might mistake the law, or they might mistake the

Court, and so no reason it should be so penal." Lord Vaughan speaking for the majority of the Judges with whom he conferred, ordered that the prisoners be discharged "for the reason given was, because the jury may know that of their own knowledge, which might guide them to give their verdict contrary to the sense of the Court.[17]

And after all this anguish there is still this contradiction: The law demands responsibility, but people are less responsible than they were once thought to be. Even if behavior is not predetermined, it is certainly dynamic, multiply motivated, and individual. We may respect both needs. But we must maintain our distinctions between the purposes of psychiatry and the purposes of the law. Psychiatry serves the individual, and is directed at restoring him to health. The law serves the community, and is designed to secure its values and preserve its safety. The law demands an essential responsibility of its citizens. It assumes with Aristotle that "what lies in our powers to do, lies in our powers not to do."[18]

The progressive liberalization of the insanity defense was an ill-conceived attempt at benevolence. It threatened to unravel the unity of the law. It regressively began to undermine the common and democratic features of the criminal code. Individualization at the current degree is already undermining equity; and equity—equalness under law—is an essential component of justice.

Of course we must allow some exemptions from responsibility to satisfy a common sense of decency, which is also a component of justice. The assumption that modern psychiatry would offer clean and accurate guidelines to the limits of responsibility has been proven false. Psychiatry in its present state cannot and, given its present direction, will not in the future. As long as psychiatry is tied to a dynamic and developmental model, it will never accommodate itself to the kind of responsibility the law must insist on. The psychiatrist can indicate the limits of rationality, of cognition, and perception, and that is about all. The M'Naghten rules, with all of their inadequacies, remain the best we can hope for. They are blunt enough instruments to make good law. They are sufficiently ambiguous to allow a jury to interpret them according to its heart rather than its mind alone; and they do clearly exculpate the most obviously irresponsible of the mentally ill. It may not be the greatest endorsement to say they do less harm—but it is not the worst either.

Professor Abraham Goldstein of the Yale Law School said, in emphasizing the importance of the concept of responsibility to the law:

> That concept is more seriously threatened today than ever before. This is a time of anomie—of men separated from their faiths, their tribes, and their villages—and trying to achieve in a single generation what could not previously be achieved in several. Many achieve all they expect, but huge numbers do not; these vent their frustration and anger, in violence, and in theft. In an effort to patch and mend the tearing social fabric, the state is playing an increasingly paternal role, trying to help as many as possible to realize their expectations and to soothe and heal those who cannot. As this effort gains momentum, there is a very real risk it will bring with it a culture which will not make the individuals within it feel it is important to learn the discipline of moderation and conformity to communal norms.[19]

I believe there is a growing public sense that there is a disbalance, that we have reached the limits of individualism. And I would argue that this, too, cuts across traditional lines of political affiliation. Liberals are upset at Reagan-type individualism, which would allow further exploitation of the environment; and conservatives are offended by the concept of the right of an individual to conform his sexual life to another individual in precisely the way he wishes, independent of a common sense of morality.

At any rate, I firmly believe that the new discovery of scarcity will demand a re-evaluation of individualism, and that is good. We have gone too far (see Chapter 9).

Justice in the killing of Bonnie Garland demands more than a concern for Richard and his fate. The community at large has a stake in this matter. And certainly the Garlands were vested parties. The Garlands were outraged with the disposition of this case. To this day they are as embittered at the results of the case as they were that day of the verdict. Remember what Joan Garland said after the trial: "If you have a $30,000 defense fund, a Yale connection and a clergy connection, you are entitled to one free hammer murder. . . . Heaven help girlfriends and boyfriends that are breaking up. *Everything is absolutely upside down.*"

Everything *is* upside down when we insist on approaching justice from the standpoint of the individual. The insanity defense was introduced to bring a compassionate mitigating limit to the concept of responsibility. The law demands responsibility. Whether there is such a thing as true or absolute responsibility is irrelevant. Proper functioning of society requires the assumption of its existence. Each individual must conform his behavior to expected models, and if he does not he must be held responsible for his violation of the code.

We must not press individualism so far either here in the criminal proceedings or for that matter in the public space—in our use of goods, in our treatment of the common resources, or in our destruction of our natural environment—so that this good state can no longer exist.

At the same time, we must not do gross injustice to the individual in our society, for our society was built to its state of imperfect nobility out of respect for individualism. If the Garlands were outraged, so, too, in an opposite appraisal, were Sister Ramona and Jack Litman. How and where do we fit compassion into the system? To what degree do the Richards of this world deserve mitigation? In that spectrum from responsibility to exculpation where do we locate Richard?

8
WHERE IS RICHARD?

A criminal trial traditionally starts with an opening statement by the lawyers in which they outline their arguments in advance. In this statement they will define a case to be documented during the course of the trial with whatever proofs they bring to bear. This is from the opening statement:

> *He walks around, looks for a weapon and finds a hammer. . . . He covers the hammer in the towel. . . . He goes about it as a fellow is to go about committing a crime. Premeditated, cool, plan it out. Cover his tracks. . . .*
>
> *He went inside, to see that she was still sleeping. Came back outside. Took the hammer and brought it into the room. Saw that she was still sleeping. . . .*
>
> *And he took the hammer—and that rage that was in him . . . now surges forth, and in one strong flow, he smashes the hammer into Bonnie's skull.*
>
> *Needless to say, the body moves. Gurgling noises. He picks up Bonnie's head, and he calls out her name . . .*
>
> *"Bonnie!" he calls. Obviously, she doesn't answer. She is unconscious. She is probably near death. Puts the head down, and then comes a flurry of blows; repeatedly hits Bonnie over*

the head. Still maybe sensing she didn't die, he tries to strangle her.[1]

From the prosecutor's opening statement?

Not at all. These are excerpts from the opening statement of the defense attorney, Jack Litman. He has admitted the murder. He has admitted the brutality of it. He has admitted the intention of it. He has admitted the calculation of it—the planning and the execution. In simpler societies, or merely in simpler times, such concessions on the part of the defense attorney would never have been made, because, having made them, the trial would have been over. What argument then can Litman use to attempt to gain either the freedom of his client or mitigation of his charge from murder to manslaughter?

In this more complicated time in which we live, in our pursuit of a more sophisticated concept of justice, we have decided that what Richard did, his behavior, could only be judged on the basis of his state of mind while doing it. The reasons and rationale for that were presented in the preceding chapter.

In order to try to understand where Richard should be placed in all this theoretical discussion of intention and insanity, it is important to raise a number of questions, most of which will be unanswerable in a precisely scientific or objective, and in that sense conclusive, manner. Is he psychotic? Was he psychotic at the time of the killing (temporary insanity)? Is he normal? If he is normal, is there nonetheless a significant pathology? If so, what is the nature of his pathology? And finally, Where is Richard? By that I mean, among this maze of behavioral, dynamic, pathologic, psychiatric, sociological, psychological, and legal descriptions, where is the essential Richard, and how does *he* fit into the scheme of things that we are calling criminal justice?

In this series of questions I have purposely avoided the concepts of insanity and extreme emotional disturbance. Those are the language of the law. Those are ultimately to be decided not by a psychiatrist but by the jury. What I am addressing here in these questions are the basic ingredients from which the jury will confect a story titled either "Guilty" or "Innocent."

In this discussion, then, I will be liberated in a way that the psychiatrist who testifies in a courtroom is not. I have no need to conform to the rules of testimony. I am free to discuss the legal considerations while I am testifying to his psychological state. I am also free to complicate the matter, where their job—and a paid job it is—is to simplify it.

Is Richard psychotic?

The damnable thing about every aspect of diagnosis in psychiatry is the inadequacy of our terms. This itself is rooted in the primitive position we still occupy in terms of etiology, the nature of the cause of the disease.

In the nineteenth century, mental illness existed in the same territory of ignorance occupied by physical illness. The modern concept of "disease" had yet to really evolve. All medicine was in that sense only descriptive. What was described were signs and symptoms. Signs being the objective measurements: swelling, inflammation, fever, or dementia, delusion, and disorientation. Symptoms are those things that a patient complains of—a pain in the belly, double vision, numbness of hand, a feeling of despair.

Out of these signs and symptoms, well before the etiological (causative) nature of the disorders was understood, a particular combination of signs and symptoms was recognized as a syndrome, a pattern, with a recognized natural history and development that occurred commonly within the population. This was then seen as a specific sickness or a disease. But a symptom, despite the juror, is not like the smoke that signals a fire. A symptom alone means nothing. Night sweats are symptoms of tuberculosis. Night sweats are also a symptom of menopause, and night sweats might simply occur when a room is too hot. When the night sweats are continuous and combined with a specific kind of cough producing a specific kind of sputum (as to color, consistency, viscosity, even odor), with a gradual and malignant weight loss and a reduction in the vital capacity of the lungs and an audible change in respiration and altered percussive signs (the thumping of the chest) indicating consolidation in the lung, plus various other signs and symptoms—then, and only then, a diagnosis of tuberculosis could be made. Because physicians had only their powers of observation, they were keen observers, and this diagnosis (like others) could be made with great assurance, even though the X ray that visualized the specific and characteristic lesion in a tubercular lung, and isolation and cultivation of the tubercle bacillus, remained yet to be done.

So, in the nineteenth century all medicine was essentially descriptive and was basically a nosological discipline—a matter of careful classification. In that massive burgeoning of scientific discovery in the late nineteenth century, primarily in Germany, the fields of pathology and physiology, bacteriology and immunology, were created, and modern medicine was born. Mental disease was left behind. The descriptions of mental conditions that we have today are no better than those we possessed in earlier times, and the ultimate causes are still unknown.

Gradually there did evolve a new concept of mental illness. After all, we could not simply remain embedded in nineteenth-century thought while the rest of science was multiplying knowledge with a fertility that put the fruit fly to shame. New scenarios were built. Some researchers continued their inquiries in the physical organic world, and we see their results in the current exciting discoveries of the anti-depressant drugs and the general biochemistry of the mental processes.

Some, following the great tradition of Pavlov, experimentally studied induced behavior and laboratory mechanisms for changing it. This led to modern behaviorism, of which B. F. Skinner is the most eminent spokesman. It also laid the foundation for the general field of experimental psychology. Some followed the genius of Sigmund Freud and expanded his exploration of mental mechanisms that bound abnormal behavior to normal behavior in a kind of continuous linked series of incremental changes.

Most of the testimony in the courtroom follows this last grand tradition; but as I have previously argued, this tradition has led, ironically, to a greater understanding of normal behavior than to that of abnormal. Further, while producing a set of brilliant deductions and speculations, they are the sort that generally remain undocumentable in an empiric fashion. We cannot titrate or measure one against the other like the bench scientists. More like the historian, we work in a tradition of continually revising our stories in light of new understanding and new developments.

One should not think in terms of which tradition is correct, only which is most useful in shaping the available data into a usable whole. The most absurd dichotomy is the psychological–physical one. The argument about whether disease is rooted in psychology or physiology is silly stuff—like previous arguments about nature and nurture. It is both, or neither. An intelligent student of biology knows that these are not exclusive or differing terms, but simply different aspects, different visions of that which is always an amalgam of both.

In the nineteenth century, mental illness encompassed psychosis of the most constricted sort. People who were deemed crazy were indeed crazy. They were different from you and me. They seemed closer to the eighteenth-century concept of possession than to the twentieth-century concept of mental disease. As it turns out, most of them were possessed not by a demon but by a spirochete yet to be discovered. The majority of admissions to mental hospitals were for tertiary syphilis.

Freud introduced the concept of neuroses. This presented a new vision of mental illness—a gradation. No longer would there be merely the insane and the normal, but a spectrum of functioning: psychoses, symptom neuroses, character disorders (nonsymptomatic neuroses), psychosomatic disorders, perversions, maladaptations, work inhibitions, significant omissions (lack of orgasm), and simply failure to fulfill one's potential.

The first step was the enunciation of the concept of the neuroses. This suggested that to be mentally ill one need not be completely "crazy." A normal person like you and me (or Freud for that matter) could have different aspects of his functioning which were "crazy," that is, inconsistent, illogical, and maladaptive. Beyond that, those of us who were completely normal could be abnormal in certain ways at certain times for limited periods.

These were all extraordinary new concepts. Without giving a detailed history of psychiatry, what happened then was that we gradually expanded the reach of psychiatry by expanding the concept of mental illness. Less and less damage had to exist in a person's behavior or perception to define him as mentally ill. By decreasing the degree of impairment to diagnose mental illness, we have gradually increased the amount and number of the mentally ill.

In a classic study of the Upper East Side of Manhattan symptoms of mental distress were found in some 60 percent of the population. Now, I grant you that the Upper East Side of Manhattan has a rather strange and unique population, but I suspect that these same researchers would have found the same statistical presence of mental illness in almost any population they would have examined.[2]

If at one time psychotic was equivalent to mentally ill, what then does it now mean when all of us, or at least the majority of us, have signs of mental illness? Psychotic is now reserved for those individuals in whom the mental illness so fragments or destroys performance because it so impedes either cognitive or emotional life that the individual loses his hold on the real world.

This does not suggest that psychotics act crazy all the time. One of the most frightening things on entering a closed ward is not the discovery of how grotesque or different the people are from oneself but the revelation of how similar they are. The psychotic can enter into a normal discussion of political events in a way that your best professional colleague can. At the same time, if cornered about the truth of a statement, he might tell you that God had told him that it was true.

Certain psychoses look different from other ones. Certain psychoses even look different from themselves. The layman is always confused by the term "schizophrenia," and perhaps we should have stuck to Eugen Bleuler's use of the plural, the schizophrenias. They simply do not look alike. Dementia does not look like catatonia, and catatonia does not look like paranoia. Common threads are seen to a psychiatrist who views all the forms of the illness as merely reparative maneuvers against the essential defect which is the fragmentation or splitting of the various functions of the human mind. The attempted repairs are different—muteness, delusions, hallucinations, irrationality—but the underlying defects are the same.

To all that, you must add the fact that schizophrenia is often a cyclic and remitting disease. We never describe schizophrenia as cured, only arrested. We refer to the person as a "schizophrenic" even when he is not psychotic or behaving with any apparent degree of emotional distress. We view the schizophrenic similarly to the way we see the manic-depressive—someone who is subject to cyclic bouts of his psychosis—recognizing that he may have one "attack" and never another, or a second in twenty years, or one breakdown and never go into remission and remain psychotic all of his life.

What, then, does one call a schizophrenic either between his attacks of irrationality or before he has had his first attack? We call him a compensated schizophrenic, or a latent schizophrenic, or a pseudo-neurotic schizophrenic, or a borderline schizophrenic. The labeling has value for medical purposes but can be harmful and unfair, because in those interstices between the acute attacks the schizophrenic *is* as rational as the rest of us. Perhaps even super-rational at times. Besides, the classical signs—the flattening of affect, the tendency for withdrawal and isolation, a concreteness—every one of those aspects (although not necessarily combined in that same way) may be present in any one of us, just as we all have sweats, fevers, swellings, and thirsts.

A psychiatrist is nonetheless likely to speak of a schizophrenic (or manic-depressive) "in remission" even though the person may have had one schizophrenic episode when he was young and never had another (roughly one-third of all cases). This kind of labeling is convenient in communication with other professionals who have no difficulty understanding that while a person is a schizophrenic he may not be behaving "schizophrenically."

The law will not tolerate such communication despite all its good intentions, and the law should not. These diagnoses may be intended as mechanisms for communication among professionals, but they can be, and have been, vehicles for depriving individuals of their essential liberties. Powerful tools can be corrupted into unjust means of social control and social engineering. In the Soviet Union "creeping schizophrenia," an actual diagnosis, can be made because of the individual's criticism of the state, and the diagnosis is sufficient to forcibly commit him. In all areas where psychiatry and the law abut, the terms "psychosis" and "psychotic" must be used stringently. We are not free to talk about a "psychotic," thereby dangerously labeling a person who does not at that moment have a psychosis as evidenced in psychotic behavior or perception. Aware of the labeling problem, we tend to use terms suggesting psychosis cautiously.

So in this period when we are expanding the concept of mental illness, we are at the same time narrowing the concept of psychosis. As muddle-headed as it may seem the prevailing practice in psychiatry is as follows: Schizophrenia is considered a psychosis, but even an acknowledged schizophrenic is not called psychotic unless he is in a specific phase of the disease.

This is all, alas, part of the question Is Richard psychotic?

The answer is, therefore, No.

Was Richard psychotic at the time of the killing?

There is no way to adequately examine the mental state of an individual in the past. Jack Litman's outrage at Dr. Halpern, for testifying without having examined Richard, was misplaced. If Richard had been tried for manslaughter, then Halpern's failure to see him would be insupportable. How could he possibly know what would produce extreme emotional disturbance in a Richard he had never seen? Litman invited Halpern into the courtroom when he insisted on also having an insanity defense. To say whether Richard was insane at the time of the murder required no special gymnastics or hocus-pocus on Halpern's part. Here he was in exactly the same position as all of the other psychiatrists. They *all* had to extrapolate from the present into the past, trying to guess what was going on in Richard's mind a week, a month, or a year before. No one can know what went on in someone's mind retrospectively—no more than we can tell you what his white blood count, his body temperature, or his pulse rate was then. We *can* ask Richard. And he is free to tell us the truth—the truth as he sees it, which may be a whole different story—or a lie.

Richard was a good boy who always told the truth, we are told. But he also told lies, according to his own testimony. (Recall his preparedness to lie in order to avoid paying money to redeem his truck at the airport.) It is over seventy-five years since Freud discovered that it was only when he stopped asking questions that the truth emerged. When you ask someone about his personal feelings, even when he is not on trial, the answers you get are most likely to be what he thinks he should feel, what he would like to feel, what he thinks is prestigious to feel, what he thinks it would be useful for you to think he feels—and only accidentally what he really feels. Asking the criminal what was going on in his mind at the time of the crime is generally not fruitful. We cannot corroborate it. There were no witnesses there. The victim is dead. We are dependent then on his observed behavior before and after the killing in order to speculate on the state of his mind during the killing.

Those who saw Richard immediately preceding the killing and those who observed his behavior immediately after the killing were in consensus that he was not behaving in a psychotic way. None of the psychiatrists even considered this seriously except Train, and he was so hard-sell in this case that I believe he lost his credibility with the jury.

The one piece of evidence that would strongly support the concept of "temporary insanity," a term that is offered with apology even when used in quotation marks, is the action itself. Surely, an act so vile, so heinous, so useless and inappropriate to the provocation, has to be a sign of craziness. It was this kind of reasoning that gave birth to the concept of temporary insanity. But if we accept this, then every crime that is vicious enough would have to be the act of a madman, albeit a temporary madman.

If the action is consistent with all of the person's preceding personality and character, if he always behaves this way, then we are dealing with a madman. If it is inconsistent, the very out-of-character quality will be evidence of the irrational. When a delusional psychotic attempts to stab to death the attendant on the ward, this is not different in kind from his attempt to enucleate, disembowel, or castrate himself. If a seemingly normal person does this, the disparity is so great that it will then be used to prove that he is one with the delusional psychotic. Who then is responsible for the irrational act? It would seem by this reasoning no one.

Jack Litman, in his attempt to juggle between self-contradictory defenses, got himself into deep water at one point in his summation. He was attempting at this point to establish the fact that Richard was operating under extreme emotional disturbance.

> Was the extremity of this based on a mere annoyance or unhappiness? No, of course not. I mean, if someone comes up to you, for example, and says, "You know, I don't like the shoes you're wearing," and as a result of that, you get emotionally upset because you like your shoes, and you kill someone—I mean, is that a reaction which is extreme? Yes, perhaps, but the law requires it to be reasonable, as well. In the killing, it is never reasonable to kill. The law doesn't require that the killing be reasonable. It requires that the reaction, the extreme emotional disturbance, be reasonable. In the situation of the man talking to you about your shoes, that clearly wouldn't be something—that is not the type of thing that provokes any sense of sympathy for reason, for a person to get upset that way. I mean, for shoes, that is not that important.[3]

No, indeed. That is nothing for someone to get upset about, and someone who would kill over a pair of shoes would have a greater claim to the insanity of the action than someone reacting out of rejection by a lover. In arguing the reasonableness of the response (reasonable in relationship to what Richard felt he was losing in losing Bonnie), Litman essentially made a case for the rationality of his client and therefore *against* his first plea of not guilty.

He then went on and said the following in the very next paragraph: "If someone calls you a dirty name or defames your religion, should that allow you to do something like this?"

Here he seemed to get caught up short. Indeed, in the Durkin case he was involved with almost precisely this situation. He recovered in the next sentence: "It is an unclear question. Maybe yes, maybe no. That would be for the determination of the jury."[4]

If Litman argued that the reasonableness should be taken in terms of significance of the event to oneself, then certainly someone who is called a spick, a nigger, a wop, could interpret it as a threat to his very existence, at least during a period when prejudicial behavior can destroy opportunity and promise. The problem remains a difficult one—how to establish a proportionality to the act, and to the provocation. Is rejection, any more than prejudice, proportional to murder?

Dr. Halpern was offended by what he sensed was the contradiction in logic.

> If Herrin had pleaded extreme emotional disturbance and looked for a manslaughter first-degree verdict, I would not have felt they were playing games. . . . Litman didn't think that in Westchester of 1978 he was going to get an acquittal. Not this kind of unlawful act.
>
> But he felt this would give him a chance to introduce psychiatric testimony easily. There are clear-cut rules for the introduction of psychiatric testimony in an insanity case, but there are actually no rules for its introduction in a manslaughter first offense. It isn't necessary, because it is presumed understandable to the average juror when a person is emotionally disturbed. You don't need a psychiatrist to testify that Mr. Jones is upset and acting somewhat irrational if he opens the door to his bedroom and finds his wife in bed with two of his best friends. In Texas at one time, Mr. Jones would have been acquitted outright.
>
> Litman was faced with a murder charge, second degree, and he probably guessed that a jury faced with an alternative of acquittal by reason of insanity and conviction of murder would compromise for choosing manslaughter one. Of course that is what they did. To me that was hypocrisy.

Whether it was hypocrisy or not, it wasn't psychosis. There is no reasonable case that can be made for temporary insanity here that would not undermine the very principle of responsibility in the law. Of course everyone who "loses control" is temporarily acting in an irrational way to those around him as well as to himself. The individual who, enraged at being cut off by another driver, speeds up in turn to cut him off once again is behaving irrationally. He is risking his own life and that of another person over an assumed affront to his space and dignity. While that may seem crazy for the moment, it cannot be called momentary insanity.

The whole concept of temporary insanity is only acceptable as a defense in a toxic hallucinatory state, when, as some side-effect of a therapeutic drug such as lithium, cortisone, and many others, a person becomes truly temporarily psychotic. To make a vile action its own defense puts the law in the position that the more disgusting and inhuman the action, the more defendable. While certain legal theories might countenance those ideas, it would inevitably be a losing case as long as there is trial by jury.

I agree with Dr. Halpern that Litman's use of the insanity defense was a tactical device and that he no more than Halpern and no more than I believed that Richard was "temporarily insane."

Is Richard normal?

If Richard is not psychotic and was not psychotic at the time of the killing, is he then "normal"? When I address this question as I do the following ones, it should be understood that I speak with the frame of reference of a psychoanalyst; I take a dynamic approach to behavior. While I do not reject the chemical causes or the physiological base of emotions, at this stage in our understanding I tend to feel it is more profitable to discuss behavior in dynamic terms. The analogy that I have used in the past is one that I borrow from Franz Alexander, who assumed that the art of acoustics and sound would be such that someday we would be able to analyze a piece of music in terms of overtones, vibrations, resonances, harmonics, counterpoints, rhythms, melodies, frequencies, and the like. The question is, he asked, Would you then be able to understand the *Eroica* better that way than simply by listening to it? In this case, I think we are at a point where we are better off just listening.

When Freud expanded the concept of mental illness, he might

well have condemned all of us to a state of psychic hypochondriasis, since we would all begin to recognize our kinship with the sick. But, with a stroke of genius, at the same time that he was enlarging the scope of illness he was also expanding the concept of normalcy. The sharp distinctions between the normal and the pathological were erased. Whereas previously sick and healthy were seen as entirely different, Freud saw them as containing similar elements where only the arrangement distinguished the sick from the healthy. Freud allowed normalcy a broader package, which now included many strange and exotic things that had never before been acknowledged as part of normalcy. At one time, sexuality was something that only men enjoyed, and then the men of lower classes were presumed more sexual. Freud pronounced sexual pleasure as belonging to men *and* women, rich and poor, child and adult—a concept that disgusted the Victorian world from which he came. He insisted that the difference between the sick and the normal was not in what they felt but in what they did. Even in the area of behavior, there is more shared than had been admitted. There is more that connects the sick with the healthy than that which separates them. Perverse sexual behavior is only perverse when it is exclusive behavior. Indeed, it is seen as the common root from which healthy normal adult behavior flowers. Perverse behavior is a part of the package of normal behavior.

So it is with every Freudian concept—the Oedipal complex, castration anxiety, death wish, voyeurism, masochism—they are all contained and carefully packaged within and under the heading of normalcy.

In the sense that Richard had no organized symptomatology—a phobia, a compulsion, impotence—and in the strictest definition of illness, we could not label Richard sick. Unless *he* felt sick we would have to include him in the company of the normal. Richard is normal. Despite the wide band in that spectrum of human behavior reserved for normalcy, there are always pieces of behavior that push one to the limits of normalcy. Mental health is like a balance scale in which one side is never empty. Despite all the pieces of "sick" behavior in one side of the pan, if it is the lighter balance we will not label the individual as sick. Then when one more minor piece of abnormality enters, and the scales tip, we make our diagnosis. Now all of those other ills that we allowed to exist under the general heading of normalcy are re-examined and seen as evidence of sickness. The sick and the healthy will share 90 percent of the same behavior. The same factors that will be explained in one as contributions to sickness may be used in the healthy as explanations of success.

With this in mind, we see the difficulty in discussing whether Richard is normal. We approach his past and personality differently after the fact of his killing Bonnie from the moment before the killing—even though it is an identical past and personality.

When I first moved to New York from the Midwest, my wife, unused to the tabloid form but addicted to human interest stories, would comment with a combination of chagrin, anxiety, and dismay at a typical article in the *New York Post,* headlined "Model Boy Kills Mother." I would then reassure her that *model* boys, by definition, do not kill their mothers, and then inevitably in the following days the newspaper would list the number of juvenile arrests, misdeeds, crimes, and offenses committed by the "model boy."

Richard *was* a model boy, and much was made in his defense of the bizarre and peculiar nature of the fact that, raised in a tough Mexican ghetto area of Los Angeles, he never lost his temper, never got angry, never disobeyed. It was presented in the most ominous terms and was a cornerstone of the structure of his defense. Had these same arguments been used in the same ominous tones in the deliberations of an admissions committee at Yale, it would have been seen as an outrage. Would it have been considered a rational and reasonable discussion in questioning Richard's suitability to become a lawyer?

His mother, Mrs. Linda Ugarte, placed great emphasis on his past and her culpability. Yet she was, by my standards, a good mother—at least I would have said so before the killing. Mrs. Ugarte described having a miscarriage after Richard was born, because: "My husband was always drinking. The bills were never getting paid, and so we moved from a house to another house." She described an incident in which Richard's father came home very drunk as she was putting Richard to bed. The father wanted him to say "sandwich," and Richard was "too little to say sandwich and he was so drunk and got so upset that he pulled his belt up—he was going to hit my son in the face—I put out my hand and instead the belt swung at my arm protecting his little face. And so I told him to get out. I never wanted him to hit my son again." An ugly incident, but I wonder how much uglier than the incidents that could be described in many of the broken homes of America. And it was not this incident that caused Mrs. Ugarte to break up the marriage. Indeed, *she* did not break up the marriage.[5] Richard's father continued to drink, and there continued to be occasional scenes, but Mrs. Ugarte endured them. Evidently they were not sufficiently disturbing for her to seek separation. Finally it was he who came to her and told her he had another woman.

Despite the fact that she was unhappy with his behavior toward their son, she evidently felt that his absence was worse than his presence, because she asked him not to leave and said, "What about Ricky? Ricky needs a father."

So Richard was abandoned by his father. As it turns out, his father had been abandoned by his father at the age of three. Not a happy childhood. Yet not one that we would want to dignify as an absolute determinant or objective predictor of untoward future behavior.

Richard was a bed-wetter until thirteen or fourteen. He suffered from a very "terrible rash when he was about four years old. He'd break out with this rash on his little legs and feet—it would usually be in the summer, sometimes just before school was going to close, he had it real bad on his little legs, and in order to keep him in school I would buy him these high stockings, which they call them knee stockings which only girls wore, he had to put on little sandals—he couldn't wear no shoes. So, I told him if he wanted to keep on going to school he was going to have to keep on wearing those high stockings and these little sandals, and that the kids would probably tease him. So he said he didn't care, because he wanted to go to school, and he wanted to finish school. So when he'd come home I'd ask, 'Did the kids tease you?' and he said, 'Yes, they would make fun of me, but I would turn around and look at them and tell them how would you feel if you had to wear . . .' "[6]

Much is made of the relationship between Richard and his stepfather, and surely this was not good. He would make fun of him; he would "humiliate" him in public; he would shout and rant, according to Richard, but he never hit. How many could say that about their own fathers? Let alone their stepfathers.

Richard's eczema, as it was diagnosed, was self-limiting. Again, we have to value the implication of the condition of an eczema to a child as either exculpation or explaining future behavior. I am not happy with this kind of exculpation to protect the individual. I do not believe it is sufficient to explain the crime. If one is this casual in mobilizing past history to exculpate, are we prepared for the use of such material to evaluate stability; are we prepared to find this evidence sufficient when it may be used *against* the individual.

I do not mean to dismiss these facts or treat them lightly, but hundreds of pages of the testimony are devoted to establishing these traumata of Richard's younger life in contrast with his steadfastness, his model behavior, his failure to lose his temper, and in general his good comportment in an effort to explain and exculpate his killing of Bonnie. I do not feel this data "explains" that behavior. And I question whether data that does explain ought necessarily exculpate.

I recognize that individual items may be insignificant but that when woven together they could have created an impelling force that predetermined his actions. Something of this sort will always be the form of explanation unless we assume strong genetic factors in operation—always a difficult and dangerous tactic (but not necessarily an impossible assumption). So one will always have to seek the roots of current behavior in the past, for that is one of the basic suppositions that we now hold about behavior.

What is important for this argument is to ask whether we want to consider this history as constituting significant evidence. Would this have made a convincing story that would have warned us in advance of the volatility and the fragility of the individual with whom we are dealing? The test of one's conviction about the entire testimony on Richard's past is whether we would have been alarmed if it had been presented without the killing. How impressive a tale of damage and deprivation is it? It is not Oliver Twist. It is not even David Copperfield.

Is there significant pathology?

From the preceding discussion it will be seen that, to a psychoanalyst, there is *always* pathology in *every* person. It will not be considered significant until the sum of the pathology drives the person to a maladaptive position, the disruption of those vital functions we define as normal to the human experience—the ability to perform sexually, to work and be creative, to relate with feeling to other people, and to gain pleasure from one's activities.

Not all of us are capable of doing all of those things to the same degree, which is why the broad definition of normalcy encompasses people who are so different in the quality of their lives. Individual histories as well as cultural differences will alter our capacities. We will never know whether on psychological examination, before the killing, Richard would have ever been deemed to have *significant* pathology. If he had walked into a psychiatrist's office seeking treatment, he would have been considered entitled to it, because we tend to assume the seeking of treatment is a significant index of the need for it.

We often define sickness in terms of a treatment. By that I mean we first discover a "cure" and then invent a disease for it. Presbyopia would certainly never have been considered a disease before there was a corrective lens. It would have been considered, like baldness, graying hair, and loss of the elasticity of the skin, a product of aging.

Richard did not seek treatment himself. He rejected the suggestion when offered. There were many who saw signs that disturbed them—many fewer than now claim to have seen, hindsight being the ultimate method of diagnosis in emotional disorders.

He did not seek treatment, so that test of illness is absent. I think that on balance we would be wiser avoiding labeling people like Richard—without the evidence of the killing—as sick. That intellectual segment of society that would be most likely to wish to exculpate Richard on the basis of the pathology demonstrated in his past would be precisely that segment of the community who would be most outraged if he were declared sick on that same evidence had there been no killing.

Nevertheless, however we would have judged had Richard never killed Bonnie, the fact is that he did kill her, and as soon as he did, the very nature of the action answers the question affirmatively. Yes, there was significant pathology.

What is the nature of his pathology?

My first real sense of Richard—and the most succinct and accurate psychological portrait of him—came from none of the psychiatrists, nor from Sister Ramona, who was too intensely involved to be an objective reporter, but rather from Jack Litman.

—Tell me about Richard.

He's a difficult person to get to know, because I think even at this time he hides his emotions and therefore you have difficulty in making a human contact with him when you discuss critical things in life. You think he's still standing apart looking at himself, giving answers to questions. It's very difficult for a lot of people to get to know him, to like him, to understand him, to appreciate him. I met him very close after the event. I could see the humanity that I knew would be there, just from knowing the type of case that I had read about. But once you get off the issue of the actual event, he still has a very difficult time expressing emotion.

—You feel it is *just* the expression—that he *has* the emotion, that he's really a warm person?

He has always been concerned, and to some extent overly concerned, with feelings of others. He's always wanted to be accepted by other people, but he has learned from a very early age never to express any emotion which is considered unmasculine. He never cries; he doesn't get angry. Richard never, ever expressed anger. Never. And I think he was taught to do that as a young child. By the circumstances of his upbringing. He had a tough time with his biological father. As a young child he developed an extraordinary dependency on his mother. He always wanted to be accepted and was always fearful of rejection. Certainly, in part as a result of that, he never did anything that would incur the wrath of other people—like being mad, crying, being angry, hostile, aggressive. He never did any of those things. He was always a good boy. He was very fearful of rejection, so he always contained his emotions.

In the beginning of this section I avoided the word "diagnosis." I asked instead, What is the nature of his pathology? The purpose of this is twofold. The concept of diagnosis already suggests an illness, and with it suggests that what I am offering represents a more objective or scientific evaluation than any of the others. This is not true. My impressions are no more "proof" of disease than other profiles. There is a traditional psychiatric means of looking at human beings that finds pathology in all of us. I am sure many of the readers find in the description of Richard some elements of themselves. Therefore, being freed of the need to fulfill some definition of a diagnosis that is part of an arbitrary and changeable code, I can discuss Richard more fully and perhaps give a better picture.

The reader has already been presented with a rich set of tapestries woven from the threads of Richard's background by the varying sets of weavers using varying sets of images. My story can be added to the list. I think it is easier to approach pathology from two entirely separate but related points of view: first, character and characteristic modes of adaptation—the defense structure of the person; and then the more dramatic world of psychodynamics.

In the first category we have an essentially withdrawn and rigid personality, flatness of affect, isolation from his own emotions, an "as if" personality, immature sexuality, strong dependence on denial, ideas of reference with a paranoid strain, concreteness.

In the second category are feelings of inadequacy as a male, fear of exposure and public humiliation, fear of confrontation, a special vulnerability to abandonment and rejection by a woman.

It seems reasonable to approach Richard first from the standard language of psychiatry and psychoanalysis and to deal with the structure of his character, his ego and its defenses. This seems to have been sadly neglected in at least the official versions of what is wrong with Richard.

Richard is a loner. Despite the outpouring of support for Richard and the genuine affection with which he is held, Richard never let anyone get close to him, with the possible exception of his mother. I think he allowed himself to get close to Bonnie, but I do not believe, as others have said, that he ever allowed her to get close to him. His unfailing courtesy, decency, and almost compulsion to ingratiate and to please made people feel genuinely attached to him, but the looseness of his own attachments is immediately apparent. Richard himself describes it best. I asked him whether he had made friends in prison. He talked about his "best friend." The quality of his talk did not indicate either true attachment or real affection. I pressed him on this:

—You say you feel close to him.
   Well, closer than any other person here.
—Is it easy for you to make friends?
   No. I honestly don't think it is.
—Why is that?
   I'm not sure. I can be friendly—I'm basically an easygoing person with tolerance towards others—but I don't believe I really make friends that easily.
—Don't you like people?
   I'd have to say yes. It would depend on my surroundings and the kind of people around me. I find it easy to not like a lot of people in here.
—But I have a feeling you didn't make friends easily even outside. Is that true?

Yeah, that's true.
—But you say you like people in general?
Yes. I would say that.

When I questioned him as to why he thought he had so much difficulty since he said that he did like people in general, he said, "I
don't know how much importance you give to childhood. When I
was growing up I didn't have a lot of kids to play with."

When I asked him why that was, the answers again seemed to
have no validity. He went to a school "out of district" for reasons he
was unaware; he lived in a business district "where there were few
children." However he had previously described neighbors next door
with children his own age. He said, "I didn't go to the playground. I
think because I was afraid. I didn't know anybody and I was afraid to
get beat up on."

When I asked about the neighborhood, he said that it was a Mexican-American neighborhood—therefore, he certainly was a member
of the majority ethnic group—that it was not particularly de-
teriorated, not the toughest neighborhood. The reasons he offered
seemed circular and inconclusive. The image that emerged was a
sharply focused one of a child who felt himself alone and isolated.
Whenever I returned to the question of whom he felt close to in his
childhood, the only one that emerged was his mother. The one time
Richard talked to me about what might have been his mother's
inadequacies—and then only because I pressed him to be critical—
he related it to his loneliness as a child.

> I think she was too smothering. I didn't, I don't think I had
> a chance to be a kid. I mentioned the fact of not having a lot of
> kids to play with. It didn't seem to bother her. She didn't en-
> courage me to go to the playground and to go find friends. I
> would stay home and read and watch television. So I substi-
> tuted reading books for playing with other children. Maybe . . .
> maybe I should mention the symbiosis thing that people have
> mentioned. Perhaps her need was to have me near her as well. I
> didn't know any better, so I was just content with whatever she
> wanted.

I asked him specifically about men in his life.

> I only had my uncle Richard, my mother's brother. Three of
> my aunts were married and I liked all of their husbands, who

290

were now my uncles, but I never really felt any rapport. Although one of the uncles had been around the longest and I kind of felt very welcome and very much at home in his house. In fact we lived there for a while when my father left us. But I definitely had no father figure. I didn't really confide in my uncle Richard.

—Did you have a favorite priest?

No. I didn't really get to know priests personally until high school, and even when I got to know them personally, I didn't really take them into confidence. Only after I met Bonnie I remember going back and talking to Father Tim and telling him how I felt.

Whatever age and whatever time period I focused on, I always returned to the question of feeling close and I invariably received a negative response. During a later period when he was discussing his relationship with Peter Fagan, who initially mobilized his defense, we had the following conversation.

—Were you close to Peter when you were at Yale?

Not especially close. But he was a man I could go to if I had a problem—I don't *recall* going to him with a problem—but I *felt* that I could have gone and trusted him and confided in him.

—Actually, were you close to any of them involved with the Church before the incident?

No. I wouldn't say I was close to anybody there. I did work with Sister Ramona on little projects and things but never really sat down and talked with her. I never got to know her as a person.

True and easy involvement with people eluded him. In one poignant episode Richard described real suffering. As things often did with Richard, it came out perversely while I was talking about nightmares. I asked him if he had any nightmares about the killing?

I wouldn't say nightmares. I would say not being able to sleep, just dwelling on the incident, what happened. I wasn't able to eliminate . . . I would let myself dwell on what happened. I would relive the scenes over and over. This would be after I got into bed and was trying to go to sleep. I would just start thinking about what happened and keep myself awake for hours on end, crying. This was while I was with the Brothers.

When that would happen, sometimes I would get up and go downstairs. At that hour almost all the Brothers would be asleep, say after eleven or twelve o'clock. Except for one, Brother Bernard [Barney] and his dog. Barney would usually be watching the TV and I would go downstairs and sit on the couch and grab and hold the dog, Okie. It was my way of getting hugged, holding someone. A lot of times I needed the hugs; needed to be just sitting in the same room with Barney. He would kind of be watching the TV and talk to me, not look back, not embarrass me by seeing I was crying but just talking to me. I would just sit there and hold the dog.

It was particularly moving, one of the rare times that I was emotionally touched by Richard. Surrounded by compassionate and loving people, he turns for comfort not to a human being but to the safety of a dog.

Flatness of affect. Affect is used in psychiatry to mean the prevailing emotional mood. It is that which you observe about a friend when you say, "You seem to be feeling down today." It is the part of our emotions that is apparent to those around us. The "ups" and "downs" define the range of emotionality within which a person traditionally operates. When we talk about a flatness we mean that an individual operates in a narrow range. He seems to have neither high ups nor low downs. It is one of the things that is most noticeable in Richard. He will talk as matter-of-factly about prying a hammer out of the head of his girlfriend with the same level of affect (actually absent) as he would about fossil classification.

It is what has struck many observers of Richard as somewhat unnerving and unsettling. The manner and form are all of unfailing courtesy, politeness, and rectitude. The very formality of the presentation when juxtaposed with the horror of the substance adds its own surrealist quality. We expect people to be defensive, evasive, apologetic, guilty, fake guilty, at least, when they discuss the details of a bludgeoning. The casual delivery that one uses in giving directions for assembling a toy is unnerving. The inappropriateness adds another dimension of horror. The words, "cool," "collected," "calm," are often used to describe Richard. It is not just that he *shows* less curiosity, indignation, embarrassment, and the like—he seems to operate with less, implying that they are not there. The following demonstrates the thinness of his emotional life and emotional responses.

As I understand it he [Richard's father] left when I was two. I remember his bringing me a bicycle for a birthday—probably three or four—my memory is vague. I don't recall. The only image I have is seeing him getting out of the car holding the bicycle.

—He never came to visit you after that?

No.

—Did you ever want to look him up?

No.

—Do you know where he is?

No.

—Do you know if he is alive?

I'm not sure. My mother got a report one day that someone had read that he had died, but it didn't mean anything to me then.

—And you never had any curiosity even as a teenager?

My curiosity was aroused for a while hearing ads on a local jazz station on the radio. One of the disc jockeys was named Jim Herrin which is my father's name.

—It would be a logical job for him, being interested in music.

Perhaps.

—Did you ever write to this "Jim Herrin"?

No. I thought about it. That was during the few weeks or few months I saw his name in the paper, whatever they were advertising. I thought about it. I didn't really have any strong feelings one way or another about it. I said, it's probably not him so . . .

—I don't understand. How could you not have strong feelings? Aren't you a curious guy?

I would say I am. Other than the time I heard of this disc jockey on the radio, I never made any plans or made any attempts to try to contact him, nor did I ask my mother to contact him for me.

—Did you have a feeling she wouldn't have wanted it?

Well, she had mentioned she knew how to get a hold of him if she had to. I guess she would know where he hung out or who he hung out with. If I had pushed her I imagine she would have tried and made the attempt in my behalf if I had asked her . . . but I never did. She wasn't interested at that time.

—Did you have any feelings when the trouble started that he might contact you or come to your aid or write you?

It flashed through my mind. What if he's still alive? What if he heard? And what if he realized I was his son? What kind of reaction would he have? I didn't carry that line of thought very far because, again, I didn't have any really strong feelings like "Gee, I need him now, or I'd like to see him now."

Isolation from his own emotions. Richard simply does not seem to know how he is feeling. "I have no conscious awareness of feeling."

Great emphasis was put on Richard's failure to get angry during his entire lifetime. I do not see this as specifically a problem with control of anger. It is part of a broader inability to touch his own emotions. In the case of anger, it is compounded with an absolute commitment to avoid confrontation. This makes the control of anger a more obvious phenomenon. Anger is a highly visible emotion, so the control of anger would be most evident to the observer, whereas guilt, for example, is a much more internalized emotion and would not make itself manifest either by its presence or its absence. Nevertheless, I found his isolation from his own guilt as eccentric as his isolation from anger. The result of the latter is that it is difficult to ascertain whether Richard is truly remorseful. He describes remorse, but one does not have the sense that he has experienced the emotion. This is not an indication that he takes the killing lightly; it is simply an extension of his failure to consciously experience emotions in general.

Psychoanalysts are used to idiosyncratic responses which are shame- and guilt-producing to one person but not to another. A patient who calmly reveals some rather exotic socially condemned behavior in one area tends to be particularly sensitive in another. But almost all people have great difficulty in talking about masturbation. Richard, not the most sexually liberated individual, had very little difficulty. I asked him about his early masturbation. It dated back to prepubescence at age ten or eleven.

—Did you feel guilty about it?
 No. In the beginning I didn't feel guilt but afterwards when I learned it was considered a sin I would confess it. I would never feel terribly bad, but I would feel compelled to admit it to the priest. I never received any kind of lecture about it. The penance was mild—five or ten of each.
—You went to church regularly?
 Yes.
—But you didn't feel guilt?
 No.

But the best example I can offer of his isolation from his own emotions (and also of his concreteness and his denial) is this small incident that happened during the interview. We were in the process of talking about his docility and why and how he was such an obedient child. His mother never hit him and he was never afraid of her. Yet she had almost complete control over him.

> I used to believe that somehow I intuitively understood her or our plight. That we were alone. That I had to behave myself and not cause any problems. That we didn't have a lot of money and therefore I shouldn't ask for things. That whatever she provided was good enough. I intuitively understood that. Like in the transition when my father left and Emmanuel came on the scene. I must have known somehow that I mustn't be a burden to her. That I should try to help her. I don't remember the time as being so difficult, because I tried to be so good and she would do everything she could for me. She'd take me places. She was always very nice and loving.

As he was telling me this, his eyes began to well with tears. His voice got huskier. I asked him if this was upsetting him and he said, "No."

I said, "But you're all choked up now."

He said, "No, it must be the remnants of a cold I caught earlier in the week."

Incredulous, I persisted. "It's not because you're upset by the subject?"

"No," he replied.

"But your eyes are tearing," I persisted.

"I'm not upset."

He then attempted to continue his narration about this period of his life, but I interrupted him. I said to him that it was apparent to me that he was getting choked up and upset. I indicated that I had no question as to the correctness of my observation, in which case that left only two possibilities: He simply did not know that he was having this emotion, or he knew it but was embarrassed to admit it.

He denied the latter. He said he did not know that he was having any feelings. "If it was there, I didn't know. I thought you said choked up meaning my voice. I didn't feel that my eyes were watering. You detected it then but I didn't feel it."

I found this so difficult to believe, I said, "You simply were not aware of it? Your eyes were more than watery, you were teary." The denial was incredible. So was the concreteness. "Being choked up" is hardly an esoteric expression, and normally has nothing to do with the quality of one's throat. I then asked him if he was sure that he wasn't just embarrassed about showing emotions. He answered, "Not any more. I did at one time. Not now. Especially speaking of the things I've spoken of today. I wouldn't hold anything back or try to cover up anything."

He honestly sees himself as a person who does not withhold emotions. And perhaps he does not. Perhaps we have to take him literally, and that which he feels is that which he expresses. What that indicates is how little of what he actually is feeling comes into his conscious mind or, more tragically, how little he is capable of feeling.

"As if" quality. Some of the most valuable terms out of psychiatry are difficult to translate in simple words understandable to the layman. Once the concept is understood it is immediately recognized. An "as if" quality may actually be a product of the first few character traits I have already described. It means literally that the individual seems to be acting "as if" he is having a good time, is sad or elated, rather than actually experiencing the emotion.

We have known that certain people who either have aberrant emotional responses or are deeply out of touch with their emotions soon learn that their characteristic response pattern is different from those around them, and that the difference often attracts attention. Therefore, they pattern their behavior on that of the majority, learning to act "as if" they were experiencing that which seems to be the prevalent and consistent emotional response to a given situation. It has an "actorish" quality about it that does not ring true. The two presidents Richard Nixon and Jimmy Carter, while different in politics and other qualities of character, seemed to share this "as if" quality, at least to many of us who observed them. They didn't seem to be quite "happy" when they were smiling and their "sincerity" did not register as true and convincing, but more like what actors in a derogatory way call "indication," as if the emotion expressed was not an accidental end product of any internal feeling but was something consciously affected to announce to us a feeling that they thought ought to be appropriate.

Immature sexuality. Richard had no sexual experience beyond masturbation and mild necking during his high school period, despite the fact that he was in a lower economic ghetto district where young men, at least, are generally exposed to sexuality at an earlier age. It may well have been that he was part of the intellectual group which traditionally has a delayed adolescence. Nonetheless, the fact that he had no sexual experience until well into college, despite strong sexual drives, points to a rather immature and inhibited sexuality.

In addition, in his experiences with both Ginny and Bonnie he was more than happy to delay, or avoid, intercourse. This has multiple meanings. Certainly it related to his fear of exposing his sexual and genital inadequacy. This may have been compounded by the fact that Richard was early exposed to pornography. This was not brought out in his discussion with the other psychiatrists. While this again is not necessarily atypical in a ghetto child, he had occasions to view pornographic films, at the flea market, of an extreme and ugly type.

Denial. Denial is a mental mechanism of defense in which the person handles an idea or an impulse that is painful or threatening by simply denying its existence. The most massive case of denial I recall occurred when I was an intern. A woman presented herself in the out-patient clinic of the hospital with a lump in her breast the size of a small grapefruit. I was astounded. Where in God's name had the woman been when the mass was the size of an orange or a plum or even a walnut. I asked her why she had waited so long. She said she came in as soon as she noticed it. She "hadn't noticed the mass." This is denial. Denial is often associated with physical symptoms.

Richard denies constantly. The incident of his tears and his being choked up is certainly an example of denial. In every area, he refuses to acknowledge influences that are unacceptable. When he was discussing his loss of faith in a God of justice and order, I asked him what he thought caused the change.

He said, "Just coming to terms with things."

I then said it obviously related to the mess he was in now.

He flatly denied it. "No, it has to do with what I am studying in school. Evolution, the fossils, paleontology. I got to study a lot about scientific explanations of how things came about and developed. That is why I have the conflict between evolution and Catholicism."

But he had previously told me that he had resolved that conflict between religion and biology by talking to a Catholic priest who explained to him the compatibility between evolution and Catholicism. It was only since the killing and the deterioration of his life in prison that he experienced a loss of faith.

He flatly insisted that it did not have anything to do with the "incident."

At another period when I asked if he had need for psychiatric treatment he answered, "Not until just before the incident. I always told myself and others that I was a person free of problems. I didn't have anything to worry about. Bonnie was one of the people who had picked up the fact that I did, indeed, have problems that probably required some kind of therapy. Any time she would bring it up I would say, 'No, you're wrong.' "

And Bonnie did bring it up and brought it up early and brought it up in relevant spheres. Bonnie was upset that he was so out of touch with his emotions, that some of his behavior seemed inappropriate, and that Richard seemed completely unaware of this.

Ideas of reference. "Ideas of reference" are part of the spectrum of paranoid feelings. All of us have experienced some range of paranoid feelings at some time. Some of us are more susceptible. An idea of reference is a tendency to interpret neutral events as being related to ourselves—but short of the conviction of a delusion. In a frank paranoid delusion, you would be sure that people were talking about you and were saying specific things. An idea of reference is vaguer. It is the sense that people are staring at you or talking about you. It is the assumption, whenever in a public space, that others are looking or noticing. Richard seemed always to assume that others were noticing. Hand-holding was clearly a symbolic announcement to the public at large about how he was feeling about Bonnie and how she was feeling about him. This assumed the public would be noting and commenting that they were or were not holding hands. Richard assumed as much. He mentioned it a half dozen times. He would not hold hands at this point, he would at that point. He wanted people to know. He did not want people to think.

A paranoid trait also shows itself in the peculiarly extended and convoluted reasoning that justifies its assumption. While in Texas, Richard performed miserably in one examination and one oral presentation, both coincident with visits by Bonnie. In discussing this with me, he did two things in tandem that formed a paranoid pattern. First, while denying that he blamed her, he created the im-

pression that somehow or other it was her fault that he was not prepared; and secondly, because of this unconscious assumption that
she had really "done this to him," he tried to protect her reputation.
He did not want anyone to know that Bonnie was visiting him in the
spring for fear they would put "two and two together." What were
the two and two? They would relate her fall visit to his difficulty in
the exam and her spring visit with his failure in an oral presentation.
Somehow the public at large would connect these two events and
condemn Bonnie for being a bad influence on him.

This is ludicrous. No one keeps this kind of track of the coming
and going of another person's friend, particularly since Richard was
careful to isolate himself and Bonnie from the community in Texas,
partly because of his protective scheming. Richard consistently assumed that people noticed more about him than they actually did or
cared to. He then compounded this with the projection of his own
feelings (that Bonnie was responsible for his failures) onto others.
Projection is a basic mechanism of paranoia.

Concreteness. This is the last and perhaps the most startling of
the character traits I detected in Richard. Startling in the sense of
being most extreme. With the preceding traits, the "evidence" may
not seem impressive. We are talking about a subjective evaluation on
the part of the interviewer. Such subjective evaluations are the most
difficult to demonstrate to a third party, yet, ironically, are those in
which a psychiatrist generally has the most confidence. The concreteness, though, was of such severe form as to be demonstrable.

Concreteness is a special kind of literalness. Concrete individuals
have trouble thinking metaphorically. They are often very attractive
people, because they are usually not devious in their thinking, sometimes being incapable of it. They are often easy to "put on." A small
amount of concreteness and literalness is charming because it is honest and naive. A larger amount becomes disturbing.

One example of the concreteness that I have alluded to was the
use of the phrase "choked up." Richard thought it meant his throat.
Perhaps that is not remarkable to a layman. It startled me. When it
occurred two or three times it was sufficient to alert me.

During a discussion about his isolation from his own feelings, he
seemed unfamiliar with even the word "feelings." He had described
discussions with his psychologist in the prison. Never once did they
discuss Richard's feelings. This was peculiar. To most psychiatrists

and psychologists feelings are the most important aspect of treatment.

He constantly balked at the subject of emotion. Whenever I asked him to discuss his feelings, he acted as though I were asking him to speak Chinese. He repeatedly tried to change the subject and I just as stubbornly resisted, insisting that he "stay with his feelings." Nothing availed. Finally, I asked him to simply list all the feelings he was familiar with. There was a long pause of at least one or two minutes and then he said, "Can I ask you what this indicates?"

The answer was that his handling of feelings in general was more important and more interesting than any "meaning" that might be ascribed to a specific feeling. This was again followed by a long pause. He seemed unable to answer, and I said, "Tell me any feeling you have had. Any at all in the last day, week, or month."

He said, "I can't think of any."

—No emotion at all?

That's right. I can't think of any.

—No emotion?

That's right. Why don't you name some?

—Supposing this were a test in school and you were asked to list all the emotions human beings feel. Would you pass the test?

What I would do is ask the person giving the test if I was sure of my definition of feelings.

—You list them and I'll tell you.

Love, hate, pain, fear, pride, joy—am I on the right track?

—Yes. That is exactly it.

Okay.

—Of course, which do you feel a lot?

How about tolerance?

—No, that's not a feeling.

Mostly I feel I'm tolerating my situation. I'm not happy with my situation. I can accept it. I can tolerate it but I'm not happy with it. I wouldn't say that I'm running around depressed or angry or fearful most of the time. I'd eliminate those. My relationship with my friends that write to me and have continued to support me all these years are sources of joy, because they send me good news about what they're doing and I can share in their experiences.

—Do you ever feel envious of them?

[Very long pause.] Not that I can realize, not that I can remember feeling.

—Do you ever feel regret?

Yeah, I would say regret, but not envy. Regret that I couldn't have been sharing this firsthand with these people. But people have asked, have written, should they tell me about things they're doing, would I not feel bad I couldn't be there. I said, "No, I want to hear what you're doing. It would help me remember things I've done and it would help me know what you're doing and thinking; sharing your joy."

—So now you're telling me you feel what you call tolerance. To me that sounds like control of feelings rather than feeling.

No.

—That you're blocking feelings so you won't feel.

Well, I can't say that I'm glad to be here. I'm glad when I hear from my friends, when I can feel that I'm loved and cared about and in turn I can care about my friends and love my friends, but I can't say that I'm happy to be here.

This last description of a feeling is again that which he doesn't feel. "I don't feel happy to be here" I suppose is one way of telling that he feels unhappy.

In the pressure to discuss feelings, Richard's readiness to accept a conspiratorial left-wing view on world affairs came out. It is not unusual in prison. Nonetheless, the language that he uses, considering he is a graduate of an Ivy League school, sounds innocent and may reflect that paranoid trace which is ready to buy conspiracy. It came out of our discussion of whether he was feeling, or aware of feeling, anger any more these days than in the past. I asked him what made him angry these days.

Anything coming out of Washington gets me angry just about. . . . Once I got my eyes opened with what I consider the real things that are going on . . . I started looking at underlying reasons for things . . . analyzing political decisions.

—Is this relatively new for you?

Yes. Politicized and opinionated. I never used to have my own opinions before.

—Like what?

Okay. Like a broad label for a lot of the real strife in the world I would say that the conspiracy of the . . . financial racketeers, the worldwide people that . . . with no allegiance to any one country who make the top-level decisions that affect the economies.

—Do you feel there is a kind of conspiracy establishment?

Yes. And below that worldwide conspiracy I feel that the "military-industrial complex" is a source for a lot of the problems in America. But it's related to the worldwide group financially.

—Would it be fair to say you've become radicalized?

I would say yes, it's the critical assessment of our government and these world financiers who call the shots. I have no proof but things that I've read and, like I say, analyzing things and looking at underlying causes, I draw my own conclusions.

—Would you say you've become a socialist or Marxist?

No. I wouldn't say that. I haven't studied political science or any ideology. I tended to stay away from that. In the past when I tried, it was too heavy—like philosophy and these abstract concepts—I really couldn't grasp it.

—You're not good at abstraction?

No.

This last statement offered me an opportunity to directly pursue the concreteness I had been detecting, as in the simple device of standard psychological testing that had evidently never been used with Richard. I asked him if he had trouble with aphorisms. He was unfamiliar with the word and I gave him some examples and changed the word to metaphor.

—What does it mean when it says, "A rolling stone gathers no moss."

It doesn't have time to establish roots and being in one place long enough to grow moss. That would be my spontaneous answer.

—Let me give you others that you may have heard. Do you know what this means: "A stitch in time saves nine."

I've heard it. You patch something up when it's a small hole and you'll save having to patch up a bigger hole later on. Try to nip the problem in the bud.

—Did you ever hear the expression "An apple never falls far from the tree"? What do you think it means?

Is that a saying? I've never heard it.

—Well, what do you think that would mean?

Well, assuming it was correct, which I believe it is, let's see. I would say it stays close to its home. It grew up in the tree and falls not far from the tree. It stays . . .

—If it were applied to people, what do you think it would mean?

I would think it means people don't stray far from the community where they grew up.

These expressions are hardly part of the common currency of modern language, and it may seem that Richard gave acceptable answers, but he did not give the answer one would normally expect. He could not take the metaphor away from the specific. A stitch in time had to do with stitches. The rolling stone and moss had to do with stones and moss. He could not understand the metaphoric nature of it. There are of course cultural differences, and the rolling stone is an intriguing one. The "proper" answer for this, in my days, implied that people who do not settle down do not prosper, and in that interpretation the moss is a positive, like money, another greenery. In my children's generation—perhaps because of the popularity of the Rolling Stones group, or simply because of the changes in culture—it was the rolling stone that was the good one and the stationary one that was bad. When I've asked people of this generation, I more often than not get an answer that if you keep moving you won't become an old fogey, a mossback. Certainly this is another interpretation of the rolling stone aphorism, but in both it is important to notice that the person quickly leaps from the literal to the figurative meaning of the aphorism.

Since my contact with Richard, I have tested this on children whenever I've met them in groups. Inevitably, as a child approaches pubescence, he moves from the literal to the metaphoric without any prompting from the questioner. Richard could only do this with the apple example and then only when I said, "Forget apples, let's talk about people."

The most dramatic example of his concreteness came in the following:

—What about the expression "People in glass houses shouldn't throw stones"?
  I've heard that one [long pause] The shattering of glass is too obvious an answer, I guess. I don't know.
—What would you think if I said to you, "This is a piece of advice, I want you to remember this. It's an important lesson. People in glass houses should never throw stones." Am I telling you any message of importance?
  [Long pause.] You'd be telling me I should be careful.
—Why?

303

Well, if I live in a glass house, it's fragile and could be easily broken.

—You don't live in a glass house, do you?

No.

—So if you don't live in a glass house would it have any meaning to you?

Yes. It would be a caution.

—What kind of caution?

[Long pause.] Caution in general.

—How does my saying "People in glass houses shouldn't throw stones" differ from my saying "People shouldn't throw stones at other people"?

[Extremely long pause.]

—If I said people shouldn't throw stones at other people would you agree with that?

Yes, I would agree with that.

—What does that sentence mean?

I would immediately apply it to physical aggression. Where one person throws at another. That you should never hurt anyone.

—Would "People in glass houses shouldn't throw stones" mean something different?

Yes.

—What would that mean?

[Pause.] I wouldn't apply it to other people being hurt by the rock. Just . . .

—Why do people in glass houses differ from other people? Nobody should throw stones, should they?

Because they live in a fragile home.

—Supposing I tell you that expression has nothing to do with homes at all. It's just a poetic way of talking. What would it mean if it has nothing to do with houses?

Well, carrying through the idea of fragility . . .

—Like what?

I don't know. It could apply to a relationship or a position, a social position or professional position.

—Like what?

Maybe a professor seeking tenureship shouldn't criticize the college.

—Good! Why not?

It might ruin his chances for tenure.

—Okay. So that in general it has nothing to do with houses, but it means people who are vulnerable shouldn't attack other people. Or you don't think it means that?

I just have a whole new picture of people in glass houses shouldn't throw stones! The first picture I had was someone inside the house throwing rocks. Now I have a picture of that person throwing a rock at someone else in a brick home and the person in a brick home throwing a rock back at the person in the glass house. That's a different picture!

—You've seen more psychiatrists than most men your age. Has anyone asked you this question before?

No.

—Any like that? When you were examined pre-trial?

No. Not that I can remember.

—Let me ask you another thing. Let me try you on another kind of problem. If I said to you that the big hand of the clock is on the eleven and the little hand is on the six. What time is it?

Five minutes to six.

—If the big hand is on the six and the little hand is on the ten and you reverse them what time is it?

Almost ten, ten minutes to six. Are you good at this?

—I'm asking the questions. [Laugh.] Do you think you're good at this?

Yes. But the little hand wouldn't be right on the six.

The last part of the dialogue was my attempt to confirm that what we were dealing with had nothing to do with intelligence. Richard was very rapid in switching hands and thinking abstractly. Indeed, he was better at it than I was. His concreteness helped him. He could tell me that "when the hands were reversed my example would not make sense" and he was right. The little hand would not be right on the six.

What does this all add up to? Richard has significant pathology, deficits that seem to alter his method of thinking and evaluating the events of the world he inhabits. Some would label him "borderline," but I have already suggested the dangers of such labeling. If Richard is to be so stigmatized, he would be joined by a host of people we honor: writers, judges, senators, and psychiatrists. The place that Richard holds on the spectrum from normal to psychotic is securely within the area we must reserve for normalcy. In so doing we recognize both the existence of a spectrum, and the vulnerability of the so-called normal person.

This method of evaluating pathology examines character and perception. It does more than that. It describes the basic thinking methods of a person, his integration, his sense of self and world, and the relationship between the two. In doing all of this, it helps us to analyze his hold on reality. If insanity were the true issue, these and like considerations would be the only factors of importance. But insanity was only one of the issues. Richard's mental status, short of insanity, would determine whether the crime he committed was murder or the killing was done in a condition of extreme emotional disturbance. In order to appreciate the latter, we must evaluate actual events in the present, in terms of the symbolic meanings that may be imposed on them. To do this we must now approach Richard from the method beloved by Dr. Train and Jack Litman, the dynamic approach. His dynamic problems can be arranged into the four clusters I previously described.

His feelings of inadequacy, particularly in the area of masculinity, were visualized by Richard in terms of genital inadequacy. He was convinced that his penis was smaller than normal. Most men have anxiety about penis size, and most men assume that they are smaller than average, which by definition is unlikely. But with Richard it was a fixation. It may have been related to a premature exposure to pornography. Richard had early access to visual film which impressed him, dogs having intercourse with women, and the like. As one can expect from pornography, there were massive close-up frames of male and female genitalia. They are intimidating enough to an adult, let alone to a child.

His eccentric reactions when Ginny was dating another man—remember she had indicated in advance that he was simply to be a useful accommodation for her during the period when she was separated from someone she seriously was interested in—were more in terms of exposure than loss. His fear with Bonnie also heavily involved his terror that he would literally not measure up. In his mind, intercourse would involve an opportunity for Bonnie to measure him phallically against another. And he "knew" he would always lose.

This does not mean that Richard did not fear losing Bonnie for her own sake, but it does mean that the total emphasis of Sister Ramona, Jack Litman, and the psychiatrist on "machismo," the cultural influence of being Hispanic, is not sufficient. Richard had specific, as well as generic, sensitivities about his manhood. He was convinced that he was genitally inadequate, and if Bonnie were to discover this she would reject him. He was as concerned with this, perhaps more so, as with the factor of his betrayal, symbolized by the humiliation of being cuckolded. Even if Bonnie were sexually in-

306

volved with another man, as long as he thought it had not come to a point of penetration he was secure. The betrayal became critical when it confirmed his sense of genital impairment.

Exposure and public humiliation are obviously intertwined with the feelings of inadequacy. It was evident in that most peculiar discussion about not wanting Bonnie "blamed" for his bad performances.

Exposure and public humiliation were the ultimate sins associated with his stepfather. The stepfather provided for Richard and his mother during hard times. He never beat Richard; Richard was not a battered or abused child. The stepfather's crimes were verbal.

—Was there a lot of physical violence?

No. There was only the psychological humiliation. Well, from the age of seven or so I was going to work with him to the Swap on weekends, Saturdays and Sundays. He's not a good person to work for. If I put something on the table wrong I would get yelled at. I would try to defend myself like "I didn't know it was supposed to go there," and I would just make it worse.

My mother would then step in and say, "Leave him alone." "He's trying to learn," and then she would get yelled at. If I packed a box wrong, or put a box in the truck wrong, anything I did wrong, or even if I didn't do anything wrong I'd get yelled at.

Now these Swap Meets are open-air markets held at drive-in theaters, so there was dozens of people around while I was being told what a stupid, no-good bum I am in front of all these people, and then having my mother being told the same thing in front of all these same people and they looking and saying, "Gee, what kind of a family is that?"

That happened constantly from the time we started loading the truck to the time we packed up and went home. It was a constant thing just being humiliated.

He was to come back and repeat these early "humiliations" constantly. When I questioned him as to why there was no affection at all for the only father he really knew, he answered:

The humiliation. Not the yelling, the humiliation. It was the hurt of being made to feel stupid in front of all these people. That just made it that much worse. All these people staring at me. The people that were selling next to us they'd hear it every week, watching me get put down. It was a constant thing, a constant hurt, constant humiliation. And I had no way to defend myself other than my mother intervening. She would shoulder the blame. If he started yelling at me, if she got in the way, he would yell at her, and it would take the heat off me.

Fear of confrontation. Again it is my contention that it is not just the show of anger that bothers Richard, but anger leads to confrontation, and any confrontation was painful for Richard. Think of the pathetic episode of his discovering his "betrayal" by Ginny and his going up to ask for a cup of water. It is Richard at his most peculiar. Confrontation was difficult for him even with someone as indulgent as his mother.

—Did you ever question your mother's decisions?
  Never. I let her make most decisions for me throughout . . . until the time I left high school I let her make most of the decisions for me.
—Did she buy your clothes, tell you to wear a rust or red sweater?
  No. I got my clothes from the flea markets where my mother and stepfather worked. Whatever they happened to be selling at the time and something would fit me, I would take it regardless of style.
—It wasn't important to wear jeans or whatever they wear out there?
  I didn't really . . . I was content with whatever I was given.
—Really content?
  I may not have been content, but I never said anything.
—But that doesn't mean you were content.
  No. I really wasn't much of a demanding person. I would never complain about the food my mother prepared. My stepfather would always complain about the food. I would never complain about the food I was eating.
—Surely there were some things you liked better than others. Beans better than rice, et cetera. They all are just as easy to make. Why wouldn't you say?
  Two reasons. One, the food was never that bad anyway. The other reason was that I would feel sorry because my stepfather was yelling at her and I wouldn't want to increase her troubles. I would take whatever she made and eat it. I was a very noncomplaining person. If I wanted to go somewhere and I knew I was supposed to work at the house, I would ask her and she would ask her husband, my stepfather. I knew if I asked him he

would say no and start yelling. So I would let her ask so he could yell at her. I never . . . She fought my battles.

Confrontation with his stepfather was out of the question.

No. He would get very angry. I could tell by his expression, seething, boiling. At first it might have scared me, but I knew later, even when he was that mad, he wouldn't strike out. I would have to say there was always that fear that when I saw him and saw that rage underneath—real, real rage—there was that fear that maybe he would strike out. He did slap me a few times but not when I was younger. Only when I was around the age of fourteen, fifteen, sixteen. There were maybe three or four occasions when he did—on the side of the face. A couple of times I felt maybe it was justified—that I'd answered back in a smart-alecky way. Another couple of times I felt there was no need for it.

—And what did you do when you felt it was unjustified?

Nothing.

Or with other children. One example is particularly interesting because it emerged in an entirely different context. It was when I was asking him about guilt. In the course of twelve hours of talking to Richard, he described four acts of "violence" in his entire life— throwing a toy shovel at the head of a young friend, smashing in the head of a rattlesnake, bashing the heads of twenty-four laboratory rats, and finally, "the incident" with Bonnie. All of these were claimed to be devoid of anger. Two certainly would seem to be non-confrontational, involving animals rather than people. Richard recalls no other episodes of confrontation. Traditionally, the absence of confrontation is viewed as fear of the other person's response—retaliation in kind or withdrawal of love and approval. But there is an alternative check on expressing anger. The primary fear may be of one's own anger, not the other person's. The most controlled people are often those who visualize loss of control in almost total terms. They fear their own anger because they feel, once released, it will be beyond their management.

The following incident is significant in that light. Richard couples the one memory of attacking another person with his more typical passivity in the face of aggression.

I remember an incident when I was very little, maybe six. I was walking home from school with my mother and I had won a little toy shovel in school for doing something, and as we were walking towards the court where we lived, about three houses down there was a little boy sitting down and playing, and I was walking with my mother, and yet I threw the shovel at him and hit him in the head. He got a little cut. He started crying and his mother came out. I remember feeling guilty for that.

—Was he a friend of yours?

Yeah.

—The shovel was something you were proud of wasn't it?

Yeah.

—Why did you throw it at him?

I have no idea.

—But you remember feeling guilty?

Yeah. I didn't intend to hurt him. I was just walking with my mother and had this shovel as a prize that I had just won in school that day and this kid was sitting on the grass playing and I just threw it and I saw that I had cut him and hurt him and felt guilty.

—Any other incidents of feeling guilty?

That was an aggressive act, by the way, for a six-year-old. At least for me it was. I didn't fight, but I did have a couple of scuffles, no slugging. I was pretty sheltered. One time I was riding my bike and a kid who was smaller than me came by and said, "Let me borrow your bike," and I had never seen him before and I let him take the bike and he didn't come back for a long time. I thought he had stolen it. I just sat there and waited and he came back. I was ten or so.

There were a couple of incidents. At the flea market where I worked with my stepfather there was a period of time where the two of us went alone to one of these markets and we were just selling these household goods and I remember one Saturday he left the stand to go walking around. A couple of tough kids came up to me and said, "Give us the money in your box or you'll be beat up." I gave them some coins. They came back again and I gave them some more and they went away. I thought they would beat me up. I was maybe ten.

In junior high school there were a couple of guys that pushed me around and I didn't fight back. They got tired of pushing me around. They shoved me, not hard.

—So you were never in a fight or fought back?

No.

There is something eerie in close evaluation of the only four acts of violence in Richard's entire life. The shovel thrown as a child at the head of his friend inevitably reminded me of the hammering of

Bonnie's head. But the coincidence extended further. I had asked him specifically how, after he had decided to kill Bonnie, he chose the method.

—You said to yourself, I'm going to kill her. What did you know about killing? Did you ever kill anything?

I killed a snake in Texas—in Mexico—with a shovel. A rattlesnake.

—When was that? What was that like?

Well, the place where we were collecting, my field partner and I, the place in Mexico where we were collecting our rock samples, doing our field work, was kind of desertlike. It was on some people's property. People who owned cattle. They said, "If you ever come across a rattlesnake, kill it. It's better for you to kill it than for us to take a chance it's going to kill one of our cattle or horses. So if you ever have a chance to kill a rattlesnake, kill it."

So one afternoon when Dean, my partner, and I were coming down from the field house, underneath the truck we saw a rattlesnake holed up. It was sitting there under the truck. It didn't rattle, but we saw it. I decided that I was going to try to kill it, so I circled around and got in the cab of the truck and backed the truck up just enough so that one of the wheels had the snake pinned under it. The snake couldn't move. I got back out of the truck. We had a shovel. I got the shovel from the back of the truck. The snake was pinned, and I used the shovel to settle the snake. I brought it down. We left the snake. We didn't cut off the rattles or anything like that or take it back to the house.

Dean was upset. He didn't appreciate my killing the snake, but I reminded him what the rancher had told us. I didn't feel it was wrong to have done it.

—You didn't feel squeamish about it?

No. I felt more frightened that I was so close to a rattlesnake.

—Dean felt somehow or other that you'd done something wrong—killed an innocent creature?

Right. Ordinarily I would have felt the same way. That's why I reminded him about what the ranchers had said. They said to go ahead and kill it even if it's not bothering you. If you have a chance to kill a rattlesnake, kill it.

—So, coming back to your decision to kill Bonnie. What did that mean? How did you visualize it?

The first visualization was both of us lying in bed together with our wrists slashed. We would die together. That was the first thought—the first image that I had of how this could be accomplished. Can I mention another killing? When I was in high school I worked for a summer in a parasitology laboratory. I was given a little project to do—to grow some parasites inside rats, and I had to sacrifice rats to extract the worms from the intestines. I killed. I sacrificed all twenty-four rats in the same day. And I sacrificed, I killed the rats by putting them in an ether jar until they were unconscious and then holding them by the tail—this is how I'd been taught by the other people in the lab—holding them by the tail and swinging the rats against the side of the sink and cracking their skulls on the sink. And I did that to twenty-four rats in the same day. . . . That wasn't a wild—a natural situation. It was a controlled laboratory situation. But I did it.

—Did it bother you at all?

No. I felt I was pursuing a scientific project. I'd been trained how to kill rats, and these professors and scientists told me how it was done. I thought I'd mention it.

I have no idea what the battering of heads may symbolically mean to Richard, but psychoanalysis is reluctant to assume "coincidence" as a possible explanation.

Special vulnerability to abandonment and rejection by a woman. This of course need not be documented, since it threads its way through Richard's entire story. This is a very special primitive dependence where it and survival are linked as in the mind (and actuality) of a child. Richard's dependency has an oral, sucking, and infantile quality. It is formed totally out of his own need and projected onto the relationship. In the beginning, Bonnie was in that sense no different from Ginny. Richard "attached" like a barnacle or a clinging infant. He did feel that his survival in some way depended on his attachment to a woman.

This has been described as "symbiosis" in his relationship with both Ginny and Bonnie, obviously in an attempt to psychodynamically link it to a description of a symbiotic relationship with his mother. But symbiosis by definition operates in both directions. It means that the person who seems to be parasitically involved with another is no more dependent for his survival on her than the one who seems to be the nurturing figure is dependent on him. In true symbiosis the two support each other through a sense of mutual interdependence.

This is ridiculous when applied to Ginny and not much less ridiculous when applied to Bonnie. Yes, Bonnie was more attached to Richard than Ginny was, and felt affection and love toward him. But symbiosis? Hardly. Bonnie was a teenager with the capacity for infatuation and romanticizing that a teenager has. But from the very beginning one senses Bonnie's awareness of other men—her readiness to flirt, her readiness to seek love, and to fall in love when Richard was not around. Her ambivalence toward the relationship with Richard was a secret to only Richard and, perhaps, the Garlands.

Beyond the nature of his dependency was also his rage with women. One of the products of dependency is often rage. If another person is that important to one's life, she has power and control over him. The threat of the withdrawal is enormously corrosive. We resent that power, even though it is we who endow that person with it.

Fantasies of harming someone we love and hate at the same time are not uncommon. "I wish you were dead" is an ubiquitous statement of feeling directed to the parent from the dependent child. But fantasies of ripped vaginas and mutilated breasts are not common. This is the stuff of the unconscious, and when allowed the credence of consciousness suggests a diminution of defenses and a general weakening of the integration of the person. Richard's rage with women was profound and long-standing. One wonders how many others, beyond Bonnie, Richard was destroying when he raised that hammer and brought it crashing down into her skull.

With the dependent child, and those who carry that form of dependence into adult life, abandonment is terrifying because it symbolically means death. The truly dependent cannot survive without those that support them.

A special component of Richard's vulnerability to abandonment by women was the fact that his feelings of identity and worth were firmly fixed and bound to their reflection in the eyes of a woman. To be abandoned was the ultimate judgment of his lack of worth. Here, abandonment also destroyed self-respect and cut to the core of his identity.

Richard's repetitive dreams of childhood are of particular interest. While they are drawn from the same categories as most childhood nightmares—falling, exposure, being chased by animals—they do have some special qualities. Richard did have typical exposure dreams, like being in public places without his pants, nothing remarkable or atypical. His dreams of falling were different. The fear was not in the fall itself, but in being "pressed down into the earth" (smothered?). Then, too, his animal nightmares did not involve the usual "lions and tigers," but a big "hairy" bear.

If a young child is asked to draw first a boy and then a girl, he will usually draw identical stick figures, with a mass of hair added to one to identify it as a girl. A hairy animal is often a figure of a mother to a child. The bear kills with an embrace.

Of course it can only be speculation as to the relationship of Richard's recurrent nightmares of childhood to the dynamics outlined above. The number of scenarios are unlimited, and most can seem attractive and plausible. Consider this doctor's opinion:

> As a boy he never had friends. He was by nature a solitary creature. When such failures of interpersonal reactions occur, a child expects that life will be filled with triumph and be free of difficulties, that everything will be done for him by others, while he is striving to surpass others.
>
> Hence for a time the person may be extremely successful . . . Sooner or later, especially when confronted by the problems of social life, of occupation, and of love, such a person gains the impression that the environment is constantly attacking him. Not comprehending the situation, he experiences this as a repeated insult, is subjected to a series of shocks until finally his resistance is completely broken down.
>
> He is not prepared for a solution of his problems that would require that he give up his asocial interest in himself and that he cooperate and contribute even when conditions are difficult and unfavorable to himself. Therefore, he cuts off his relationships to the world reality and, directed solely by his style of life, is guided by the fancies and imaginings of his childhood.

This is not another evaluation of Richard. It is an analysis of the breakdown of the famed dancer Waslaw Nijinsky, written in 1936, by the distinguished Dr. Alfred Adler.[7] It is as reasonable a dynamic summary of Richard's behavior as mine or that of Dr. Train.

And that is precisely the problem. It is not that Train is wrong or that I am wrong or that Adler is wrong. It is that the nature of such a description is usually broad enough to include the healthy as well as the sick, the successful as well as the defeated. This kind of explanation—whether derived from character traits or from a psychodynamic background—can only be an adjunct in understanding an event after the fact. It can never predict the development of the event, nor is it even sufficient to causally explain the event. It is a descriptive adjunct.

My view of Richard is different from the others because it is shaped by the perspective of a different viewer. Is it a truer one? I do not know. It has the advantage of having been conceived by an observer with no pressure to conform to either side of the argument.

The same facts are available to all, except that the facts are almost unlimited, and different viewers will preselect those that are consonant with what their training and experience have told them to be crucial factors in shaping personality. Since each psychiatrist's training and experience differ somewhat, the events he looks for will be different, and therefore the incidents he discovers will differ. The design he makes with these raw materials will be influenced by his purposes. If his purposes are the pursuit of truth, there will still be his internal biases to contend with. If his purposes are, however, to make a case, almost inevitably he will "see" things that are supportive of the case. No one wants to consider himself a gun for hire, but every psychiatrist will simply find a way of seeing those things that conform to that which makes the life of the defense or prosecutor easy. They will rationalize away nonconforming evidence. Those that have become pros in the field are evidently artful dodgers in this particular device. Some, like Rubenstein, are obviously too discomfited to continue in a courtroom career.

Do we know Richard any better for having examined this kind of material as distinguished from simply observing his behavior? I think we do. I think inevitably a psychological and psychoanalytic point of view adds another dimension toward our understanding of a human being. It is not necessarily a truer picture—simply a different one.[8] To probe the unconscious of an individual and then to ignore his behavior is to distort the real truth as much as to do the opposite. A person may not always be what he seems, but what he seems to be is always a significant part of what he is. We would not want to substitute the X ray of Grandpa's head for the portrait that hangs above the mantel. But each dimension and each approach gives us a fuller understanding of a person's purposes and motivation.

Does this understanding in a new way help us in determining the disposition of this case? It is my contention that it does not.

It is ridiculous to offer dynamic factors in an insanity defense. They can never exculpate. Insanity must be defined more narrowly, and more specifically, and in the long run probably within the constricted confines of the old M'Naghten rules.

As a mitigation, dynamic factors can be of limited use. In seeking evidence of extreme emotional disturbance, they can offer a framework in which to examine the behavior in order to judge whether it warrants a mitigation of punishment. Psychodynamics may only serve the purpose of allowing the introduction of information that would technically not otherwise have been admissible and thereby permit the jury to use its emotions rather than its rationality in coming to a decision. I am not sure that is unwise; I am not sure that I do not trust emotionality as well as rationality.

As a psychoanalyst, I am trained in a tradition that places the individual at the center of things, and that, too, is a problem. If one thinks in terms of the individual, a warp will be introduced into the concept of justice that will distort the very purposes of justice. It is not just that we are forced into a single perspective rather than a collective one—which is bad enough—but it will always be the same individual whose perspective is dominant. It is only a criminal whose sensitivities, whose unconscious, whose hopes and ambitions and aspirations will be explored. Never the victim.

A system of justice cannot forget Bonnie Garland, because it was designed originally to protect her and to serve her needs. It was designed to serve the purposes of the law-abiding, not the offender.

A system of justice must consider the victim even though she can no longer be helped, in order to protect others who also may become victims and unhelpable. To be beyond help must not mean to be beyond thought or compassion. Otherwise we lose the focus of the very intentions of our laws. And justice demands more. A system of justice must speak to righteousness. It must not just defend the good; it must proclaim the good. It must announce our moral purposes.

9

WHERE IS JUSTICE?

In one impassioned moment in his closing argument, Jack Litman reminded the jury that Richard was "entitled to your impartial fairness, and he is entitled to justice." In the end Litman was to feel that Richard received neither. At this point Richard shares his feeling. Two separate words, "equity" and "justice," are often used interchangeably and are presented as synonyms for each other in the dictionary. The two related concepts must be distinguished. They have a different feeling, and for purposes of clarity can be assigned separate meanings.

Equity, as distinct from justice, refers to a form of fairness and impartiality. For most of us, righteous indignation and moral outrage are first sensed in that frustrating and ubiquitous experience of early childhood when some damnable manipulative sibling gets off whistle-clean for the same infraction for which we were "always" made to pay the full measure. "It's not fair!" vibrates with a moral fervor and conviction that "I'm sorry" rarely does. Even within the confines of the benevolent and loving family situation, it is a humiliating and alienating experience, and if indeed true, and repeated sufficiently, can destroy that sense of identity necessary for our reasonable relationships with other people. If we violate a sense of fairness, we undermine that concept of order necessary for communal living. What is true in the family is equally true in the less benevolent structures of authority. Equity is susceptible to some objective measurement; we can compare the way one person is dealt with under law with others who have committed like offenses and measure the standards of judgment and distributions of punishment. In that sense we can decide whether he was dealt with equitably, i.e., in an impartial manner.

"Justice" refers to the broader social concept. Like most of the supremely important things in life, it resists measurement and titration. Justice refers to the quality of being right, to righteousness and the rightness of things. Of course an important ingredient of justice is the sense of impartiality and fairness. But people may be treated equitably in an unjust society. With equity we will compare an individual's treatment under law. With justice we will question the rightness of the law. In justice we occupy both the legal and moral territories.

If all homicides were punishable by death—whether the result of criminal intent, psychosis, drunken driving, or self-defense—there would be an absolute and impartial equality as to disposition. It would be a morally blind society that could not distinguish among those homicides—and as such cruelly unjust. The legislative code which introduced extreme emotional disturbance into the laws of homicide was an attempt to introduce a more humane concept of justice or, at least, a more relative sense of right and wrong than had previously existed in our criminal law.

In an earlier era, when there was more confidence in our capacity to define right and wrong, individual responsibility was assumed, and each person was answerable for his actions. It was an objective standard. Unless you were truly "insane," the presence or absence of mental illness was of little interest to the courts. As Justice Holmes said, "Men who are not insane nor idiotic [are expected] to control their evil passions or violent tempers or brutal instincts, and if they do not do so, it is their own fault."[1]

Your mental anguish and distress were as irrelevant as your physical comforts or the state of your liver. While said with irony and at its most extreme, the statement of the judge in Samuel Butler's *Erewhon* is a more dramatic version of sentiments that were shared by Justice Holmes.

"You may say that it is not your fault. The answer is ready enough at hand, and it amounts to this—that if you had been born of healthy and well-to-do parents, and been well taken care of when you were a child, you would never have offended against the laws of your country, nor found yourself in your present disgraceful position. If you tell me that you had no hand in your parentage and education, and that it is therefore unjust to lay these things to your charge, I answer that whether your being in a consumption [tuberculosis] is your fault or no, it is a fault in you, and it is my duty to see that against such faults as this the commonwealth shall be protected. You may say that it is your misfortune to be criminal; I answer that it is your crime to be unfortunate."[2]

In the twentieth century, with the decline in the power of the religious vision and our abandonment of religious values, we began to approach questions of right and wrong sociologically and psychologically. Rules of conduct became fudged by consideration of the events that led up to the conduct: the state of mind of the individual, his perceptions of right or wrong. This relativism began to erode previously held sets of absolute principles. We began to individualize our concepts of justice, and in so doing we inevitably made them more subjective and relative.

"Whatever became of sin?" Dr. Karl Menninger eventually asked.

We were entering a more understanding age, and it was beguiling to assume that greater understanding would somehow or other bring more justice. In certain areas it inevitably did. But often increments of individualization, which when considered independently seemed steps in the direction of a more humane and just society, in accretion and aggregation led to a greater injustice. This will not be apparent if we only examine the individual case. Each gain for the individual must be weighed for its impact on the common good. This is precisely what remains to be explored in the story of Bonnie and Richard—and applied in principle to our society as a whole.

Society has established a hierarchy of crimes. We indicate our revulsion for the crime and the importance with which we consider it by the degree of punishment imposed. We do not send people to prison for jay walking, and when some aberrant judge attempts to do so, his action is treated with the contempt it deserves. Recently a zealous and publicity-hungry prosecutor charged the parents and physician of a set of hopelessly deformed Siamese twins with murder for their decision not to try to sustain the life of those children. The community reacted with contempt—even those within the community who may have felt morally outraged at the decision of the parents. We reserve the charge of murder for a special kind of killing or induction of death. We distinguish among homicides. We recognize this action of the parents as quite different from that of the professional criminal who gratuitously shoots to death the storekeeper he has just robbed.

Consider the following theoretical case: A man has just seen his wife beaten to death resisting a robbery in their store. Since this is a theoretical case, rather than the real world, the police arrive in time to apprehend the criminal. As the body of the man's dead wife is being removed he notices the assailant being led away by the police, and in a rage he grabs a knife and stabs his wife's killer. He has committed a homicide with precisely the same degree of intention and calculation as the killer of his wife. Most of us, however, draw a moral distinction between the acts of these two men. Some of us would even exculpate the action of the bereaved widower, but even those who would not, would want to introduce into their judgment some concept of his mental state at the time of his act. Independent of whether he was insane or not, we would want to consider the provocation for the act.

It is through this desire to introduce provocation that a relativistic and subjective approach to mental illness has been introduced into the law. "The irresistible impulse" was one such attempt. It offended many scholars of jurisprudence because it seemed to elevate the impulsive nature of the act over the provocation for action. Would it have been essentially different if the grieving husband, instead of picking up a knife that happened to be at hand, had gone back to his closet, taken a chair, retrieved a gun hidden on a top shelf, loaded it, walked out, and shot the man? Perhaps it would have made a difference to some observers, but even then they might still acknowledge a difference between the action of the nonimpulsive husband and the "cold-blooded" killer. The very term "cold-blooded" implies a lack of provocation and therefore a seeming lack of justification. It was for this humanizing reason that the concept "extreme emotional disturbance" was introduced into the law of New York State to mitigate a charge of murder and convert it into a charge of manslaughter. This was not simply a matter of relabeling. It reduced the crime from a Class A felony to a Class B felony, where the range of discretionary punishments allowed the judge were different. Remember that while the judge has discretion in sentencing it is always within the maximum and minimum range set by law. He is bound by the collective judgment of the people. It is the legislature that decides the seriousness of crime and sets the limits of punishment available to the judge.

The example just given was designed to show the origin and intention of "extreme emotional disturbance." The emotional disturbance must be something with which the general public can empathize. Is that what a reasonable person—and of course this means you and I—would have done at the time? Remember Jack Litman saying, If someone does not like your shoes that is not a provocation. In order for extreme emotional disturbance to be a mitigating factor, the provocation must be sufficiently outrageous for all of us to identify with it. If we stuck to this very clear interpretation of provocation the questions and statements about Richard's particular susceptibility—his rejection, his illegitimacy, his hypersensitivity to abandonment by women—all would have been irrelevant. We simply would have examined the provocation as it *was*, not as it was perceived by him. And we would ask whether we thought rejection by one's lover was sufficient provocation for killing to warrant our compassion. And whether we wished to establish that as a precedent in law. Was Richard's response a reasonable one? Not reasonable given Richard's background, but reasonable in our own objective sense of what is, or ought be, provocation.

This original intention became lost in practice. We began to introduce the *criminal's perception* of what happened into our concept of provocation. That kind of data, if carried to extreme, can certainly and logically allow the exculpation of some people whose taste in shoes was questioned.

The Model Penal Code attempted to strike a compromise position between the subjective and objective evaluation of provocation, and it created a muddle. It asked that reasonableness be considered from the viewpoint of the actor in the situation, and under the circumstances as he *believed them to be*. Evidently realizing that this opened Pandora's box to its widest, it hedged in the specific by the seriousness of the examples selected: "If you were blind or distraught with grief." "If you were experiencing an unanticipated reaction to a therapeutic drug."

Even under modifications of the Model Penal Code it is questionable whether Richard's background would have been seen as significantly altering the circumstances "as he believed them to be," to the degree that demands mitigation. The Model Penal Code emphasizes drugs, physical disability, and severe life-wrenching situations, i.e., the death of a child, the death of a wife. Its intentions normally would not be stretched to rejection by a college sweetheart. Nonetheless the jury is free to act with its emotions, and it certainly has a right to see Richard in a more compassionate light than a hired killer, and this is what it did. Where then is the inequity? Litman would say in the sentencing.

The Garlands saw the decision of the jury as an inequity, and in the opposite direction. Certainly the average killer of his girlfriend does not get the services of Jack Litman or the support of a religious community such as that which Richard was offered. A sufficient percentage of killers are of the Catholic faith that it would tax even the extensive resources of time, money, and compassion of an organization like the Catholic Church. It was the fact that he was from Yale, young, a member of a minority group but still identifiable as "one of us," attractive, and newsworthy that contributed to the fact that he was treated differently from others.

Richard *was* treated differently. The difference was viewed as special privilege by the Garlands and as special punishment by Richard's friends.

The fact is, had Richard stayed in the barrio of Los Angeles, as Paul Garland once proposed that we consider, he would probably have received a *lesser* sentence. A bargain would have been struck between his Legal Aid counsel and the harried Prosecuting Attorney of Los Angeles County. Richard would have pled guilty to a lesser charge of manslaughter in agreement for a sentence of a few years. Depending on how busy the prosecutor's office was, and how ready they were to bargain, the defense lawyers could have negotiated lesser and lesser sentences. Many killers have bargained their way out of a felony charge into a misdemeanor, and some have served no time in prison at all, either because of age, the difficulty in presenting the case, or simply the mechanics of an overburdened jurisdiction.

It is an assumption often repeated by those who should know better that blacks and other minorities suffer discrimination in sentencing in homicides. It is an assumption that is accepted without question by the intellectual community because it seems consistent with the knowledge of prejudice in our society. In actuality it is not true and has not been true for years.

As far back as 1964 one respected sociologist reported that "Negro offenders against Negro victim crimes resulted in the mildest penalties, with half as many penitentiary sentences and four times as many probations as either the Negro-White or a White-White offender, who got approximately the same degree of punishment for the different possible penalties."[3]

That this may indicate a different kind of bias is of course true. It may imply that the black lives lost are valued less than the white lives lost, although, if so, it seems to imply that they are valued less by black juries as well as white juries. Even if it is evidence of the racism persistent in our society, it does not point to inequity in that direction which is so often assumed and so often cited by those who ought to know better. More likely, it is the product of makeshift justice in high-density crime areas.

Plea bargaining is both inequitable and in a more profound sense unjust. It is inequitable because the chance of where a crime was committed will arbitrarily determine what will happen to the criminal, even while under the jurisdiction of the same state laws. In the Bronx, Brooklyn, and Manhattan the courts would be choked with felons if everyone who committed a felony were charged correctly. So, many felonies are traded away to become misdemeanors. It is the knowledge of this that repels much of the law-abiding population in larger cities. On the other hand, if one is convicted of a felony in a low-crime area, one may see it as inequitable. Richard and his lawyer were prepared to plead guilty to manslaughter, a plea that would have been accepted ten miles south of Scarsdale. In Westchester County there is little plea bargaining, for there is little homicide; and, in addition, this case was a dramatic one. There is profit for all in prosecuting such cases.

At the Association of American Trial Lawyers (AATL) Convention held in San Francisco on July 29–30, 1981, this was acknowledged. One criminal lawyer said that he advised his clients to "drag the body across the border" into a district that was more amenable to a defense. The cynicism of these trial lawyers—as distinguished from the typical professional meeting—made their convention a newsworthy event. Lawyers talked with joy of getting the most flagrantly guilty acquitted and shared devices one could use. As one said, "When you have that rare person, the innocent client, anything goes." Richard (Racehorse) Haynes went so far as to say, "It is better not to know whether your client is planning to commit crimes in the future, because the attorney-client privilege does not carry over into discussion of prospective criminal conduct." If the client seems on the verge of confiding some criminal plan, Mr. Haynes suggested, "I don't want to hear it."

Many of us reading that in *The New York Times,* Saturday, August 1, 1981, would wonder whether the lawyer ought not tell his client not to contemplate committing future crimes. It would seem he might be serving his client better that way. He would certainly be serving society better.

The public is offended by plea bargaining, and they clearly have a right to be. While it is no violation of the law, it is a flagrant violation of the will of the people. The legislature defines the code of conduct and imposes criminal sanctions that express the moral consensus of that which is evil or intolerable. The degree of seriousness is fixed by definition, and the range of permissible punishment is established. The law allows for special cases by granting discretion and mitigation all down the line. But to call that which is known to be one thing another thing for the pragmatic convenience of the court is a way of evading the legal definition of the crime and the public will. Bargaining in terms of the sentence is possibly defensible, but to bargain in terms of charge is an outrage against the public sensibility and will inevitably produce the kind of public backlash which we are now seeing.

If plea bargaining continues in crowded jurisdictions at the current level, it may force prescribed punishments to go even higher, beyond that which the public might otherwise feel just. They will build into the law an erosion factor to allow for the expected dilution of punishment. This will inevitably increase the inequity between the disposal of a crime in a busy jurisdiction and one in a leisurely county.

Litman felt that Richard had been treated unfairly *and* unjustly. "He was treated unjustly by the manner in which he was tried and the way sentence was imposed." He then went beyond that, saying it was unjust that he was in prison at all at that point, considering what rejection by Bonnie had meant to Richard and also that it was a first offense.

Justice often requires inequity. Two drunken husbands decide to "teach their wives a lesson." Both sock their wives in the jaw. One snaps the neck and kills her, the second "merely" breaks her jaw. The former is likely to spend a few years in jail for manslaughter (unless it is a *very* busy jurisdiction), and the latter is unlikely to be arrested at all.

Both men did the same thing, with the same intention, in the same level of clouded judgment. It is "unfair" that they be treated differently for the same act and in the same state of mind. But a woman is dead in one case. If it is the first man's "misfortune" that his wife died, as Samuel Butler said, "I answer that it is your crime to be unfortunate." Society cannot countenance the death of an innocent. I do not think we should tolerate the beating of a helpless person by a bully either, but others may feel differently, and society in this case may weigh differently the damage to its values here against concern and compassion for the individual attacker. He may have been depressed by unemployment, frustrated sexually, insecure in his manhood by past intimidation by other women (mother, older sister, former wife), and truly loving of the wife whose jaw he broke.

But for certain crimes, punishment is required. To be "merciful to the cruel is to be indifferent to the good." A life was lost, an innocent life, and society must indicate the precious nature of that loss.

It may be that the man who killed his wife did not *deserve* punishment. That is not the point. We—the collective we—require it. What may seem unfair when considering the criminal in splendid psychological isolation may be essential in a sociological concept of justice.

Richard, at this point, has joined the group that seems less disturbed by what he did than by that which was done to him. He now seems more indignant than contrite.

> I feel the sentence was excessive.
> —Let's talk about that a little.
> Well, I feel that way now and after the first years. The judge had gone overboard. Again, at the very beginning, they could have done anything to me and I would have accepted it.
> —Why was that?
> Because I felt the need to be punished for what happened.

325

That was right after my arrest, while I was sitting there in the police station and I could foresee being locked in a room and the key being thrown away for ever and ever, and no one ever hearing from me again. But that was not paramount to me at the time. What I was concerned about was hearing the reports on Bonnie's condition. And getting my hopes up that she would recover, survive and recover. The reports about her survival—she was alive all that day and the chief at Coxsackie had given me the reports from the hospital that she was alive, she might have some permanent damage but she was alive and that's what was carrying me.

—If I remember when that report came in your response was totally different. You were totally disbelieving. You said, "It's impossible, it can't be. Her head split open like a watermelon." I don't recall any expression of joy or relief.

Right. They took portions of my statements. The feeling behind that statement was that I can't believe that she didn't die, and I'm so *glad* that she didn't die. I mean, having these vivid recollections of what happened it was unbelievable to me that she didn't die, but I was hoping that she would recover.

—At any rate, you say that at that time you felt any sentence would have seemed equitable?

Yes.

—What happened as time went on?

Considering all the factors that I feel the judge should have considered: prior history of arrest, my personality background, my capacity for a productive life in society—you know, those kinds of things—I don't think he took those into consideration. He looked at the crime itself and responded to a lot of public pressure or maybe his own personal feelings, I don't know. I'm not going to accuse him of anything, but I was given the maximum sentence. This being my first arrest and considering the circumstances, I don't think I should have been given eight to twenty-five years.

—What do you think would have been a fair sentence?

Well, after a year or two in prison, I felt that was enough. At the time of the sentencing I don't think I could have said, Well, two years will be enough to repay society, or four years. After my first few months I didn't think that I had served enough time. I didn't think, "Gee, I'm tired of prison." But after a certain amount of time I did start feeling that I've waited long—that I've had enough. This is, they shouldn't require more of me. If I've given them so many months or so many years, I don't know what else I can do or what they want of me. There's no purpose to this. I felt that I had repaid adequately already.

—How would you answer the kind of person who says, for Bonnie, it's her whole life; for you it's eight years. What's eight years compared to the more years that she might have had?

I can't deny that it's grossly unfair to Bonnie but there's nothing I can do about it.... She's gone—I can't bring her back. I would rather that she had survived as a complete person, but she didn't. I'm not, again, I'm not saying that I shouldn't have been punished, but the punishment I feel is excessive. I feel I have five more years to go, and I feel that's just too much. There's no . . . I don't see any purpose in it. It's sad what happened, but it's even sadder to waste another life. I feel I'm being wasted in here.

—But what about the people who say, Look, if you got two years, then someone who robs should get only two days. You know, the idea of commensurate punishment. If it is a very serious crime it has to be a very serious punishment. Are you saying two years of prison is a very serious punishment considering what you did?

For me, yes.

Albert Camus might have felt differently. Even while defending the concept of a just assassination, he clearly indicated that what lent justice to the assassins' actions was their readiness to die for the crime. Not simply to be punished, but to die for it. In discussing his purposes in writing the play *The Just Assassins*, he stated:

> I wanted to show that action itself had limits. There is no good in just action but what recognizes those limits and, if it must go beyond them, at least accepts death. Our world of today seems loathsome for the very reason that it is made by men who grant themselves the right to go beyond those limits, and first of all to kill others without dying themselves.[4]

Sister Ramona also feels that an injustice has been done to Richard and he has suffered enough, as do most of the people still nobly struggling on Richard's behalf. Obviously for all of these people there exists a specific concept of justice that only looks forward; it is concerned with what purpose would be served by punishment in the future. It starts with the death of the victim, and looks forward from there. This is an incomplete and imperfect consideration of the complexity of the concept of justice. A worthy concept of justice would demand that we look backward as well as forward. This concept of justice would require a respectful consideration of punishment.

While some might question the value of punishment, few would argue that the state does not have a right to punish. We exist as a government under laws. The authority of those laws is established by announcing and enforcing a set of punishments, the price that must be paid, that will be visited upon those who violate them. In modern times the chief justification for punishment has been a utilitarian one: what measurable utility will arise by inflicting this punishment, usually visualized in its potential deterrent effect on future crime.

There are five traditional reasons for incarcerating a criminal: the protection of society; specific deterrence; general deterrence; rehabilitation; and retribution, vengeance, deserts, et al. Punishment, until very recent times, has specifically been seen as serving the purpose of deterrence, both specific and general. Specific deterrence simply means that when you fail to pay your income tax, if you are forced to spend three months in jail you will be less likely to cheat on your income tax in the future. The action will have a specific effect on you.

General deterrence refers to the influence your imprisonment will have on society at large. If a respectable person like you can be made to go to jail, it is a warning to a respectable person like myself that I too can suffer that terrible humiliation. General deterrence is a fundamental concept in controlling behavior; and while there was a time when it was fashionable to think that nothing was deterred by punishment, common sense indicates that this is sheer nonsense. If not common sense then the diminution of drunken driving in the Scandinavian countries, where a severe and absolute punishment based on the fact of alcoholic content in the blood—as distinguished from intention, motive, purposes, or rationalization—has been dramatically effective in reducing drunken driving. Common sense in raising children, in the knowledge of human motivation, indicates that while punishment is not the only, and perhaps not the best, method of influencing behavior, it certainly works.

The deterrent value of punishment has been questioned most in crimes of violence. Here again the blithe assumption that it does not work is constantly made because despite incarceration crime continues. Obviously the crime rate is multiply determined. In order to truly state that punishment does not work, we would have to conceive a society where there is no punishment for assault, manslaughter, or homicide.

To most of us, punishment seems the *only* thing that works; and while it may not work with a grand degree of efficiency, it works.

The utilitarian argument is purely future-oriented. It is not concerned with the crime that has been done but the crimes that might be done. Punishment of the individual is justified only in terms of its relationship to other crimes. It is in this respect that Dr. Karl Menninger wrote of *The Crime of Punishment*. It was his firm conviction that punishment of criminals would not cure them of their criminal habit and his like-minded conviction that it did not have a general deterrent effect on potential future criminals that led him to see it as a self-defeating exercise. He combined his pessimism about punishment with a grand optimism about the potential for rehabilitation and treatment.

In none of the foregoing discussion is there any justification remotely resembling retribution or vengeance. I would hope that deterrence works, but even if it does not—particularly when it does not—I am prepared to say, "I don't care what good it may or may not serve. You deserve to be punished." That attitude has been seen as immature and beneath the dignity of a just state. While the modern state did not turn the other cheek, one would have to search far and long to find any defense for arguments that say, The state has a right to punish because it is just to do so; it feels good to do so; a sense of fairness requires it. In other words, whether it helps the criminal or not, it makes me (the state) and the general public feel better and more secure. That would have been rejected as emotional, inefficient, and nonpragmatic in this age of scientific understanding of behavior—beneath the dignity of the collective self.

It therefore came as somewhat of a shock to the intellectual community when an essentially left-of-center group, the Goodell Committee, sponsored by an essentially liberal-radical pair of foundations (the Field Foundation and the New World Foundation) published its report asking for re-evaluation of the concept of just deserts.[5]

One of the unpredicted products of this commission was an articulated defense of punishment, independent of its value as a deterrent. The arguments in defense of the independent concept of punishment are multiple—some of them still clinging to a strongly utilitarian rationale. They have in common that they extend the legitimacy of punishment beyond its deterrent effect, and the justification begins and ends with the incident being punished, not some other incidents. These arguments are prepared to look backward as well as forward.

One of the earliest arguments for retribution was that it served as an alternative to personal vengeance. It was a means of placing restraint and control on those who identified with and loved the victim. Vengeance, even when expressed by the most aggrieved of individuals, seems ugly and unattractive. Our compassion for the loss of others is a short-term and ephemeral phenomenon. We comfort our friend in the immediate period of mourning and then somehow or other we become impatient with him if he does not "get on" with his life. We are offended by the self-indulgence and the self-involvement. After all, the husband, daughter, wife, brother, died a "good six months ago." The sustaining loss to the individual involved in the death, even a nontraumatic one, is never totally appreciated by one who has not been in that position. Time does not heal all wounds, and the amount of time needed to heal the majority of serious wounds is well beyond that which the unwounded could ever anticipate.

I have heard more criticism of the Garlands over two and a half years of research than I have of Richard Herrin. In all honesty, they are not easy people to relate to. I do not know how this would have been before the fact—what their "premorbid personality" might have been. Suspicious, angry, resentful, conspiratorial in their view of the world around them and its indifference to them, they invite rejection and they get it. One has the feeling that they constantly feel betrayed, but it is a known fact that a constant feeling of betrayal breeds betrayal. It is the nature of a persecutory view of life. People sense it, and they comply with your image of the way the world operates.

This was especially true in the Yale community. Paul Garland, in hurt anger, severed all of his ties with the Yale community.

In his letter of resignation publicly released to the newspapers, he wrote:

As you know, our daughter Bonnie, who would have been Yale, '78, was hammered to death in the middle of the night as she slept, by Richard Herrin, Yale '75. He has confessed in writing to this horrible crime and has been indicted.

My expectation from the Yale community was that it would cry out against this brutal act and demand justice be done. What has happened, incredibly, is largely to the contrary. Yale people, past and present, have rushed to the aid and support of the killer, in an organized and systematic manner, and have succeeded in clothing him with the aura of Yale sponsorship and support, as well as that of the Catholic Church.

While we seem to live in an increasingly insensitive society, I cannot believe either the University or the Church really stands for the kind of reckless and irresponsible behavior involved.

Few, if any, of the Yale community have stepped forward to denounce the sponsorship given to the killer. Those who have stepped forward seem to have been able to block out the horrible crime involved and to write the type of letters which a candidate for a job or college might receive.

Surely a murder is an occasion for moral outrage and not for attestations of the fine character of the confessed killer, nor is it occasion for standing silent lest one be viewed as "taking sides."

In the face of this cruel, thoughtless, and dishonorable behavior by members of the Yale community, I am overwhelmed. They do not represent the concern for God, country and Yale which has meant so much to me for so many years.

These people have lent themselves to a cause which in my opinion is lacking in any justification: the freeing of a brutal confessed killer without psychiatric examination, with bland assumption as to what he will do next, the disregard of the impact upon our family of what the killer's being free represents, and of the risk to society that he may represent, as just too much to condone or forgive.

I never could have imagined Yale people would do such a thing. Since they have, I add the loss of my college to the loss of my daughter.

I talked to a number of Yale faculty members about Mr. Garland's action. One of them said to me:

> It's simple to call Paul Garland unreasonable, because you're not the one involved. I have daughters of my own, so heaven knows how I would have reacted. Maybe it could have flipped me just the way it seems to have flipped him. Quite ob-

viously the way he behaved once the terrible shock of the thing should have been passed was irrational. He still is irrational. He will always be irrational about this situation. He's never going to change. I'm not going to blame him. I just feel sorry for him, because I think he's made it difficult for everyone around him.

In the view of another professor:

I must say at the time I thought it was pretty incredible that anyone would go to these lengths to protect a confessed murderer. I just never will understand that! And, of course, that's what Paul Garland felt. I don't blame him a bit. I just blame the way he acted beyond the point that I thought he should act that way. It simply ruined him.

Another said:

I just get very tired of the whining and complaining and criticism.

And yet another said:

He totally fell apart, as though she was his whole world, thus making for one thing the other children in the family feel rotten. That to me is unforgivable. To put everything in that basket. What are the other kids supposed to say or do if the father is going to rant and rave like this without any real thought about those kids that are left. Why not give a little of yourself to them and not spend the whole time moaning about something that cannot return. And it went on beyond the normal period of course when you are naturally grief-stricken. It went so far beyond that it became psychopathic. That's the way I feel about it.

At Yale, Paul Garland's chief offense seems to be that he dared incriminate the Yale community. It is as though they were more offended by his attack on Yale than the attack on his daughter.

I think it's childish for a man of his intelligence and maturity to lash out at Yale University, which any thinking person would understand that Yale is not going to champion anything like that. Anything so personal. It stays out of these things. It simply doesn't get involved in it.

Beyond the Yale community all the concern for the Garlands is tinged with reproach. It seemed particularly true in the same Catholic community that so embraced the concept of forgiving in Richard. It may be understandable in terms of Paul Garland's particular bitterness about the Catholic Church. He has been neither polite nor prudent in his attack on them. He sees them as the enemy, and then perhaps in a self-fulfilling way they have become that. Not that every member of the religious community that I talked to did not mention compassionate concern for the Garlands. I simply never *felt* much of it. And they were not at all above being judgmental.

Brother Robert expressed it when he described his chagrin that Richard's presence in the Christian Brothers community had been made public because of Paul Garland's investigation. He felt that Richard was having a "positive experience." That he was well on his way to a healing process with his attendance at school, making new friends, and that Paul Garland's vindictiveness interrupted this for no useful purpose.

I asked him:

—Don't you feel he was entitled to a certain amount of anger and bitterness after having his child hammered to death?

Oh, I think that you are . . . But I do think that time should heal!

—This was a very short time after.

It was a very short time later. But he kept on and on and on. And it has yet to change!

He then went on to suggest that his only understanding of why the Garlands should have persisted with their bitterness was that perhaps they felt guilty for attempting to break up the affair.

"They are the ones that wanted to break it up, so I think that changes the color of things."

The Garlands did not "break up" the affair. And even if they had, that would not change "the color of things." The Brothers' store of forgiveness and charity seemed spent on Richard, with very little left for the Garlands. They were sorry for them, but one sensed no love for these sinners—perhaps their sins were insufficient.

Nor was the Scarsdale or the Yale community demonstrative in its support of the Garlands. The Reverend Gary Brown of Scarsdale Community Church, acknowledging the Garlands' sense of isolation, explained Bonnie's friends' "reluctance to get involved."

"Bonnie's gone. Her friends don't have anyone to hang in there with. . . . He's the one that needs the help. . . . You can motivate people to help someone in trouble."

He is absolutely correct. Bonnie was gone, and it is the nature of human empathy to require a human focus—only Richard remained. Repeatedly, throughout this book, Bonnie's absence in the proceedings following her death was commented upon with dismay. And it must be said again here. Richard dominates this discussion, not Bonnie.

In the real world, a psychological presence is required for passion—whether it be love, compassion, or even hatred. All the more reason, then, for an institutional stand for Bonnie. It must be the function of the state to do that which individuals find difficult to do, to maintain its primary concern for the life that was not lived. It must announce the value of that life in its attitudes toward the destroyer of it. It must not be beguiled by a humane concern for the criminal into trivializing the death of the victim. Beyond emotion, it must announce the moral purpose of the law.

Yale, as an institution of education, took a most peculiar position. It played no role and seemed proud to deny any institutional involvement. Yale acted as though someone had inadvertently dumped a load of manure on its front lawn. It was embarrassing, an annoying inconvenience, and Yale was particularly offended by the importunity of the neighbors in complaining of the stench. "After all, it wasn't Yale's fault" was a constant refrain. Yale's official attitude remains constant to this day. While the mess was on their doorstep, it was not of their doing. If they managed with good form and proper manners to carry on, why could not those less discommoded neighbors behave with the same grace?

Well, the mess, whether of their making or not, *was* on their doorstep. And that, like it or not, does require some institutional involvement. Besides, there are questions beyond the scope of this book, as to whether they did not contribute an inadvertent but significant share to the tragedy. They recruited Richard while still a junior in high school. Should a university pursue an affirmative action program and insensitively assume that a boy from the barrio is no different from that young lad from Hotchkiss who brings his experience, his culture, his know-how, his friends, his manners, and his sense of self and place along with him to an environment that was designed for him by people like him?

Richard was in academic—and social—trouble from the day he arrived. First in his class in high school, he botched his college work from the first class. Makeup examinations, incompletes, special exceptions, pushing through, and finally graduation despite incomplete work are not appropriate substitutes for awareness, supervision, guidance, and even discipline. Richard was in culture shock from the beginning. He needed an institutional mother. Where *is* alma mater these days?

The same lack of emotional involvement and understanding for the Garlands' loss was evidenced in my interviews with the psychiatrists, and ultimately even Richard himself.

This is not to suggest that the concern of all involved about vengeance is not very real, nor that preoccupation with vengeance is not destructive. This is not the central point. The point is that individual vengeance is totally ineffective in terms of serving any purpose of reprobation, reproach, pointing the finger of guilt, establishing a moral principle. If anything, it does the opposite, confusing the ethical issues.

The shrillness of the shriek of vengeance makes one begin to lose patience with those demanding it, driving one to sympathize with the victimizer. The poets were well aware of this and the ugliness of the Erinyes (the Furies) who pursued Orestes, demanding blood for blood, for the murder of his mother, whom he had been obligated to kill to avenge his father's death, makes Orestes flee from the very concept of such "justice." The Erinyes are only converted to the Eumenides (the Gracious Ones) when their desire for revenge is mitigated by their acceptance of mercy.[6] We do not generally rally round the vengeance seekers for long. In this case the defensive personality of Paul Garland did not make it easy, but in any case the nature of their needs is not such to attract support. Richard needed comfort and compassion. The Garlands did not want that. They wanted vengeance. It is harder to mobilize people for an assault, except in the passion of a lynching or a revolution. The desire for vengeance cannot be privately "financed." There are few prepared to emotionally invest in such a cause. Vengeance must be channeled into the retributive mechanisms of the state.

Besides, the dangers of vigilante justice are obvious. The law recognizes that it is difficult for people to contain their anger at times of anguish and pain. This is the justification of the principle of "extreme emotional disturbance." It might well anticipate a parent's killing the killer of his child. Living in a state of laws, we are constrained and restrained by the assumption that the state will mete out punishment for us. Because it will, it will not tolerate our taking the law into our own hands. The state must punish not just because it might serve some other purpose, not because it will do some good for some future other, but simply because the killer of our child deserves to be punished.

It was Kant who insisted that the "last murderer" on earth still ought to be punished, thus showing his contempt for a pure utilitarian argument. The moral order demanded it. There was a rightness to it.

Herbert Morris goes even further. He not only insists that we have a right to mete out punishment but insists that those of us who transgress have a right to *receive* punishment; if we are not punished adequately for our crimes, we are being treated as less than persons. He is saying not just that "justice requires a person be punished if he is guilty," but he is arguing for "the criminal's right to be punished."[7] Human dignity is based on that freedom and autonomy that elevates us above the animal host. In recognition for that autonomy, we must punish the transgressor. As a tribute and testament to his freedom, we must dignify him by making him pay for the evil actions he commits. We show our respect by making him accountable.

There are other arguments that extend the right and purpose of punishment. One is the reprobative one—pointing a finger. It is important that the society enunciate clearly its moral principles and supply a forum for moral outrage. It is the purpose of reprobation and reproach to publish the moral statement—publicly announce, "This is evil; this is a crime; this we abhor."

What was needed was a poet in the courtroom describing Bonnie Garland's childhood, as Richard's was described by the psychiatrists; a prophet in the courtroom describing Bonnie Garland's unlived future, the daughters she might have had and the sons she might have raised; we needed a miracle worker in the courtroom to raise her from the dead. Bonnie's feelings and thoughts, her loss and her suffering—the verities of Bonnie Garland as a person—had to be introduced into that balance of justice. It is an impractical scenario for a court of law. There are few poets left, and those that are left are often trapped within the narcissistic cage of themselves.

Instead we must be content with a statement that prosaically but precisely announces the seriousness with which we take the tragedy of Bonnie Garland by treating her death and her killing not just as a vehicle—as a means to some end—but as a thing in itself.

The claim for punishment against Richard and like criminals is the social equivalent of a moral statement about Bonnie Garland's death. It is also a public statement of righteousness.

Sister Ramona is offended by a waste of another life "to compound the waste of the one he took." She would not even have added one life to balance six million; thirty years after the fact, she would feel no justification for the punishment of Eichmann.

In defense of a concept of righteousness over utility, consider for a moment a colleague of Eichmann's, Adolf Hitler. Supposing he had survived at the end of the war? What would have been the proper justification for punishing Hitler?

Protection of society? Hardly necessary. We could insure that he would not once again rise to power. He was an older man, and the time to mobilize another course of action would be insufficient.

Specific deterrence? No, for the same reasons, it is not a serious consideration. We do not have to worry about Hitler redux.

General deterrence? In the world in which he operated it was unlikely that the fate of a Hitler would influence the fate of a future Hitler any more than the fate of a Napoleon influenced Hitler.

Rehabilitation? There was nothing to rehabilitate. Hitler might well have led a peaceful and fruitful life in retirement in Argentina in the company of his colleagues. Who knows, he might have resumed his painting career and a promising talent might have been discovered—a latter-day Grandpa Moses, although the name would no doubt have been offensive to him.

Yet the concept of Hitler in retirement on a ranch in Argentina painting landscapes is simply intolerable. Even if it cannot be justified on purely utilitarian grounds, that man deserved to be punished with all the righteous wrath of an outraged community sensitivity. It cheapens the Holocaust to suggest that his punishment must be justified in terms of prevention of some future pain and destruction. There was enough pain and destruction in the past to warrant that punishment. We must not mobilize utilitarian justifying excuses. He must be punished because the moral order of things demands it, because it would be unbearable to see a man like that rewarded and allowed to go unpunished. Righteousness demands it.

Now where is forgiveness in all this? Wherever it is, it must not displace responsibility. The same Christ who preached forgiveness insisted on human freedom. Dostoevski has his Grand Inquisitor berate the returning Christ, "Instead of taking men's freedom from them, Thou didst make it greater than ever!"[8] "Go and come no more. Come not at all, never, never!"[9]

Freedom demands responsibility; autonomy requires culpability.

In the Jewish tradition the holy days between the New Year and the Day of Atonement are spent in contemplating the preceding year and praying to God asking forgiveness for transgressions. But God forgives only sins against Him and His Law. One must seek forgiveness in the affairs of people from those whom you have wronged. Only they can forgive you.

Aryeh Neier, that staunch civil libertarian, worded it well: "Public forgiveness and private vengeance suffer from the same vice: They depreciate the victim. Respect for those who suffer requires that no one usurp the victim's exclusive right to forgive his oppressor. Similarly it requires that the duty to punish must be assumed by everyone other than the victim. That is what is meant by the rule of law."[10]

We must also consider the limits of individualism. The concept of community is not a creation of man. He was born into it and of it. We do not *choose* to live in social relations; we are obliged to. As Adolf Portmann has said:

> Man comes to sociability not by arrangement, by rational decision, but from the natural, primary disposition he shares with all higher animals. Attraction to other members of the species precedes all hostility and repulsion; solitariness is always secondary, a flight from the natural bond.[11]

One of the truly unique aspects of human development is the total helplessness of the human infant and the uncharacteristically long period of time in which he remains floundering in this helpless state. A guppy must face life at the moment of birth. Autonomous and independent, it must avoid its first predator—its mother! More remarkably, a sea urchin is prepared to face a hostile environment only hours after the egg has been *fertilized*. Generally, the more complicated the animal the longer the gestation period. The human species has an inordinately abbreviated gestation period for an animal as complicated as it is. A higher mammal like an elephant may take twenty-two months to produce its infant; and when the child is born, limbs are developed, it is capable of standing and walking by itself. It moves freely and readily with the general herd.

Why is it that human beings are born in such a purely helpless state with practically no instinctual capacities for survival? The answer lies in that other extraordinary endowment of the species, the human brain. The rapid physical growth of that huge brain *demands* birth at nine months of gestation, otherwise it could not pass through the peculiarities of the birth canal, which in itself was necessitated by the upright posture of the human mother. In other words, given the nature of the human pelvis, and the extraordinary size of the fetal brain at nine months, it is essential that the fetus pass through at that time, even though this may mean that in comparison with other animals it is born with a particular vulnerability. Big as the brain is at birth—350 grams—by the end of the first year of life it has grown to 825 grams, over half its total eventual size.

It is for this reason that the first year of life has been referred to by many authors as the final stage of fetalization. The kangaroo child is also born tiny and helpless. The marsupials, however, have a protective pouch—an open uterus—to protect the fetus during this extra-uterine gestation. Mere evidence of survival indicates that the human creature must have some equivalent protective mechanism. Since survival does not reside in the infant itself, it must exist in protective and communitarian impulses of the species. We did not create the family. We are all born into a "good family." It is not just luck or learning. The mother does not decide when she is hungry to devour the tender child as the guppy mother does. Nor does the father, even though in the most primitive times he had yet to learn of his relationship with the child.

Because of the bizarre and peculiarly long dependency period that only human animals are born to, we could not survive as a species, let alone develop as individuals, were there not a social structure to support us. While homo sapiens is not quite a colonial animal like coral, he is certainly not a true individual like an amoeba. He rests somewhere in between, and no theory of the nature of man and no public policy based on that theory is completely adequate that does not recognize the obligate social structure.[12]

The need to live in some group, combined with possession of the only kind of brain that could evolve a technological society, dictated the advantage of living in even broader communities than the family.

The family became an extended family; the extended family a tribe; and the tribes became a nation.

With the evolving community came an evolving set of laws to facilitate community.

At one time, if you invaded the cave of one household, you would have had a rock thrown at you which bloodied your nose; in another cave you may have been dragged out and beaten to death by clubs. All depended on the size or mood of the individuals whose domicile had been invaded. This individual justice had little of the quality of commensurate punishment, or reasonable deserts, that we associate with equity and true justice.

Over the years there emerged codes of communal living couched in the language of myth, totemic taboos, religion, and ultimately the emergence of a state under law. The giving of the law was in the vision of the old Bible the greatest testament of God's love of man.

The emergence of a law of the land is the foundation of a just society. It establishes the first step of equity, by dictating that all people will be considered equally under the law and insisting that violators of the same law be punished in like manner. Of course it is only the first step in the establishment of a just society. It is also necessary that the nature of the law define a set of values that are good. But it is a first step. Impartiality is a form of fairness that supports whatever our definition of justice will be.

In America, our law is in great part dependent on "common law." The protection of the common law, with its massive body of precedents and inherent inertia, has been cursed for its inconsistencies and unwieldiness. It is hard to move that law. But that, too, can prove to be beneficent and advantageous. The German system of justice, with its elegant individualization of each case as a thing in itself to be evaluated against certain absolute principles of right and wrong, and its freedom from encumbrance from the past, became only too accommodating to the present. The judges of the courts in Nazi Germany, unencumbered by obligations to conform to common law, were prepared to find rationalizations and legal justifications for the destruction of the Jewish population in the Nazi state.

In a peculiar way the intrusion of psychological arguments—the consideration of each individual as a universe in himself—by de-emphasizing action and emphasizing state of mind, is fragmenting the common factors in the law. It is undoing the generalizing, and thereby civilizing, aspects of common law. No longer will each action be judged against similar action, but rather each action will be interpreted and redefined according to the truth as it is visualized in the psychological world of the criminal. We are substituting the thing as perceived for the thing that happened.

The new psychological definition of human beings that had each of us operating in a reality different from those around us destroyed the actual world. But it is in the actual world that the law must operate in order to preserve equity. In our search for individual justice we must not destroy the sense that we are living in a fair and just state. All of us are prepared to accept individual inequities. We all know that life is not always fair. Still, somehow, we expect that generally the good prevails. A deepening cynicism on that point can deteriorate into the disaffection and desperation that presage riots and anarchy. The anger and outrage generated by a sense of ubiquitous injustice could lead to an abandonment of all humanitarian and altruistic concerns for the criminal and, beyond that, for the disadvantaged and disenfranchised in general. We must not attempt to purchase an elegant and individual justice for each person at the expense of the concept called social justice. It would turn out to be a very costly exchange.

We must always balance individual good against the need for social justice. We have learned that in other ways. We have contaminated our public space too often and in too many ways. We are now gasping for clean air, clean water, and safe movement. A just society traditionally does some disservice to its individual members. The common good demands sacrifice of the individual. That is the lesson in the most moral of doctrines. The community under Jehovah is a community of law and justice, and yet the prophets may demand the ultimate sacrifices, even unto death, for the preservation of the law and the people of the law. The sacrifice of the firstborn under the Egyptian host was an awful price to pay, visited on the most innocent—the children of a population. The readiness of a God of Justice to sacrifice even them to insure the survival of his people—people chosen to support a vision of the law—is a measure of the value the ancient Hebrews placed on the importance of community.

The ultimate test is always the willingness to sacrifice that thing of greatest worth. And the sacrifice of the innocent, whether it is the virgins sacrificed to a primitive god, or Iphigenia to Zeus, or Isaac to the Lord God Jehovah—the sacrifice of the innocent implies a *respect* for the individual. It is because the Old Testament stresses the pride of the father for the son, and only because of that, that Abraham's readiness to sacrifice his son represents the value he places on the will of God, and the trust he invests in the word of God.

It was that other aspect of justice, the concept of doing good rather than doing right, that led us into this individualization. It was part of the humanistic spirit and optimism of our time. Like many other things, we may be finding out that we cannot "afford" this individualization. We are reaching the limits of individualism. We are learning an increased respect for the community by the necessity of certain shortages. We drive in smaller, unsafe cars, calculatedly enhancing the amount of mutilation and mayhem on the roadways for pursuit of a common good, which is the conservation of energy.

We must not wait until we reach a scarcity level in our trust and confidence in the essential fairness and decency of the state. We must conserve the sense of the rightness of our social order, even to the point of sacrificing some of that very respect for the individual which makes our order one that is worth preserving.

We have been moving toward that brave new world of Aldous Huxley, in which the announcement that someone had committed a crime elicited a compassionate response: "I did not know he was ill." This approach was always under attack from the conservative community, to which it had appeared as a mollycoddling, bleeding-heart outrage; but now the liberal community, with different motives, has joined the argument for its abandonment.

It is not easy to abandon the rehabilitative model, for it was a scheme born in optimism and faith and humanism. It viewed the evils in man as essentially correctable and only partially the responsibility of the individual. While we may grieve for the lost illusion and the death of a dream, we need not mourn the reality. It is really no great loss. The rehabilitative model abounded with internal inconsistencies that inevitably offered opportunities for exploitation—which were just as inevitably accepted. It produced unexpected abhorrent consequences and numerous unpredictable side effects that were less humane or liberal than its proponents had anticipated.

The problems inherent in the subject of incarceration are formidable. Prisons are, after all, part of the broader institution of society—a criminal-justice system. The purposes of that system have been particularly obscured by much of the current discussion, which tends to focus exclusively on the offender. But the system is, at its base, designed to serve not his needs but rather the needs of society.

Laws are established to maintain and preserve the social structure. In that sense, at least, the chief purpose of law is order, and the justice system is designed to serve the ends of the society at large. One of the sad consequences of the appropriation of the term "law and order" by the extreme right wing as a euphemism for racist feelings that were unfashionable to articulate was that the intellectual community, repelled by the implicit racism, turned away from the legitimate rights that such words imply. The authentic need to investigate the essential importance of both law and order was slighted. Instead, the intellectual community focused all too exclusively on the neglected rights of the criminal offender, forgetting that, while this was a compassionate and necessary pursuit, the welfare of the community was the primary concern of a system of criminal justice.

But if the primary purpose of law is order, it is not merely law *for order*. The orderly society is not necessarily the most desirable. A concentration camp is more orderly than a town meeting. Law, in a good society, must preserve not only the society but its ideals and values as well. And, in so doing, it must balance its desire for stability and order against its other values. Security, safety, and survival may be fundamental—but there are limits. A good society must examine the methods of its survival to make sure that that which survives is still worthy. For that reason, one of the truest indices of the quality of life in a state will always be the way it responds to those who defy the law.[13]

There was no winning with the rehabilitative model. The public at large was infuriated at its failures; the intellectual community could not tolerate the ambiguity of maintaining someone indefinitely in prison for a rehabilitation that might or might not be working; parents and friends of the person maintained in total institutions were outraged at the length of time for treatment. And finally treatment was not only ineffective, it was excessively costly.

Early release, when premature, satisfied neither the public nor the advocates of the criminal. The foster mother of Stephen T. Judy, a twenty-three-year-old construction worker convicted of raping and killing a twenty-one-year-old woman and drowning her three children, blamed "the system," for not giving Stephen the kind of support and help he required in childhood.

> Mr. Judy was repeatedly admitted and released from institutions, beginning at age 12, when he was charged with burglary.

Later that year he was charged with assault and attempted rape. He was convicted twice for attacking young women and was freed on bail five days before the Chastine killings after being arrested on a charge of attempted robbery.

"Our system helped nurture this, helped turn him into a murderer," Mrs. Carr said. "You know a twelve-year-old boy who attacks a woman needs help, but Steve was back on the streets nine months after that attack."[14]

No, the rehabilitative model was no bargain. It denied the legitimate claims of society for reprobation. If all crime is "sickness," all criminals are nonculpable, and we live in an essentially amoral state. The public has a right to enunciate its values, to denounce as immoral, in public space and in common terms, those actions which clearly violate its standards. Where, indeed, is sin?

The symbolic value of the reprobative approach in these dramatic cases must not be minimized. Though they are small in number, their leverage is such that they disproportionately influence the public consciousness. Because of the high visibility, the decisions in these cases are indices of the way "things are working." They contribute to or diminish the general sense of law, fairness, equity, and order. To shake the public faith in these areas is to risk the abandonment of goodness in the pursuit of safety.

A relatively unsafe state may be tolerated if it is necessary to secure values we respect. Freedom of speech and travel may weaken national security, but they are minor risks compared with the inherent value of freedom. If the relative risk is perceived as preserving only the evil and meretricious, why should we not all elect security. The capacity to embrace authoritarian and fascist solutions in the name of a kind of equality and security is evidenced in the communist and fascist monoliths which dominate Africa, South America, Asia, and half of Europe. But it is also evident in the manifest hungers of large portions of our own population for the security, particularly moral security, represented by the growing appeal of cults and saviors—both religious and political—with their simplistic prescriptions.

"As ye sow, so shall ye reap" is a basic tenet of a democratic faith. It is, of course, violated; but we label those violations "injustices." We cannot abandon our basic belief in the principle without seriously altering the structure of our society. Good guys must—at least on average—win. Crime ought not generally pay. And we must, for the most part, be held responsible for the consequences of our actions. The unseemly flight of Norman Mailer and his colleagues from responsibility in the case of Jack Henry Abbott offended our sense of rightness from two standpoints. Abbott had been paroled on the urging of an intellectual group who had been impressed by his writing talents. In so doing, they evidently confused talent with decency, and flights of fiction with documentation. One would have thought that Eldridge Cleaver would have been sufficient evidence that writing ability is neither an exculpation of past crimes nor a predictor of future behavior. Within days of his parole, Abbott was charged with killing a young actor, Richard Adan. The death of Adan was an individual tragedy, but the action of one of our most distinguished creative talents was a social tragedy.

Mailer's command of words is unsurpassed in living writers of fiction. It is for this we respect his work and listen to his advice. We therefore expect him to treat "words," and his word, with reverence. On April 15, 1980, Mr. Mailer wrote to Utah parole authorities, urging that Mr. Abbott be given a state parole. "I am aware of the responsibility of what I propose," Mr. Mailer wrote, "and propose it in belief that Abbott is in need of a special solution that can reach out to his special ability." After the tragic killing, Mailer acknowledged "feeling" responsible. But responsibility is not just a feeling.

What, then, is responsibility? Responsible means "accountable," "answerable," "liable." It suggests "duty," "obligation," or "burden." At least in the dictionary it means that. Does Mr. Mailer hold himself "accountable" to the state for this killing? Is he "answerable" to the homicide; will the patron serve the protégé's time? How does he view his obligation to the victim's mourners? Is he liable for the loss of that young man? What duties does he owe those bereaved? Will he support them financially and emotionally in partial compensation for their loss? How was Mr. Mailer using the word "responsibility"? It is still not clear.

But Mailer is in the tradition of modern thinking about criminality: Romanticize the criminal, trivialize the crime, and ignore the victims.

In addition to responsibility we must value the importance of symbols. Serious criminologists tend to neglect the cases that dominate the front pages of newspapers and support the evening news on television, correctly pointing out they represent a small percentage of the crimes that plague the community. But to ignore the psychological meaning of events in this most psychological age is to be dangerously narrow-sighted. The Boston Strangler, the Son of Sam, and the Atlanta Slayer may represent a small percentage of the homicides in this country, and certainly a small percentage of the crimes of violence, yet they haunt public consciousness and influence our social policy disproportionately to their numbers. The power of the symbol must never be underestimated.

The fifty-four American hostages held in Iran were an inconsequential group in terms of numbers. Yet they dominated the news for a year and may have been a determining factor in defeating a President. They symbolically presented a concrete example of a national feeling of impotence and hopelessness. They gave credence to a general fear that our powers were declining, and gave expression and focus to our daily sense of frustration in the face of irrational forces that limit our aspirations, diminish our pleasure, and reduce our sense of pride.

It is amazing that the symbolic significance of crimes of violence has been generally left unexamined by the same community that has been almost obsessionally devoted to another statistically insignificant number. Compare the attention paid to murders on death row and the general devotion to the issue of capital punishment.

The interest in capital punishment has generally exceeded my own emotional investment in this field. Practically, I find little in favor of capital punishment. Theoretically, I find little to oppose in it. In the past I have been convinced that on a procedural basis it was unjust, although I have never shared most of my colleagues' feelings that the principle of capital punishment is morally indefensible. In order to protect itself from real or imagined enemies from the outside, the state assigned thousands of innocent young men to certain death in war. I do not see any rationale that allows for this which would not allow the sacrifice of guilty men for reasons of internal security.

If it were done trivially it would be offensive. It ought be reserved for "capital crimes." If it were done casually, even for so serious a crime, as indeed it has been in the past, it would be a moral outrage. But if it were deemed to be necessary for internal operation of the state—and I am not saying that case has been made—I can find no moral position (short of a total commitment to pacifism) that would support an absolute indictment of this procedure.

Nonetheless, most of my friends, and all of my betters, disagree with me and are united in their opposition to capital punishment. The justification then for the ardor—and the commitment of funds and energy—to save such a small number (compare the number of men killed by capital punishment with those who are killed by irresponsibility in the work place) must be based on the symbolic meaning of the act. Even one death, if it were a lynching, represents a scar on the body politic. If beyond that there were an authorized murder which was unjust and inappropriate, it would be a scar on the soul of the state.

It is this symbolic rationale that would justify an organization like the American Civil Liberties Union, year in and year out, committing its scarce and needed funds to fight capital punishment—all in a cause that is only peripherally part of its domain—civil liberties. For it is a cause recognized by large groups of our population as containing within its symbolic bounds certain crucial statements about the sanctity of life and the relationship of the state to the individual.

So, too, crimes of violence, particularly those which lead to the slaughter of the innocent, must be seen as more than tabloid entertainments or aberrant phenomena. They are capable of channeling the public's emotionality, its impotent rage and frustrated sense of injustice, into a personal vengeance of the ugliest sort.

Certain crimes demand public censure and reprobation that is commensurate with the seriousness with which the public holds that which has been done. The price, and an appropriate price, must be paid. The state must tell the Garlands, their friends, and those of us who are parents of daughters that it abhors that which was done. In order to do that we may, even while sympathizing with a Richard Herrin, demand that he pay a serious price. And one should not underestimate the seriousness of a long prison sentence.

The penalties the state sets for crimes represent the public's opinion of the gravity of the crime. If eight and one-third to twenty-five years is the price we wish to place for the killing of an innocent, it is because we see that as a proportionate one. When we do not, we are allowed to raise or lower it, until our sense of justice is met. We must hate the sin and—while free to love him—punish the sinner.

We have a primary responsibility to protect the good society from the antisocial act and the antisocial person. We are conceived in the care of others. We are sustained by love and attention during the prolonged period of our helplessness. We learn love, empathy, compassion, and conscience through our interrelationships with those around us; and our very survival is always dependent on the huge network of supporting people who represent the communities in which we abide.

An individual human being is only a useful social myth. We achieve humanness only in and through our relationship with others. We exist through our attachments. We can never protect the individual while destroying the community. We cherish the community not merely because it protects us but because it defines the nature of our species. And it is with our species that righteousness resides.

The killing of Bonnie Garland was not just the theft of a young girl's birthright, not just an unbearable pain inflicted on her family and friends; it was an assault on the social order that makes human life possible. The killing of Bonnie Garland, first by Richard Herrin and then again by a legal and cultural process, which seemed to forget that she had ever existed, endangers us all. In our compassion for the criminal, we must remain vigilant in defense of the social good, for the sake of those innocents living and yet unborn.

AFTERWORD:
THE
HINCKLEY CASE

On June 21, 1982, within weeks of the publication of this book, the trial of John W. Hinckley, Jr., for the attempted assassination of President Reagan came to an end. The jury found him not guilty by reason of insanity. The public was stunned. The moral outrage that poured forth was exactly the kind of backlash that had been anticipated in this book. What had not been expected was that it would happen so quickly, and that it would be followed by a hysterical rush to legislation.

I, like most Americans, assumed that Hinckley would be found guilty. After all, conviction or acquittal on the insanity defense has very little to do with the actual mental state of the individual. Certain crimes are deemed by the public so reprehensible—the Son of Sam, the Speck, the Manson, and the Gacy cases, for example—that a jury simply will not hear, know, or acknowledge that the individual is innocent. Thus, typically and traditionally the "craziest" of those who are brought to trial are found guilty. A jury is prepared to deny its sense of logic to satisfy its disgust and revulsion, and to express to the public its condemnation of the offense. The Hinckley case should, predictably, have fit this category.

What happened in the Hinckley case? Two things we know for sure. In most jurisdictions, in order to establish a defense, it is necessary for the *defense* to prove beyond reasonable doubt that the defendant is insane. But in certain jurisdictions—and the District of Columbia is one of them—it is up to the *state* to prove that the individual is responsible or healthy. That this has been tolerated for so long is merely one more testament to how difficult it is to remove even a foolish standard from the precedent of law once it has been established. The idea that anyone can prove any other individual healthy or normal is preposterous. Psychiatry has never been able to successfully define what is normal. I would not testify to the absolute normalcy of most of the people I know. Although I may be convinced of the normalcy or good mental health of my wife, children, and a handful of my best friends, I have no idea how in the world I would go about proving that. The statute itself placed the trial in a jurisdiction of the absurd.

Then the judge, interpreting the law scrupulously but legalistically, gave so insistent and intimidating a charge to the jury that it ensured acquittal, except at the hands of the most vindictive or the most courageous of juries. And acquittal is what actually happened. It is interesting to speculate about what conceivably *might* have happened in the minds of the jurors. It has been my experience that jurors in general are swayed more by their emotions than by logic. It is now close to one hundred years since Freud discovered that man is a less rational animal than he chooses to believe. Nonetheless, there is something about the process of serving on a jury that brings out the responsible, perhaps the noblest, aspects of simple, ordinary people. I suspect that this jury wanted to convict John W. Hinckley with all their heart, but having heard the judge—in his awesome explicitness, with his certitude and authority—these simple people overrode their own emotions and "did their duty." I suspect they suffered for it, wanting, as did the public at large, to see Hinckley convicted.

What an irony that this group, who probably left the courtroom feeling that they had unselfishly done exactly what the state demanded of them, should have been vilified, accused, and attacked. In post-trial interviews, some jurors expressed their shock and chagrin that they were treated as villains when obviously they felt that they had denied their own feelings to do their duty.

In any event, what happened immediately after the Hinckley trial was as nothing compared with the mounting crescendo of outrage and indignation. Within weeks there were demands for abolition of the insanity defense from leading figures in the Reagan administration, and within months there was a virtual torrent of legislative proposals on both state and federal levels, constituting a fundamental rupture with the general legal tradition in which the insanity defense had evolved. By the fall of 1982, three states—Idaho, Alabama, and Montana—had abolished the insanity defense altogether. Eight states—including Connecticut, Illinois and Michigan—had adopted statutes that would permit a verdict of guilty but mentally ill. In the Congress, no fewer than eleven pieces of legislation were proposed that would either eliminate the insanity defense or allow for a verdict of "guilty but insane."

David H. Leroy, the Idaho attorney general who was instrumental in passing the legislation that abolished the insanity defense (effective July 1, 1982) in his state, cited the strong public opposition to the insanity defense: "In legislative polls between 85 and 96 percent of the constituents measured in Idaho favor the abolition of the insanity defense."[1]

The people of Idaho are not alone. In a survey for ABC News taken on June 22, 1982, some 80 percent of the people polled disapproved of the insanity defense. And, more dangerously, in a July 12–15 survey conducted by Audits and Survey for The Merit Report, 71 percent of those surveyed said that the Hinckley verdict "weakened [your] faith in this country's system of justice."[2]

It is this latter problem that is the most worrisome. It was a central point of this book that while the insanity defense is employed in a minimal number of cases, its impact is vast. The intellectual community has sadly neglected this disproportionate psychological effect. While few in number, these trials are precisely the kinds of cases that gather public attention and incur public wrath. They then become conflated and confused with the public's already existing anxiety about law and order and contribute to the general feeling that "things are not working." The sense that justice is not prevailing, that the system is failing, is a terrifying and dangerous phenomenon. It encourages simplistic, impulsive solutions and creates a mood of susceptibility to demagoguery, rhetoric, and quick-fix quackery. And oh, how the politicians have responded!

[1] *The Mental Disability Law Reporter*, vol. 6, no. 5, September–October 1982, p. 342.
[2] As reported in *Public Opinion*, August–September 1982, p. 27.

First let's look at the abolition of the insanity defense. I have just made an exhaustive case for why I feel the insanity defense should be restricted and allowed only for the truly insane, in the most limited sense of that word. Let me repeat why it should not, and cannot, be abolished. It should not be abolished because we are a humanistic society and we ought not want those who are truly not knowledgeable, truly not responsible, and therefore truly not culpable to be punished. At an extreme, the individual in a toxic delirium induced by a drug that was prescribed by a physician for a disease is not responsible for the havoc that is a product of that delirium and ought not be punished. It would make more sense to punish the prescribing doctor. There are psychological cases analogous to this that clearly place the individuals outside the general intentions of the law.

Even were we so heartless or so pragmatic that we still wished to exclude the insanity defense, we could not anymore. The concept of *mens rea* (criminal intent), with its insistence that we examine the intention of the individual and the condition of his reasoning, has so permeated the criminal law that there is simply no way back. The person who gives someone cyanide to inherit his wealth is not committing the same crime, even though he is committing precisely the same action, as the person who unwittingly gives someone the same poison introduced into a Tylenol capsule. Nor for that matter is it the same crime if the person intentionally gives cyanide in the mistaken assumption that cyanide in small doses is a curative to a specific disease.

What will happen, then, in those states that have abolished the insanity defense? Well, obviously, it will simply be introduced in different language. Instead of arguing about whether a person is sick or not, we will argue about his rationality, reality testing, judgment, intentions, and state of mind. One difference may be that instead of having psychiatric testimony, since a psychiatrist by definition is a member of the medical profession and speaks in terms of health, we will have the testimony of psychologists, who need not at all be concerned with sickness or the sick role. It is highly unlikely that, aside from vocabulary, the testimony of psychologists will differ appreciably in quality or kind from that of psychiatrists. The arguments presented in this book for a rational and reconsidered discussion of where we want to set the limits of responsibility, how we want to apportion the rights of the individual versus the rights of the social group, will still demand the same reappraisal.

Now what about the increasingly popular concept of guilty but insane? If the abolition of the insanity defense is simply an example of furnishing the same problem with a new label, this surely is a different problem, and to my mind a regressive movement with dangerous and ugly potential consequences. The guilty-but-insane concept is morally offensive, legally unsound, and politically dangerous. Since classic times we have accepted the fact that an insane person is different from the rest of us and cannot be judged for his actions under full concepts of responsibility. The nature of the sick role is such that the sick person cannot be culpable: You are held responsible and morally judgeable for your political or social acts; you are not ordinarily blamed for your fever, your cancer, your heart attack, or your psychosis. Do we really want to be in the position of taking the truly nonculpable and throwing them into a prison? This is a disservice to a political system that has thrived on a respect for individual dignity under a philosophy in which dignity rests greatly on the concept of autonomy. The values that underlie our political system could not tolerate the punishment of the truly not responsible out of mere expedience or convenience.

Well, suppose instead we took the guilty but insane and committed them not to prison but to a mental hospital. This would have even more destructive consequences. It would make one branch of medicine, psychiatry, a punitive and judicial arm of the state. Medicine cannot survive that way. We must not convert a percentage of our physicians into jailers. We have battled too long for the distinctions between asylums and prisons to allow this corruption of a branch of medicine. As a physician, I deplore the concept of converting our mental institutions into instruments of our state justice system. But even if this could be justified as a price the physician must pay to serve the common good (after all, there are physicians who serve the courts, armies, corporations, airlines, and the like and are faced with problems of dual loyalty—the role I once designated as the problem of the double agent), there are other grounds for opposing it.

The use of mental institutions in the Soviet Union for control of political dissidence has shown what a powerful tool this can be in the service of a totalitarian state. It permits the circumvention of law, limits of punishment, constitutions, and legislation. The argument has been presented that all definitions of mental health include the values of the culture, that we hospitalize people by our definitions of mental health and the Russians by *their* definitions of mental health. This is a specious argument based on a partial truth. Of course all definitions of mental health incorporate values, and the values of one society will be different from those of another. So it may be true that our definition of schizophrenia—the most common psychotic designation—will differ from that of the Russians because the reality that is being tested in each case is different. To the Russians, criticism of the state is deemed a form of "creeping schizophrenia," evidently on the assumption that in so perfect an environment as the Soviet Union anyone who would have something of which to complain must be crazy. They argue that we are just as political, that we merely define schizophrenia according to a different set of values. And I'm sure we do. The flaw, though, is in the extension of the argument for hospitalization. In the United States we do not hospitalize people because of *diagnoses*. We do not even hospitalize people because they are clearly psychotic, let alone because they are schizophrenic, which may or may not imply psychosis. We hospitalize them only when they are clearly a danger to themselves and others, and then only with great difficulty for short terms. Every individual has a constitutional right as defined by the federal judiciary to be released from a mental hospital unless the government can prove by "clear and convincing evidence that he is both mentally ill and dangerous." Those are extraordinarily stringent standards and in certain jurisdictions make it almost impossible— given the current state of predictability about behavior—to institutionalize *anybody*. To convert mental institutions into instruments of the court would be a dangerous stage in the confusion between individual treatment and social control, between healing and punishment.

There is a tendency in this country to avoid moral issues by converting them into legal ones, to reduce all difficult problems to a question about rights and therefore force all moral solutions into litigation and legislation. We must not be so afraid of moral discourse. We must be prepared to face the issues of our responsibility to the individual and our responsibility to the social structure that supports and defines that individual. Neither abolishing the insanity defense nor inventing a chimera called the guilty-but-insane verdict will get us off the hook. What is needed is what I have asked for here: a careful reconsideration of the limits of individualism. The hysteria about the Hinckley affair will pass, and we will then get on with intelligently facing this profound dilemma.

NOTES

PROLOGUE

1. Willard Gaylin, *In the Service of Their Country: War Resisters in Prison.* New York, Viking, 1970.

2. My first article in jurisprudence was "Psychiatry and the Law: Partners in Crime," *Columbia University Forum,* New York, vol. VIII, no. 1, spring 1965.

3. Jessie Kornbluth, "A Fatal Romance at Yale," *The New York Times Magazine,* May 7, 1978, p. 88.

4. Sam Rosensohn, "Bonnie's Parents Fight to Keep Killer in Jail," *New York Post,* June 19, 1978, p. 1.

5. Whenever direct quotations are not cited, they represent that which was said during personal interviews with the author.

1: RICHARD AND BONNIE

1. I have retained the actual names of most principals, since they were extensively published. Occasionally, an actor in the drama is present whose anonymity may be protected from recall by altering a name and the place names of background. This is the case with "Ginny."

2. J. Kornbluth, p. 82.

3. Ibid.

4. Kathleen Hendrix, "Chicano Honor Student Center of Controversy," *Los Angeles Times,* August 6, 1978.

5. J. Kornbluth, p. 83.

6. Ibid.

2: THE END OF THE AFFAIR

1. Trial Record: Herrin Direct Examination, pp. 834–37.

2. Ibid., pp. 837–59.

3. Trial Record: Tartaglia Direct Examination, pp. 145–43.
4. Ibid., pp. 161–62.
5. Suppression Hearings, p. 8.
6. Trial Record: Porcelli Direct Examination, pp. 179–80.
7. Trial Record: Joan Garland Direct Examination, pp. 267–69.
8. Trial Record: Oestreich Direct Examination, pp. 222–25.

3: THE TELLER AND THE TALE

1. Philip Berrigan quoted in *The New York Times*, July 19, 1981.
2. This concept was first articulated and popularized by Erik H. Erikson.

4: THE GOSPEL TRUTH: CHRISTIANITY

1. Peter Ellis, "Cardinal Cooke OK's Meeting," *New Haven Register*, January 22, 1978.
2. P. Ellis, "Garlands' Plea to Cardinal," *New Haven Register*, February 21, 1978.
3. Sister Mary Ann Walsh, "Local Catholics Demonstrate Compassion," *The Evangelist*, August 3, 1978.
4. Karl Menninger, *Whatever Became of Sin?* New York, Hawthorn, 1973.
5. *The Star*, July 11, 1978.
6. *National Catholic Reporter*, September 4, 1977, p. 4. Here Father Russell was quoting Pope John XXIII.

5: A NEW TESTAMENT: PSYCHOANALYSIS

1. Sigmund Freud, *Studies on Hysteria*, vol. 2, Standard Edition, ed. James Strachey. London, Hogarth Press.
2. William Barrett, *Irrational Man*. Garden City, New York, Doubleday, 1962.
3. Trial Record: Train Direct Examination, vol. III, pp. 964–67.
4. Ibid., pp. 967–71.
5. Ibid., pp. 972–74.
6. Ibid., pp. 974–78.
7. Ibid., pp. 978–80.
8. Ibid., pp. 980–81.
9. Ibid., pp. 983–85.
10. This letter was not admitted in evidence. It was dated by Bonnie November 1974.
11. Trial Record: Train Direct Examination, p. 1001.
12. Ibid., pp. 1007–09.
13. Ibid., p. 1008.
14. People's Exhibit 15-D.
15. Trial Record: Train Direct Examination, pp. 1009–10.
16. People's Exhibit 15-E.
17. Trial Record: Train Direct Examination, pp. 1014–15.
18. People's Exhibits 15-G, 15-H, and 15-I are three almost identical letters written by Richard and left unmailed.

19. Trial Record: Train Direct Examination, pp. 1015–16.
20. Ibid., pp. 1019–20.
21. Ibid., pp. 1021–22.
22. People's Exhibit 13.
23. People's Exhibit 12.
24. Trial Record: Train Direct Examination, p. 1025.
25. Ibid., p. 1026.
26. Ibid., pp. 1030–33.
27. Ibid., p. 1035.
28. Ibid., p. 1039.
29. Train's direct testimony occupies pp. 960–1054 in vol. III of the court transcript.
30. Train, pp. 1039–41.
31. Ibid., p. 1047.
32. Ibid., p. 1048.
33. Ibid., pp. 1048–49.
34. Ibid., pp. 1053–54.
35. Trial Record: Herrin Cross Examination, vol. III, p. 957.
36. Trial Record: Abrams Direct Examination, vol. IV, pp. 1247–60.
37. McKinney, *New York Penal Law*, Sec. 125.25.
38. Hal Davis, "Herrin Trial Going to Jury," *New York Post*, Thursday, June 15, 1978.
39. Trial Record: Schwartz Direct Examination, vol. IV, pp. 1307–08.

6: THE ADVERSARIAL CREDO: GUILT OR INNOCENCE

1. For a fuller discussion of the sentencing prodcedures see Willard Gaylin, *Partial Justice*. New York, Knopf, 1974.
2. Trial Record: Litman Summation, vol. V, p. 1371–73.
3. Ibid., p. 1373.
4. Ibid., pp. 1376–79.
5. Ibid., pp. 1384–85.
6. Ibid., p. 1392.
7. Ibid., pp. 1397–99.
8. Ibid., pp. 1404–07.
9. Ibid., p. 1409.
10. Ibid., pp. 1411–12.
11. Ibid., p. 1416.
12. Ibid., p. 1419.
13. Ibid., pp. 1420–21.
14. Ibid., p. 1421.
15. Ibid., p. 1422.
16. Ibid., p. 1424.
17. Ibid., p. 1427.
18. Ibid., pp. 1431–32.
19. Ibid., pp. 1436–37.
20. Ibid., pp. 1441–42.
21. Ibid., pp. 1443–44.

22. Ibid., pp. 1446–47.
23. Ibid., p. 1450.
24. Ibid., p. 1452.
25. Ibid., p. 1455.
26. Ibid., p. 1456.
27. Ibid., pp. 1472–73.
28. Trial Record: Fredreck Summation, vol. 5, pp. 1479–80.
29. Ibid., p. 1482.
30. Ibid., pp. 1482–83.
31. Ibid., pp. 1483–84.
32. Ibid., pp. 1486–88.
33. Ibid., pp. 1488–89.
34. Dan Kaferle, "Juror: Psychiatrists Swung It to Defense," *New Haven Register*, June 19, 1978.
35. Trial Record: Fredreck Summation, pp. 1490–91.
36. Ibid., pp. 1493–94.
37. Ibid., pp. 1494–95.
38. Ibid., pp. 1495–96.
39. Ibid., p. 1496.
40. Ibid., pp. 1496, 1497–99.
41. Ibid., p. 1498.
42. Ibid., pp. 1506–08.
43. Ibid., pp. 1508–09.

7: RATIONALITY AND RESPONSIBILITY

1. For a fuller discussion of coercion see W. Gaylin, "On the Borders of Persuasion: A Psychoanalytic View of Coercion," *Psychiatry*, vol. 37, February 1974, pp. 1–9.
2. For a good brief summary of the history of legal reliance on psychiatry see Jonas Robitscher, *The Powers of Psychiatry*, chapter 3, Boston, Houghton Mifflin, 1980.
3. Nigel Walker, *Crime and Insanity in England*. Edinburgh University Press, 1968.
4. *The New York Times*, July 27, 1981, "Issue and Debate."
5. The argument that follows immediately is developed from ideas first presented in "Psychiatry and Law: Partners in Crime," *Columbia University Forum*, vol. VIII, no. 1, spring 1965.
6. Model Penal Code of the American Law Institute proposed in 1962.
7. Durham v. U.S. 312F. 2d 847 (D.C. Cir. 1962).
8. Exodus 20:13.
9. Nigel Walker, p. 63, as cited in Robitscher, *The Powers of Psychiatry*, p. 22.
10. Blocker v. U.S. 288F. 2d 853 (D.C. Cir. 1961).
11. James Gleick, "Getting Away with Murder," *New Times*, August 21, 1978, p. 24.
12. Ibid.

13. Ibid., p. 21.

14. *The New York Times*, July 27, 1981.

15. Herbert Fingarette, *The Meaning of Criminal Insanity*, p. 211. Berkeley, University of California Press, 1972.

16. Abraham Halpern, "On Closeting the Conscience of the Jury," *Psychiatric Quarterly*, vol. 52, no. 2, summer 1980.

17. Bushell's case as quoted in Ibid. p. 155.

18. Aristotle, *Nicomachean Ethics III*.

19. Abraham Goldstein, *The Insanity Defense*, p. 223–24. New Haven, Yale University Press, 1967.

8: WHERE IS RICHARD?

1. Trial Record: Litman Opening Statement, pp. 64–67.

2. East Side Cornell Study, *Mental Health in the Metropolis: The Midtown Manhattan Study*, Leo Srole and Anita K. Fisher, eds. New York University Press, 1978.

3. Trial Record: Litman Summation, vol. 5, pp. 1468–69.

4. Ibid., p. 1469.

5. Trial Record: Ugarte at p. 694.

6. Ibid., pp. 701–02.

7. As reported in *The New York Times*, August 5, 1981, p. A9.

8. For a fuller discussion see "Will the Real Adolf Hitler Please Stand Up," W. Gaylin, *Hastings Center Report*, October 1977, vol. 7, no. 5, p. 10.

9: WHERE IS JUSTICE?

1. A. Goldstein, *The Insanity Defense*, p. 192.

2. Samuel Butler, *Erewhon*, pp. 93–94. New York, New American Library, 1960.

3. Edward Green, cited in W. Gaylin, *Partial Justice*, p. 30.

4. Albert Camus, *Caligula and Three Other Plays*, author's preface, p. x. New York, Knopf, 1958.

5. The Goodell Committee, named after its chairman, former U.S. Senator Charles Goodell, included Marshall Cohen, Samuel DuBois Cook, Alan Dershowitz, Willard Gaylin, Erving Goffman, Joseph Goldstein, the late Harry Kalven, Jr., Jorge Lara-Braud, Victor Marrero, Eleanor Holmes Norton, David J. Rothman, Simon Rottenberg, Herman Schwartz, Stanton Wheeler, Leslie T. Wilkins. Its report was published under the authorship of its staff director, Andrew von Hirsch, *Doing Justice*, New York, Hill & Wang, 1976.

6. Aeschylus, *Eumenides*.

7. Herbert Morris, "Persons and Punishment," Monist, vol. 52, no. 4, p. 475.

8. Fëdor Dostoevski, *The Brothers Karamazov*, p. 246. New York, Modern Library.

9. Ibid., p. 278.

10. Judy Freed, "Notes on Getting Even," *The Dial*, October 1981.

11. Adolf Portmann, *Animals as Social Beings*. New York, Viking, 1961. As quoted in *Caring*.

12. For a complete discussion of the biological roots of human dependency see W. Gaylin, *Caring*. New York, Knopf, 1976.

13. This argument was first expressed in the introduction (W. Gaylin and D. Rothman) in Andrew von Hirsch, *Doing Justice*, pp. *xxvii–xxviii*. New York, Hill and Wang, 1976.

14. *The New York Times*, "Murderer of Four Awaits Electric Chair in Indiana," February 18, 1981.

INDEX